Civil Society a

MW00779620

Blending history and social science, this book tracks the role of social movements in shaping German public memory and values since 1945. Drawn from extensive original research, it offers a fresh perspective on the evolution of German democracy through civic confrontation with the violence of Germany's past. Told through the stories of memory activists, the study upends some of the conventional wisdom about modern German political history. An analysis of the decades-long struggle over memory and democracy shows how grassroots actors challenged and then took over public institutions of memorialization. In the process, confrontation of the Holocaust has been pushed to the center of political culture. In unified Germany, memory politics have shifted again, as activists from the former East Germany have brought attention to the crimes of the East German state. This book delivers a novel and important contribution to scholarship about postwar Germany and the wider study of memory politics.

Jenny Wüstenberg is DAAD Visiting Assistant Professor of Politics at York University in Toronto. She is the co-founder of the Memory Studies Association.

Civil Society and Memory in Postwar Germany

Jenny Wüstenberg

York University, Toronto

 CAMBRIDGE
UNIVERSITY PRESS

CAMBRIDGE
UNIVERSITY PRESS

University Printing House, Cambridge CB2 8BS, United Kingdom

One Liberty Plaza, 20th Floor, New York, NY 10006, USA

477 Williamstown Road, Port Melbourne, VIC 3207, Australia

314-321, 3rd Floor, Plot 3, Splendor Forum, Jasola District Centre, New Delhi - 110025, India

79 Anson Road, #06-04/06, Singapore 079906

Cambridge University Press is part of the University of Cambridge.

It furthers the University's mission by disseminating knowledge in the pursuit of education, learning and research at the highest international levels of excellence.

www.cambridge.org
Information on this title: www.cambridge.org/9781316628379
DOI: 10.1017/9781316822746

First published 2017
First paperback edition 2018

A catalogue record for this publication is available from the British Library

ISBN 978-1-107-17746-8 Hardback
ISBN 978-1-316-62837-9 Paperback

For Ben Scott

Contents

List of Figures   *page* viii
Preface   xi
Acknowledgments   xiii
List of Abbreviations and German Terms   xvi

1 Civil Society Activism, Memory Politics and Democracy   1

2 Memorial Politics and Civil Society since 1945   32

3 Building Negative Memory: Civic Initiatives for
   Memorials to Nazi Terror   76

4 Dig Where You Stand: The History Movement and
   Grassroots Memorialization   127

5 Memorial Aesthetics and the Memory Movements
   of the 1980s   178

6 A Part of History That Continues to Smolder:
   Remembering East Germany from Below   206

7 Hybrid Memorial Institutions and Democratic Memory   262

Interviews   294
Bibliography   301
Index   326

Figures

1.1 Banner at the Topography of Terror site in 1989:
"We need an Active Museum!" *page* 2

1.2 The cross memorial installation at Checkpoint Charlie
in Berlin: activists chained to the crosses to prevent
their removal in 2005. 5

2.1 Inauguration of a Memorial in Fischbachau/Birkenstein
near Brannenburg in Bavaria on the "Tag der
Heimatvertriebenen" (Day of Expellees) on 6 June 1948.
The banner reads "Give us back our homeland!" 46

2.2 Heimkehrermahnmal at Friedland, erected by the
veterans group VdH in 1967. 48

2.3 Heinrich Lübke at the Steinplatz memorial in 1960. 52

2.4 The Memorial to the Victims of Stalinism (built in 1951)
and the Memorial to the Victims of National Socialism
(built in 1953) are on opposite ends of the Steinplatz,
Berlin-Charlottenburg. 54

3.1 Demonstration to demand the safeguarding of
Neuengamme as a memorial, January 28, 1984. 77

3.2 Protest sign erected at Neuengamme, January 28,1984. 78

3.3 Flyer/invitation to demonstration at Neuengamme,
January 28, 1984. 79

3.4 Unveiling of a memorial at the Bergen-Belsen
concentration camp during the first congress of survivors in
the British zone, September 25, 1945. 83

3.5 Memorial seminar, with participants from across West
Germany, Essen 1984. 100

3.6 Activists of the Memorial Site Movement visit the future
site of the Topography of Terror in Berlin as part of the first
international memorial seminar, October 1985. 101

3.7 Installation intended to show all the purposes of a future
Active Museum, 1989. 106

3.8 Activists of the Active Museum on top of a construction crane at the Topography of Terror site. The banner reads "End the halt to construction now!" 2004.   113

4.1 Policemen remove the sign put up by the Berlin History Workshop from a bridge in Berlin-Tiergarten, 1987.   128

4.2 Members of the Berlin History Workshop celebrate the official naming of the Rosa-Luxemburg-Bridge on January 1, 2013. The small memorial with flowers is visible in the foreground.   129

4.3 "History workshops of all regions – unite!"   146

4.4 The alternative historian, as depicted in a History Movement publication.   151

4.5 Activists of the Berlin History Workshop assembling the exhibit "Rote Insel," April 1989.   155

4.6 Graffiti on a military memorial in Marburg: "Being a soldier is a shameful profession – N.Tolstoy."   158

4.7 Opening of the Berlin History Workshop's Mobile Museum exhibit "Von Krenz zu Kohl," summer 1990 at the Alexanderplatz Berlin.   159

4.8 Activists of the Marburg History Workshop protest during a commemoration of the Marburger Jäger, September 1989.   160

4.9 "How do you feel in such organically grown structures?"   169

5.1 Members of *Bürger gestalten ein Mahnmal* work on asphalt panels for the memorial in Hanover-Ahlem in 1988.   179

5.2 One of the signs of the Memorial around Bayrischer Platz in Berlin: "Postal workers married to Jewish women are forced into retirement, 8 June 1937."   185

5.3 A Stolperstein before its placement in the offices of the Berlin citizens' initiative *Bürgerverein Luisenstadt e.V.*   187

5.4 The Mirror Wall Memorial in Berlin-Steglitz.   190

5.5 Memorial to the Baum resistance group, with Plexiglas addition, Berliner Lustgarten.   198

5.6 Activists of the Marburg History Workshop protest the removal of their monument to the unknown deserter, September 1989.   201

5.7 Singer Wolf Biermann performs at the inauguration of the deserter memorial in Potsdam in 1990. The banner reads: "This sculpture is to be the only German soldier that moves East ever again."   203

6.1 Protesters at Leistikowstrasse 1 form a human chain on the
    occasion of the opening of the new permanent exhibit,
    April 18, 2012.   208
6.2 A protester wearing his prison camp jacket at the same
    rally, holding a UOKG sign, April 18, 2012.   209
6.3 DDR Museum in central Berlin.   230
6.4 Art installation to show how tight quarters were in prison
    cells, Cottbus Human Rights Center.   241
6.5 Commemorative ceremony at Leistikowstrasse, May 16,
    2014.   253
7.1 Topography of Terror memorial in the heart of today's
    Berlin.   264

Preface

My fascination with memory and particularly with the complex politics surrounding the competition between various "pasts" is rooted in narratives about my own family during the Nazi era. My mother's father was a committed member of the Nazi party and pressured his wife to have numerous children, ultimately resulting in her death in childbirth. She posthumously received the "Mutterverdienstkreuz" (mother's cross for accomplishments) by the Nazis. As I was growing up, my mother grappled with this legacy, which shaped her commitment to anti-authoritarian pedagogy – as a parent and as a professor at the University of Applied Sciences in Frankfurt. My paternal grandfather, by contrast, escaped from Nazi Germany to England after his father – a trade union leader – was murdered by Nazi thugs in 1933. He then met my British-Jewish grandmother, who followed him to Australia after he was deported there on a ship called the *Duneera* along with other German and Italian refugees suspected of disloyalty. Resettling in England after the war, he never wanted to return to Germany. This background no doubt compelled my father to become a specialist on migration. Overall, our family's stories and their contradictions underpinned my parents' attitude toward politics and compelled them to be part of critical social movements – the milieu within which I grew up. Attending high school in Frankfurt am Main after the fall of the Berlin Wall, I was exposed to some key debates about memory, most importantly those about the crimes of the Wehrmacht and about Daniel Goldhagen's surprise bestseller *Hitler's Willing Executioners*. I believe that these experiences and family narratives laid the groundwork for my interest in memory and my skepticism toward straightforward readings of the conflicts involved.

The field research for this book was carried out during numerous trips to (and a period of residence in) Germany between 2005 and 2016. During this time, I frequented archives and libraries, undertook site visits, and practiced participant observation at public hearings and expert conferences on memorialization. Above all, I conducted over ninety "semi-structured" in-depth interviews with academics, government officials, memorial staff, members of parliament, artists, and, of course, memory activists. The largest part of the interviews were conducted in Berlin, but I also traveled to other cities for interviews, conferences and site visits, including to Hamburg, Stuttgart, Pforzheim, Weimar, Dresden, Erfurt, Magdeburg, and Jena (among others).[1]

I analyzed transcripts or notes of my interviews, archival materials, and other documents with the help of the qualitative software package *Atlas.ti*.[2] Whenever possible, I sought to "triangulate," that is, to corroborate information by using different types of evidence. Taking a cue from writings on "process-tracing,"[3] I worked to understand and explain the chronology of relevant events, how they were linked together, and how they led to certain outcomes. The processes of meaning-making that surround memory activism cannot be directly "observed" in an interview. As Joe Soss writes "the interview, in a sense, stands outside the stream of interactions we seek to understand and, thus, offers only an indirect basis for accessing them."[4] For this reason, the emotional investments, the contradictions, jealousies, and varying accounts given by interviewees are crucial to provide clues about what memory means in the interaction between different agents. The question that I try to answer is not necessarily "Who is right?" when there are contradictory accounts, but what sorts of politics result from these different understandings and how they impact what memory means to democratic practice. A commitment to democratic practice is ultimately what motivated this study and I believe that memory activism plays a crucial role in this – even in those cases when I fundamentally disagree with some of my interviewees' views and politics.

---

[1] All translations from German, unless otherwise noted, are my own. With one exception, all interviews were conducted in German.

[2] See Lewins and Silver, *Using Software in Qualitative Research. A Step-by-Step Guide.*

[3] George and Bennett, *Case Studies and Theory Development.*

[4] Soss, "Talking Our Way to Meaningful Explanations. A Practice-Centered View of Interviewing for Interpretive Research," p. 139.

Acknowledgments

This book has been in the works for a long time and through several stages of life. Accordingly, numerous people deserve acknowledgement for help and encouragement along the way is long. First, I would like to express my sincere thanks to my interview partners and the many competent staff of archives and libraries. Without their generosity of time and insight, this project would have neither been possible nor as intellectually and personally rewarding. Speaking to those involved in memory initiatives and institutions and hearing about their passion and commitment never failed to reinvigorate my own enthusiasm for this project. In particular, I would like to thank Jürgen Karwelat, Diethart Kerbs, Thomas Lindenberger, Andreas Ludwig, Sonja Miltenberger, and Gisela Wenzel (*Berliner Geschichtswerkstatt*), Michael Heiny (*Marburger Geschichtswerkstatt*), Christine Fischer-Defoy and Kaspar Nürnberg (*Aktives Museum*), Thomas Lutz and Ulrich Tempel (*Topographie des Terrors*), Gerd Koch and Beate Meyer (*Geschichtswerkstatt Hamburg-Eimsbüttel*), Detlef Garbe (*Gedenkstätte Neuengamme*), Christian Albroscheit and Gisela Rüdiger (*Gedenkstättenverein Leistikowstrasse Potdam*), Volker Römer (*DDR Museum Pforzheim*), Renate Bauschke (*Arbeitskreis Bürger gestalten ein Mahnmal, Hannover-Ahlem*), Peter Boeger (*Erinnerungs- und Begegnungsstätte Grenzkontrollpunkt Dreilinden-Drewitz*), Jochen Voit (*Stiftung Ettersberg Erfurt*), Carl-Wolfgang Holzapfel (*Vereinigung 17. Juni 1953*), and Benjamin Baumgart (*Union der Opferverbände Kommunistischer Gewaltherrschaft*) for generously providing me with material and images, answering additional questions and inviting me to events.

This project was made possible through financial support from the University of Maryland, College Park graduate student fellowship program, an American Institute for Contemporary German Studies AICGS/DAAD summer fellowship in 2006, and a postdoctoral fellowship at the Free University's Berlin Program for Advanced German and European Studies from 2012 to 2013. The Berlin Program, with its fellows and its coordinator Karin Goihl, made for an especially productive environment within which to carry out the final phase of field research and discuss results. York University in Toronto and the *Deutscher Akademischer Austauschdienst* (German Academic Exchange Service) have provided a fabulous environment to wrap up the manuscript during my time as a DAAD Visiting Assistant Professor here.

My thanks go to the many individuals who shared comments and gave me advice over the years. In particular, Professor Martin O. Heisler was always ready to provide encouragement and read many draft chapters thoroughly. Professors Ken Conca and Jeffrey Herf also offered indispensable guidance from different perspectives. Professors Miranda Schreurs and Vladimir Tismaneanu accompanied me throughout graduate school. Professor Jim Hollifield has been a mentor from my earliest graduate school days. Professor Martin Will allowed me much freedom to write while working with him as part of the "Independent Academic Commission at the Federal Ministry of Justice for the Critical Study of the National Socialist Past." In addition, various discussants and participants in countless conferences and workshops made helpful suggestions on different incarnations of the project. I would also like to thank Lewis Bateman, John Haslam, and Sarah Lambert of Cambridge University Press for their editorial advice and support. Two anonymous reviewers provided extremely constructive and encouraging feedback.

Sylee Gore, Amy O'Hanlon, and Professor Jennifer Dixon all provided feedback on Chapter 1, and I thank them for doing such a thorough job in a short amount of time. Jennifer's comments were especially astute. Many friends, but most importantly Professors Christina Morina and Jennifer Sciubba, provided both substantive and practical counsel throughout, for which I am very grateful.

My family deserves a lot of credit for providing logistics and comfort. My adopted grandmothers, Ruth Nowak and Gisela Hermann, became a regular audience for my research findings during weekly coffee visits in Berlin-Lichterfelde. My parents, Stephen Castles and Wiebke Wüstenberg, encouraged me throughout research and writing. A very special thank you goes to my mother for kindling my interests in politics and history early on, for giving me so many opportunities to explore them, and for unflagging practical support. In fact, this study would not have been possible without the love and energy with which my mother took care of my kids (and me) on both sides of the Atlantic.

I began this research project as a graduate student in Political Science at the University of Maryland. I finish it now as a Toronto-based scholar and a mother of three. Though the juggling of parenting, research, writing, conferencing, or transatlantic flights is never easy, the combination certainly makes life more rewarding and fun. I thank my daughters for allowing me to leave on research trips without too much complaining, for many much-needed breaks from writing and for giving me a healthy perspective on the importance of academia. Their comments and questions on memorials we visited together also provided some comic relief when the weight of thinking about what was being remembered there threatened to overwhelm me.

Since we met almost twenty years ago, my husband Ben Scott has read and discussed with me most of what I have written – and this book is no exception. He accompanied the entire process – discussing with me the first ideas, planning field research, listening to interview war stories, and helping to manage all the ups and downs of the writing and editing process. He came along for portions of the research or encouraged me from afar. In the final stages, he was a huge source of strength and he proofread the entire manuscript patiently. Very often he took on more than his fair share of family and household obligations – but still found the time to be the most interesting guy I know. All along, he got the balance right between support, motivation, humor, and stress reduction. I could not have asked for more and it is only logical to dedicate this book to him.

Abbreviations and German Terms

ABM	Arbeitsbeschaffungsmassnahmen (government subsidized positions)
ABR	Arbeitskreis Berliner Regionalmuseen (working group of Berlin local museums)
AG	Arbeitsgruppe (working group)
AGN	Arbeitsgruppe Neuengamme (Working Group Neuengamme)
AIN	Amicale Internationale de Neuengamme (main survivors group at Neuengamme)
AK	Arbeitskreis (working group)
AL	Alternative Liste (West Berlin branch of the Green Party)
APO	ausserparlamentarische Opposition (nonparliamentary opposition)
ASF	Aktion Sühnezeichen/Friedensdienste (Action Reconciliation/Service for Peace) in West Germany
ASTAK	Anti-Stalinistische Aktion (Anti-Stalinist Action) – group that runs Stasi Museum in Berlin
ASZ	Aktion Sühnezeichen/Friedensdienste (Action Reconciliation/Service for Peace) in East Germany
BdA	Bund der Antifaschisten (Union of Anti-Fascists)
BdV	Bund der Vertriebenen (League of Expellees)
BGF	Bundesministerium für gesamtdeutsche Fragen (Federal Ministry for Pan-German Questions)
BGW	Berliner Geschichtswerkstatt (Berlin History Workshop)
BKM	Bundesbeauftragte(r) der Bundesregierung für Kultur und Medien (Federal Commissioner of the Federal Government for culture and the media)
BpB	Bundeszentrale für politische Bildung (Federal Agency for Political Education)

BRD	Bundesrepublik Deutschland (Federal Republic of Germany)
BStU	Bundesbeauftragte(r) für die Unterlagen des Staatssicherheitsdienstes der ehemaligen Deutschen Demokratischen Republik (Federal Commissioner for the Records of the State Security Service of the German Democratic Republic)
BSV	Bund Stalinistisch Verfolgter (Association of those Persecuted by Stalinism)
Bundesland	State of the Federal Republic of Germany
Bundestag	Federal Parliament
Bürgerbewegung	(citizens' movement) refers to East German opposition movement of the 1980s
Bürgerkomitee	(citizens' committee) refers to oppositional governing committees that sprang up during the revolution of 1989
BVN	Bund der Verfolgten des Naziregimes (Association of the Persecuted of the Nazi Regime)
CDU	Christlich Demokratische Union (Christian Democratic Union party)
CID	Comité International de Dachau (International Committee of Dachau)
DDR	Deutsche Demokratische Republik (German Democratic Republic)
DGB	Deutscher Gewerkschaftsbund (Confederation of German Trade Unions)
DHM	Deutsches Historisches Museum (German Historical Museum)
DPs	Displaced persons
e.V.	eingetragener Verein (legally registered association)
FDJ	Freie Deutsche Jugend (Free German Youth – East German communist youth organization)
FDP	Freie Partei Deutschlands (Liberal Party of Germany)
Förderkreis	Support association
Förderverein	Support association
FRG	Federal Republic of Germany
GDR	German Democratic Republic
GDW	Gedenkstätte Deutscher Widerstand (Memorial to German Resistance)
Gedenkstätte	Memorial (also *Gedächtnisstätte*) – usually an institution, rather than merely a monument

IBA	Internationale Bauaustellung (International Building Exhibition)
KPD	Kommunistische Partei Deutschlands (Communist Party of [West] Germany)
KUD	Kuratorium Unteilbares Deutschland (Council for an Inseparable Germany)
LpB	Landeszentrale für politische Bildung (State Agency for Political Education)
LStU	Landesbeauftragte(r) für die Unterlagen des Staatssicherheitsdienstes der ehemaligen Deutschen Demokratischen Republik (State Commissioner for the Records of the State Security Service of the German Democratic Republic)
Mahnmal	Monument (in the sense of a monument that warns or admonishes)
MdB	Mitglied des Bundestages (member of the federal parliament)
MEP	Member of the European Parliament
NATO	North Atlantic Treaty Organization
Neues Forum	New Forum, key East German opposition group
NKVD	Soviet service (abbreviation based on the Russian acronym). Its successor was the KGB.
NSMs	New social movements
OdF	Opfer des Faschismus (Victims of Fascism)
OdN	Verband der Opfer der Nürnberger Gesetze (Association of Victims of the Nuremberg Laws)
PDS	Partei des demokratischen Sozialismus (Party of Democratic Socialism, emerged from SED, now called Die Linke after a merger with a West German party)
RAF	Rote Armee Fraktion (Red Army Faction), radical left-wing terrorist organization, operating in the 1970s to 1990s.
SBZ	Sowjetisch besetzte Zone – zone occupied by Soviet forces
SDS	Sozialistischer Deutscher Studentenbund (Socialist German Student Association)
SED	Sozialistische Einheitspartei Deutschlands (Socialist Unity Party of Germany)
SEW	Sozialistische Einheitspartei West-Berlins (Socialist Unity Party of West Berlin)

SPD	Sozialdemokratische Partei Deutschlands (Socialdemocratic Party of Germany)
Speziallager	Soviet Special Camp(s) (run by NKVD in East Germany after 1945)
SRP	Sozialistische Reichspartei (right-wing Nazi successor party after 1945)
Stasi	Staatssicherheit der DDR (State Security of the GDR) Stiftung Aufarbeitung or Bundesstiftung zur Aufarbeitung der SED-Diktatur (Federal Foundation for Working Through the SED Dictatorship)
ThürAZ	Thüringer Archiv für Zeitgeschichte (Thuringian Archive for Contemporary History)
UOKG	Union der Opferverbände kommunistischer Gewaltherrschaft (Union of Victims Associations of Communist Dictatorship)
VdH	Verband der Heimkehrer, Kriegsgefangenen und Vermisstenangehörigen (Federation of Homecomers, POWs and Relatives of the Missing)
VDK	Volksbund Deutsche Kriegsgräberfürsorge (Popular Alliance for the Care of German War Graves)
Verein	Civic association
Vertriebene	Expellees
VOS	Vereinigung der Opfer des Stalinimus (Union of Victims of Stalinism)
VVN-BdA	Vereinigung der Verfolgten des Naziregimes/Bund der Antifaschisten (Union of the Persecuted of the Nazi Regime/Association of Antifascists)
WG	Wohngemeinschaft (living community)

1 Civil Society Activism, Memory Politics and Democracy

On the 5th of May 1985, a small group of activists from the *Active Museum – Fascism and Resistance in Berlin* gathered with shovels near a mound of overgrown rubble in West Berlin. They stood on the site of what had been the headquarters of the Gestapo and several Nazi ministries until 1945. Here, thousands of political dissidents had been interrogated and tortured in the Gestapo's subterranean prison cells. Among them were Jews, Social Democrats, Communists, trade unionists, and other political opponents of the Nazi regime. Key resistance groups, including the conspirators in the July 1944 plot against Hitler, were brought here before they were moved to execution sites or concentration camps. In a different part of the building complex, major elements of the plans for the Holocaust and the war of aggression were drawn up and implemented. And yet, the place had been all but forgotten in the postwar era. The site was used to pile wartime rubble, and one section had been cleared to practice driving without a license.

Three days before the fortieth anniversary of the end of the Second World War, the activists began – symbolically and literally – digging up the past. These regular citizens, teachers and students, and several victims of the Nazi regime, no longer wanted to leave the task of remembrance to the authorities. They chose this location in central Berlin to highlight the failure of the government to commemorate the grim history of such centers of Nazi power. Their publicity stunt was highly effective in propelling the city's leaders to address the Nazi past. The memory activists' demand was to found an "active museum," which would offer research facilities, meeting places, and opportunities for collective deliberation, where visitors would not merely learn about history, but actively engage with it and reflect on its meaning for the present (Figure 1.1). Plans for the site where part of a rising tide of civil society activity at the time, the collective force of which made it unacceptable for the state *not* to reckon publicly with this history. Over the decades that followed, what is now called the Topography of Terror became one of the most important and

1

Figure 1.1. Banner at the Topography of Terror site in 1989: "We need an Active Museum!"[1]

highly frequented memory sites in Berlin. In 2013 alone, the memorial was visited by over one million people, including locals and tourists.[2]

I begin with the *Active Museum*'s digging protest – and depict it on the book's cover – because it is emblematic of the kind of civil society-led activism that has transformed the memorial culture in Germany. The Topography of Terror is especially important because it exemplifies the crucial role played by grassroots action in propelling both a normative shift and institutional change in how the Nazi past and the Shoah were confronted in a society that was initially unwilling to accept responsibility. The *Active Museum* was part of a highly successful movement that gained momentum throughout the 1980s and 1990s to transform the meaning and content of commemoration from the ground up and in every location. Its motto was "dig where you stand." And yet, these efforts were certainly neither the first nor the last time civil society intervened in postwar memory politics. Over the course of the postwar period, grassroots groups have profoundly shaped public commemorative politics and memory culture in Germany. In the immediate aftermath of the Second World

[1] Monika Rummler, Aktives Museum Faschismus und Widerstand in Berlin e.V.
[2] www.topographie.de/topographie-des-terrors/presseservice/pressemitteilungen/.

War, Holocaust survivors demanded the commemoration of victims. Throughout the decades that followed, victims' associations and interest groups representing German expellees and veterans erected their own monuments and lobbied state agencies to officially remember their experiences and suffering. In East Germany there were similar impulses toward memory activism – but they were quickly squashed by the regime.

These early efforts resulted in countless memorial markers across West Germany, but they did not succeed in overturning the mainstream and official memorial regime. The early 1980s, however, marked an inflection point when West German memory politics underwent both a qualitative and quantitative transformation. Myriad citizen initiatives and history workshops sought to investigate local and everyday history, uncover traces of the past, mark the sites of National Socialist terror and make their findings relevant to political education. According to a survey by Brigitte Hausmann, during the 1980s "about half of the monuments were initiated by history working groups, homeland associations (*Heimatvereine*), peace groups and citizen initiatives, by associations for Christian-Jewish cooperation and memorial initiatives"[3] – in other words, by civil society. The memory landscape that resulted was decentralized, antimonolithic, self-reflexive – and profoundly different from contemporaneous "official" monuments. For the first time, perpetrators, sites of crimes, and the range of Nazism's victims were explicitly named and commemorated. Much of this memorialization activity was driven by two key West German social movements – the Memorial Site and the History Movements – and took place against the resistance of state authorities. These movements became two of the most important instigators of new memorials about the Nazi past and had a lasting effect on the state institutions that govern how memory "is done" in the united Germany.

After the fall of the Berlin Wall in November 1989, a new wave of civic activism emerged – this time to memorialize the victims of East German authoritarianism – that was just as momentous in transforming German memory politics as the movements of the 1980s. The contested sites of memory now focused on former crossing-points between East and West, the locations where the East German regime had incarcerated its opponents, and the places that had become emblematic of resistance to dictatorship. Once more, civil society organizations emerged to challenge the government to do more to commemorate the central sites of repression. And again, the political contest over public memory commanded national media attention and steered a heated public debate. Fluctuating between the meticulous work of commemoration – making exhibits, holding vigils,

---

[3] Hausmann, *Duell mit der Verdrängung?* p. 13.

interviewing witnesses – and the contentious quality of protest actions – occupying sites, illegally erecting monuments, holding hunger strikes – these new memory activists have profoundly shaped the memory landscape of the Berlin Republic. Through these strategies, civic advocates have both pressured state actors to address the legacies of the East German dictatorship and challenged the prevailing norms about what "democratic remembering" means in unified Germany. A very clear example of this was the installation of a memorial dedicated to those who died trying to cross the Berlin Wall by a coalition of activists at Checkpoint Charlie in Berlin. The controversial director of a decades-old private museum at Checkpoint Charlie had been instrumental in erecting over one thousand black crosses, some marked with names of the dead, on leased land at the former crossing point in 2004. Critics argued that this kind of remembrance was neither historically accurate – a study later put the number of Wall victims at 138[4] – nor in line with the aesthetic sensibilities of a diverse and multireligious public. But the site was defended vigorously by organizations representing victims of repression in East Germany. When the crosses where ordered removed (mainly due to a dispute about real estate), former political prisoners and their supporters chained themselves to the crosses in protest (Figure 1.2). These memory activists viewed the authorities' reluctance to defend the installation as a sign of its general unwillingness to adequately honor their experiences and grant them prominence in public space. They demanded that the East German dictatorship receive a level of attention comparable to the Nazi past. The clash between different memories – and between civic activists – becomes even more poignant at locations with a "double past." These are memorial sites that hold meaning both for victims of the Nazi regime and for those who experienced repression in East Germany. The Buchenwald and Sachsenhausen concentration camp memorials are the most well-known. Such sites encapsulate the tensions created by the commemoration of diverse pasts after the fall of the Berlin Wall.

This book analyzes the role and long-term impact of memory activists from 1945 to the present, examining a broad range of remembrance from that of the Holocaust and the Nazi past, to Germans' war experiences, to repression under the East German regime. The confrontation with history as an arena of modern German politics has long featured hotly contested debates and attracted intense scholarly scrutiny. Nonetheless, scholars have neglected the work of grassroots, civic organizations, which have played a central role in determining the evolving landscape of memorials and commemoration. Directly addressing this gap, this book

---

[4] Hertle and Nooke, 'Die Todesopfer an der Berliner Mauer.'

Figure 1.2. The cross memorial installation at Checkpoint Charlie in Berlin: activists chained to the crosses to prevent their removal in 2005.[5]

examines the tensions between state institutions and memory activists representing different views of the past. I show why and how such activists shape outcomes in German memory politics and argue that the continuing contention about Germany's "dark past" and its meaning for democratic governance cannot be understood without considering civic memory activism.

By focusing on civil society action in memory politics, I examine the link between memory and democracy in two ways. First, through the study of grassroots activism, I offer a novel explanation of why Germany's approach to commemoration changed so dramatically in the course of the postwar period and followed a trajectory that is unique when compared to other countries. I examine how civic engagement has become interwoven with state institutions, transforming both in the process. Throughout, I detail the shifting balance between public remembrance that is *representative of majority opinion* and remembrance that promotes *norms that may challenge that majority*. My account traces how the normative regime of

[5] Roland Brauckmann, Union der Opferverände kommunistischer Gewaltherrschaft.

memory – those practices and narratives about the past that are considered acceptable by the public and by state institutions – changes over time through civic action.

Second, in this first comprehensive account of memory activism in Germany, I home in on the practice of memory initiatives and contend that it is precisely when the work of memorialization is contentious – *when memory work becomes memory protest* – that civil society challenges norms and institutional structures and directly impacts the course of democratic societies. This is not to say that civil society single-handedly drives normative change. In fact, it makes little sense to regard grassroots groups as separate from their institutional context. Rather, in postwar memory politics, civic initiatives of various kinds have pushed normative innovation by identifying and highlighting where memorial practices conflicted with contemporary public norms about what makes up a functioning and sustainable democracy.

Investigating the influence of memory activism in postwar and postunification Germany requires weaving together many and diverse stories about activist groups and local contexts into a coherent narrative in order to substantiate my broader arguments. As such, my conclusions cannot easily be generalized: my book is unapologetically about Germany, and Germany only. However, the concepts and mechanisms I identify – most notably the balancing act between representative and normative components of democratic memory and the tipping point between memory work and memory protest – should find fruitful application beyond the German context.

Memory Activism and Democracy

This introductory chapter explains how I employ key social scientific concepts and how they guide my analysis. However, the question of how memorialization relates to democracy is not solely an abstract one: most of the over ninety individuals I interviewed for this study are deeply invested in how their engagement and identity matter for the quality of Germany's democracy. The current Director of the Topography of Terror, Andreas Nachama, stressed the importance of activism in the memorial's history, arguing that "much like connected pipes in physics, if you put more civic engagement in on one side, more democracy will also come out the other end."[6] The causal link between public remembrance and democratic institutions is made explicit here, highlighting the importance of reckoning with the past for the stability and deepening of German democracy. Though Nachama made this statement in the context of

[6] See Interviews, Andreas Nachama.

remembering the Shoah, civic and governmental actors across the spectrum of remembrance have argued that greater civic engagement in memorialization leads to better democratic outcomes.

But is it possible to say that memory activism – irrespective of its aims or strategies – strengthens democracy? What do we make of activism of the kind that challenges the commemorative primacy of the Holocaust for German democracy? Can we regard civic engagement to commemorate the plight of wartime expellees as democracy-enhancing if it laments the location of the current border between Germany and its Eastern neighbors? What happens when victims justly commemorate the harm done to them by Communist perpetrators, but do so using the rhetoric of the extreme right? Does civic activism always translate into a more democratic memorial culture? In other words, is Nachama's equation a universally applicable formula?

The relationship between memory and democracy turns on two axes: first, the capacity and representativeness of state institutions to commemorate publicly; and second, the normative values of democracy (e.g., justice, human rights, and equality), which may or may not characterize popular memory or officially implemented memory at any given moment in time. State-supported commemoration can be (and in practice often is) broadly representative of public opinion, even while memorializing pasts or groups whose values are not democratic. The tension between representation in democratic institutions and the normative values of democracy form a central theme in this book.

To elaborate on this problematic, consider that a minimalist definition of democracy emphasizes the procedural provisions that ensure the "rule of the people" through elections, as well as other institutional safeguards against the abuse of state power. Thus, applying the idea of representative government to public remembrance might mean the representation of the historical experiences and symbolic references of the *majority* of society in public space. In other words, memories that are widely and strongly shared in society (though not necessarily "historical truth") dominate the memorial landscape. This, I argue, was the case in the early postwar period, when memorials to German "victims" of war far outnumbered those to the victims of Nazism. At the time, liberal elites feared that an honest confrontation with the crimes of the German majority through the honoring of Jewish and other victims would endanger the nascent institutional structures of the Federal Republic (FRG). As Jeffrey Herf writes, the "inherent tension between memory and justice on the one hand and democracy on the other would appear to have been one of the central themes of postwar West German history."[7]

---

[7] Herf, *Divided Memory* p. 7.

In contradistinction to such a majoritarian approach to memory, it is precisely the extent to which memories of *minorities as well as of historical failures of the majority* (the perpetration of crimes, racism, anti-Semitism, collaboration, profiteering, etc.) are represented publicly that characterizes a "deeply" democratic society. Hence there is a basic tension between a *representative* and a *normative* regime of remembrance. This tension can be captured in the distinction between a *democratic process of memory*, which is staked on the breadth of public support, and the *democratic content of memory*, which is found in the democratic values expressed through commemoration. Civic initiatives hold the potential to mediate this tension and create spaces outside of representative institutions that can host alternative democratic processes. At the same time, such spaces can be used to challenge prevailing norms about acceptable ways to confront the past.

A society that acknowledges its own wrongdoings and calls for respect and protection for the memories of its victims engages in what Konrad Jarausch has called "inner" democratization.[8] I argue that civic efforts to work through the Nazi past, to examine the crimes and name the perpetrators, and to mark sites of suffering and resistance in public space have contributed to such "inner" democratization in the Federal Republic. Since the early 1980s, the two social movements mentioned earlier – the Memorial Site and the History Movements – were particularly instrumental in shifting this form of remembrance from the margins of civil society to the central memorial institutions of the German state. Such normative change was driven to a crucial extent (though not exclusively) by memory activists. In order for this normative change to happen, the local *work of memory* – historical research, archiving, interviewing, presenting results – had to be become contentious action, or *memory protest*. Memory became protest both because the content of the commemorative work challenged the prevailing notions of what was acceptable remembrance in public space and because activists used confrontational tactics to force public change. These conflicts drew responses from the state (and sometimes other memory activists) and ultimately led to change through gradual resolution, compromise, concession, and sometimes even through the more rapid transformation of memory institutions.

By the 1990s and 2000s, I argue, the *normative regime of remembrance had become largely representative*. By "representative," I mean that a particular set of mnemonic values were evident in the practice of official memory institutions. This was a victory for the many civic initiatives that

---

[8] K. Jarausch, *German Studies Association Annual Meeting*, Denver, CO, October 3–6, 2013.

had fought for a critical reckoning with the Nazi past. However, their success also led to a decline in the power of mnemonic civil society and a concomitant decline in its critical potential. Moreover, despite the strong civic and state support now enjoyed by the "Holocaust-centered" memory regime, it has been challenged by new civic memory claims, with implications for the evolving norms of public remembrance.

Illustrating the unintended consequences of memory activists' successes, recent calls to recognize the plight of "ordinary Germans" during the war and under Communist dictatorship have often been derided as attempts to dismantle the work done to confront the Nazi past or even to relativize the memory of the Shoah. Victims of Communist repression have in turn decried the trivialization of their suffering. These debates are important reminders that public memory must strive to be representative of the different historical experiences present in society without violating the norms that are constitutive of a democratic political culture. Dealing with the commemoration of suffering in Soviet camps and East German prisons poses new challenges to mnemonic norms that have gone largely unquestioned since the 1990s. As with earlier periods of memory activism, the content of the commemorative activity of initiatives focused on the German Democratic Republic (GDR) challenges prevailing mnemonic norms. Furthermore, these new activists have explicitly adopted protest tactics, effectively triggering another wave of memory protest and memory work with the potential to change commemorative practices and norms of public remembrance.

The question now is whether the existing institutions, actors, and norms that constitute German memorial culture will allow a new generation of memory activists to shape a portion of public space – without prescribing rules of remembrance that have congealed in the course of earlier struggles. The task is to integrate the plight of victims of Communist repression in a way that takes seriously their own interpretation of history and does not impose an existing normative narrative on them. The democratic quality of German commemorative culture and its ability to address the complexity of history will be put to the test. There are no simple answers to the question of how the politics of memory interact with ongoing processes of democratization. However, this book contends that an understanding of the role played by civil society in the politics of memory does much to explain the link between memory and democracy. Civil society has a potentially decisive role in transforming the political culture of democracy – either toward or away from deeper democratization.

In a book seeking to bring grassroots actors "into" the study of memory politics, it would be tempting to regard civil society involvement as a straightforward path to the creation of a democratic memory culture. As Andreas Nachama of the Topography of Terror would have it, the more activism you put into a memorial, the more democratic it will be. Though I stress the deep impact that activists have had on public memory, civil society is neither always the source of laudable impulses to memorialize, nor are there particular memories that are automatically beneficial to democracy. There are many instances of civic activism pushing for public memory that commemorate perpetrators or bystanders to violence above its victims, that deny or gloss over historical facts, or that support an exclusionary or antidemocratic political agenda. In other words, civic engagement is not virtuous in and of itself (as some theorists would have it), but depends upon its institutional context and substantive goals.

Another central argument is that the definition of democratic memory is not clear-cut. The history of German memory activism underscores that interpretations of the past that are widely felt in society (even if they are problematic from a normative standpoint) *and* those memories that evoke a deeper consideration of democratic values (even if they are felt only by a minority) must find their way into a negotiated public memory. Democratic memory politics can therefore be either representatively or normatively democratic (or both), and sometimes in contradictory ways. The arguments made by activists and others about the relevance and meaning of their own proposed commemorative approach must therefore be investigated without an a priori assumption about the democratic value of a particular narrative about the past.

Key Concepts

This study is situated at the intersection of scholarship about public memory, civil society and social movements, and the requirements of democratic institutions. In using concepts and theories from these three bodies of scholarship, my work draws from several complex and long-standing intellectual traditions. In the remainder of this chapter, I discuss the existing theories and arguments that provide a frame for understanding the interrelationship between memory activism and democracy.

Given the multidisciplinary nature of memory studies and the terminological baggage that scholars from different fields bring to the table, the lack of agreement on terms is perhaps not surprising. This situation compels every work on remembrance to begin with a clarification of concepts – mine is no exception. Central to my analysis is "public memory," which can signify any expression or result of efforts to mark events, individuals, or lessons learned from the past *in public space*. Public memory is the subject of contention for memory actors. Remembrance or commemoration (and this includes forgetting) are the active processes on the part of individuals, groups, and institutions that leads to public memory.

Pierre Nora argues that the fascination with the past is manifested most prominently in *lieux de mémoire* (realms of memory). The need for representation and place-creation exists because the memory of our past is no longer an integral part of everyday life and rituals.[9] Thus, memory is a historically contingent concern and its present strength as a cultural mode explains in part why many groups now seek memorialization when they previously might have expressed their identity and interests in other ways. The cultural and political importance of having a particular moment or version of history represented drives political competition and social conflict over public memory.

Though some authors use the term "memorial" interchangeably with a *lieu de mémoire*[10] and thus broadly include any result of remembrance, I take it to mean physical and purposely built manifestations of memory in public space. These include museums, monuments, commemorative plaques, art installations, signs with historical information, and more. Memorials are initiated by "memory actors," a term I will use as an umbrella concept for any type of actor (state, individual, or group) that seeks to shape public remembrance. My concern with the contentious politics and grassroots mobilization that drives memorialization processes accounts for my focus on *memorials*. Other manifestations of public memory – such as anniversaries, debates, educational policies, representations in media, fiction, or historiography – are of course also relevant. However, physical memorial sites are especially significant for being the subjects of intense civil society mobilization. They can be highly visible and thus hold key symbolic value due to their placement in (more or less) prominent locations. In disputes over memorials, civic actors directly encounter agents and institutions of the state. The politics of memorialization are closely related to more general politics of memory, but their outcomes in the form of monuments do not neatly correspond to individual or intersubjectively held memories. What makes the politics of memorialization fascinating is that through them, decisions are made about what gets "set in stone" in public spaces. Memorials evoke the contention and power relationships that brought about their construction.

[9] Nora, 'General Introduction' for work applying Nora's framework to Germany, see Reichel, *Politik mit der Erinnerung*; Borsdorf and Grütter, 'Orte der Erinnerung' Francois, 'Deutsche Erinnerungsorte.'

[10] Nora and Kritzman, 'Realms of Memory.'

Another important motivation for my concentration on public monuments is the tension inherent in them with respect to the symbolism of democratic politics. As the Director of the Buchenwald concentration camp memorial Volkhard Knigge points out, the monument was traditionally a predemocratic form; a cultural symbol that was erected to evoke loyalty and identification with a state or community.[11] The debates between memory activists, artists, state representatives and others about the aesthetics, placement, and design of memorials are thus instructive as to their intended meaning in democratic societies. Most strikingly, the skepticism about monuments and the resultant ideas for "countermemorials" during the 1980s signify a new requirement that remembrance sites be self-reflexive, inclusive, participatory, and critical. In other words, memorials are especially important for my examination of memory activists' transformation of the link between remembrance and democratization: memorials are sites in which the actions of representative and normative democracy are staged.

The notion of a "politics of memory" has also been highly contested in scholarship. There are several different approaches to the idea. For example, Norbert Frei's use of the concept in German (*Vergangenheitspolitik*) has a specific meaning connected to his work on the first five years of the Federal Republic. Far from acknowledging the plight of Nazism's victims, the purpose of *Vergangenheitspolitik* in the early 1950s was to institute a break with the occupation period and to reintegrate convicted or "purged" Germans into society and, through this indiscriminate exoneration, to dispel feelings of collective guilt. While not a coherent policy, this *Vergangenheitspolitik*, was promoted by political elites and broadly supported by the public. Though other scholars have used *Vergangenheitspolitik* in a broader sense (to include policies to compensate victims for example), it has usually retained a relatively short temporal focus, concerning the first years after regime change.[12]

By contrast, two other approaches to memory politics – *Geschichtspolitik* (history politics or policy) and *Erinnerungspolitik* (memory politics or policy) – have come to be associated with symbolic and discursive reckoning, rather than with judicial or material policies. History/memory politics are not temporally limited by the presence of witnesses to or participants in history.[13] Some commentators attach to it a pejorative air that suggests manipulation and instrumentalization.[14] As Erik Meyer

[11] V. Knigge "Denkmäler demokratischer Umbrüche nach 1945," 12th International Symposium Stiftung Ettersberg, Weimar, 18–19 October 2013.
[12] Meyer, 'Memory and Politics' p. 175, Wolfrum, *Geschichtspolitik in der Bundesrepublik*
[13] Meyer, 'Memory and Politics.'
[14] Wolfrum, *Geschichtspolitik in der Bundesrepublik*; Meyer, 'Memory and Politics.'

puts it, "the question is not if the image of history communicated is scientifically truthful. Instead, the crucial factor is how and by whom, as well as through which means, with which intention, and which effect past experiences are brought up and become politically relevant."[15]

Another body of scholarship reverses the model of top-down instrumentalization of memory and begins at the individual level, focusing on the subjective processing of historical experience. Individual memory is often a crucial factor motivating memory actors to become engaged in the shaping of public memory. Nevertheless, I am not directly concerned with individual (or even "collected") memory[16] because I am interested in cases where memory becomes the object of public controversy and is thus necessarily intersubjective. In such cases, civil society-driven memory politics come into play, challenging and molding state-driven memorialization. Temporal and generational factors are relevant to these contentious interactions. Jan Assmann has popularized the distinction between communicative and cultural memory, where the former refers to the immediate processes of confronting past history (akin to *Vergangenheitspolitik*) and the latter denotes the long-term and more symbolic perspective.[17] The primary difference is based on generational variation among actors and the amount of time that has elapsed since the past in question. Though one should not overstate the distinction between communicative and cultural memory, it is useful because some of the most intensive memory struggles occur during the shift from one to the other.

My focus on periods of contentious memory politics explains the use, throughout this study, of analytical tools borrowed from social movement theory. In particular, I use the concepts of political opportunities, mobilizing structures, and frames to systematically analyze memory initiatives and to make them clearly visible as social movements – something that is rarely done in research on remembrance.

In sum, my study is delineated in several key ways. I am interested in the contentious politics of memory, that is to say in the interactions of memory activists with state and other actors in their struggles to have a particular interpretation of the past receive public attention. I am not concerned with individual memory or that of specific social groups; rather, I want to understand the processes by which societal commemoration is negotiated. Finally, I focus in particular on memorials (physical markers in public space) because conflicts over these sites are especially well suited to examine the role of grassroots activists and their impact on democracy.

---

[15] Meyer, 'Memory and Politics' p. 176.   [16] Olick, 'Collective Memory.'
[17] Assmann, *Das kulturelle Gedächtnis*see also Assmann, *Religion and Cultural Memory*.

Agency in Memory Studies

Political science has been a late addition to the field of memory studies, which continues to suffer from a lack of conceptual clarity.[18] Some political scientists have sought to demonstrate that remembrance affects power balances and political decisions and should thus be subject to the same scrutiny as any other policy field.[19] Despite these welcome contributions, memory studies remains notable for the lack of systematic attention paid to agency and to grassroots agency in particular. Much of the literature on memory in Germany is made up of descriptions and analyses of public discourse. This concentration is partly a result of the genuine role that public debates have played in the memory politics of the Federal Republic, such as the *Historikerstreit*, the scandal concerning the exhibition about crimes of the German *Wehrmacht* or over the *Black Book of Communism*. Accordingly, some of the most insightful analyses have happened in this context.[20] However, this scholarship is often curiously silent on *who it is* that is defending certain lines of arguments and by which strategies and alliances they have come to be successful – as if the outcome of public deliberations were based solely on verbal competition between individuals. Though authors often mention various actors, they seldom provide a more detailed account of their role. As Jan-Werner Müller has pointed out, however, "remembering ... *is* a form of action," and it is always a product of ongoing intellectual and political negotiations between the social "carriers of memory."[21] The term "carriers" is somewhat of a misnomer as memory actors are not merely passive transmitters of history – they reshape images of the past in the course of struggling for their acceptance. Alon Confino has advocated for "writing the history of memory's construction as commingling with that of memory's contestation."[22]

Most historians and social scientists, however, take the view that collective memory is written and sustained by political leaders from the top down. But the political speeches and ribbon-cutting for new memorials mask a more complex history of bottom-up initiatives and social

---

[18] Roediger and Wertsch, 'Creating a New Discipline'; König, *Politik und Gedächtnis* p. 16.

[19] See for example Berger, 'The power of memory and memories of power'; Schrafstetter, 'The Long Shadow of the Past'; Markovits and Reich, *The German Predicament*; Cruz, 'Identity and Persuasion'; Art, *The Politics of the Nazi Past*; Levy and Dierkes, 'Institutionalising the past.'

[20] For instance Maier, *The Unmasterable Past*; Art, *The Politics of the Nazi Past*, Assmann and Frevert, *Geschichtsvergessenheit – Geschichtsversessenheit*, Sabrow and others, 'Wohin treibt die DDR-Erinnerung?', Brumlik, Funke, and Rensmann, *Umkämpftes Vergessen – Walser-Debatte, Holocaust-Mahnmal und neuere deutsche Geschichtspolitik*, Cullen, 'Das Holocaust-Mahnmal', Jeismann, 'Mahnmal Mitte'

[21] Müller, 'Introduction: the power of memory' p. 30.

[22] Confino, 'Collective Memory and Cultural History' p. 1398.

movements that – more often than not – do the real work of making memory. These initiatives operate with a particular logic and according to patterns of political practice that recur over time. For instance, the same kinds of processes that built Germany's powerful memory culture around the Holocaust are now contesting that culture. New organizations demanding the commemoration of the victims of East Germany's dictatorial state are challenging established institutional structures. These clashes showcase the practice and importance of social movements in making memory.

To some extent, the elite focus of the memory literature can be explained by the fact that members of the state have long dominated commemorative politics. According to the philosopher Agnes Heller, since the eighteenth century, nation-states (in addition to religions) have been the primary proponents of cultural memory. She writes that "the work of building and preserving cultural memory became first and foremost the employment of the state, or governments. States, or more precisely governments, began regularly enlisting so-called intellectuals – teachers, poets, painters – in the production of cultural memory, and continue to do so."[23] The erection of monuments, the staging of public celebrations, the naming of streets and memorial days have long been activities of state agencies, and of political and religious leaders.[24] Since the French Revolution, the state has skillfully used public remembrance in order to unite a population behind a common war effort or national cause.[25] In the course of the twentieth century, with the questioning of unrestrained hero-worship and the increased visibility of victimhood narratives, the making of memory has gradually become more inclusive. Memory is no longer simply imposed from above, though it is probably misleading to assume that it ever was; it is the result of a societal negotiation between "official" memory actors, elites, and nonelite groupings and individuals in the context of prevailing networks of meaning.

So far, few scholars have adjusted their research focus to this diversification in memory actors; most studies still concentrate on the actions of the state – its agencies and individuals at various levels of organization – as well as those of intellectual elites.[26] Erik Meyer writes, for example, "Not only representatives of the political administrative system are involved [in controversies about the past], but also individuals and groups who possess a privileged access to the political public sphere. In addition to

---

[23] Heller, 'A Tentative Answer' p. 1033.
[24] See Le Goff's description of the development of memory from pre-historic to modern times: Le Goff, *History and Memory*.
[25] Mosse, *Fallen Soldiers*, Koselleck, 'Die Transformation der politischen Totenmale.'
[26] Wolfrum, *Geschichtspolitik in der Bundesrepublik.*

politicians, this elite includes journalists, intellectuals, and scholars."[27] Noetzel directs his attention to lobbying efforts.[28] While this is a noteworthy approach, it assumes that "the state" is the main memory creator that must be persuaded to act by other actors that are separate from it. In other words, such studies depict an image in which the state is the (only) definitive institution for the politics of the past in which only elites participate. Social movements, civil society, and "ordinary people" are peripheral, as are more complex understandings of what it takes to mobilize in order to achieve public remembrance.

The most sophisticated attempt at grappling with the question of agency in memory politics thus far is Michael Bernhard and Jan Kubik's *Twenty Years After Communism*, in which they provide a typology of mnemonic actors. The authors categorize those involved in memory politics through their normative approach to the past, calling them mnemonic warriors, pluralists, abnegators, and prospectives. This is a significant approach, because it allows a better understanding of the intractability of the contention between different memory actors in the German case and elsewhere. However, Bernhard and Kubik adopt a relatively narrow instrumental reading of memory politics, which is not always about manipulation. Memory agency is not exclusively aimed at strategies "to make others remember in certain, specific ways."[29] Their typology also does not differentiate how various actors are situated with regard to power structures in society, particularly the state, and thus does not reference specifically the role of civic actors.

When scholars do connect civil society and memory, the latter is often regarded as "a form of communal *property* that, in circular fashion, reconfirms the identity of the group" in the sense that Michael Rothberg has criticized.[30] Barbara Misztal for instance argues that the past is used to define a group's self-understanding: "Collective memory in civil society provides a source of categories through which a group constructs its identity; a necessary step in the development of the group's ability to speak in one voice or be a political actor in the process of its mobilization."[31] Ron Eyerman similarly provides a range of examples in which social movements have used references to the past as a way to support their struggles or help define their identity.[32] Such work has little to say about how grassroots actors become engaged in shaping memory for the society writ-large.

---

[27] Meyer, 'Memory and Politics' p. 176.   [28] Noetzel, 'Erinnerungsmanagement.'
[29] Kubik and Bernhard, 'A Theory of the Politics of Memory' p. 7.
[30] Rothberg, 'Multidirectional Memory' p. 126 (emphasis in original).
[31] Misztal, 'Memory and Democracy' p. 1329. A similar approach can be found in Uehling, 'Social Memory as Collective Action.'
[32] Eyerman, 'Social movements.'

Many accounts of memory politics in Germany do make note of societal contention, but without digging deeper. For instance, Thomas Berger's explanation of why some states issue apologies for past wrongs (while others do not) suggests that various groups are involved in the making of collective memory. However, collective memory is seen as separate from official memory: states suppress or manipulate societal memory and "insurgent narratives" may challenge official ones.[33] Moreover, Berger does not regard societal groups as integral to the making of the state institutions that govern memory. David Art also proposes a top-down model of ideational change that is elite-driven and may open windows of opportunity for the participation of other actors, but these are also identified as elites.[34] Wulf Kansteiner notes that "decentralized memory activities accelerated in the 1990s," but thereafter returns to official memory policies.[35] All these authors seem to regard nonelite activity as a symptom, rather than a possible cause, of the changing nature of memory.

There are some notable exceptions to this neglect of civil society activity. Rudy Koshar, in his careful study of changing memorial forms in Germany from 1870 to 1990, grants grassroots initiatives an important role in the memorial politics of the 1980s and accurately identifies the institutional consequences.[36] Jay Winter and Emmanuel Sivan "examine collective remembrance . . . as the product of individuals and groups who come together, not at the behest of the state or any of its subsidiary organizations, but because they have to speak out."[37] The authors rightly contend that there has been an overemphasis on state agency and manipulation at the expense of civil society, but their work accounts only for the actions of victims during a period of transitional justice. This excludes both long-term projects and civil society activities not centered on victims.

Matthias Haß, Karen Till, and Claus Leggewie and Erik Meyer have all written studies on memory campaigns in Berlin, in which civil society plays an important role,[38] but they do not move beyond their specific cases to an assessment of the larger importance of these practices. Jennifer Jordan places the "memorial entrepreneur" (together with public resonance, land use and ownership) at the center of her account of Berlin

---

[33] Berger, *War, Guilt, and World Politics.*   [34] Art, *The Politics of the Nazi Past.*
[35] Kansteiner, 'Losing the War' p. 126. Other major works on the topic similarly mention civil society only peripherally: Wolfrum, 'Die beiden Deutschland', Reichel, *Vergangenheitsbewältigung in Deutschland.*
[36] Koshar, *From monuments to traces.*   [37] Winter and Sivan, 'Setting the framework' p. 9.
[38] Haß, *Gestaltetes Gedenken,* Till, *The New Berlin,* Leggewie and Meyer, *"Ein Ort, an den man gerne geht."*

memorial politics and clarifies the processes by which some memorials are built while others are not.[39] Going beyond Germany, Birgit Schwelling brings together a diverse set of case studies on the participation of civil society in transitional justice processes. Anna Reading and Tamar Katriel focus on how nonviolent struggles have found their way into – or been excluded from – cultural memory. In both volumes, civil society plays a central role, but the authors do not offer a joint framework for how to conceptualize it in relation to memory.[40] This scholarship offers important insights, however, to my knowledge, there are no systematic studies of civic activism that provide a framework for analysis and an in-depth examination of civil society engagement in memory politics. By putting grassroots front and center in the story of how memory politics changed in postwar Germany, this book aims to fill that gap.

In studying memory activism, we must pay particular attention to moments when memory becomes contentious, that is, when *memory work* becomes *memory protest*. I distinguish between these two *modes of action* in mnemonic civil society, in order to highlight that it is the contentiousness of memory – rather than memory per se – that propels normative change. I define *memory work* as those activities that are the primary occupation of memory initiatives, including: holding meetings; networking with stakeholders and potential benefactors; creating forums for debate; lobbying; conducting historical research (through archival work, interviews and the collection of materials); safeguarding of evidence (sometimes under adverse conditions); presenting findings in exhibits, publications, and guided tours; and organizing commemorative events (large and small). These kinds of activities are, by definition, undertaken by memory activists, and often take place outside of broader public view. Memory work can become contentious for two reasons: first, because the content of commemorative activity clashes with existing mnemonic norms or challenges the government's official line (this is the case particularly in nondemocratic regimes). Thus, the mere voicing of an alternative memory makes it contentious. Second, memory can become protest because activists employ contentious tactics, intentionally provoking a reaction from society. Often, this shift occurs for both of these reasons. Memory protest tactics can involve the whole range of the social movement repertoire and are linked with the explicit publicization of historical information or the staging of public commemoration. Common for the grassroots actors examined in this book are: staging

---

[39] Jordan, *Structures of Memory.*
[40] Schwelling, 'Reconciliation, Civil Society', Reading and Katriel, 'Cultural Memories of Nonviolent Struggles.' See also Margry and Sanchez-Carretero, 'Grassroots Memorials' for an account of spontaneous bottom-up memorialization.

rallies and other protest actions such as occupations or sit-ins; putting up exhibitions and memorials in provocative places or manners; undertaking hunger strikes (a tactic used especially by early memory activists and more recently by GDR victim groups); repurposing existing memorials through signs or graffiti; and illegally placing monuments or commemorative symbols. The distinction between work and protest is not always straight-forward, nor is it regarded as such by activists. Crucially, however, grass-roots memorialization challenges and transforms norms about the past most rapidly and profoundly when it is contentious. *Noncontentious memory work* is either in line with mainstream memory narratives (as was the case with expellee or veteran activism in the immediate postwar era) or is not visible enough and so can easily be ignored by elites and by society at large (like that of some Holocaust survivor groups during the same period). Memory activists have struggled to have their interpretations of the past acknowledged throughout the postwar period, but they have not always succeeded in transforming mnemonic norms in the emerging democratic society. They are effective when their actions provoke public outrage or pressure on other actors to either shift positions or dig in their heels, thereby producing more protest.

Civil Society, Movements, and Memory

Grassroots actors are the primary protagonists in this book, and my empirical research shows how their initiatives shaped memory politics in postwar Germany. However, they cannot be understood in isolation from the state. As historian and former activist Thomas Lindenberger argues, "where there is civil society, there is always also governmental action that addresses civic structures and the civil society structures themselves know this. You always have to include this, otherwise you may construct auton-omous grassroots action in a way that has never existed in reality."[41] The relationship between civil society and the state is highly complex as they clash over and negotiate about how to interpret and implement competing values in the memorial landscape. Civil society action in Germany today is funded and praised by state actors and is at the same time subjected to control. Civic activists regard "the state" with suspi-cion, and yet work closely with its representatives or even inside its agencies. Activists identify with memorial institutions they helped create, and bureaucrats contend that these same institutions are not "state-like." Through such (at times uneasy) cooperation, state and civil society actors have participated in the establishment of a strong framework of rules

---

[41] See Interviews, Thomas Lindenberger.

about what is legitimate, democratic, and fund-worthy memorialization. My larger point is that the analytical division between civil society and the state in the memory field is unhelpful for understanding the struggle over public remembrance. Neither state nor civil society is a monolithic party in memory politics. Both need to be disaggregated in order to understand the actual social relationships and interactions that underpin and shape public memory. The experience of transforming the commemorative landscape in Germany holds many insights for practitioners in other countries – but it does not suggest a straightforward path for how to achieve "democratic memory."

As I discuss below, the scholarship on civil society and social movements offers opposing assessments of the relationship between civil society and the state. A strong current in the civil society literature sees civic engagement as a fundamental part of building social capital that supports and reinforces strong state institutions that are representative and participatory pillars of democracy. The social movements literature develops the view that civil society actors serve as a check on state power and are the bottom-up disciplinary force that democracy requires to challenge state institutions. The history presented here shows that both of these assessments come into play. The memory movements I detail in the chapters that follow did in fact emerge in opposition to the state and serve as a check on the top-down instrumentalization of memory politics. Yet these civil society groups also engaged deeply with state institutions and became increasingly integrated with them over time.

Both lines of reasoning ultimately offer a normative reading of the implications of activism for democracy. Civil society as a concept is historically bound up with the rejection of barbarity, as well as the establishment of decency, human rights, and tolerance. Moreover, the idea of civil society as an arena that is *autonomous* from other spheres (familial, economic, religious, governmental) is an extraordinarily strong normative force that permeates scholarship and activist communities alike. Though Jeffrey Alexander conceptualizes civil society as "contradictory and fragmented" and as "created by social actors at a particular time and in a particular place," it is nevertheless an "independent sphere" which offers the "possibility of civil repair."[42] By this Alexander means that actors, especially social movements, within the civil sphere function as guarantors of democracy when elites abuse their power. "To maintain democracy, and to achieve justice, it is often necessary for the civil to 'invade' noncivil spheres, to demand certain kinds of reforms, and to monitor them through regulation in turn."[43] Nancy Bermeo makes

[42] Alexander, *The Civil Sphere* pp. 6,7.   [43] Ibid. pp. 33–34.

a similar point, arguing that the "connectedness of civil society" to other spheres is crucial for its democratic functioning.[44] Thus, both the autonomous identity of civic actors and the values that have been nurtured within civil society have the potential to infuse the institutions of the state with much-needed democratic spirit. Theorists of democracy, too, have argued that democratic institutions thrive only when challenged by "counter-democracy."[45]

Rather than conceptualize the civic sphere as separate from and somehow more "pure" than other spheres, I conceive of civil society as a kind of "imagined community"; a sphere that activists (and many academics) believe to be "a world of values and institutions that generates the capacity for social criticism and democratic integration."[46] Although "base" motivations such as hunger for power, profit, and emotion of course play a role in this arena, it is the *appeal* to solidarity and community purpose that is key to civil society. It is this normative identity that sets memory activists apart from the state. This makes the distinction between state and civil society no less real, but it does mean that the distinction can shift or blur in the course of contentious action.

Formal as well as informal groups operate in civil society. Civic associations (*Vereine*) have a defined legal status, whereas citizens' initiatives are not (yet) registered with the state. Social movements are usually larger and more dispersed than civic groups, though the latter may form part of a social movement. I use the term "(grassroots) activists" as an umbrella for all these variants. Again "the grassroots" tend to have a strong identity that sets them apart from "the state," but this does not negate the possibility of an intermeshing of civic activity with official institutions. One of my arguments is that civil society and state are often not neatly separable, that individuals move back and forth between the two and can identify with both. In the realm of memory politics, this has produced what I call "hybrid institutions," which combine characteristics commonly associated with both civil society and the state. Nevertheless, in my analysis of memory contention, I routinely write of "civil society" and "the state" – not because they are analytically always separable, but because they are important "categories of practice," that help constitute actors' sense of their struggles and loyalties. This distinction between concepts used in scholarly analysis versus in political practice is crucial and should be kept in mind throughout my account.[47]

---

[44] Nancy Bermeo cited in Kubik, 'Hybridization as a Condition' p. 112.
[45] Pierre Rosanvallon cited in della Porta, *Can Democracy Be Saved?* p. 4.
[46] Alexander, *The Civil Sphere* p. 4.
[47] I borrow this useful distinction from Brubaker, *Nationalism Reframed*.

Despite the close association of civil society and social movements, and their considerable overlap in practice, scholarship about them has developed within two relatively distinct research programs. A central concern of both, however, has been the relationship of activists with the state.

Theorists of civil society since Tocqueville have grappled with understanding the relationship between "state" and "civil society" in general and between civic engagement and democratic governance in particular. Some have hailed civil society as the solution to our democratic woes.[48] Robert Putnam is the most well-known proponent of the notion that civic engagement through associations makes for effective institutions. He argues that collective action problems that routinely hamper the functioning of institutions can be alleviated through civic community: since citizens who are part of a strong community expect better government, they are more likely to get it, partly because they strive for it, partly because representative government is supported through a vibrant social infrastructure.[49] For Putnam, effective institutions equal democratic ones.

In addition to the belief that civil society leads to the smoother functioning of institutions, scholars have contended that the internal dynamics of civic associations socialize members and equip them with key skills and "habits of the heart" needed for active citizenship.[50] According to Putnam, trust and reciprocity are all nurtured in civil society, while the absence of these norms (which he encapsulates in the concept of social capital) breeds distrust, shirking of responsibility, isolation, and disorder.[51] Applied to memory politics as a realm of civic activity, this approach might suggest that civil society is an unequivocally positive force for democratizing public remembrance. In a democracy, civil society can help guide the project of representative commemoration by compelling citizens to become engaged. Civil society is also the place where a critical approach to commemoration can be fostered. However, closer scrutiny of the relationship between "civil society" and "democratic state" suggests that, in practice, matters are not so straightforward.

First, civil society is by no means automatically beneficial to democratic institutions, even when associations foster a community spirit. Early on, Samuel Huntington argued that the mobilization of society without corresponding institutional development leads to social disorder and can endanger democracy.[52] Sheri Berman contends that civic engagement can undermine democracy. She demonstrates that due to the weakness of

---

[48] Barber, *A Place for Us* p. 6.   [49] Putnam, *Making Democracy Work.*
[50] Tocqueville, *Democracy in America* p. 497.   [51] Putnam, *Making Democracy Work.*
[52] Huntington, *Political Order in Changing Societies.*

Weimar institutions and political parties, citizens shifted their allegiance to nongovernmental organizations. The Nazi Party was able to tap into these civic networks and thus establish deep roots of support in German society.[53] This suggests that activism – about memory or otherwise – is not necessarily "civil" in a normative sense: "The discourse of civil society can be as repressive as liberating, legitimating not only inclusion but exclusion."[54]

Second, social movement scholars are skeptical of the benefits of activist cooperation with the state. An underlying assumption is that movements start out in a relatively unstructured manner, then gradually solidify, and finally become static institutions (and so the opposite of a movement).[55] Such images derive from Robert Michels' classic work on German Social Democracy, which argued that every large organization tends toward oligarchy, characterized by a differentiation between leadership and membership, the development of a professionalized operation, and a shift away from movement goals toward the corporative interests of the organization.[56] Sidney Tarrow, however, has a more differentiated perspective on the relationship between movements and institutions, arguing that

> ... movements [closely] interact with institutions. This is not simply a question of challenging institutions – although this is the central image the social movement cultivates – but also of collaborating with institutional actors and, at various times, gaining support from institutions ... But institutional participation is, as we have seen, a double-edged sword. Social movements that are too alienated from institutions risk isolation and sectarianism; but those which collaborate too closely with institutions and take up institutional routines can become imbued with their logic and values.[57]

The role of activism in democracy, then, has been assessed divergently: Putnam and others see civic engagement as supportive of the state, while social movements scholars have regarded civic engagement as a counterweight to the power of the state. In practice too, activists routinely face the dilemma of cooperating with elements of the state while maintaining their autonomy and critical function. As we shall see, this predicament is at the heart of the relationship of many memory activists with formal institutions. Activists often see their key contribution to democracy in watching and checking "the state's" moves in the field of memory politics, and in providing alternative memory solutions. When

[53] Berman, 'Civil Society and the Collapse,' see also Brubaker, *Nationalism Reframed.*
[54] Alexander, *The Civil Sphere* p. 4.   [55] Rucht and Roose, 'Von der Platzbesetzung.'
[56] Michels, *Soziologie des Parteiwesens,* Rucht and Roose, 'Von der Platzbesetzung' p. 176.
[57] Tarrow, *Power in Movement* p. 208.

successful, they see their mnemonic proposals realized in public space. Frequently, however, they also receive material and normative support from state agencies and government officials. The problem of possible cooptation by the state has led to serious conflicts within many memory initiatives. However, my research also raises another question: what happens to state institutions when they become imbued with the logic and values of activists? Conversely, what does it mean for democratic governance when state actors take over memory sites that were initiated by civil society?

Memory and Democratic Institutions

In the field of democratization, and in transitional justice in particular, there has been a considerable amount of work done on the relationship between memory and democracy, which intersects with my own concerns. I emphasize here the debate about whether institutional structures or normative changes are more likely to result in more sustainable democracies. I contend that this is a false separation because it ignores the interactions and contradictions that can exist between the two. This point is important to my argument that attention to memory activism helps us understand precisely how the tension between majoritarian and normative cultures of remembrance plays out in practice. Once again, the question arises whether it is the state or civil society that plays the decisive role in controlling memory politics. And once again, the more complicated reality is that it is both, and it is the interaction between the two that emerges as the focal point of study when these ideas are applied in actual case studies.

Anne Sa'adah contends that during democratization, two goals stand side by side and often compete with each other: the aim to create a "community of behavior" in which citizens respect the rules and institutions of the state, and the objective to foster a "community of conviction" in which democratic values are internalized. The former is established through an "institutional" strategy, which is concerned primarily with the absence of violations and the reliability of the citizenry. The latter is the result of a "cultural" strategy that seeks to create a trustworthy citizenry with a self-sustaining democratic spirit.[58] According to Sa'adah, a community of behavior draws lessons from the past by erecting strong institutions and regards "too much" memory as potentially detrimental to those institutions. This was very much the conviction of many leaders in postwar Europe, where myths of resistance and anti-German heroism

---

[58] Sa'adah, *Germany's second chance.*

glossed over the extent of complicity and collaboration. In the newly founded Federal Republic, Chancellor Konrad Adenauer feared a right-wing revolt against the democratic system, and thus felt that the price of integrating compromised Germans was silence about Nazi crimes.[59] A community of conviction, by contrast, is dependent precisely upon the confrontation with the past, even if it is still painful and fresh. Such a reckoning forces individuals and groups to reevaluate their beliefs about democracy and membership in the community, thereby leading to cultural change.

Scholars of transitional justice have focused overwhelmingly on institutional strategies, with the partial exception of work on truth commissions and apologies.[60] Experts in this field tend to be most concerned with the risk of authoritarian reversal during early phases of democratization, as well as with the inherent uncertainty of transitions. The reigning assumption, according to Sa'adah, is that "in a contest between (democratic) institutions and (nondemocratic) mores, institutions can win."[61] In other words, institutions are thought to have an "integrative effect" by which they can shape citizens' attitudes over time and bind them to the democratic system.[62]

This institutional perspective, however, is limited by a short-sighted concentration on the immediate needs of democratic governance, focusing mainly on recent atrocities and concrete accountability policies: There is an implicit assumption that long-established liberal states do not confront similarly fundamental questions when dealing with the past.[63] For Jarausch, "the negative fixation on the effort to cope with the terrible legacies of dictatorship has largely prevented a critical look at the creation, character and role of memory culture in *maintaining* democratic societies."[64] While the transitional justice literature has made the most sustained contribution to our thinking about democracy and memory, it has also resulted in a short-term and institutional bias.

Theorist Gesine Schwan takes the opposite stance. In *Politics and Guilt*, Schwan worries that with traditional institutions such as political parties in decline, the "silenced guilt" felt by Germans will endanger democracy through a decline in trust and self-esteem, and the rise of scapegoating and isolation within society. Consequently, she argues that accumulated guilt for Nazi crimes must be dealt with in order to avoid scapegoating

---

[59] Judt, 'The past is another country', Herf, *Divided Memory*.
[60] Berg and Schaefer, 'Introduction', Torpey, 'Introduction: Politics and the Past'
[61] Sa'adah, *Germany's second chance* p. 4.   [62] Schwan, *Politics and Guilt* p. 142.
[63] Torpey, 'Introduction: Politics and the Past.'
[64] Jarausch, 'Critical Memory and Civil Society' p. 12 (emphasis added).

and alienation. After all, she suggests, "the traditional alternative to better institutions has been better citizens."[65]

While the "cultural" approach favored by Schwan and Sa'adah has the advantage of a long-term perspective and regards democracy as more than a set of rules and structures, it suffers from an artificial separation of institutional and cultural, or, in my terminology, representative and normative commemoration. Rather than the question of whether institutional rules or the norms of democracy should be prioritized; it is more *crucial to understand the ways in which the prevailing tension between the two is negotiated in practice.* While it is important to study institutional solutions in the aftermath of dictatorship and violence, investigating public memory offers the appealing opportunity to focus precisely on those processes that cannot be pigeonholed into either the state or the societal category. An understanding of the politics of memory as a public performance of democratic identity and civic power reveals how conflicting interpretations of the past are part and parcel of the continuous cultural struggle that shapes institutions from inside and out. Far from viewing contention around memory as a sign that the "correct" lessons from the past have not yet been ingrained in society, negotiations over memory should be regarded as fundamental processes in and determinants of democratic societies.[66]

Civil Society and the State

Throughout this review of theories of civil society, social movements, democracy, and memory, the interaction between activists and state actors, and their impact on democracy have been recurring themes. Most scholars posit state and civil society as neatly separable entities that either help or harm one another. Instead, I contend that we must examine how civil society and state actors play off each other and use one another to legitimate their preferences in the memory field. What happens to institutions when civic activism and civic norms "infiltrate" the state apparatus? And what are the (memory) political outcomes of this?

As I have argued, the image of civic autonomy from the state is critical to the identity of grassroots activists. State agencies, meanwhile, regard civic engagement as a field of policy-making and a space in which to intervene. German policy-makers, for instance, have actively sought to create support structures for civic initiatives and have tried to outsource some of the traditional tasks of the state to this sector.[67]

---

[65] Schwan, *Politics and Guilt* p. 146.
[66] Dowe, 'Geschichtspolitik als wesentliche Aufgabe' p. 185.
[67] Alscher and others, 'Nähe und Distanz' p. 18.

Michael P. Brown argues that civic organizations can become closely intertwined with state agencies in the course of efforts to provide services or transform public policy. He conceptualizes such hybrid institutions as a "shadow state" that is staffed and shaped by civil society but has complex ties to the state apparatus.[68] The intermediary character of such hybrid institutions makes them more effective than either "pure" state or civil society actors. "By drawing on their grassroots origins, volunteer organizations can better identify with the needs that the state had failed to acknowledge; yet, by drawing on their state-like qualities, they can better accommodate the heightened levels of demand for services that inevitably accompany increased needs."[69]

The development of this shadow state can have both empowering and disempowering effects. On the one hand, activists may be able to provide critical services and address policy challenges with vastly improved resources. This means that the usual distinctions – between work and politics, citizen and bureaucrat, and state and civil society – may no longer be very meaningful. On the other hand, the growth and complexity of these organizations may make them more "state-like," reducing the informality of interactions and giving activists less control over their work or forcing them to defend state interests.

There are several important lessons here. First, Brown reminds us that the state is not a monolithic actor but rather a multifaceted one.[70] In the field of memory, bureaucracies, parliaments, agencies, and local authorities become active across a wide array of memory political activities in civic life. The state is thus encountered in many forms and in diverse spaces, including symbolic ones such as public memorials and museums. Second, state and civil society are not clearly separate and distinct. This means examining closely where civic activity takes place, rather than automatically assuming that it occurs outside the boundaries of the state.[71] Moreover, as Timothy Mitchell points out, "we need to examine the political processes through which the uncertain yet powerful distinction between state and society is produced."[72] As I will show, this is key to understanding the development of hybrid memorial institutions. During the 1980s and 1990s, citizens' initiatives created pressure on public institutions to adopt a critical approach to the Nazi past. This resulted in the partial institutionalization of key principles of memory activism – manifested through staff, organizational structures, and memorial principles. The same happened even more rapidly after 1989, when advocates for GDR memory appeared on the scene.

[68] Brown, *RePlacing citizenship.*   [69] Ibid. p. 117.   [70] Ibid. p. 18.   [71] Ibid. p. 119.
[72] Mitchell, 'Society, Economy, and the State Effect' p. 77.

The institutional arrangements of memory work matter not only because of how they translate into the memorial landscape and contemporary political culture, but also because they provide a framework for future memorialization efforts. New activists must contend with (or try to alter) existing institutional structures. Memory initiatives since the 1980s impacted not only *how* the Nazi past is commemorated, but also changed institutions in ways that – over time – influenced how the memory of East German Communism, and other "pasts" are represented in public today. The ideals, values, and processes that were born from opposition to "official" commemorative practice were then integrated into hybrid activities within the state. This has created a novel normative model for enacting public memory within governing institutions. This model – which was shaped by the last generation of memory activists – is now under challenge from the next generation, and so the cycle appears to repeat.

The realization that the state is inseparable from civil society and that it has been "infiltrated" by the grassroots should not suggest that it ceases to be a realm for the exercise of power. The salient question is: how is power exerted in the arena of memorialization when state representatives intermingle and often identify with memory activists? Lindenberger argues that the German federal state "has established a regulatory frame of orientation," implementing "persuasive authority rather than application of sheer force or formal rules." This is done by enabling others – including civil society groups – to act on the state's behalf in matters of memorialization, using guidelines for action based on "specific rationalities" in order to coordinate activities of various actors.[73] The establishment of such "neutral" guidelines was particularly important at the federal level after 1989. Memory leaders at the federal level during and after reunification were faced with the challenge of recasting large GDR memorial sites and accommodating demands from new memory activists. Meanwhile, they were held to a high standard by West and East German activists to live up "to the democratic credentials of West Germany's reflexive history culture and East Germany's Peaceful Revolution."[74] Local authorities faced a similar challenge when negotiating the future of memorial sites in their communities, especially with a double dictatorial past from before and after 1945. Such contention has been characterized by bitter conflicts about the relative meaning of atrocities under Nazism and Stalinism.

Lindenberger's observation is astute but incomplete. The state governs memory politics indirectly, by establishing rules and outsourcing concrete policy-making to nonstate actors. But the state in his conception is

---

[73] Lindenberger, 'Governing Conflicted Memories' pp. 79–80.   [74] Ibid. p. 77.

regarded as the primary source of regulation – no matter how subtly exercised – and as relatively distinct from civil society. Instead, I contend that we must pay attention to *how actors within the state and the civic sphere jointly construct a framework for legitimate memorialization* – and what happens when actors from either realm come into conflict with this system of rules. This point challenges the assumption that civil society simply confronts state behavior from an autonomous position. Government policy-makers, memorial officials, and activists all have to demonstrate that they can operate within this framework and conflict erupts when they violate its norms. The result can be either exclusion from the legitimate memorialization "scene" (with important implications for support and funding) or a transformation of the rules themselves.

To reiterate, my analysis of memory activism from 1945 to the present is built on the assumption that the *boundary* between state institutions and civil society is *a category of practice*. Actors define and imagine this boundary through their contentious interaction. The boundary is thus real and meaningful, but it is not static. To paraphrase Rogers Brubaker: it is important not to take a concept inherent in the *practice of memory activism* – namely the idea of separable and idealized spheres of civil society and state – and make it part of the *theory of memory activism*.[75] Both civic memory activists and the leaders of state institutions hold these views about the boundaries between their respective "spheres." And yet, both sides consistently work across those boundaries in a hybrid space through which civic values are transmitted into public remembrance. I argue throughout this book that a construction of narratives about democracy and memory happen in this hybrid political space. This activity is especially meaningful and transformative of existing institutional arrangements when the work of memorialization turns contentious, when memory work becomes memory protest. Close attention to hybrid spaces, their inhabitants, and how they interact highlights the balancing act between representative and normative memory and clarifies the link between memory and democracy.

Outlook

The next chapter provides an account of civic initiatives aimed at building memorials since 1945. The goal is to examine the entire breadth of memory activism of the early, postwar period – including the efforts of victims of Nazi persecution, reconciliation initiatives, anti-Communist campaigners, expellee groups, and veterans. In this way, I assess not only the incidence of civic involvement, but also its outcome in terms of

---

[75] Brubaker, *Nationalism Reframed* p. 15.

concrete memorial spaces. This chapter demonstrates that while the history of memory in Germany is incomplete without due attention to these groups, the state maintained the upper hand in struggles over memory during this time. The examination of the early memorial activists of the Federal Republic (and of attempted civic action in the German Democratic Republic) is couched in the broader context of the history of German memory politics. I also discuss how memorial debates have developed from the 1960s to the present in order to contextualize the arguments I make about civic memorialization in subsequent chapters.

In the third chapter, I focus on the initiatives that helped to transform the sites of Nazi terror – most importantly concentration camps on German soil – into large, state-funded institutions with educational missions and political cultural weight. I discuss the changing role of victims' associations in the governance and design of these memorials and their interaction with the *Gedenkstättenbewegung* (Memorial Site Movement) that gained in strength since the 1980s. I trace the process by which civic pressure has shifted these sites of Nazi terror from the margins to the heart of German public policy and commemorative culture. I focus particular attention on the case study of the Active Museum, the citizen's initiative in Berlin discussed at the outset of this chapter, which was instrumental in achieving what is today one the most important memorial sites of the Federal Republic: the Topography of Terror.

The fourth chapter offers the first comprehensive account of the left-wing *Geschichtsbewegung* (History Movement). It was composed of myriad local "workshops" and "alternative archives" that were networked with each other and sought to practice a new type of historical research and public education. I detail the Movement's emergence, milieu, goals, practices, development, outcomes, as well as its gradual decline in the 1990s. Through their local work, the History Movement became one of the most important initiators of memorials throughout West Germany. Through lobbying efforts, protest action, and their "long march" into the institutions of the state, these activists have transformed both memory landscape and institutions from the ground up, emphasizing the importance of critical remembrance for democracy.

Chapter 5 examines how the Memorial Site and the History Movement have jointly influenced the German memorial landscape. I discuss and illustrate the design principles promoted by these closely allied movements, including decentrality, authenticity, antimonumentality, and the diversity of the victims of Nazi terror. A common theme is the attention paid to the nonemotionality of approach and the primacy of historical research, which is an emphasis that will later clash with the aesthetics of some GDR victim groups.

The sixth chapter shifts attention to memory politics after the fall of the Berlin Wall. I investigate both the institutional context and many important civic initiatives to commemorate the GDR, which were closely intertwined from the outset. I detail the roles played by victims groups, former GDR oppositionists, "pragmatic" activists, and for-profit memory entrepreneurs. I analyze the ways in which civil society initiatives have framed their work in terms of democratic memorialization and the need for recognition, as well as the tools used to implement their goals. I then trace how civic memorial projects have become institutionalized and how state and civil society have become interwoven. To illustrate these processes, and the difficulties that can arise along the way, I discuss the case of the Leistikowstrasse Memorial in Potsdam – the site of a former Soviet prison. Throughout the chapter, I argue that remembrance of the GDR must be viewed in the context of the institutional structures and individuals that have become significant in the course of the struggle to commemorate the Nazi past. Thus, the antecedent history of civil society engagement in the field of memory politics shapes current developments.

In the concluding chapter I bring together evidence from the study as a whole to construct an argument concerning the mechanisms by which memory activists engage with and transform state institutions. I examine how left-wing memory activists have made their mark on memorial institutions through institution-building, staffing, and normative transferal. I also trace the processes of institutionalizing those civic initiatives that have campaigned to commemorate different facets of the GDR legacy. Overall, I emphasize the importance of mnemonic civic action, its long-term influence on institutions, and its crucial function in explaining the ongoing competition between Holocaust and Communist memories in the Federal Republic. Moreover, I stress the analytical leverage gained from the focus on civic activism for understanding the complex relationship between memory and democracy. I argue that the relationship between civic activists and the state in the cultural field of public commemoration has important implications for our understanding of the memory-democracy nexus. Unlike unabashed champions of civil society such as Putnam, I argue that the interventions of activists in memory politics do not have an automatically positive impact on institutions. Nevertheless, it is crucial to take seriously the demands of memory activists – whether civil or "uncivil" – if our goal is to build a truly democratic culture of remembrance.

2   Memorial Politics and Civil Society
       since 1945

On the ninth of September 1945, thousands gathered in the Berlin neighborhood of Neukölln to remember those who had not survived Nazi persecution. Amid the flags of the countries that had endured German occupation, former prisoners and relatives erected a monument, mourned their losses, and solemnly vowed to eradicate fascism and build a democratic Germany.[1] This was the first time the "day of the victims of fascism" was marked and survivors showed their ability to mobilize for the cause of memory. The second Sunday in September subsequently became an official commemorative date in both German states and was decisively shaped by the civic groups that emerged from the ad hoc initiatives of 1945. These victims' organizations were the memory activists of the first hour – and their rallies marked the beginning of the contention over the meaning of memory between civil society activists and the state. It was a struggle that crucially influenced the ways in which the Second World War, the Holocaust, and the historical consequences were commemorated.

This chapter examines how East and West Germans maneuvered their respective (and later united) paths of memory politics. Most importantly, I investigate to what extent civil society activists have been involved in the shaping of public memory and in particular in the creation of the physical landscape of memorials. I provide the historical context necessary for the central arguments of this book, specifically exploring four distinct periods of public memory. In each case, the analysis calls attention to the crucial (and underresearched) role played by civil society actors in memory politics throughout the postwar era.

First, even in the immediate postwar years, there was significant civil society activity that aimed to construct memorials in both East and West Germany. In the West, most of the Holocaust memorials inaugurated 1945–1960 were not initiated by state actors. They were organized by the victims and relatives of victims of Nazi persecution. Initially, the West

---

[1] "Der zweite Sonntag im September. Zur Geschichte des OdF-Tages" http://odf-tag.vvn-bda.org/ausstellung.php3?id=2.

German government was tolerant, though not supportive of these groups. Several had left-wing leanings that were deemed suspicious in the anti-Communist climate of the time. The state reserved most of its assistance for civic activists campaigning to engrain the memory of German soldiers and civilian victims. These groups – expellee and veterans organizations most prominently – were vocal, well funded, and held a high status during the 1950s in the FRG. They successfully worked to establish a dominant narrative whereby everyone had suffered under Hitler and, apart from a few bad apples, all were to be honored for having served the fatherland. The Holocaust and its perpetrators were virtually absent from this discourse. Memory activists with a critical perspective laid the groundwork for successors during this period, but their ability to influence mainstream institutions of memory was limited.

In the East meanwhile, though the same impulses for activism (and some of the same organizations) existed as in the West, the state rapidly seized control of the memorialization process. The government outlawed even leftist survivor organizations, marginalized uncomfortable memories, and generally suppressed dissent. The memory of Communist resistance against Nazism was harnessed to serve state ideology. The rulers quickly erected a landscape of antifascist memorials intended to place them on the victorious side of history and enhance popular allegiance to the regime. This approach to memory – official instrumentalization and suppression of societal initiative – was continued until the mid-1980s, when a careful opening was allowed. There is considerable evidence that members of the GDR opposition movement at this time undertook a more critical reading of the past that could be labeled "memory activism."

The second major period of postwar memory activism began in the 1960s. It was a pivotal time for the development of critical memory, but less due to the confrontation with the past that took place and more because of changes in society writ large. Building on the societal liberalization made possible by rising prosperity and a host of liberal intellectuals during the 1950s, the sixties saw not only the radicalization of students and their call for transformation, but also a series of events that moved the Nazi past onto the public agenda. The combination of widespread social mobilization with a more general societal opening laid the foundations for more detailed memory work later on. Moreover, the failure of the student movement and the splintering of the left that resulted in the formation of an "alternative scene" of "new social movements," created the social backbone of the civic initiatives discussed in Chapters 3 and 4. However, the memorialization work of the 1968ers themselves was limited in impact. This is reflected in the scant numbers of monuments that were initiated during this period.

The third and decisive period of transformation in German memory politics and landscape began in the late 1970s and extended to the fall of the Berlin Wall. New social movements were at the height of their vibrancy and met with a rising interest in memory and history in diverse sectors of society. From about 1979 to the late 1980s, there was both a *quantitative* and *qualitative* change in memory activism. Initiatives to scrutinize local, regional and national history emerged in all kinds of organizations, while the fascination with the past engulfed the entire political spectrum. Most importantly, myriad independent initiatives collectively became the single most effective force for critical commemoration. More memorials were inaugurated during the 1980s than during all the postwar years combined.

The current period of memory politics in Germany begins with the fall of the Wall in 1989 and continues to the present. Three overall trends shape the events and debates of this period. First, I argue that the memory of the Nazi past has become "representative," not only in the sense of being reflective of a widely held attitude to German history, but also in that it enjoys sustained support by the state. The activists and intellectuals who fought to direct attention to the Holocaust and its perpetrators during the 1980s have moved into the mainstream and many of them hold positions of power within the institutions that administer public memory. Second, Holocaust remembrance has acquired prominence in the public landscape – this is most immediately demonstrated by the Berlin "Memorial to the Murdered Jews of Europe." In other words, the Nazi past holds a place at the very center of German political life.

However, the third major trend has emerged that challenges the first two. The post-Wall era brought a diversification in memory activists and the landscape that they have helped to produce. Remembrances of German suffering and of victims of the Communist regime have emerged from their previously right-wing domain and are also finding a novel home in public space. These memories have been supported most importantly by civil society groups that today represent the critical voice vis-à-vis the memory politics of the state – much like the citizens' initiatives did as part of the Memorial Site and History Movements during the 1980s. I argue that this pluralism has brought with it competition between different memories and their advocates. This struggle has impacted what I have called "normative memory" and which had – primarily through hard-fought civic action – been moved from the margins into the mainstream of German political culture. The demand to remember the suffering of victims of the Communist regime has brought to the scene a new kind of normative memory.

This chapter provides an analytical history of the civic memory initiatives from 1945 to the present that made their impact on memory politics. Each period is shaped by its historical context and influenced by what came before. But common central themes emerge that repeat in different forms since 1945. Most important is the constant struggle between the state and different civic and social movements over the decades. These contests form the central political terrain on which the meaning of public memory is negotiated, formulated, and implemented in public space. And within this fight, again and again, a central role in shaping public memory is played by civic memory activists and their ability to make memorialization into a contentious activity.

Confronting the Past in East and West After 1945

After the war, the majority of Germans rapidly shifted from being supporters of the Nazi regime to portraying themselves as victims of Hitler. Germans' resentment of Allied measures and their – no doubt real, if self-inflicted – suffering from the general societal collapse made many feel part of a "community of fate" again. Estimates suggest that Allied bombing raids killed up to half a million civilians and had produced about three million evacuees who were housed mainly in barracks and with other families. About a quarter of the housing stock (in some cities up to three-quarters) had been shattered.[2] The new authorities also had to deal with about 12 million refugees or "expellees" – ethnic German populations from former German territories in Eastern Europe. Millions of men were absent – having died in battle or held as prisoners of war. Many of those prisoners of war (POWs) interned in the Soviet Union never returned. These experiences became the primary foci for memorialization in the postwar era. The political elites of the two new states founded in 1949 were therefore faced with the challenge of legitimizing their rule and winning the allegiance of their populace. Though they dealt differently with Germans' wartime experiences and their responsibility for National Socialism, they both harnessed memory politics for the purposes of reaching this objective.

The Federal Republic of Germany

In West Germany, government authorities did not maintain strict control over memory politics, but neither was there much in the way of justice for and reconciliation with the victims of Nazism. The changing international

[2] Schildt, 'The Long Shadows.'

climate of the early Cold War years curtailed the pursuit of transitional justice begun by the Allies. In the 3.6 million trials during the Allied occupation and then in German courts, 95 percent of defendants were exonerated, amnestied, or classed as harmless "fellow-travelers." Only 1,667 persons were given prison sentences or severe fines.[3] Norbert Frei contends that this almost indiscriminate absolution was driven by a high level of consensus in the population that rejected any responsibility for Nazi atrocities, as well as by the negative electoral implications of forcing a confrontation with the past. The amnesty enabled the new leaders to emphasize the break with the occupation period and harness the support of the population – all in the name of democracy.[4] Jeffrey Herf argues that Konrad Adenauer "struck a bargain with compromised Germans: in exchange for his reticence about the Nazi past, they would agree to accept the new democracy, or at least not try to destroy it."[5] This arrangement was seen by Western Allies as a tolerable price to pay for the FRG to be firmly rooted in the anti-Communist camp.[6] While there were important exceptions, such as philosopher Karl Jaspers, President Theodor Heuss, Social Democrat Kurt Schumacher, and publicist Eugen Kogon, most Germans were not keen to discuss the Nazi catastrophe.[7] The call for justice and the memorialization of Nazism's victims was therefore left mostly to survivors of the Shoah – and among these, many did not have the material and psychological resources for this mission.

Hermann Lübbe contended that the "communicative silence" about recent history extended the solidarity of Nazi society into the democratic state after 1945 and made possible its survival.[8] However, as Robert G. Moeller argues, it would be misleading to present the immediate postwar period as one of complete muteness about 1933–1945. In fact, Germans intensively commemorated when it came to their own dead. POWs and fallen soldiers, those "expelled" from Eastern Europe, and the victims of Allied bombing campaigns were all mourned and seemed to justify a collective narrative in which Germans themselves were the victims of Hitler and Allied reprisals.[9] "West Germans collectively mourned the suffering of these groups, and their experiences became central to one important version of the legacy of the war; their private memories structured public memory, making stories of Communist

---

[3] Ibid. p. 36.   [4] Frei, *Vergangenheitspolitik*, Frei, *1945 und Wir.*
[5] Herf, *Divided Memory*, p. 389.   [6] Kansteiner, 'Losing the War.'
[7] Herf, *Divided Memory*, Assmann and Frevert, *Geschichtsvergessenheit – Geschichtsversessenheit*, Jarausch, *Die Umkehr.*
[8] Lübbe, 'Der Nationalsozialismus im politischen Bewußtsein.'
[9] Moeller, *War Stories*, Moeller, 'Remembering the War', Assmann and Frevert, *Geschichtsvergessenheit – Geschichtsversessenheit.*

brutality and the loss of the 'German East' crucial parts of the history of the Federal Republic."[10]

Popular culture reinforced this mainstream account of who had suffered most during the war and many towns erected memorials to the dead.[11] Expellees were one of the most visible forces in federal and state politics in the FRG, with their party entering the *Bundestag* in 1953 and becoming part of chancellor Konrad Adenauer's coalition government.[12] Veterans and expellees founded numerous organizations as soon as this was permitted by the Allies and actively cultivated their cultural heritage, erected memorials,[13] and in some cases demanded the return of lost lands. Indeed, one might call the expellees the most effective "memory activists" of the early postwar period. The state ensured that the narratives of expellees and soldiers became part of public memory: their stories were included in school curricula and the government funded cultural and scholarly institutions designed to safeguard the culture of the "German East." It even commissioned two massive research projects that collected testimony from thousands of expellees and POWs.[14] Neither study included the experiences of the victims of National Socialism. Though Jews and others were not completely forgotten, their plight and their identity remained faceless.[15]

Participation in the policy-making processes of federal institutions legitimized the concerns of various constituencies. From unions to expellees, organized interests soon felt they had a stake in the new system.[16] In the early years of the Federal Republic, allegiance to the democratic state was possible despite (or maybe because of) the absence of a vigorous confrontation with the Nazi past. The building of democratic institutions and of public memory that represented the majority of Germans was thus privileged over the fostering of democratic norms that would have been symbolized in the commemoration of the Shoah. This concession, of course, was made at the expense of Nazism's victims and the continued presence of authoritarian elements in culture, daily life, and administrative structures.

[10] Moeller, 'Remembering the War' p. 86.
[11] Mühl-Benninghaus, 'Vergeßt es nie!,' Schornstheimer, *Bombenstimmung und Katzenjammer*, Schissler, 'The Miracle Years,' Ullrich, 'Weltuntergang kann nicht schlimmer sein.'
[12] Ahonen, *After the Expulsion*, Holtmann, 'Politische Interessenvertretung von Vertriebenen', Ther, 'The Integration of Expellees,' Stickler, 'Die deutschen Vertriebenenverbände.'
[13] Panne, 'Erinnerungspolitik – Erinnerungsspuren', memorials, www.bund-der-vertriebenen .de/information-statistik-und-dokumentation/mahn-und-gedenkstaetten.html.
[14] Moeller, 'Remembering the War,' Schulze, 'Zwischen Heimat und Zuhause.'
[15] Moeller, 'Remembering the War.'
[16] Jarausch, *Die Umkehr*, Moeller, 'Remembering the War.'

When addressing an international audience, on the other hand, Adenauer acknowledged German responsibility and culpability, although he did not name perpetrators directly. Agreeing to restitution payments and support for Israel was designed to convince partners that the FRG was permanently reformed and trustworthy. This two-sided approach was reflected in the political elite's handling of sites of Nazi persecution. While most of these locations were not safeguarded, the most important ones (such as Dachau and Bergen Belsen) strategically underwent minimal memorialization in response to pressure from German, but especially international, victims' organizations.

In sum, during the early 1950s, the democratic regime in West Germany was not guaranteed popular support and therefore carefully sought to cultivate the allegiance of its citizenry as well as the assurance of its international guarantors. The result was a complex and somewhat paradoxical approach to the Nazi past in which German responsibility was not denied outright, but its meaning was not actively impressed upon the German population. The dominant civic voices in the memory politics of this period were not the victims of Nazism, but rather the war veterans and expellees with their narrative of common German suffering. This fit with the larger political frame of Adenauer's Germany, defining the new Germany on terms other than Nazi crimes. Edgar Wolfrum argues that West German leaders were able to capitalize on the apparent popular rejection of Communist rule during the uprising in 1953 – for instance by declaring the 17th of June as a "Day of German Unity" – in order to strengthen their legitimacy. Without resorting to traditional nationalism, the FRG thus began to establish an identity of its own, as well as popular loyalty.[17] As a consequence, critically questioning the past now became more feasible – and indeed a host of journalists and intellectuals began to do just that.

The German Democratic Republic

Though the memory of victims of Nazism was not actively promoted by the majority of West Germany's elite, the emerging pluralism of that society nevertheless allowed some groups to begin the work of remembrance on the margins. In East Germany, meanwhile, there was a deliberate official strategy to instrumentalize memory politics in a monolithic framework. The memory of most Shoah victims was sidelined, whereas the Communist resistance was granted a special place in state ideology. The Communist leadership saw themselves on the

---

[17] Wolfrum, *Geschichtspolitik in der Bundesrepublik.*

victorious side of history and the GDR as the appropriate answer to a Nazi regime that had been rooted in the evils of capitalism.[18] The Communist leaders, who after all had mostly returned from exile, deeply mistrusted the general populace and used this as a justification to impose dictatorship. Nevertheless, and to a lesser extent than in the West, they quietly reintegrated many Nazi perpetrators and fellow-travelers. Jeffrey Herf writes that,

> remarkably, within only three years the Communists had removed the Germans from the ranks of those "millions and millions" who had been complicitous with the perpetrators of mass crimes and transformed them into a nation of innocent victims of American imperialism. Communist nationalism went hand in hand with the task of unburdening the Germans of their difficult past.[19]

This "unburdening" also meant sidelining the truth about the Holocaust, in particular the overwhelmingly Jewish identity of Nazism's victims, and refashioning the tradition of antifascist resistance into a Stalinist state-ideology. To this end, as Herf has demonstrated, the Politburo leadership purged its ranks of those Jews and non-Jews who had shown solidarity with Jewish victims or advocated restitution. This "anticosmopolitan" campaign resulted in the decision of a quarter of the remaining Jewish population to leave the country.[20] The campaign was closely linked to similar purges in other Soviet bloc states and was nourished by Stalinist paranoia and continuing anti-Semitism.[21] Not until the 1980s was the prohibition against Jewish memory work weakened. According to Herf, "while some East German novelists and filmmakers addressed anti-Semitism and the Holocaust, these issues remained on the margins of East Germany's official antifascist political culture."[22] Mark Wolfgram's work on East German television and film confirms how infrequently the issue was confronted in popular culture.[23]

From the beginning, the state invested scarce material resources into the construction of a legitimizing national narrative in which the GDR took on the legacy of the Communist resistance against fascism. A national museum of German history and a range of representative memorials were erected where Communist and German achievements could be celebrated. These moves were central to the ideological competition with West Germany that began even before the founding in 1949 and lasted for the duration of the German partition. Both governments sought to harness revolutionary or democratic traditions for their purposes and struggled to define the character of current events (the 1953

---

[18] Reichel, *Vergangenheitsbewältigung in Deutschland.*   [19] Herf, *Divided Memory* p. 110.
[20] Ibid.   [21] Ibid. p. 113.   [22] Ibid. p. 161.
[23] Wolfgram, *Getting History Right*, see also Fox, *Stated Memory.*

uprising especially). As late as the 1980s, the two states competed for the historical "upper hand," claiming the legacies of Prussia (1981) and Berlin as a city (1987) for themselves in parallel exhibitions. Apart from icons of the Communist movement such as Rosa Luxemburg, Karl Liebknecht, and Ernst Thälmann, the Communist resistance to Nazism took center stage in East German public memory. Communists and workers were regarded as the primary victims of Hitler and reverence to them became the central ritual legitimizing the dictatorship.

The way the GDR handled the memory of the three largest concentration camps on its territory, Buchenwald, Sachsenhausen, and Ravensbrück, typifies the selective and carefully controlled memory politics of the regime. In the immediate postwar period, these sites were used by the Soviets as "special camps" and for military purposes. Though the special camps were also used to intern Nazi perpetrators, many of the internees had been arrested because of actual or purported opposition to the new regime. Thousands perished and were tortured here. The history of the special camps and other Stalinist facilities was not addressed until after 1989.

After the closing of the special camps, the three concentration camps were made into National Memorial Sites (Nationale Mahn-und Gedenkstätten) between 1958 and 1961. The GDR victims' organizations, such as the International Ravensbrück Committee,[24] were centrally involved in this process, though their endorsement and infiltration by the East German secret police makes it problematic to regard this as grassroots action. For example, Buchenwald survivors began efforts to memorialize the site immediately after liberation, drawing on the organizational structure that had developed during incarceration. The Buchenwald Committee of the Vereinigung der Verfolgten des Naziregimes (VVN – Union of the Persecuted of the Nazi Regime) was initially nonpartisan and representative of all victims, but quickly became an instrument of the SED regime. As early as 1947, commemorative events portrayed Buchenwald as primarily a site of Communist resistance, glossing over the diversity of camp inmates.[25] Buchenwald subsequently became one of the most important memory spaces reinforcing the new state identity.[26] It was well known to every young GDR citizen because part of the induction ritual (*Jugendweihe*) for the Free German Youth (FDJ) took place here.[27]

---

[24] Beßmann and Eschebach, 'Das Frauen-Konzentrationslager Ravensbrück' p. 306.
[25] Gedenkstätte Buchenwald, 'Die Geschichte der Gedenkstätte Buchenwald.'
[26] Assmann and Frevert, *Geschichtsvergessenheit – Geschichtsversessenheit*, Leggewie and Meyer, 'Shared Memory.'
[27] Wegner, 'In the Shadow of the Third Reich: The "Jugendstunde" and the Legitimation of Anti-Fascist Heroes for East German Youth.'

The VVN did make a few attempts at non-regime-sanctioned memorialization. For instance, as a site of Nazi political justice, incarceration, and execution, the judicial complex at Münchener Platz in Dresden was proposed by the VVN as a memorial in 1950. However, at this time it was being used by the Soviet Secret Police (NKVD) and continued to be used for abusive purposes by the GDR regime. In Torgau, where over 1,400 people were sentenced to death by the central Wehrmacht special court since 1943, efforts by the VVN to safeguard evidence of these Nazi crimes were silenced. The site continued to be used as a Soviet special camp, then to incarcerate political prisoners in the GDR. After 1975, the site became a notorious site for the imprisonment of "troublesome" youth, subjecting them to physical and emotional abuse.[28]

This instrumentalization of Communist resistance was reproduced throughout the memory landscape of the GDR. Martin Schönfeld argues that memorial plaques (*Gedenktafeln*) in East Berlin were thoroughly integrated into the public rituals of the state.[29] Over 60 percent of these were dedicated to Communist resistance fighters, while Social Democrats made up 6 percent; "nonaffiliated" victims 14 percent; Jewish victims 10 percent; religious resisters 3 percent; and deserters, emigrants, and "interbrigadists" (those who fought in the International Brigades during the Spanish Civil War) made up 13 percent. On special occasions, delegations of youth or workers would attach wreaths to the plaques and use the opportunity to praise the policies of leaders. The historical meaning of the text was secondary – the plaque symbolized the "better Germany."[30]

In the early GDR especially, dissent and autonomous civic activity was severely curtailed. As Anne Applebaum argues, the GDR leadership regarded civil society as a basic threat to its power – a notion that had a long tradition in Communist ideology.[31] Workers were deprived of representation through the forced unification of the left-wing parties into the Socialist Unity Party (SED) and their protests brutally suppressed in 1953. Jewish identity was tightly circumscribed. Even the memory of "German victimhood" was prohibited – discussing the expulsion from the East, after all, could conjure up negative feelings against the Soviet brethren. Manfred Wille explains that,

> Public reference to the former territories was forbidden and subject, in the immediate postwar years, to investigation and prosecution by the police and the NKWD. Radio stations in the SBZ [Soviet Occupied Zone], for example were ordered not to play songs (*Heimatlieder*) associated with the

---

[28] Stiftung Sächsische Gedenkstätten, 'Spuren Suchen und Erinnern.'
[29] Schönfeld, *Gedenktafeln in Ost-Berlin*, See Interviews, Hans Coppi.   [30] Ibid. p. 13.
[31] Applebaum, *Iron Curtain*.

eastern provinces or the Sudetenland or to play their melodies with different lyrics. After all, the SBZ was now the expellees' new homeland ... They were supposed to integrate themselves into their new society as a-historical beings, officially forbidden to keep memories of their homeland alive or preserve their cultural and intellectual heritages.[32]

Until the building of the intra-German border in 1961, dissent was mitigated by the "exit" option[33] – of which Jews, expellees, oppositionists, and others took advantage. For those who remained, the East German state's maintenance of control over memorialization was part of the ubiquitous presence of ideology in public space. Civic efforts at more critical remembrance and even narratives about German homelands in the East or negative war experiences were suppressed.[34] The GDR government's heavy-handed approach to memory blocked both normative and representative approaches to democratic commemoration. This largely prevented a negotiation about the meaning of the past for democratic governance – until East German dissidents picked up this issue during the 1980s. Their critical perspective helped to empower the GDR opposition and continued to influence memory politics after 1989.

Early Memory Activism in East and West

Different as they were, both West and the East German state actions proscribed civil society activists in their efforts to commemorate autonomously and harnessed memory politics to their own political ends. Nevertheless, memory activists continued to organize whenever they were granted space, particularly in the West. They challenged the state's dominant narratives and offered alternative views. Though they had only limited success and visible results at this time, these early efforts to check state power in memory politics proved an important foundation for the memory activists of later years.

Despite especially harsh restrictions in the East, a few activists attempted to undertake memory work beyond the purview of the GDR state. The main victims' organization VVN had been founded before the German split and so existed in both states, making it inherently suspect. The VVN stood for thoroughly communist and antifascist convictions, but it did address the suffering of non-Communist victims. After a period of toleration and infiltration by the Stasi, the state outlawed the VVN

---

[32] Wille, 'Compelling the Assimilation of Expellees' pp. 271–72.

[33] Hirschman, 'Exit, Voice, and the Fate of the GDR.'

[34] However, Jan Palmowski has argued that despite the regime's efforts to control society, citizens were not entirely powerless and learned to "'play by the rules' of the political system." Palmowski, *Inventing a Socialist Nation* p. 9.

in February 1953 in the wake of the anticosmopolitan purges.[35] Publicly, the justification was that in the antifascist state such an organization was superfluous; internally, the regime accused the VVN of subversive activity and even treason.[36] The VVN was replaced by the *Komitee der Antifaschistischen Widerstandskämpfer* (Committee of Antifascist Resistance Fighters), which was tightly controlled and carried out the commemorative agenda of the state. Local historical committees of the SED were tasked with researching and memorializing the resistance.[37]

The regime also prevented the Christian initiative *Aktion Sühnezeichen/ Friedensdienste* (ASZ in the GDR – Action Reconciliation/Service for Peace) from acting effectively and liaising with its Western counterpart. Until the mid-1960s, ASZ was restricted to church and internal reconciliation: it was not allowed to work in former concentration camps or with East European partners. Even after that, the government argued that ASZ's efforts were unnecessary in an antifascist state.[38] Thus, the GDR severely hampered the most promising sources of grassroots memory activism and critical remembrance. A reckoning with the Nazi past that was independent of the state did not truly emerge until the 1980s when some in the oppositional *Bürgerbewegung* (citizens' movement) started grappling with the issue.

In West Germany, the potential for protest was much greater and memory activism existed, though it was limited compared with the levels of activity that existed in later years. Civil society efforts to memorialize took place both in line with the mainstream attempts to foster the narrative of German victimhood and in a more critical vain, by those who sought to remind Germans of their responsibility for crimes committed during the Nazi period. The result was a certain level of memorial pluralism. As Martin Schönfeld writes in reference to Berlin, "The memorial plaques in West-Berlin were no less political in function than in East-Berlin. But . . . in East-Berlin, the memorial plaques to the victims of National Socialism articulated the ubiquitous nature of state power, while West-Berlin plaques denote the complex differentiation of society."[39]

This pluralism notwithstanding, the most prominent memory activism in the FRG of the 1940s and 1950s was clearly focused on what Birgit Schwelling has called "memorials for the consequences of war" (*Kriegsfolgedenkmäler*). Thousands of (mostly) locally relevant monuments were erected during this time, commemorating POWs, flight and

---

[35] Herf, *Divided Memory* p. 133.   [36] Reuter, 'Die VVN in der SBZ/DDR.'
[37] Schönfeld, *Gedenktafeln in Ost-Berlin*.
[38] www.asf-ev.de/de/ueber-uns/geschichte/shnezeichen-ost-und-west/asf-geschichte-nach-teilung.html.
[39] Schönfeld, *Gedenktafeln in West-Berlin* p. 12.

expulsion from the formerly German territories of Eastern Europe, reconstruction efforts after the war, the 1953 uprising in the GDR, and the
separation of Germany.[40] The large number of suggestions for the erection of memorials received by the *Bundesministerium für Gesamtdeutsche
Fragen* (BGF – Federal Ministry for Questions of German Unity) likewise
indicates the broad scope of memory activity taking place. Most proposals
came from individuals and were aimed at commemorating fallen
Germans or celebrating the glories of German history.[41] More organized
initiatives were undertaken by organizations of expellees and veterans.

Vertriebene in the West actively voiced their concerns in organizations as
soon as the Allies allowed political associations in 1948 in the context of
heightened Cold War tensions (*Vertriebene* were thought to be staunch
anti-Communists). One of the primary responsibilities of the BGF was
providing support and financing to civic associations dedicated to keeping
the memory of the German East (on both sides of the Oder-Neisse line)
alive.[42] The *Vereinigte Ostdeutsche Landsmannschaften* (the federation of
all regional and ethnic expellee groups) with many local branches, as well
as the *Bund der Vertriebenen* (BdV – League of Expellees) were founded in
1950[43] and enjoyed widespread institutional and societal support in these
early years. Indeed, in his study of the main Silesian expellee organization,
Christian Lotz has found that "the basic attitude in the Federal Republic
was favorable for the Landsmannschaft: All political forces, with the
exception of the Communists, seemed to be unified in the territorial
goals ... Unlike in later years, the minutes [of Landsmannschaft meet-
ings] only rarely indicate memory-political controversy within West-
German society until the mid 1950s."[44]

In his recent comprehensive survey study of expellee monuments,
Stephan Scholz found that local branches of the BdV, as well as other
expellee associations and affiliated civic groups, were the primary initiators.
Where local governments were the official creators, Scholz found that
individuals and groups with close ties to the expellee community were
nevertheless the driving forces behind memorials. Scholz argues that the
intermeshing of expellee organizations with local power structures, for
example through dual memberships in political parties and expellee
organizations, was standard in the postwar period.[45] Often, memorials
were erected in the context of sponsorship programs, of which there were
about four hundred in the Federal Republic. Towns and cities adopted

---

[40] Schwelling, 'Die "Friedland-Gedächtnisstätte"' p. 189.
[41] Wolfrum, *Geschichtspolitik in der Bundesrepublik.*
[42] Lotz, *Die Deutung des Verlusts* p. 41.
[43] Schulze, 'Zwischen Heimat und Zuhause', Ahonen, *After the Expulsion.*
[44] Lotz, *Die Deutung des Verlusts* p. 72.   [45] Scholz, *Vertriebenendenkmäler* p. 83.

sister communities in the formerly German territories. Almost all of them erected a memorial as part of the sponsorship, as was recommended by the federal government.[46] During inauguration and subsequent commemorative ceremonies held at these memorials, the local (and sometimes national) leadership of expellee organizations was present, as were representatives of politics and churches. On remembrance days such as the "Volkstrauertag" (Day of National Mourning), the "Tag der Heimat" (Day of Homeland), or "Tag der deutschen Einheit" (Day of German Unity), gatherings took place simultaneously across the country and were often kicked off by a central event in Berlin.[47] The linkage of the local memory of expulsion with prominent public rituals and their support by mainstream politics clearly indicates that expellee civic organization were highly influential at this time.

This broad acceptance of the goals of expellee memory and its local embeddedness is also evident in Katrin Panne's case study of the district of Celle. She shows that those areas that saw a large influx of expellees became home to numerous memorials, recalling the war dead, the home regions, and the struggles of the *Vertriebene*. Many of them merely added inscriptions to war memorials of the 1920s; others were built in the 1940s and 1950s, but retain the traditional language of "honor" and "fatherland." Inaugural ceremonies, such as the one seen in Figure 2.1, attracted large portions of the local population, whose donations also provided much of the funding for the monuments. Panne notes the significance of these sites as focal points of identity for these communities, as well as the absence of critical interrogation of the past that is evoked by them.[48]

While veterans' groups were disbanded or organized into state-run associations in the GDR, they were crucial and successful memory activists in the West. By no means did these groups remain silent about their war experience. As Christina Morina argues:

> At the expense of historical truth, war veterans could forge their narratives of the war without addressing explicitly its criminal history and legacy. Claiming that fighting on the German side in World War II was just as patriotic a duty as fighting on the other sides of the war, veterans could imbue their experiences and memories with meaning. The criminal character of the aggressive wars waged by Nazi Germany was persistently brushed aside. Moreover, the Cold War provided this discourse with the necessary interpretive framework within which World War II, and particularly the war against the Soviet Union, took on political meaning, even retrospective legitimization.[49]

The most important veterans' group in terms of memorialization was the *Verband der Heimkehrer, Kriegsgefangenen und Vermisstenangehörigen*

---

[46] Ibid. p. 84.   [47] Ibid.   [48] Panne, 'Erinnerungspolitik – Erinnerungsspuren.'
[49] Morina, *Legacies of Stalingrad* pp. 160–61.

Figure 2.1. Inauguration of a Memorial in Fischbachau/Birkenstein near Brannenburg in Bavaria on the "Tag der Heimatvertriebenen" (Day of Expellees) on 6 June 1948. The banner reads "Give us back our homeland!"[50]

(Federation of Homecomers, POWs and Relatives of the Missing – VdH). Founded in 1950, it sought to influence policy concerning veterans that remained imprisoned (including convicted war criminals) as well as lobbying for compensatory legislation. Moreover, the VdH sought to shape the public memory of POWs in the Federal Republic. Birgit Schwelling writes that,

> In the first half of the 1950s, the Federation organized, with financial help of the federal government and under strong participation from the general population, "POW commemoration weeks" where the release of POWs was demanded. It initiated a travelling exhibit on POWs, which was shown in over 100 German and some non-German cities between 1951 and the 1960s and was seen by a total of 1.7 million visitors. The VdH was also strongly engaged in memorial projects, erecting about 1800 local monuments recalling the plight of POWs, of which only few remain today.[51]

The narrative put forward by the VdH in the traveling exhibit and elsewhere did not critically interrogate the circumstances under which

---

[50] Bayrisches Hauptstaatsarchiv, Sudetendeutsches Archiv, Bildersammlung 22043.
[51] Schwelling, '"Verlorene Jahre"?' pp. 55–56.

Germans became POWs; it highlighted the experiential dimension of imprisonment, clearly depicted POWs as victims and even deployed imagery reminiscent of concentration camp inmates.[52]

The VdH was also instrumental in the erection of a number of memorials near the transit camp Friedland, through which expellees, emigrants from the GDR, and POWs released from Soviet imprisonment entered the Federal Republic. According to Sascha Schießl, "in the first half of the 1950s, the Friedland camp was a central venue for negotiating various memory political debates ... In view of the symbolic and emotional meaning of the topic of POWs, local actors made repeated efforts to inscribe Friedland into contemporary victimhood discourses. The same is true of the Verband der Heimkehrer ... "[53] Next to the *Friedlandglocke*, the bell tower of the Protestant camp ministry, the *Friedland-Gedächtnisstätte* (Friedland Memorial) with its monumental *Heimkehrermahnmal* (Monument to Homecomers) was most important. The Memorial had been initiated by Adenauer in 1957 as an official site honoring primarily the experiences of Germans in and after the Second World War, obscuring the plight of Nazism's victims and responsibility for the war. Schwelling contends that the early plans for the memorials must be seen in the context of the extraordinarily high identification of the West German public with the POWs.[54] As public attitudes about the meaning of the Nazi past began to shift in the 1960s, the German government put plans for the memorial on hold, allowing the VdH to take the lead. When the Monument was inaugurated in 1967 – a large concrete structure with panels that stressed German victimhood and barely mentioned non-German suffering – not a single representative of the federal government could be persuaded to attend (Figure 2.2). The VdH remained impervious to criticism of its memorial approach and decried the lack of attention received for *Friedland*, as well as the dismantling of smaller memorials to the consequences of war.[55]

The *Volksbund Deutsche Kriegsgräberfürsorge* (VDK, roughly translatable as Popular Alliance for the Care of German War Graves) – a partially state-funded group that was founded in 1919 to care for graves of fallen First World War soldiers and had been taken over by the Nazis – also consistently worked to ingrain the memory of the "honorable" soldiers. Over the course of the FRG's life, the VDK was the pivotal force behind the commemorations on the National Day of Mourning every November and consistently lobbied for the erection of traditional, patriotic monuments imbued with Christian

---

[52] von Hegel, 'Der Sinnlosigkeit einen Sinn geben.'
[53] Schießl, *"Das Tor zur Freiheit"* p. 288.
[54] Schwelling, 'Die "Friedland-Gedächtnisstätte"' p. 193.   [55] Ibid. p. 209.

Figure 2.2. Heimkehrermahnmal at Friedland, erected by the veterans group VdH in 1967.[56]

symbolism. The memory of the *Wehrmacht's* victims did not figure prominently in this memory advocacy. This is not surprising considering the organizational continuity through the Weimar, Nazi and postwar periods.[57] As the late George Mosse wrote,

[56] Jenny Wüstenberg, 2016.   [57] www.volksbund.de/volksbund.html.

The *Volksbund* itself had collaborated closely with the Nazis, and even for some time after the war its personnel did not change. The chief architect of the *Volksbund*, Robert Tischler, in office since 1926, was himself close to the Nazis (he had, for example, designed a Germanic shrine for a martyr of the Hitler Youth), and he continued to design some *Totenburgen*, those fortresslike memorials and mass burial places so popular under the Nazis ... However, their inscription now exalted peace and friendship among former foes.[58]

Another group, the *Volksbund für Frieden und Freiheit* (Popular Alliance for Peace and Freedom), which was part of an international anti-Communist organization, made plans and collected donations for a large memorial after the 1953 uprising in the GDR.[59] While the responsible ministry rejected these schemes as premature, its own bureaucrats made similar plans for memorialization, indicating that these societal initiatives were largely in line with official memory discourse. Indeed, some of the earliest memorials of the FRG commemorated not the Nazi period, but the immediate past of the Cold War conflict. Most prominently, the city inaugurated the memorial to the Berlin Airlift (1948/49) next to the airport in Berlin-Tempelhof in 1951.

The *Kuratorium Unteilbares Deutschland* (KUD – Council for an Inseparable Germany) worked to "prevent the affirmation of the two-state system and to strengthen the idea of national unity in people's consciousness" by organizing commemorative events around the 17th of June every year and by erecting unity monuments in hundreds of cities.[60] Smaller groups were also actively involved in the creation of the German memorial landscape. Shortly after the 1953 uprising, participants erected the first memorials to the victims and heroes of that day. Together with the *Verein 17. Juni 1953* (Association 17 June 1953), activist Carl-Wolfgang Holzapfel reports responding directly when someone was killed at the Wall. They erected wooden crosses, laid wreaths, and even conducted hunger strikes to create publicity.[61] This group continues its efforts to commemorate 1953 to this day.

One of the most important and successful civic initiatives of the early years was the *Vereinigung der Opfer des Stalinismus* (VOS – Union of Victims of Stalinism), which was founded in West Berlin in February 1950 by former internees of the Soviet zone. Initially, the group's primary purpose was to support their members in practical ways, to facilitate their social integration and to advocate for their recognition by the federal state. From the beginning and increasingly as years

[58] Mosse, *Fallen Soldiers* p. 214.   [59] Wolfrum, *Geschichtspolitik in der Bundesrepublik.*
[60] Wolfrum, 'Die Massenmedialisierung.'
[61] See Interviews, Carl-Wolfgang Holzapfel.

went by, the VOS and its local subgroups became vocal memory activists as well.[62] An important example is the Memorial to the Victims of Stalinism that was inaugurated in 1951 at the Steinplatz in Berlin-Charlottenburg by the VOS (Figure 2.4). Local chapters of the VOS formed rapidly in all the states of West Germany, saw a rising membership, and considerable support from state actors. In October 1954, the VOS held its first national meeting, attended by over one thousand former political prisoners. This meeting was one of many events that was partially funded by the Federal Ministry for Pan-German Questions (BGF). High-level politicians, including former Chancellor Adenauer, regularly joined VOS events. In VOS historiography, the consistent support received by the authorities is stressed. For instance, the Berlin Senate is regarded as a reliable partner that provided funding and that was fostered the community of political prisoners across the divided city: "It was not unusual for the Senate to send a competent representative to our forums or rallies. Especially the Mayors of Berlin, no matter of which political party, supported us through receptions or speeches to the Berlin chapter of the VOS."[63] This sense of recognition stands in stark contrast to the feelings of marginalization dominant among the victim organizations of the Nazi regime.

Memory work addressing the plight of Nazism's victims indeed had little institutional support in West Germany and was often actively discouraged by the authorities. The task of commemoration fell to a small minority in civil society, made up mainly of survivors and relatives of victims. Despite being hampered by official intransigence, local victims' groups gathered almost immediately after the liberation of the concentration camps. Pan regional groups also formed relatively quickly. The *Verband der Opfer der Nürnberger Gesetze* (OdN – Association of Victims of the Nuremberg Laws) was founded in June 1946 in Berlin and emerged out of a collection of groups that had existing during the Nazi period to support the interests of the persecuted (such as the Association of non-Aryan Christians). This group later became the Berlin section of the *Bund der Verfolgten des Naziregimes* (BVN – Federation of the Persecuted by the Nazi Regime).[64]

The *Vereinigung der Verfolgten des Naziregimes* (VVN),[65] the Eastern sister organization of which I have already mentioned, was formed in 1947 by victims of Nazism who sought compensation, justice, and

---

[62] Richter, 'Aus der Geschichte der VOS.'   [63] Ibid. p. 98.
[64] Faust, 'Vorläufer des BVN', Goldberg, 'Gerechtigkeit und Sühne.'
[65] Union of those Persecuted by the Nazi Regime. It was later called VVN-BdA (*Bund der Antifaschisten – Union of Antifascists*).

remembrance for their plight. Due to its far-left image, the organization was marginalized by mainstream politics from its inception.[66] In 1950, all VVN members were expelled from the civil service, in 1951 the group's "central council" was forbidden, and in 1959, there was an (unsuccessful) attempt to ban the whole organization through an administrative court order.[67] Notwithstanding the fact that it was outlawed in the GDR, the VVN in the West was never able to shake the suspicion of being an agent funded by the Stasi. Nevertheless, the VVN was a vocal advocate for victims' rights and memory and became part of the peace and student movements in later years.[68]

According to Martin Schönfeld, the VVN was the main initiator of memorial plaques in Berlin in the postwar years, though implementation was often carried out by local authorities.[69] The identity of the initiators is reflected in the inscriptions of the early memorials. Their texts express the personal bond felt with the murdered and the mission of those still alive to uphold their memory. Most of the memorials are in (especially Jewish) cemeteries or close to former concentration camps; others mark mass graves and are difficult to find. Their design tends to be traditional – a boulder, an obelisk, a flame, or a suffering figure – and inscriptions are simple and not very informative about the identity of victims or perpetrators or reason for murder. Most common are texts such as "To the victims of fascism."[70] This dearth of information reflects both the lack of societal support extant for the memorials and the immediacy of their creation – when it may have seemed unnecessary to explain what had happened.

Because of its close ties to the Communist Party of West Germany (KPD), some members left the VVN and founded other victims' initiatives such as the *Arbeitsgemeinschaft Verfolgter Sozialdemokraten* (Working Group of Persecuted Social Democrats).[71] From the outset, the efforts of victims' groups were caught up in the intensifying politics of the Cold War. For example, the authorities of the Soviet-occupied sector in Berlin would allow the OdN/BVN to exist only if the Western Allied authorities would permit the VVN in its sectors – and vice versa. The BVN was the non-Communist counterpart to the VVN, and had taken a nonpartisan stance on the need to compensate and memorialize victims, as well as struggle for a liberal democracy in contradistinction to the GDR.[72] This group erected the first memorial to the victims of the Nazi dictatorship in

---

[66] Schneider, 'Die VVN in der BRD.'   [67] Baukloh, 'Nie wieder Faschismus!'
[68] See Interviews, Hans Coppi, Christine Fischer-Defoy.
[69] Schönfeld, *Gedenktafeln in West-Berlin.*   [70] Haß, 'Mahnmaltexte 1945 bis 1988.'
[71] Baukloh, 'Nie wieder Faschismus!'
[72] Nikoline Hansen '60 Jahre Bund der Verfolgten des Naziregimes Berlin e.V.' www
     .bvnberlin.de/60.html.

Figure 2.3. Heinrich Lübke at the Steinplatz memorial in 1960.[73]

West Berlin in 1953 at the Steinplatz in Charlottenburg, constructed from stones of a destroyed synagogue (though there was no explicit reference to Jewish victims). The memorial was financed by donations of BVN members and seen as part of the group's mandate to safeguard the memory of the victims. The Steinplatz illustrates the tension between the efforts of memory activists to create public spaces of remembrance and official Germany's ambivalence toward this memory. In 1960, Federal President Heinrich Lübke, who resigned in 1968 because of his Nazi past, laid a wreath at the Steinplatz NS memorial, indicating that the site was relevant to the political elite (Figure 2.3). At the same time, the

---

[73] Bundesregierung/Gert Schütz.

federal government's statement on the occasion of the Volktrauertag (Day of Mourning) in November continued to emphasize German war victims and argued that only a small minority was to blame for the crimes of the Hitler regime.[74]

The placement of the BVN memorial at Steinplatz directly opposite to the VOS monument of 1951 therefore makes perfect sense in the context of the West German memorial culture of the time (Figure 2.4). A competition of memories was already at play and the (sometimes fierce) contest between state and civil society actors over what and how memory should be demonstrated publicly characterized the process from the start. The link between remembrance (and the Steinplatz memorial in particular) and democracy is made explicitly in the historiography of the association. As its leader, Nicoline Hansen said in a speech marking BVN's sixtieth anniversary:

> In a living democracy there is always a need to act to safeguard human rights, so that they exist not only on the patient paper of the constitution, but are also engrained in people's heads. That is why it is important not to forget, but to remember again and again. To remember especially one's strengths, but also one's weaknesses, without pointing a finger at others.[75]

A very successful example of early memory activism is that of the *Hilfswerk 20. Juli 1944*, a group founded by relatives of the military opposition, particularly those murdered after the failed attempt on Hitler's life in July 1944. In the immediate postwar years, these resisters were still defamed as traitors, but by the 1950s, the group had succeeded in making the 20th of July central to the commemorative culture of the FRG.[76] The *Hilfswerk* proposed to Berlin Mayor Ernst Reuter that the men and women of 1944 be memorialized in the *Bendlerblock* – the building where the Nazi defense ministry had been located, the resistance group was centered, and where its leaders were shot. In 1953, a large sculpture of a man was inaugurated there and from then on, the *Hilfswerk* conducted commemorative ceremonies there every year, complete with military rituals and *Bundeswehr* honor guards.[77] Moreover, the 20th of July became the most important holiday recalling the victims of National Socialism, replacing the 11th of September that East Germans continued to mark as the *"Gedenktag für die Opfer des Faschismus"* (remembrance day for the victims of fascism). Despite this elevation of

---

[74] 'Gedenken am Volkstrauertag' *Deutsche Politik 1960 – Tätigkeitsbericht der Bundesregierung*, Presse- und Informationsamt der Bundesregierung (ed.)
[75] Hansen '60 Jahre Bund der Verfolgten des Naziregimes Berlin e.V.'
[76] Schönfeld, *Gedenktafeln in West-Berlin*, Dowe, 'Symbol des Widerstandes.'
[77] Schönfeld, *Gedenktafeln in West-Berlin*.

Figure 2.4. (a) The Memorial to the Victims of Stalinism (built in 1951) and (b) The Memorial to the Victims of National Socialism (built in 1953) are on opposite ends of the Steinplatz, Berlin-Charlottenburg.

resistance to part of the official remembrance repertoire, the Bendlerblock did not become a major memory site until the 1980s. At this point Mayor Richard von Weizsäcker tasked the historian Peter Steinbach with the creation of an exhibition (opened in 1989) on the entire breadth of resistance against the Nazi regime. From this developed the institution *Gedenkstätte Deutscher Widerstand* (GDW – Memorial to German Resistance) that conducts research and administers the memorial at *Plötzensee* (where over three thousand people were executed) and the *Museum Otto Weidt's Workshop for the Blind* that recalls the resistance of "little people" to Nazism. Moreover, the GDW hosts a number of civic organizations, including the VVN, the Active Museum, the International Auschwitz Committee, an initiative for "stumbling blocks," and more.[78]

Unlike in the GDR, September 11 in West Germany became the "Day of Germans," a day to foster patriotism and an occasion for expellee organizations to march with torches and recall their homeland.[79] The transformation of the commemorative calendar in East and West illustrates the extent to which memory on both sides was instrumentalized in the context of the block confrontation. In this climate, only very particular segments of the Nazi past were deemed useful to mainstream West German narratives. 1950–1960 is the decade during which the fewest new Holocaust memorial sites and monuments were erected,[80] indicating that civil society activity was limited or unsuccessful. The state was largely in control of the process of memorialization – and its ambitions were intentionally limited and directed at highlighting only particular values and selective engagement with the past to support a particular vision of the present.

Toward the end of the 1950s, mnemonic civil society became somewhat more vibrant. An important example is *Aktion Sühnezeichen/ Friedensdienste* (ASF – Action Reconciliation/Service for Peace), a group that was based on Christian ideals of reconciliation, but was not overtly religious. It was founded in 1958 on the initiative of two members of the small church-based resistance to Nazism and sought to confront the complicity of church and society with the fascist regime. While it was founded as a pan-German organization, cooperation across the East-West divide was in practice not possible. In the late 1950s and early 1960s, ASF was the first to organize contacts between German youth and survivors of the Shoah, particularly in Israel. Directed by the wishes of its partners, they helped build nursing homes, synagogues, churches, and more, thus offering whatever practical assistance was useful and in

---

[78] See Interviews, Johannes Tuchel.   [79] Schönfeld, *Gedenktafeln in West-Berlin.*
[80] Haß, 'Mahnmaltexte 1945 bis 1988.'

the process fostering a spirit of reconciliation and cooperation. A considerable number of protagonists in the History and Memorial Site Movements and in present-day memorial institutions were politically socialized through the ASF – its Executive Director Christian Staffa estimates up to 50 percent.[81] Local societies for Christian-Jewish cooperation also became active in the commemoration of sites of Nazi terror.[82] ASF sent thousands of volunteers abroad and became a significant force in the peace movement into the 1980s.[83]

In sum, during the first postwar decades, the majority of the population did not remain silent about the past, but remembrance was highly selective. In East Germany, challenges to official anti-fascist memory policies – be they from Jewish victims of the Holocaust or expellees – were suppressed along with other forms of dissent. Here, then, neither did the state allow a free expression of memory that was representative of public opinion, nor was there a fostering of the kind of memory that might have encouraged a normative reckoning with responsibility for the Nazi past. Instead public memory fully served the ideological *raison d'état*; it was not until the 1980s that official narratives were effectively confronted by oppositional memory activists.

In West Germany, civil society activists were active in memory politics from the outset. The most visible of them were those that echoed the population's focus on their own wartime suffering – expellees, veterans, anti-Communist campaigners – and they received the most support from state actors. In this sense, the early memory politics of the FRG were highly representative, but they marginalized the memory of Nazism's victims. Nevertheless, memory activists critical of mainstream narratives remained vocal and increasingly were able to challenge dominant interpretations of the recent past. Through their own initiative, effective lobbying and pressure exerted on local authorities, civic initiatives, and victims groups managed to influence the memorial landscape and erect monuments.

Thus, the memory politics of the early Federal Republic were played out in the tension between state and civic action. This tension was a complex one, shaped both by the normative pressure exerted by a minority to use remembrance as a part of the democratization process but also the demand to represent the loudest mnemonic voices in society, partly in order to shore up support for democratic institutions. In this situation, those who sought to remember the Holocaust were not able to

---

[81] See Interviews, Christian Staffa.
[82] Stiftung niedersächsische Gedenkstätten, 'Bergen-Belsen' p. 68.
[83] See Interviews, Christian Staffa; www.asf-ev.de/de/ueber-uns/geschichte/shnezeichen-ost-und-west/asf-geschichte-bundesrepublik.html.

profoundly influence the institutions of commemoration – but they could not be ignored altogether. They undertook important groundwork, on which later critical memorial movements could build.

1968 as the Turning Point for Memory Politics?

There is no consensus on the meaning of "1968" for German society or for the politics of the past. I suggest here that the student movement cannot be credited with much concrete and grassroots memory work. What it did do, however, is to build on earlier efforts to foster societal liberalization and critical attitudes toward the past that resulted in the social movement "scene" of the late 1970s and 1980s and ultimately made the History and Memorial Site Movements possible.

The strengthening of institutions, economic advancement, and liberal political and artistic engagement during the 1950s no doubt facilitated the social transformations of the later 1960s. Diethelm Prowe has gone so far as to suggest that the real miracle of the 1950s was not economic but the "basic political transformation that led within less than a generation to a genuinely democratic society."[84] The continuities of Nazi party members in positions of influence and widespread positive views about Nazism found in public opinion surveys during this era warrant some skepticism about this argument.[85] However, despite the marginalization of critical memory work during the postwar years, rising prosperity, accelerating cultural change, and a few key political developments made possible the growing attention to the Nazi past during the 1960s.

According to Jarausch, the Adenauer period equipped the FRG with a new *Bürgerlichkeit* (civility), the necessary infrastructure of a free media, and the mechanisms to found associations.[86] Overall, societal developments by the mid-1960s had led to what Chancellor Ludwig Erhard called "the end of the postwar era" and a concomitant liberalization and cultural opening. For historian Edgar Wolfrum, it was "unmistakable that the Federal Republic was well on its way to achieving self-confidence in its identity as a state in its own right and that, in the perception of its citizens, West Germany had lost its provisional character."[87] By 1967, 81 percent said they had gotten used to the German division.[88] This newfound self-assurance and the resulting de-intensification of the societal competition with East Germany enabled a more critical approach to the Nazi past.

---

[84] Prowe, 'The 'Miracle' of the Political-Cultural Shift ' p. 451.
[85] Frei, 'Hitlers Eliten nach 1945.'   [86] Jarausch, *Die Umkehr.*
[87] Wolfrum, *Geschichtspolitik in der Bundesrepublik* p. 241.   [88] Ibid.

By the 1960s, a new generation of political and cultural personalities was moving into positions of power. Dirk Moses has called this cohort the "forty-fivers" and it includes such figures as Chancellor Helmut Kohl, novelist Günter Grass, philosopher Jürgen Habermas, historian Hans-Ulrich Wehler, and sociologist Ralf Dahrendorf.[89] This group was between ages fifteen and twenty-five when the war ended, but shaped most decisively by the new possibilities of the postwar period. Even before 1968 there was therefore a societal force that could drive the reform of memory narratives. In fact, Moses argues that the strong elements of antiliberalism central to the student movement were effectively countered by the forty-fivers who protected the liberal foundations laid in 1949 against the students' attacks.[90]

These leaders helped to open up German society and thereby prepared the way for a more aggressive reckoning with the past that began during the 1960s. In 1959, a wave of anti-Semitic graffiti prompted many to address the Nazi past for the first time. In direct response to the vandalism, tens of thousands protested in January 1960 in Berlin against anti-Semitism and neo-Nazism – an unprecedented level of mobilization in this issue area.[91] In 1962, all but one of the eleven *Bundesländer* made the study of 1933–1945 a mandatory subject in school and the numbers of school groups visiting concentration camp memorials expanded by more than a factor of ten.[92] Already in 1958, a special prosecutorial agency for Nazi crimes had been set up in Ludwigsburg and led to new trials against war criminals, most importantly the Auschwitz trial in Frankfurt. Mainstream politics also turned toward the Nazi past; Willy Brandt's dramatic gesture of kneeling silently at the Warsaw Ghetto memorial was a case in point. But there was also President Gustav Heinemann's effort to transform Germans' values through his school essay competitions initiated in 1973. The intention was to foster a positive democratic tradition, and by 1980 over ten thousand pupils participated.[93] Intellectuals such as Günter Grass and Rolf Hochhuth drove an artistic interrogation of memory, and the media also began to be more inquisitive. Herf argues that the relationship between memory and democracy had now shifted. For the first time, politicians could envision an electoral majority in favor of confronting the past.[94] All this moved the unfinished business of the

---

[89] Moses, *German Intellectuals and the Nazi Past.*   [90] Ibid.
[91] Baukloh, 'Nie wieder Faschismus!,' see also Wolfrum, *Geschichtspolitik in der Bundesrepublik.*
[92] Judt, *Postwar.*
[93] Assmann and Frevert, *Geschichtsvergessenheit – Geschichtsversessenheit*, Paul and Schoßig, 'Geschichte und Heimat.'
[94] Herf, *Divided Memory* p. 390.

Nazi past into the public sphere – though this was not yet manifested in the physical landscape of memory. For this to happen, the memory movements of the 1980s had to drive normative change on the ground.

The contribution of "1968" to the democratization of German political culture was crucial mainly in an indirect sense. The student movement is widely credited with placing the Nazi past on the agenda and thus cata-pulting Germany into a new era. Indeed, the students exposed professors and other figures of authority that had collaborated with Nazism, and they protested against what they saw as quasi-fascist social and political struc-tures. In 1967, the movement was radicalized by the shooting death of a Benno Ohnesorg – an event that was read by many as a signifier of the fascist elements in the West German state and its servants.[95]

However, Ute Frevert argues that though many 1968ers had joined the movement in order to confront the previous generation and its selective silence of the past, their own efforts to "work through" the past remained limited. Structural and economic theories of fascism were especially popular in the 1970s.[96] Michael Schmidtke writes:

> Subject at once to inflationary use and simplification, the concept of fascism was transformed into a "collective symbol" that various actors – students, intellectuals, the press – competed to use. The concept of fascism no longer served primarily to explain a historical phenomenon, and the more widely the concept was used the more common it became for antagonists to see fascist tendencies in one another's behavior.[97]

As Thomas Lindenberger remembers, many on the Left were openly hostile toward the historical discipline, regarding it as reactionary, as well as ignorant of its professional standards. "There were a lot of people who spoke of fascism, but only had second or third hand information and who thought nothing of using the most fatuous stuff coming out of the GDR."[98] There were thus few attempts to examine the details of Nazi-history – to trace particular perpetrators, their motives, and the historical context.[99] The focus was on the system not on individuals. This may have been a popular narrative at the time, but it did not contribute to an understanding of the historical and personal circumstances that made the Holocaust possible. As Kansteiner writes, "the provocations of the students did not quickly transform Germany's historical culture. As the students entered into divisive and circuitous discussions about the nature

---

[95] Recent revelations have complicated this history: *Die Zeit* 23/2009.
[96] Assmann and Frevert, *Geschichtsvergessenheit – Geschichtsversessenheit*, Herf, *Divided Memory*.
[97] Schmidtke, 'The German New Left' p. 180.
[98] See Interviews, Thomas Lindenberger.
[99] 'Aufbruch in Nietenhosen' in *ZEITGeschichte* No. 1, 2009, pp. 46–54.

of fascism, descended into terrorism, or opted for the long march through the institutions, the Nazi past temporarily disappeared from the media headlines."[100]

The mobilization of the 1960s, then, did not immediately leave a significant mark on West Germany's memory landscape. Most of the memorials dedicated during this decade had been initiated during the 1950s and their design features reflected as much.[101] For example, the concentration camp memorial at Dachau was inaugurated in 1968, but was the product of a long struggle of camp survivors to safeguard the site.[102] Jochen Spielmann sums up the students' impact on the memorial landscape as follows: "In contrast to the 1950s, when monuments were built, but there was a hardly a reckoning with National Socialism, during the 1960s there was a more intensive confrontation of the past, but hardly any built monuments."[103] He goes on to explain:

> In the years 1968 to 1979, there was an intensive reckoning with National Socialism that did not express itself through monuments. The historical consciousness of the "generation of 68" examined – next to structure and ideology of National Socialism – especially its continuities into the present and could not use memorials for these intentions. Subsequently, the memorial form was subjected to extended discussions and was rejected as a medium for a discourse free of power [*herrschaftsfreien Diskurs*].[104]

Ulrike Haß, in her analysis of Holocaust memorial inscriptions, argues that the era of 1960 to 1979 was marked not by the creation of a critical memory culture expressed through memorials, but, by contrast, was a time of "memorials without remembrance." By this she means that the memorials of this time overwhelmingly had the intention, not of remembering or explaining, but of controlling the interpretation of the past in particular ways. For example, most memorials were built away from public view, often in cemeteries, so that they blurred the distinction between victims and perpetrators and sought to alleviate guilt by referencing the universal problems of death and violence, rather than historical specifics.[105] Until the 1980s, the West German memory landscape continues to "reflect primarily the ruling societal attitudes, and primarily bourgeois and military resistance, soldiers, and the bombing dead are commemorated. This memory epitomizes the identity of the Federal Republic."[106]

---

[100] Kansteiner, 'Losing the War' p. 120.   [101] Hausmann, *Duell mit der Verdrängung?*
[102] Marcuse, 'Das ehemalige Konzentrationslager Dachau.'
[103] Spielmann, 'Gedenken und Denkmal' p. 14.   [104] Ibid. p. 15.
[105] Haß, 'Mahnmaltexte 1945 bis 1988.'
[106] Marcuse, Schimmelfennig, and Spielmann, *Steine des Anstoßes* p. 4.

The significance of 1968 for the reckoning with the past, then, has less to do with the students' own debates about fascism or their limited memorial activities, and more with the long-term impact they had on the democratization of German society as a whole. There was no immediate revolution in terms of memory politics as a result of the 1968 protests, but more important was "the concrete experience of a qualitatively different way of life, the exposure to non-hierarchical modes of social interaction, the lived environment of solidarity, the heated atmosphere of open debate, the concrete strivings for a common and mutually beneficial system-transcending goal."[107] These experiences stayed with the "1968ers" and also influenced the next cohort, while the student movement itself fragmented into small factions of orthodox Marxist "K-groups," as well as an unorganized milieu of anti-authoritarian projects.[108] The latter formed the breeding ground for a host of "new social movements" – of which the History and the Memorial Site Movements were two.

The 1970s were a time of busy activity at the grassroots level, despite the widespread disappointment with the "failed revolution." Furthermore, during this decade, the chasm between left- and right-wing notions of democratic governance – including its manifestations in memory politics – deepened. Unable to respond adequately to the call for an expansion of democracy into new arenas, the West German state was facing a crisis of legitimacy. This presented an opportunity for grassroots initiatives of all kinds – from alternative living communities, to environmentalists and history initiatives. Leftists influenced by the ideals of 1968 founded publishing houses, alternative archives, and research projects all aimed at establishing autonomous institutions to counter the conservative establishment.[109] While the 1970s are not usually noted for important developments in the realm of memory politics, it is then that the groundwork for the memory boom of the following decade was laid. This broad sweep of social and institutional contention created a fertile environment for the ground-up debate over memorialization to begin. This debate would push to the forefront the memory of minorities and of the victims of Nazism – who had been marginalized in public space up until now. The memory activists of the 1980s transformed memory work from an activity at the margins to one with protest potential. Making the memory of the Holocaust contentious and prominent through activism was crucial for the *normative grounding* of German democracy.

---

[107] Horn, *The Spirit of '68* p. 194.　　[108] Jarausch, *Die Umkehr.*
[109] von Saldern, 'Markt für Marx.'

The 1980s: The Pivotal Decade

In the early 1980s, two contrasting developments occurred. On the one hand, the *außerparlamentarische Opposition* (APO – nonparliamentary opposition) was at its peak in terms of mobilization, visibility, and society-wide impact.[110] Andreas Wirsching calls the 1980s a "decade of protest," writing that "parties and parliaments, politicians and functionaries, saw themselves confronted with waves of protest in response to practically any larger political undertaking . . ., significantly narrowing the range of policy options."[111] Two of the movements at the center of this book – the History and Memorial Site Movements – are part of this wave of contention: they applied the critique of the status quo to processes of historical research and public commemoration.

On the other hand, the "*geistig-moralische Wende*" (roughly translatable as "spiritual-moral transformation") announced by the new Chancellor Helmut Kohl heralded a consolidation of power by the state in tandem with the implementation of a more formal notion of democracy and a conservative cultural style.[112] This new conservative self-confidence was mirrored in historiography with calls for a "normalization" of German discourse about the past. A return to conservative moral traditions as opposed to the critique and emancipatory goals of left-wing intellectuals was the clear intention of Kohl's political shift.[113]

Notwithstanding some divisions internal to the Christian Democratic Party (CDU), the conservative resurgence in academia and politics explains why left-wing activists felt the need to safeguard their ideals and achievement from a "right-wing onslaught." This perception greatly aided the left's ability to mobilize. As a consequence, the conservative majority was faced with a vocal "alternative scene" that even acquired its own parliamentary representation (the Green Party). During this time also, the general resurgence in popularity of all things historical shifted memory politics squarely onto the political agenda for both ideological camps. Memory was becoming a key policy field that could not be left unattended.

The Memory Boom

The 1980s saw a veritable boom in all manner of memorial activity. Publishers saw great successes in historical book sales. Historical documentaries became a much more common feature on television. Between

---

[110] Eley, *Forging Democracy.*   [111] Wirsching, *Geschichte der Bundesrepublik* p. 393.
[112] Jarausch, *Die Umkehr* p. 199.
[113] Wolfrum, *Geschichtspolitik in der Bundesrepublik.*

1982 and 1990, the numbers of museums and exhibitions increased by about a third. By the end of the decade, there were 74 million museum visitors annually (up from 52 million in 1982).[114] Museum planners sought to offer more accessible exhibits for a mass audience, making displays more interactive and visual. A prominent example of an exhibition that both benefited from the renewed interest in history, as well as understood the new trends in representation was *Preußen – Versuch einer Bilanz* (Prussia – Attempt at an Assessment). This show was opened in 1981 in West Berlin and drew half a million people.[115] There were efforts, in both East and West, to reclaim elements of Prussian tradition and thereby enhance its standing vis-à-vis citizens as well as the Cold War adversary.[116]

The new resonance of history was also manifested in changes in urban lifestyles. In large cities, squatters occupied and refurbished old buildings (calling this *Instandbesetzung*) and citizens' groups prevented the razing of run-down historical neighborhoods. In West Berlin, this scene was an especially important breeding ground for history initiatives. All this gradually sparked the interest of municipal authorities, which began to see the new social movements as potential opportunities to reinvigorate their cities and attract tourists.

The general hunger for history was accompanied by a surge in public interest in the Nazi past in particular. Most important was the screening in 1979 on public television of the fictional miniseries "Holocaust," which depicted the everyday experience of persecution and genocide, as well as individual responsibility and resistance, under the Nazis. Twenty million Germans watched the series. In addition, a set of anniversaries provided occasions for remembrance – most importantly in 1983 (fiftieth anniversary of the Nazi takeover of power) and in 1985 (fortieth anniversary of the end of the Second World War). On the latter occasion, Christian Democratic President Richard von Weizsäcker for the first time officially acknowledged many "forgotten" victims of Nazism, though the traditional commemoration of all "victims of war and dictatorship" continued to be supported by Kohl and others.

The memory boom was nowhere more pronounced than in the arena of Holocaust monuments. During the 1980s, more memorials and plaques commemorating those murdered between 1933 and 1945 were established in West Berlin than in the period of 1945 to 1980 combined.[117] Existing sites of Nazi persecution saw unprecedented numbers of visitors

---

[114] Wirsching, *Geschichte der Bundesrepublik*.
[115] Assmann and Frevert, *Geschichtsvergessenheit – Geschichtsversessenheit* p. 251.
[116] Rosenfeld, 'A Mastered Past? '   [117] Spielmann, *Denk – Mal – Prozesse.*

and were redesigned and expanded as a result of pressure by the Memorial Site Movement.[118] This Movement, as I show in Chapter 3, also marked myriad locations of local Nazi terror. When this work began in the early 1980s, erecting a Holocaust monument meant questioning established narratives about local history and struggling against the resistance of local leaders. For the leftist memory activists, these local authorities were representative of the federal history politics of the Kohl era. Again, we see contention between civil society actors and the state over which norms and processes to use in demonstrating public memory. By the 1980s, there was an explicit claim to the democratizing process of ground-up, local history work, which was set in contrast to the dominant narrative of memory politics practiced by the Kohl government (see Chapters 3 and 4).

Kohl's History Politics

Helmut Kohl's inimitable stance kept history at the center of political contention without interruption during the 1980s. His approach was to explicitly accept German responsibility, but to "organically link it with the positive aspects of German history and, in particular, a commitment to its future."[119] Under Kohl, the CDU also continued to advocate on behalf of German war victims, especially the expellees. The official desire to define German history as more than a source of shame was not new. However, as Jeffrey Olick argues,

> Kohl's style of normalization was more aggressive [than that of his predecessors], embodied in an ideological program for cultural change, which included pride in German history, the celebration of heroes, national museums and monuments, and a distancing of past misdeeds, which now have lost their specificity – all the victims are the same. On this basis, West Germany sought to undertake a greater role in world politics.[120]

During a visit to Israel, Helmut Kohl invoked the "mercy of late birth" (*Gnade der späten Geburt*), through which he sought to absolve his and younger generations of responsibility for the Nazi past, and which are reflected in Kohl's memory policies.[121] A number of well-known controversies exemplified the government's efforts, including that over the visit with President Reagan to Bitburg; the "*Historikerstreit*" (a prominent dispute between conservative and liberal intellectuals about the comparability of Nazi crimes); the debate over the creation of a new

---

[118] Wirsching, *Geschichte der Bundesrepublik.*   [119] Ibid. p. 474.
[120] Olick, 'What Does It Mean to Normalize'
[121] Assmann and Frevert, *Geschichtsvergessenheit – Geschichtsversessenheit.*

traditional war memorial in Bonn (later reincarnated in Berlin as the refurbished *Neue Wache*); and plans to build a national history museum in Berlin, which was strongly opposed by local memory activists (Chapter 4). All of this led the left to suspect that Kohl was attempting to impose an official version of history in an undemocratic manner. However, it is often overlooked that the Chancellor also worked to marginalize the radical right within the CDU.[122] Jan-Holger Kirsch notes that Kohl himself underwent a learning process during this decade, gradually coming to understand that the memory of National Socialism would not weaken with time and that he had to respond accordingly.[123] Kohl is a more complex figure in memory politics than he is often made out to be and despite the perception of a united conservative front, reality was more multifaceted. There were a host of conservative politicians and thinkers, President von Weizsäcker among them, who advocated a critical approach to the Nazi past.

This point notwithstanding, Kohl and his allies did provoke a series of public debates that helped to transform German political culture in an unintended direction. They also inadvertently provided the left with a target; the image of a conservative offensive in history politics was crucial to the Memorial Site and History Movements' ability to recruit and motivate activists. This theme will reappear in the analyses of these movements in Chapters 3 and 4.

Efforts to lay claim to the interpretation of history on both governmental and civic sides were symptomatic of the fact that, by the 1980s, the Federal Republic had acquired an independent state identity. Though officially the goal of unification had not been abandoned, in practice all political forces had accommodated to the expectation that the German division would continue. Conservatives and liberals alike had bid farewell to the notion of a "provisional" state – ironically only briefly before unification became a reality.[124] The official museum and memorial plans, as well as the memory work of grassroots initiatives, reflected this through their lack of attention to developments in the GDR and mostly ignored human rights violations in the Communist bloc. It was in this era of memory-political flux during the 1980s that the *Gedenkstättenbewegung* and the *Geschichtsbewegung* made their marks on the German memory landscape. For the first time, the top-down approach of state-directed memory was successfully challenged by grassroots driven movements of civil society actors.

---

[122] Kirsch, "'Hier geht es um den Kern'" [123] Ibid.
[124] Wolfrum, *Geschichtspolitik in der Bundesrepublik*, Wirsching, *Geschichte der Bundesrepublik*.

Memory Activism in the German Democratic Republic?

What was happening on the other side of the Iron Curtain while memory activism was booming in West Germany? Official policy in the GDR from the outset celebrated Communist resistance against the Nazis, while sidelining the memory of Jewish and other victims. The antifascist state regarded itself as a victor of history and projected all responsibility for the Nazi regime, as well as all purported continuities of fascism in the present, onto the Federal Republic in the context of Cold War competition. Thus, official antifascism became a key component of East German state ideology. The memorial landscape reflected this.

In the late 1970s, this official approach to the past underwent some careful and gradual changes. There was an increased interest in *"Erbe und Tradition"* (heritage and tradition), which allowed for a less ideological take on history and took into account a longer span of German history in an effort to win emotional support for the GDR system.[125] At this time, there were also individual attempts to examine the legacies of the Holocaust in East German society. For example, writers Heinz Knobloch and Günter Kunert were able to publish texts – marginalized but nevertheless available – about the Jewish history of Berlin.[126] In 1983, Knobloch also initiated the marking of the site on Bebelplatz in East Berlin were the Nazis had burned books in May 1933. He succeeded in having a plaque attached and later, the GDR government made plans for a more elaborate memorial true to State Socialist commemorative style. These plans were halted by unification, but Micha Ullmann's celebrated underground room with empty bookshelves was inaugurated there in 1995.[127]

It was not until the late 1980s, however, that Jewish memory was paid more official attention and was manifested in memorialization practices. The reconstruction of the New Synagogue in central Berlin was begun and in 1988 the *Centrum Judaicum* was founded as a state-sanctioned institution of Jewish culture.[128] At the same time, several projects sought to commemorate Jewish victims of the Holocaust, most of which were not completed until after 1989. For example, the memorials at Rosenstrasse (commemorating German women who had protested the arrest of their Jewish husbands in 1942)[129] and at Koppenplatz (an "abandoned room" recalling the Holocaust and the cultural void it created) originated in this period.[130] For the first time in 1988, the anti-Jewish pogrom of 1938 was

---

[125] Wolfrum, *Geschichtspolitik in der Bundesrepublik*.
[126] Knobloch, *Mißtraut den Grünanlagen!*, See Interviews, Matthias Rau.
[127] Jordan, *Structures of Memory*.   [128] See Interviews, Hermann Simon.
[129] Stoltzfus, *Resistance of the Heart*.   [130] Jordan, *Structures of Memory*.

commemorated through an exhibition in the Berlin Ephraim Palais and
thus shifted to the center of public memory about November 9, while the
German revolution of 1918 became secondary.[131]

There is evidence that Jewish history also gained increased prominence
among members of the opposition during this period. Due to the important role of antifascism in state ideology, the questioning of this interpretation of history and an interest in Jewish suffering in itself amounted
to a subversive act. Moreover, some dissidents were motivated by their
historical awareness to question their own role under a dictatorship.
As member of the opposition Maria Nooke relates,

> There was this tradition in the GDR – we were an anti-fascist state, had
> nothing to do with the Third Reich and were "on the good side," so to speak.
> Therefore, it was very difficult to confront these issues without conflicting
> with the state doctrine. ... For me for example, the question of "how do
> I behave in a dictatorship without having to face questions from my children
> later about why I participated?" was crucial – in other words, the question
> that the 1968ers in the West asked their parents, I asked myself ... For me,
> this was one of the primary motives to position myself against this state and to
> try to voice my opinion, to publicize certain things – ecological questions,
> human rights questions, questions about democracy.[132]

There were instances where oppositionists practiced memory activism as part of their resistance to the regime. For example, the first
peace forum took place at the Kreuzkirche in Dresden on February 13,
1981, the anniversary of the bombing of the city. The activists thereby
sought to harness the memory of civilian suffering in war to take a stand
against the militarism of the GDR regime.[133] Further, Ruth
Leiserowitz reports that her group *Frauen für den Frieden* (Women
for Peace) protested against the building of a road through the Jewish
cemetery in Berlin-Weissensee and that she was confronted with overt
anti-Semitism.[134] One of the most prominent instances of the use of
memory for antiregime action was an unpublished paper written by
Markus Meckel and Martin Gutzeit on the occasion of the fortieth
anniversary of the end of the war on the 8th of May 1985, which was
discussed in opposition circles. The authors argued that despite the
antifascist identity of the state, National Socialist ideas continued to
exist and that an acknowledgment of guilt had to entail an analysis of
current political and social structures. They contended that "coming to
terms with the past includes the obligation to actively oppose the

[131] Spielmann, *Denk – Mal – Prozesse.*   [132] See Interviews, Maria Nooke.
[133] Baum, 'Für Meinungsfreiheit und Mitbestimmung – Die Friedenswerkstatt vor 25
Jahren.'
[134] Leiserowitz, 'Eine eigene Öffentlichkeit herstellen.'

system of fear and threat and injustice and misuse of power within our own society."[135]

Despite these individual examples of using the memory of the Nazi past as an instrument of opposition against the regime, there does not seem to have been a sustained effort at memory activism in the GDR at this time. Though the regime's approach to history was certainly a focus of critique, the repressive conditions for civil society in East Germany, as well as the many restrictions on the flow of information and scholarly research severely hampered the development of anything that could have resembled a memory movement. Moreover, there were plenty of current problems and human rights violations for the opposition movement to address, so that attention was directed away from an analysis of the past. Matthias Rau, who found an early interest in the Jewish history of Berlin and conducted clandestine tours of the city, mostly for Westerners, remembers that though he talked to others from the *Bürgerbewegung* about his activities, there was no widespread concern for historical questions. The role of memory in the East German opposition is an area of research that deserves further study.

When the Wall fell in 1989, it suddenly became possible not only to critically examine the regime's history of repression, but also to reevaluate its approach to the Nazi past. The first act of the democratically elected East German parliament in 1990 was to accept responsibility and apologize for the hypocrisy of the GDR state, and to announce willingness to pay compensation to its victims.[136]

Post-Wall Memory Politics

During the early 1990s, debates over this past acquired a particular urgency as the remaining survivors of the Shoah sought to establish the meaning of their history for future generations,[137] and policy-makers and activists struggled over how best to institute united remembrance. The large concentration camp memorials, in addition to a few others, including the Topography of Terror, the Memorial to German Resistance, and the Memorial House of the Wannsee Conference, received a sudden boost: in its first unified Gedenkstättenkonzeption (memorial concept), the federal government guaranteed 50 percent funding for ten years initially.[138] This was an unprecedented level of state

---

[135] 'Der 8. Mai 1945 – unsere Verantwortung für den Frieden (Februar/April 1985)' Meckel and Gutzeit, 'Opposition in der DDR ' pp. 271–72, translation taken from Herf, *Divided Memory* pp. 363–64.
[136] Herf, *Divided Memory.*   [137] Kirsch, "'Hier geht es um den Kern.'"
[138] Garbe, 'Die Gedenkstättenkonzeption des Bundes.'

support and thus an official endorsement of the work done by organizations that had begun against the resistance of the government. Over the next few decades, funding was regularized and extended to more sites, though many smaller memorials continued to struggle and rely on volunteers. Nevertheless, the 1990s witnessed the renewal of existing memorials, the overall expansion of the memorial landscape, and increased opportunities for employment in this sector. This process was strongly shaped by the West German approach to remembrance work, which by this time was becoming institutionally rooted and culturally mainstreamed. Any newcomers to the memory politics of the now unified Federal Republic had to devise strategies and frame their arguments with reference to the established memory culture in order to be effective.

From the beginning of the end of the GDR, citizens were crucially involved in the reckoning with repression under the SED-regime. In late 1989, in most larger towns in East Germany, oppositionists demanded the release of political prisoners and the opening of secret police files. The buildings and archives of the crumbling state were rapidly seized in order to safeguard the evidence of misdeeds – often through citizen occupation. Many of the ad hoc groups involved over time formalized into civic associations that continue to shape the memorial landscape in the former GDR (Chapter 6).

Early efforts to confront the legacy of communism no doubt also benefited from the experience accumulated in West Germany. Postwar denazification (or its failure) was seen as a precedent for "de-Stasification" of the civil service, prompting the creation of the Stasi file authority (BStU) and a series of expert commissions (*Enquete-Kommissionen*) as mechanisms for reckoning with the forty years of Communist rule. In the early years, the focus was less on memorialization than on a judicial and political reckoning, as well as the *removal* of the physical reminders of the division and the old regime; many potential memorial sites were never considered as such. Soon after 1990, a feeling of crisis emerged: questionable privatization schemes, rising unemployment, inequalities between East and West, and cultural differences were at the top of the agenda.[139]

By the early 2000s, *Ostalgie* (Nostalgia for the East) in popular culture seemed to be the most visible manifestation of public of the GDR past – and serious reckoning marginal. As a rule, West Germans tended to regard the GDR as part of regional rather than national history and thus not universally important for all Germans. Pollsters and educators alike noted a disconcerting lack of knowledge, especially among those

[139] Jarausch, *Die Umkehr.*

who did not have a first-hand memory of the time before unification.[140] It seems that, with *political* and *judicial* processes of transition mostly complete, Germans were finding it difficult to establish a memory *culture* that incorporated the experiences of both the Nazi and the Communist regimes. Once again, it was a new cohort of memory activists nevertheless that drove commemorative change and propelled the unified state to action.

For the first decade after the fall of the Wall, then, the memory of Nazism remained centerstage in public discourses and in the monumental landscape and state financing for memorial institutions. The 1990s saw more memory debates, including those about the traveling exhibit on crimes of the Wehrmacht (1995),[141] the publication of Daniel Goldhagen's book *Hitler's Willing Executioners* (1996),[142] and the speech by writer Martin Walser with an ensuing dispute with head of the Central Council of Jews Ignatz Bubis (1998/99).[143] All of this meant that questions of responsibility, the identity of perpetrators, and the significance of the Nazi past for the present remained prominent in the German public sphere.

Jan-Holger Kirsch contends that the memory of the Nazi past, in the course of the 1990s, morphed into a positive resource for German identity and thus enabled a new form of national self-confidence.[144] Moreover, this development took place in the context of a wider European process of reappraising the meaning of the Holocaust and various forms of resistance and collaboration. The German experience has become embedded in attempts to craft a common European memorial culture (at least at the elite level) and enabled Germans to become less cautious in their assertions of national identity.[145] As a result, more traditional national monuments – such as that for the dead of the German Federal armed forces in Berlin (inaugurated in 2009) – have become possible.[146] Another, the "Monument for Freedom and Unity," was sanctioned by the federal parliament as a prominent and positive national memorial, was then put on hold in 2016 due to an explosion of costs, only to be revived again in 2017.[147]

---

[140] Leo, 'Keine gemeinsame Erinnerung.'

[141] Hartmann, Hürter, and Jureit, 'Verbrechen der Wehrmacht,' Heer and others, *Wie Geschichte gemacht wird.*

[142] Goldhagen, *Hitler's Willing Executioners*, Goldhagen, 'Modell Bundesrepublik'; Habermas, 'Über den Öffentlichen Gebrauch,' Jeismann, *Auf Wiedersehen Gestern.*

[143] Brumlik, Funke, and Rensmann, 'Umkämpftes Vergessen.'

[144] Kirsch, '"Hier geht es um den Kern."'

[145] On European memory politics, Wüstenberg, 'The struggle for European Memory', Sierp and Wüstenberg, 'Linking the Local.'

[146] Hettling and Echternkamp, 'Bedingt erinnerungsbereit.'

[147] Apelt, 'Der Weg zum Denkmal ', www.freiheits-und-einheitsdenkmal.de/, 'Streit um Denkmal' *Der Tagesspiegel*, 16 June 2016; 72. Sitzung des Haushaltsausschusses am

One consequence of this emergent "normality" is the highly effective use of memory by German state actors. The government of Chancellor Gerhard Schröder and his Red-Green coalition was by and large less proactive in the realm of history politics than Kohl, but understood the importance of actively supporting the pivotal position of the memory of the Holocaust in German public life. Schröder noted in his speech on the sixtieth anniversary of the liberation of Auschwitz: "the memory of the war and the genocide are part of our life. Nothing will change that: these memories are part of our identity."[148]

Memory has also remained important in cultural and political discourse since Angela Merkel became Chancellor in 2005, though the Nazi past seemed to have lost some of its previous salience. Recent European crises over Greek economic woes, the "Brexit" vote in the United Kingdom, concerns over the vibrancy of right-wing populism, and especially the challenge brought by the arrival of refugees since 2015 have reignited debates about German identity. Inevitably, Germany's multiple legacies of confronting its past have featured prominently in these discussions.[149]

In hindsight, several trends can be identified in the recent memory politics of the Federal Republic. First, and most fundamentally, memory politics have become a regular and routinized field of contention in the Berlin Republic. In particular, the confrontation with the Nazi past is part and parcel of official politics and the landscape of remembrance. Memory-making in general and the confrontation with the Nazi past in particular, have arrived in the mainstream of politics and culture and are today backed by powerful proponents. It is no longer the primary domain of the left or of civil society. Seen as a development of decades of contention over memory played out in the public sphere, this new status quo is significant, because it suggests that there has been a significant shift in the balance between the majoritarian and normative components of democratic memory. The memory of the weak, of minorities, of victims of Nazism, and the remembrance of the perpetration of these crimes by ordinary Germans has moved from the margins into the mainstream. What was previously a highly moral but politically unpopular standpoint, has become not only widely accepted, but representative of official German memory policy. The critical representation of the Nazi past in public space, which was fought for by civil society for decades and was

13 April 2016, 18. Wahlperiode, Ausschussdrucksache 3125; 'Einheitswippe wird doch gebaut' Deutschlandradio Kultur, 14 February 2017.
[148] Quoted in Judt, *Postwar* p. 827.
[149] Winkler 'Es gibt kein deutsches Moralmonopol', Martin Sabrow 'Es geht nicht um Moral.'

long highly controversial, is now an almost unquestioned part of political culture. Challenging its dominance means challenging the norms of democratic memory itself.

The second major trend is that a more diverse set of memorial actors have gained easier access to official recognition and funds since 1989. The federal government, under Schröder and especially Merkel, has reacted to developments that had been brewing for several years. The most prominent are the increasing demands for a representation of the suffering of Germans during and since the Second World War. These include a diverse set of histories, including the memories of repression in the GDR, the trauma of division, the experience of "expulsion" from Eastern Europe after the war, as well as the various war experiences – from the primarily civilian remembrance of bombings and rape to soldiers' recollections of violence and imprisonment. As I have argued, the memory of German suffering was by no means repressed during the early period of the Federal Republic. However, during the 1980s, as the Nazi past came to dominate memory culture, experiences of German suffering were primarily recounted by organizations and individuals in the right wing of the political spectrum. Due to their linkage with the long period of silence about German crimes, memories of German hardship and their advocates became inherently suspect to those who moved into positions of power in memorial institutions of the post-Wall era. Similarly, those who pursued the memorialization of East German repression – traditionally also a concern of conservatives rather than the left – were seen as a dubious political entity and a potential threat to what Eric Langenbacher has called the "Holocaust-centered memory regime."

> Once representatives of the Holocaust memory regime established its political cultural dominance, they undertook numerous efforts to insure its continued power, especially after the country unified in 1990, given the widespread fear that the changed national circumstances would threaten their achievements. Importantly, the nature of the actors and their arguments changed; they no longer struggled to establish their preferred memory regime but rather defended it from a position of power. Representatives labored to ensure that the Holocaust became an even more central part of the school curricula, political education, and the memorial landscape of the country.[150]

In much of this book, I tell the story of how the memory of the Nazi past was moved to the center of political culture. Though some prominent intellectuals and politicians on the left such as Nobel laureate Günter Grass, Social Democrat Peter Glotz, and writer W.G. Sebald have helped to bring the issue of German suffering back into the mainstream public

---

[150] Langenbacher, 'Changing Memory Regimes' p. 58.

sphere and the topic has been treated extensively in media and culture, representatives of German victims have voiced dissatisfaction. It is important to distinguish between the memory of the expulsion which has been a continuous reference point of West German politics and that of repression in the GDR, which had to find its place and meaning in the unified polity. However, both have in common that they have been regarded with apprehension by those in civil society, the government, academia, and memorial institutions who were socialized through the struggle to institute the memory of the Nazi past in German public life.

This conflict manifested itself at the highest level, as well as in the competition over resources and recognition for different historical experiences at the "activist level." It came to the fore during many of my interviews. This clash of historical narratives, memory cultures, and political objectives continues to shape the relationship between state and civic actors in the arena of memory politics today.

Conclusion

Without claiming that a neat succession of developments led to the state of memory as it exists today, it is useful to view post-1945 memory politics as a series of phases. In East Germany, after initial attempts at broader activism and memorialization, a static official narrative emphasized Communist resistance to National Socialism and elevated it to the center of state ideology. This did not truly change until the mid-1980s, when there was an increased interest in Jewish history, though this also apparently had an instrumental explanation. Oppositional interest in history existed, but did not amount to sustained memory activism. In the West, there was civil society memory activism from the beginning, though its most successful incarnation in the first postwar years could be found in the arena of German victimhood. The discourse of German suffering was initially supported by the state, while the victims of Nazi crimes received little encouragement and only sporadic attention from political elites, usually on official days of remembrance. Though the victims of National Socialism kept up their activism throughout the postwar decades and managed to establish some memorials, their influence on official remembrance policy was limited until decades later.

The 1960s saw a great societal interest in the crimes of the Nazi era and concomitantly, concern for German suffering and for repression in the East was relegated mostly to conservative and special interest organizations. The 1960s did not, however, result in significant memorialization activities – such concrete manifestations of the changing memorial culture came to the fore during the 1980s. This decade was pivotal due to the

dispute between Kohl's conservative history politics and left-wing intellectuals, as well as the protest activities of the new social movements,
particularly the Memorial Site and History Movements. These activists,
as I show in later chapters, sought not merely to commemorate or honor
victims, but to transform memorial culture from the ground up, in the
context of everyday life. After the end of the Cold War, the prominence of
the Nazi past in public life was further strengthened and became a routine
and professionalized component of German politics – a circumstance that
state and politicians knew to harness to their advantage. Simultaneously,
there has been a diversification both among the memory activists and the
historical experiences at play in the public sphere. This has resulted in
a competition of memories for public space, recognition, and resources,
as well as in a renegotiation of the norms about democratic memory.

Memory politics in the Federal Republic has all along been determined
to a considerable extent by partisan politics – the stances of left- and right-
wing parties, politicians, and groups concerning the German past were
usually quite clear-cut. Most commonly, conservative politicians were
staunch supporters of expellees, of traditional war commemoration, of
anti-communism. The Nazi past was not irrelevant, but it was not
a priority for the right. Social Democrats and later Greens, by contrast,
were as a rule more supportive of an examination of the Nazi past and less
concerned with victims of communism or of expulsion. These alle-
giances have remained in place until the present, though they are often
exaggerated. It is important not to miss the complexities of this story. For
example, some commentators tend to overemphasize the importance of
the leftist "1968" while the 1980s are often falsely regarded as primarily
the domain of conservative – and elite – figures. Without doubt, today's
memory politics are the product of path-dependent developments that
cannot be understood in isolation. It is also crucial to stress the importance of the changing context within which memory activism took place at
every stage. Without a favorable local, national, or international framework for action, even the most strategically savvy civic group cannot be
effective. Without generational change and a rising awareness of the Nazi
past, the Memorial Site Movement would not have been able to recruit its
participants. Without the fall of the Berlin Wall, the campaign for the
Holocaust Memorial in Berlin would not have been successful. I argue,
however, that grassroots left-wing actors were absolutely crucial to the
process. In other words, this activism was a necessary, if not a sufficient,
condition of the transformation of German memorial culture.

Throughout the overview of the postwar history of memory politics
outlined in this chapter, we can see recurrent themes of political contestation over the normative values that different groups and actors believe

ought to be displayed in the public memorialization of the German past. Each decade witnessed new developments that built on the work of past actors. Different actors moved from opposition to institutions; new values emerged from political movements that drove commemoration strategies; top-down versus bottom-up motives for memorialization clashed in the public sphere. Ultimately, even as a new memory of the Holocaust became accepted in the mainstream, it was challenged by the need to commemorate the crimes of the Communist regime and the German victims of the Second World War.

The features and patterns of this flowing contest between different "pasts" are fundamentally shaped by the interaction between state actors and civil society. This is the consistent theme throughout all four of the postwar periods of memory politics sketched out here. The next chapters offer deeper analyses of the most important movements in German memory politics, including the key debates over normative values of democracy and political representation in public memory that were driven by them.

3 Building Negative Memory: Civic Initiatives for Memorials to Nazi Terror

In early 1984, five hundred activists of the *Initiative Documentation Center Neuengamme* staged a symbolic occupation of the site of the former concentration camp on the outskirts of Hamburg (Figures 3.1–3.3). They had collected over twelve thousand signatures from eighteen countries, including from such prominent personalities as former Chancellor Willy Brandt and playwright Heinrich Böll. The activists' goal was the safeguarding of a key building on the former campgrounds that was in serious disrepair due to decades of neglect.[1]

From 1938 to 1945 Neuengamme was the largest concentration camp in northwestern Germany. Here and in its many satellite camps, over one hundred thousand inmates from all over Europe were incarcerated, of which over 42,900 perished. After the war, the camp had been used to intern Nazi perpetrators before being converted to a regular prison facility.[2] It remained as such until 2003 with only marginal concessions to victim groups in the first four decades in the form of memorials on the periphery of the former campgrounds. The *Initiative* was founded in 1979 with the goal of achieving official protection of Neuengamme as a place of historic importance and to pressure the city's authorities to create a comprehensive institution dedicated to public education. Until then, the survivors' organization *Amicale Internationale de Neuengamme* had been the main driver of commemorative activity, seeking to establish an appropriate monument to their fallen comrades. Unlike the members of the *Amicale*, the participants in the *Initiative* were not themselves victims of the Nazi regime. They were of a different generation, mostly emanating from the thriving peace movement, and brought to the table a new set of political tactics. Though one might think that *Amicale* and *Initiative* would be natural allies, the *Amicale* was not supportive when longhaired and jeans-wearing activists carried out the occupation. The leaders of the *Amicale* had worked for decades to gain respect and access to the local

---

[1] Garbe, *Die Arbeit der KZ-Gedenkstätte Neuengamme* p. 22.
[2] KZ-Gedenkstätte Neuengamme, 'Die KZ-Gedenkstätte Neuengamme' p. 6.

Figure 3.1. Demonstration to demand the safeguarding of
Neuengamme as a memorial, January 28, 1984.[3]

government and did not want to see these efforts undone through non-
conventional politics.[4]

The scene of an occupied former concentration camp and the conflicts
that surrounded it are emblematic of the development of memory activism to establish sites of "negative memory"[5] recalling the Holocaust and
Nazi terror from the postwar period to the present. This moment in 1984
marks a tipping point not only in Neuengamme, but more generally in the
civic efforts to achieve official commemoration of Nazi crimes. All over
West Germany, we see two things happening right around this time: first,
there is a generational and political shift in who is most vocal in calling for
commemoration from the grassroots level. Citizen initiatives that are
grounded in new social movements – above all the peace and history
workshop movements – spring up at locations with a historical link to
Nazi repression. These new groups adopt a more contentious approach to
commemoration and become arguably more effective than the traditional

[3] KZ-Gedenkstätte Neuengamme, F 1986–6830.
[4] See Interviews, Detlef Garbe.
[5] Historian Reinhard Koselleck coined the term "negative memory," see Assmann, *Der
lange Schatten der Vergangenheit.*

Figure 3.2. Protest sign erected at Neuengamme, January 28,1984.[6]

victims' organizations. Nevertheless, they stand on the shoulders and often ally with the traditional groups, once the initial culture clash is overcome. Second, these initiatives emerge in the context of a larger

[6] KZ-Gedenkstätte Neuengamme, F 1986–7113.

Figure 3.3. Flyer/invitation to demonstration at Neuengamme,
January 28, 1984.[7]

---

[7] KZ-Gedenkstätte Neuengamme, Ng 9.5.1.1.

"memory boom" which provides the activists with both a target and an interested audience. This combination of factors explains why, almost across the board, former concentration camps and other sites of Nazi terror in the Federal Republic see victims groups and citizens' initiatives as their dual foundational forces. However, the successful transformation from marginal memorial to well-funded official institution clearly has its origins in the *Gedenkstättenbewegung* (Memorial Site Movement) of the 1980s.

In this chapter, I provide an analysis of how memory activists have shaped the German landscape of memorials recalling the Nazi dictatorship. First, I examine the commemorative efforts of the victims of the Nazi reign. I argue that these groups played a pivotal role in marking these locales and beginning a process of remembrance. Their approach to memory was determined by the immediacy of the experience of Nazi persecution and by the wish to honor the dead as their comrades and family members. In addition, they were concerned with achieving justice, helping survivors master life after liberation, and preventing the repetition of history. Without these activists of the early years, many of the worst places in Nazi geography would have fallen prey to the dominant West German drive to "move on." However, the victims only achieved a marginal level of recognition during the first forty years after the war. Very rarely did their efforts lead to the creation of a large and official memorial institution and most local authorities either did not prioritize or actively opposed their demands. This lack of power can be explained primarily by the context within which they had to operate. In the language of social movement scholarship, the political opportunity structure was not favorable to these early memory activists.

I analyze how this opportunity structure changed during the 1980s. At this time, a rising general interest in the Nazi past and the conservative Kohl government's efforts to harness this past for its history political purposes coincided with the emergence of myriad citizens' initiatives. In Chapter 4, I demonstrate how the History Movement focused on the "working through" of local history and blossomed in the context of a larger scene of left-wing movements. Closely associated with the History Movement – but also with a vibrant collection of union, church, and youth organizations – was the Memorial Site Movement. This Movement was similar in motivation, political orientation, and decentralized structure as the History Movement. However, it was exclusively focused on the Nazi past and composed of initiatives that had sprung up in response to what were seen as unacceptable failures to mark sites of Nazi rule in the local landscape. As these groups realized that they faced comparable political obstacles, they increasingly networked and exchanged ideas. Thus materialized a decentralized movement that has over the years developed a coherent identity and has been highly effective in pressuring state actors at various levels to commemorate officially. Though the Memorial Site Movement was composed of many diverse groups, I identify patterns in their mobilization and demands that facilitated their interlinking through the larger Movement. I first illustrate these patterns with examples from across the Federal Republic. I then discuss in detail the case of the "Active Museum," which initiated the Topography of Terror memorial in Berlin, in order to give a face to the development of the Movement and to make an argument about the intermeshing of civic and state efforts at memorialization.

In the final part of this chapter, I discuss the large symbolic memorial projects concerning the Nazi past that have been undertaken in Berlin since 1989. These efforts – especially the Memorial to the Murdered Jews of Europe, the Sinti and Roma Memorial, and the Memorial to the Homosexual Victims of the Holocaust – have become part of the Federal Republic's *raison d'état*. However, they were kicked off by civic initiatives of various kinds and this circumstance is carefully stressed by these memorials' supporters. This interesting interlinking of the critical potentials of civil society with a commemorative culture that has been fully embraced by state actors supports one of the central arguments of this book: it is crucial to disaggregate both civic and state involvement in public commemoration in order to understand its impact on democratic governance. Moreover, we see here that the *normative* memory regime that was marginal in the first decades of the Federal Republic has now become representative. The memory of the Nazi past is *representative* in two senses: first, it is supported by a large proportion of the population – encouraged by strong policies of political education in schools and through visits to memorial sites – and second, it has acquired an important function for German state actors, allowing for a more positive collective identity and more confident foreign policy stance. Thus, those norms in memory culture that helped to foster a deepening of democracy are now powerfully backed up by political interests.

Early Activism to Mark Sites of Nazi Terror

In the Soviet zone of occupation from 1945 onward, the authorities used Buchenwald, Sachsenhausen, and other facilities to incarcerate not only Nazis, but also suspected opponents of the regime. Their usage as "special camps" for and the abuse and killing of thousands there was not confronted until the 1990s. Ravensbrück became a barracks for Soviet troops. The former Wehrmacht court at Torgau was also used by the

Soviets, then as a GDR prison and as the notoriously brutal youth correctional facility.[8] During the late 1950s, some of these places were made into local or even state memorials of the GDR (Nationale Mahn- und Gedenkstätten) with high ideological value to the East German government. The problematic triple pasts of these sites as markers of Nazi and Soviet/GDR repression, as well as part of the East German commemorative agenda, were only addressed after 1989 (see Chapters 2 and 6).

The need to commemorate those who died and suffered in Nazi con- centration camps and torture chambers was on the immediate agenda of survivors after their liberation. Even in the first days, former concentra- tion camp inmates erected provisional memorials and sought to bury (or rebury) the dead in a dignified manner.[9] Moreover, survivors sought to document and publicize the crimes committed, sometimes reenacting what they had experienced. In some locations, survivor organizations were founded quickly, often drawing on structures that had formed inside the camps. For example, the International Camp Committee at Buchenwald conducted a first commemorative event and proclaimed a political appeal on the 19th of April, 1945 (only eight days after libera- tion by American troops).[10] At Bergen-Belsen, survivors first placed personal memorial markers on graves and in September 1945, the Bergen-Belsen Jewish Committee inaugurated a monument recalling the thirty thousand Jewish victims of this camp (Figure 3.4).[11]

In addition to the makeshift memorials of the survivors, Allied troops took first steps at commemoration, partly in an effort to underline the guilt of local German populations. In Flossenbürg, US commanders forced citizens to create a cemetery to concentration camp victims in the middle of town.[12] In Weimar, residents were marched through Buchenwald to witness what had been done there.[13] At Dachau, the US Army ordered local officials to build a memorial. Though initial plans for this were grand and quickly drawn up, the Bavarian authorities chose to "forget" to proceed with its erection.[14] British troops erected memorial signs immediately after taking the Bergen-Belsen camp and ordered the Hanover authorities to create a more lasting monument. In December 1945, the Soviet military mission erected a monument to

[8] Stiftung Sächsische Gedenkstätten, 'Spuren Suchen und Erinnern.'
[9] Myers Feinstein, *Holocaust Survivors* p. 70.
[10] Gedenkstätte Buchenwald, 'Die Geschichte der Gedenkstätte Buchenwald.'
[11] Stiftung niedersächsische Gedenkstätten, 'Bergen-Belsen' p. 32.
[12] Schikorra, 'Sommer 1945–1950. Übergang und Neuordnung' p. 34.
[13] Gedenkstätte Buchenwald, 'Die Geschichte der Gedenkstätte Buchenwald' p. 6.
[14] Marcuse, *Legacies of Dachau.*

Figure 3.4. Unveiling of a memorial at the Bergen-Belsen concentration camp during the first congress of survivors in the British zone, September 25, 1945.[15]

Soviet prisoners of war there.[16] Margaret Myers Feinstein argues that this early alliance between survivors and Allied troops for remembrance purposes allowed the victims to assert their agency and moral claims against the Germans. Paradoxically, however, it also meant that Germans were able to transfer "their hostility toward the occupying powers onto the DPs [displaced persons]. This may have been what Federal Republic President Theodor Heuss had in mind when he denounced the desecrations of Jewish cemeteries in 1949 as attempts to undermine West German democracy."[17] Thus, there certainly were those political elites in the Federal Republic who recognized the link between a commemoration of the victims of German aggression and the consolidation of democracy. This helps to explain the inauguration of Bergen-Belsen as an official memorial in 1952 in a climate otherwise disinclined to confront this legacy. At the inaugural ceremony, Heuss held a much-noted speech in which he argued that Bergen-Belsen was to be a "thorn" to keep memory alive and that Germans "had known about these things."[18]

[15] Yad Vashem Archive, Jerusalem, Josef Rosensaft Collection, FA 185/167.
[16] http://bergen-belsen.stiftung-ng.de/de/geschichte/gedenkort/gedenkzeichen.html.
[17] Myers Feinstein, *Holocaust Survivors* p. 106.   [18] Baumgärtner 'Schuld oder Scham?'

Most prominent Nazi sites, however, did not find their way into official West German remembrance policy until much later. Even Bergen-Belsen did not become a site that was prioritized by the German state in its commemorative politics when compared to the treatment of expellees, bombing victims, or veterans. While survivors of Nazi repression labored to have their plight commemorated, the mainstream approach remained one of neglect. Local authorities all over West Germany conceded small memorial markers or graveyards, while not letting the legacy of the concentration camps on German soil enter public consciousness or spawn political action in any major way.

After the most immediate of commemorative phases, the West German camps were used pragmatically to meet postwar needs. At Neuengamme and Flossenbürg, SS-men and other members of the Nazi apparatus were initially interned; Dachau functioned as a camp for expellees (as did part of Flossenbürg later on). Bergen-Belsen and Flossenbürg were used to house displaced persons. For DPs, these sites acquired a new meaning as a transitory location on the way to a new life in Israel or elsewhere. It may have been this future perspective that emboldened some DP organizations to demand commemoration. In Flossenbürg, Polish DPs founded a memorial committee in June 1946 and were the driving force behind the demand for adequate remembrance.[19] Despite the fact that they succeeded in erecting a memorial, survivors were not in control of the message that was put forward through memorialization. The woodcarving that was placed in a Flossenbürg memorial chapel in 1948 depicted one camp inmate being hit by another, perpetuating the contemporary public narrative about prisoners abusing one another and being criminals in general. The question of actual perpetrators was sidelined entirely.[20] In Bergen-Belsen, memorial planning was at first assigned to a landscape architect who had previously designed an SS memorial – prompting protests from survivors' organizations. During the construction in 1948, memory stones placed by Jewish survivors were removed.[21]

Despite early impulses to memorialize, the new uses of the sites and the general lack of will to acknowledge German guilt quickly lead to their neglect. Moreover, historical structures of camps and torture chambers that might have served as physical aides-mémoire were often quickly destroyed by Allied troops or survivors themselves. In Bergen-Belsen, for instance, prisoner barracks were burnt down as part of a victory celebration in 1945.[22] When the prison at Neuengamme was opened,

---

[19] Schikorra, 'Sommer 1945–1950' p. 54.   [20] Ibid. p. 55.
[21] Myers Feinstein, *Holocaust Survivors* p.87, Stiftung niedersächsische Gedenkstätten, 'Bergen-Belsen' pp. 42, 46.
[22] Stiftung niedersächsische Gedenkstätten, 'Bergen-Belsen' p. 26.

a high-level judicial official welcomed that this "sign of our past shame is being wiped out."[23] At Dachau, the main victim group, the Comité International de Dachau (CID) called for the destruction of most of the camp. In 1955, the planned demolition of the crematorium was regarded as a way to put "an end to the defamation of the Dachau area."[24] At times, the survivors' desire to destroy the sites where they had suffered interlinked with locals' desire to cover up their homeland's criminal topography. In Flossenbürg, the construction of expellee settlements on the former campgrounds was celebrated in the local press, with headlines such as "On Sites of Suffering – Home of Happiness" (August 1961) and "Settlers Made Dead Landscape Bloom Again" (August 1969).[25]

When the DP camp in Flossenbürg was closed, discussions had arisen – not about the need for commemoration – but about a commercial and residential usage of the site. Nevertheless, the international scandal surrounding the inadequate burial of concentration camp victims at the Dachau Leitenberg, propelled the Bavarian state government to redesign many of the graves around Flossenbürg as well. Thus, in 1957, the dead of satellite camps and death marches were reinterred at an honor cemetery (Ehrenfriedhof) at the former quarantine camp of Flossenbürg. In the process, the few remaining original structures of the camp were destroyed. The park-like cemetery was intended to "make less stark the memory of that which was" and according to Anja Fritz functioned as an alibi to enable the noncommemorative usage of the remainder of the space.[26]

For sure, attempts to "master" the past were not equally successful everywhere. Bergen-Belsen may be seen as an exception to the rule of mainstream silence about German complicity in Nazi crimes. Here, a memorial was in the works early on and was utilized by West German political elites for conciliatory gestures toward the victims. The Bergen-Belsen memorial had been agreed upon by an international commission that included survivor organizations and representatives of countries that had suffered Nazi occupation. The clash of memorial cultures in this commission and debates surrounding the memorial form and inscriptions delayed opening until November 1952.[27] Subsequently, the Memorial faded from public attention until 1960, when, after a wave of anti-Semitic graffiti, Chancellor Konrad Adenauer, along with several of his ministers, visited Bergen-Belsen in response to the international outcry,[28] thus again

---

[23] Behling and Möller, 'Gegen das Verdrängen' p. 43.
[24] Marcuse, *Legacies of Dachau* p.184, see also Sierp, 'Memory, Identity and a Painful Past.'
[25] Skriebeleit, 'Was bleibt' pp. 104–105.
[26] Fritz, '1950–1958. Schlussstrich und Integration' p. 75.
[27] Stiftung niedersächsische Gedenkstätten, 'Bergen-Belsen' p. 56.   [28] Ibid. p. 72.

elevating the site to national prominence. Despite this public attention, Bergen-Belsen had no permanent staff, except one caretaker, until 1987. Historical research about the camp was also rare, with a book published in 1962 by Eberhard Kolb being the only major work to come out before the late 1980s.

During the 1950s and '60s, local victims' organizations and national ones, such as the *Vereinigung der Verfolgten des Naziregimes* (VVN) and *Bund der Verfolgten des Naziregimes* (BVN),[29] continued their commemorative work – with little impact on the mainstream culture of remembrance. The efforts undertaken at Neuengamme were typical: the organization of German victims, the *Arbeitsgruppe Neuengamme* (AGN – Working Group Neuengamme), was founded in June 1948. It did not initially have much political weight and was suspected as being infiltrated by Communists (just as the VVN). Under such difficult conditions, the group nevertheless held annual commemorative ceremonies on May 8.[30] The first memorial was erected in response to pressure from the French High Commission, rather than from the AGN, which regarded the memorial as inadequate: the column, five meters high and without inscription, was located at the periphery of the former camp. Soviet and Polish victims' groups had not even been invited to the inaugural ceremony.

In 1958, the *Amicale Internationale de Neuengamme* (AIN) was founded in Brussels. This enabled German activists to increase pressure on German authorities; they immediately demanded an appropriate memorial and the funding of research on Neuengamme. Though the victims were not granted their demand of a memorial at the former location of the crematorium (which was then on prison grounds), they did succeed in the creation of an international monument outside the prison. In consultation with the AIN, the city of Hamburg placed a sculpture, a wall of remembrance with all the nations of Neuengamme concentration camp inmates, and a brief information plaque. It was inaugurated in November 1965 with many survivors in attendance. Despite this concession to the victims, the memory of the concentration camp did not seem to impact Hamburg's policy planning. In the late 1960s, without a word to the AIN, the Senate decided to build a new prison building at Neuengamme.[31] A genuine willingness to turn over the space of Neuengamme to remembrance and educational work did not come until the 1980s.

---

[29] VVN and BVN can both be translated as "Association of the Persecuted by the Nazi Regime," but they represent different sides of the political spectrum.
[30] Behling and Möller, 'Gegen das Verdrängen' p. 44.
[31] Ibid. and see Interviews, Detlef Garbe.

Another case in point is that of the Villa where the notorious "Wannsee Conference" had taken place, when the Nazi leadership had set in stone the "final solution." The initiative was led by Auschwitz survivor and historian Josef Wulf in the mid-1960s and was unsuccessful at the time. In 1966, together with about thirty other intellectuals including philosopher Karl Jaspers, Wulf founded the "Association for an International Documentation Center for the Study of National Socialism and Its Consequences," to be housed at the Villa.[32] Wulf's efforts faced strong resistance from the West Berlin establishment, though Mayor Klaus Schütz acknowledged the need for such an institution and offered alternative sites. The Villa was at that point an educational facility for school children. This circumstance was used by the opponents of the project to argue that Wulf wanted to oust innocent children in order to erect "yet another" site of horror.[33] In the early 1970s, the German interior minister rejected the idea of turning the site into a museum, arguing that the topic had already sufficiently been discussed and exhibited.[34] Distraught about his perceived ineffectiveness, Wulf dissolved the association – a disappointment that may have contributed to his decision to commit suicide in 1974. In 1986, Berlin Mayor Eberhard Diepgen announced plans to turn the Villa into a memorial and it was inaugurated in 1992, on the fiftieth anniversary of the Conference.[35] The founding Director was Gerhard Schoenberner, also a Holocaust survivor and a member of Wulf's original initiative.[36] Nevertheless, the creation of the House of the Wannsee Conference "from above"[37] after many years of unsuccessful civic efforts is emblematic of the difficult situation faced by memory activism until the late 1970s – and the shift in political opportunities after that.

This pattern was repeated all over the Federal Republic. Local and international victim groups carried out their own commemorative agendas where possible – organizing "private" remembrance, for instance through joint trips to sites of suffering. These groups also continuously lobbied the relevant authorities, demanding respect and action. Local politicians either refused to respond entirely or acknowledged the need to remember in nonspecific terms. Sometimes there were minor concessions

---

[32] *Der Aufbau*, New York, 18 November 1966, www.ghwk.de/deut/hausgeschichte/auf bau_18-11-1966.pdf.

[33] *Christ und Welt* 12 January 1967, www.ghwk.de/deut/hausgeschichte/christ_und_welt-1 .12.1967.pdf.

[34] Reichel, *Politik mit der Erinnerung.*

[35] www.ghwk.de/deut/hausgeschichte/hausgeschichte.htm; see also www.stevenlehrer.com /joseph_wulf.htm, Kühling, 'Die Auseinandersetzung.'

[36] See Interviews, Gerhard Schoenberner.

[37] See Interviews, Norbert Kampe.

that lead to the creation of memorials at peripheral locations and that did not provide much or any information about the extent of crimes or identity of perpetrators. This form of remembrance certainly did not lead to widespread public education nor did it require policy-makers to revise development plans that often further undermined the integrity of Nazi sites of terror. In a few cases – Bergen-Belsen, Dachau, and the Memorial to German Resistance in Berlin – tireless efforts by German and international survivor organizations succeeded in the erection of more substantial memorials. In the Dachau case, Harold Marcuse has documented the decades-long process of negotiations between the CID and the Bavarian authorities, which were complicated by divisions among the victims themselves.[38] In 1968, the memorial was dedicated with military honors – against which students protested and which led to confrontations between them and survivors.[39] This situational conflict is indicative of the beginning shift in understanding of what the memory of National Socialism was supposed to represent.

This account of the Federal Republic's early memory politics supports my argument that during this period, we see a minority of activists struggling against widely held memory stances. As the director of the Memorial to German Resistance in Berlin, Johannes Tuchel, argues,

> when it comes to memory work in the Federal Republic of Germany after 1945, little would have happened without civic engagement – of this I am convinced. This is the case for all areas of persecution, just as for the area of resistance against National Socialism: if there had not been relatives of the victims, some of them persecuted or resistors themselves, who pointed out the importance of remembrance in the 1950s, the state would have done this only very hesitantly, if at all. The history of how resistance against National Socialism was perceived cannot be written or understood without the civic aspect. The official Germany had to be pushed forward, carried forward in many arenas.[40]

For both victims and those Germans who bore responsibility for Nazism's crimes through action or inaction, memories were still fresh (communicative, in Assmann's terms) and perpetrators and witnesses still around. This immediacy made the remembrance of Nazism's victims a practical matter of justice as well as of democratic symbolism. In the context of general uncertainty about the strength of democracy, however, memorial institutions remained *representative* of the *majority's interpretation of the past*. A more *normative* memory politics, which acknowledged the experience of the victims and made them part of a *deeper* understanding of democracy, could not yet be achieved by victims' groups. This shift came during the 1980s.

---

[38] Marcuse, *Legacies of Dachau.*   [39] Sierp, 'Memory, Identity and a Painful Past.'
[40] See Interviews, Johannes Tuchel.

The *Gedenkstättenbewegung*: Commemorating Nazi Terror at the Local Level

The 1980s were a time of grand gestures, reacquired national confidence under the Kohl administration, and a widespread countercultural mobilization amid the protests of the new social movements. The clash between these two sides was mirrored in memory politics. The decade saw a series of large and state-funded projects that picked up on the rising interest in all things historical and in turn augmented this memory boom. Such projects included plans for the German Historical Museum (DHM) in Berlin, the "House of History of the Federal Republic" (*Haus der Geschichte*) in Bonn, and extensive plans for regional museums. The local Bonn memorial to victims of 1933–1945, at which state dignitaries had laid their wreaths since the 1950s, now did not appear sufficient.[41] The association for tending German war graves (VDK) and conservative politicians demanded a central memorial to the "victims of war and dictatorship" first in Bonn and later in Berlin. The VDK proposal emphasized the need to construct a national monument that could be identity-forming and the size of which would be proportional to "the suffering experienced by the German people." Accordingly, the memorial was to be 40,000 square meters in size and include, among other facilities, a military parade ground.[42] There was sufficient opposition among Social Democrats, Greens, and others to make such a monument unfeasible, but the lines of conflict had been drawn.

Such efforts were complemented by less controversial but elaborate celebrations of anniversaries of various kinds. For instance, the 750th anniversary of the city of Berlin, was carefully orchestrated in both East and West and involved the refurbishment of entire neighborhoods. Further, there were a whole series of grand exhibitions – such as that on the Wittelsbach dynasty in Munich (1980) or Prussia (1981) in Berlin – which attracted unprecedented numbers of attendees.[43] The overall theme of this official drive for public history was to highlight the "big picture" of German history: to rediscover the grand narrative of the past without denying the horrors of the Nazi period. By the end of the decade the number of museums, exhibits, and visitors had risen by a third compared to 1982.[44]

These large-scale projects should not be seen in stark terms: both among elites and in popular culture, an interest in an honest confrontation with the Nazi past was rising. The screening of the television series *Holocaust* in 1979 and President Richard von Weizsäcker's speech on the

---

[41] Hausmann, *Duell mit der Verdrängung?*   [42] Heinrich, *Strategien des Erinnerns* p. 41.
[43] Rosenfeld, 'A Mastered Past?'   [44] Wirsching, *Geschichte der Bundesrepublik* p. 421.

fortieth anniversary of the end of the Second World War are just the most prominent examples. At the local level too, there were increasing numbers of politicians and bureaucrats who supported a critical reading of history. This recognition notwithstanding, the overall principles of official memorial projects and the rising tide of grassroots activity were clearly divergent – and this divergence manifested itself in the kinds of memorial sites that resulted. Günter Morsch, head of the Sachsenhausen Concentration Camp Memorial, gave me the following assessment of these two trends:

> We actually have in the '70s and '80s two "movements": on the one hand the museum movement, which is primarily state-organized – Rhineland Museum of Industry, German Historical Museum, the Bonn "House of History," and all the city museums that were founded at this time – all these are obviously state institutions. In contrast, there are the *Gedenkstätten* in West Germany that were entirely bypassed by this movement. These were in fact founded by grassroots initiatives, by union movements, party groups, victims organizations, and absolutely crucially also by history workshops. So we must recognize that there is a time lag in Germany and that the movement for *Gedenkstätten* only really takes off when the museum movement has already had some grand results. And the former is also much smaller – while the museum movement builds sites costing multiple millions, the *Gedenkstätten*-movement that emerges from the history workshops has much less funding . . . But it has to be said clearly: without the history workshops, the *Gedenkstätten*-movement in late 1980s would not have existed at all.[45]

An important point here is that though there was certainly a strong *Zeitgeist* during the 1980s that supported historical work in general, the development of marginal Nazi sites of terror into important components of the German memory culture, *cannot be explained without the grassroots initiatives* that sprang up all over the country. While what Morsch calls the "museum-movement" resulted in well-funded and representative museums and memorials; then, history workshops and other initiatives challenged not only this drive for grand representation but also developed new forms of commemoration and memorial design (Chapter 5). The string of newly opened or redesigned *Gedenkstätten* – most importantly former concentration camps such as Dachau and Neuengamme and other "authentic sites" such as the Topography of Terror in Berlin[46] – were only the most high profile outcomes of this grassroots activism. Many of these locations were concerned primarily with documentation, so that the local research conducted by the initiatives fed directly into the public presentations. The developing institutions also championed the use of oral history and a central role for *Zeitzeugen* (witnesses) who

---

[45] See Interviews, Günter Morsch.
[46] Lutz, 'Von der Bürgerinitiative zur Stiftung.'

became an integral part of the educational mission. At these sites, the shift of civic initiatives from conducting research and ad hoc exhibits toward creating permanent markers of memory is most obvious. Bernt Roder, Director of the local museum in Berlin-Prenzlauer Berg, contends:

> There was an in-depth confrontation of the topic, people became professionally qualified through the concrete research, but simultaneously they fought civically – politically, if you will – that this research did not just end up in a book, but that is was secured institutionally . . . It was supposed to be about more than studying the Nazi period in all its facets – it was about: how do we engage future generations in this history?"[47]

All over the Federal Republic, citizens' initiatives emerged that targeted specific sites of Nazi terror. Unlike the history workshops that were usually eclectic in their historical interests, the memorial initiatives were single-issue and explicitly had the creation of memorials as their goal. Another distinction with the workshops was that these (at least initially) espoused a very clear undogmatic brand of leftism, while the Memorial Site Movement was more politically diverse. The *Gedenkstättenbewegung* drew on previously existing civic organizations, especially from within the peace movement, labor unions, church groups, and leftist youth clubs, in addition to history workshops. Though politically, Social Democratic and Green affiliations dominated, the *Gedenkstätten* initiatives were more culturally heterogeneous than the workshops.[48] Nevertheless, both movements interlinked in many ways, including through individuals and groups that participated in both; their related philosophical approaches of working from the ground up through the use of oral history, local research, and work with witnesses; and their common social milieu.

The Memorial Site Movement targeted two main categories of sites. First, there were those sites, mostly large and notorious, that had already become the focus of activism by victims' groups since 1945. During the 1980s, initiatives were founded with the goal of reinventing these places to transform them from relatively traditional (and publicly neglected) sites of mourning to modern and prominent institutions of commemoration and education. All the locations I have discussed here – Neuengamme, Bergen-Belsen, Dachau, as well as the Memorial to German Resistance and the Plötzensee Memorial in Berlin – fall into this category. The second type of sites targeted by the Memorial Site Movement is what might be called "forgotten" ones. Here local initiatives researched the history of places that had previously not been the focus of much (even unsuccessful) activism.

[47] See Interviews, Bernt Roder.
[48] Behrens, Ciupke, and Reichling, "'. . . und im nachhinein ist man überrascht.'"

Here, places such as the Judengasse in Frankfurt am Main, the EL-DE House in Cologne, the Gestapo headquarters at the former Hotel Silber in Stuttgart, the many sites of death marches and satellite camps, Nazi military tribunals, locations where Nazi euthanasia was practiced, and more come to mind. Included here are also civic efforts to erect memorials in central locations in towns and cities that recall the plight of victims of the Nazi regime and publicize the identity of perpetrators. The Mirror Wall in Berlin Steglitz or the Aschrott Fountain in Kassel are good examples here. Most of these confrontations took place during the 1980s and resulted not only in large memorial sites, but also in many smaller markers such as commemorative plaques or artwork. As Rudy Koshar has noted, more than three-quarters of the plaques recalling resistance to National Socialism in West Germany were dedicated during the 1980s. However, many of the initiatives that were founded during the 1980s continued their work throughout the following decades, kicking off new projects and accompanying the memorials they had initiated. When successful, previously grassroots and improvised groups sometimes turned into official support organizations of established memorials. Moreover, in East Germany and also in some places in the West, the main phase of civic memory activism came after 1989. For example, the campaign to establish a memorial and documentation center in the Hotel Silber in Stuttgart began in earnest only in 2010, but nevertheless has similar characteristics as efforts two or three decades earlier.

Typical for the core activist period of the 1980s was the previously rare focus on the "forgotten victims" of National Socialism, including Sinti and Roma, gays, the disabled and chronically ill, slave laborers, and later in the decade, deserters from the Wehrmacht. Specific victims groups also came on scene that often allied with citizens' initiatives and used similar tactics, such as occupations and unconventional demonstrations. In 1980, for example, a Sinti survivors group carried out a hunger strike at Dachau to protest their continued discrimination in West Germany.[49]

However, the forgotten victims also had to struggle with the established survivors organizations that were usually quite conservative and shaped by the prejudices common in the postwar era. With rising societal recognition of these groups, they were able to demand their inclusion in the memorial landscape. Harold Marcuse explains that "new" victims "were able to use their social recognition to press the survivors of political repression to change their exclusionary stance. The political survivors' reluctance to broaden the category of victims of Nazism is not surprising,

---

[49] Marcuse, *Legacies of Dachau* p. 354.

since they had faced decades of competing claims of victimization from Germans who had overwhelmingly supported the Nazi regime."[50]

Another key innovation driven primarily by memory activists was that perpetrators were spotlighted.[51] This meant raising the question of responsibility (rather than merely asking the public to be empathetic with the victims). The Memorial Site Movement activists – much more so than earlier civic groups – utilized these topics to link the memory of the Nazi period with a political reflection of the present. They demanded of the public to reflect on contemporary discrimination, on their responsibility in the face of racism or homophobia, and on the importance of vigilance and civil courage. In other words, here we see an explicit link made between civic memory politics and democratic values. In ways similar to the History Movement, the Memorial Site initiatives emphasized their own procedural and democratic practice; they debated the democratic symbolism of memorial design; and they demanded state recognition and funding for sites that were deemed indispensable to democratic ethics and education. These local initiatives thereby collectively made a crucial contribution to a "deepening" of German democratic culture.

Though those activists who sought to create "new" sites may have had an initially tougher time with persuading local and regional publics and decision-makers that these locations warranted preservation and funding, the conditions faced by all these initiatives were in fact quite similar. Each local campaign had to confront idiosyncratic political constellations and had to form various alliances, but there were recurring patterns.

In most cases, activism was triggered by governmental or commercial plans for development of a site.[52] At Neuengamme, protests arose in response to Hamburg's plans to either commercially utilize or demolish the Klinkerwerk (brick factory) of the concentration camp. Though a documentation center had been opened in 1981, most of the original campgrounds remained closed for remembrance and educational purposes.[53] In Wuppertal, authorities were planning the construction of a parking garage on the site of a destroyed synagogue, thus crystalizing the mnemonic opposition.[54] Memory activists were galvanized by plans in 1987 to turn the former Nazi party rally grounds in Nuremberg into a shopping mall with residential housing.[55] In Stuttgart, activism for the Hotel Silber began when a local department store made plans to rebuild a whole city block in response to the notorious renewal of the `Stuttgart central station

[50] Ibid. p. 355.   [51] See Interviews, Thomas Lutz.
[52] Jordan, *Structures of Memory*.   [53] Behling and Möller, 'Gegen das Verdrängen' p. 45.
[54] Behrens, Ciupke, and Reichling, '"... und im nachhinein ist man überrascht."'
[55] Jaskot, 'The Reich Party Rally Grounds' p. 151.

("Stuttgart 21"). The historic building that once housed the Stuttgart Gestapo headquarters would have been destroyed in the process and was saved by the protests.[56] In Frankfurt/Main, a broad coalition of activists resorted to the occupation of the grounds of archeological remains of a Medieval Jewish ghetto in order to prevent its razing for the purposes of building a public transportation administrative building. In the Frankfurt case, the occupation was mostly futile, but it brought into stark relief the conflict between city authorities and leftist cultural and political circles.[57] The protest movement resulted in efforts to acknowledge the legacies of Jewish life in Frankfurt and to commemorate the persecution of Frankfurt Jews. One result was the "New Börneplatz Memorial to the Third Jewish Community Destroyed by the National Socialists."[58]

To make the formation of such protest possible, two antecedent conditions had to be met: first, at least a small group of individuals had to have a sense of the local topography of National Socialism, as well as an understanding of the larger and developing debate about the need to "work through the past." In the Frankfurt case, for instance, several articles about the role of the Börneplatz in local Jewish history had appeared in the late 1970s providing some level of existing knowledge when the city's plans became public.[59] In places where older victims organizations had been active, these could function as a source of eyewitness and documentary information for the new activists. In Stuttgart, efforts to safeguard the Hotel Silber were preceded by history workshop research into the local history of Nazi persecution that had already resulted in another memorial (the deportation memorial "Zeichen der Erinnerung"), as well as many "stumbling blocks" and smaller markers.[60]

Second, there had to be a rudimentary awareness in the public about the importance of these issues – an awareness that was shaped by media events such as the Holocaust series or the various history political moves of the federal government, or more locally relevant happenings. For example, the Bergen-Belsen Working Group was founded in 1985 in "response to what was perceived as a lack of commitment to the Memorial on the side of the state."[61] It was composed of members of the churches, trade union, the VVN and the University of Hannover. In protest of Chancellor Kohl and US President Reagan's visit to the

---

[56] See Interviews, Jupp Klegraf and Elke Banabak.
[57] Best, 'Der Frankfurter Börneplatz.'   [58] Schönborn, 'The New Börneplatz Memorial.'
[59] Ibid. p. 279.
[60] Ostertag and Schairer, '70 Jahre Deportation'; 'Zeichen der Erinnerung'. For an overview of the Stolperstein project, see www.stolpersteine.eu/en/.
[61] Stiftung niedersächsische Gedenkstätten, 'Bergen-Belsen' p. 110.

Bitburg cemetery (where SS men were interred) and to Bergen-Belsen (for balance), activists demonstrated at the site and some occupied the documentary building.[62] Similarly, the first meeting of groups and individuals that aimed to persuade the Cologne authorities into finally realizing a six-year-old decision to create an educational site came after Richard von Weizsäcker's much regarded speech in 1985. The Cologne activists proceeded to augment the pressure by distributing flyers, holding candlelight vigils, and organizing events about various aspects of the Nazi past, before becoming a formal civic association in 1988. The result was the El-De Haus, a documentation center located in the city's former Gestapo headquarters.[63] The Weizsäcker speech was also a catalyst for a citizens' initiative in Wolfsburg to demand the rededication of a cemetery where forced laborers used in the Volkswagen factory were buried. The result was the "Memorial to the Victims of National Socialist Tyranny" as well as a longer process of research and company-driven reckoning with the past.[64] In 1999, the Volkswagen Company opened an official exhibit detailing its use of forced labor.[65]

Another common feature of civic memorialization was that it was usually a drawn-out process with much back-and-forth between activists and authorities over several years. Activists, after mounting publicity work, lobbying, and staging protests against political recalcitrance, might have been able to achieve an initial success of a small memorial marker or limited funding for an historical project. With growing public awareness and activist self-confidence, as well as a shift in attitudes within political and bureaucratic circles, more became possible. Thus, in many cases, we see either several rounds of commemoration of one particular site or an activist group expanding their memory work to other local sites. At Neuengamme, the local initiative, even after succeeding in acquiring the documentation center, kept demanding the prison be closed and the entire territory be handed over to become part of the memorial. They also increasingly included Neuengamme's satellite camps in their purview.

While Memory Site Movement activists most frequently met with refusal or at least reluctance on the part of state actors, they also sometimes found individual allies within political parties and bureaucracies. This situation became more common as the topic of the Nazi past rose to prominence in the public sphere and there is a generational shift inside the

[62] Ibid., p. 116.
[63] '20 Jahre Verein EL-DE-Haus' El-DE Info Nr. 10 (September 2008), available at www .museenkoeln.de/downloads/nsd/EL-DE-Info-10–08_klein.pdf.
[64] Fischer, 'Memento Machinae' p. 100.
[65] www.volkswagenag.com/content/vwcorp/content/de/the_group/history/remembrance.html.

governing institutions. As Norbert Kampe, then-Director of the House of the Wannsee Conference, told me:

> Two things come together: there are these citizens' movements, that have fought [for remembrance] and then a shift amongst the politicians to people who were not burdened by the past – not in terms of being burdened as perpetrators – but in the sense of a generational membership in the Third Reich. Now there were people who had a less clouded perspective. And as you can see, most of the memorials in the old Federal Republic are not actually founded until the 1980s.[66]

Another important development was that members of new social movements (and the Green Party) acquired positions of power within the state during this time. A case in point is that of the *Initiative Haus Wolfenstein*, founded in 1987, which aimed to transform a former synagogue building in Berlin-Steglitz into a memorial and community center. Though the Initiative was successful in having the privately owned building designated as historically protected, they could not achieve its conversion to a memorial. However, they did have important allies inside the local government, most notably Green politician and Cultural Senator Sabine Weißler, who helped the activists push through the Mirror Wall memorial. This was located in front of the former synagogue on a public square and was inaugurated in 1995.[67]

Early on, the Memorial Site Movement was composed of whatever constellation of individuals and groups became locally engaged to work through the Nazi past. Very much in line with the History Movement's beginnings of grassroots democracy and ad hoc alliance formation, these initiatives were often not immediately formally organized. However, in the course of mobilization and discussions with state actors, it quickly became clear that more formal organization would make for a stronger negotiating stance and also would enable activists to collect donations and to operate officially as a sponsor of a future site. Elke Banabak, the vice chair of the "Initiative Learning and Memorial Site Hotel Silber," told me that when the Roundtable was formed with the city of Stuttgart and the state of Baden-Württemberg, their representatives leaned on the activists to found a formal association so that they might be a legally and politically reliable partner.[68] As I will discuss further, such formalization presents not only advantages to memory movements, often demotivating members and triggering fundamental debates about activist identity and democratic practice.

---

[66] See Interviews, Norbert Kampe.
[67] Initiative Haus Wolfenstein, 'Von Juden in Steglitz', Seferens, *Ein deutscher Denkmalstreit*, see Interviews, Sabine Weißler and Friedrich Hossbach.
[68] See Interviews, Elke Banabak.

Key to the development of activist memorials were the debates about memorial design and democratic purpose of the sites. Previous generations of activists, including the victims of National Socialism, had been concerned mostly with a traditional honoring of victims and martyrs, and had espoused a conventional memorial aesthetic. Christian symbolism of suffering, obelisks, and gravestone-like monuments were dominant. Inscriptions remained relatively uninformative. The Memorial Site Movement emerged during a time when artists were calling the artistic format of the memorial itself into question and "countermonuments" were developed.[69] The activists of the 1980s were correspondingly concerned less with remembrance for its own sake, but with engaging the public in a critical process of rethinking the past. The memorial designs that were advocated for reflected these priorities, emphasizing authentic spaces, rejecting monumental and overly emotional designs, and insisting on the provision of information about the diversity of victimhood and the identity of perpetrators (see Chapter 5). Moreover, memorial activists did not only initiate new structures, but also triggered reflections about existing ones. In Hamburg, a citizens' initiative began questioning the meaning of a large monument to the 76th infantry regiment that, they argued, glorified war. As a result, a memorial designed by Alfred Hrdlicka was (incompletely) erected next to it as a counterpoint, depicting the less glorious consequences of war.[70] In Bremen, die Friedensinitiative Ostertor invited submissions of designs to alter the warrior memorial at Altmannshöhe in 1986 (though the winning design was rejected by authorities). Local groups also worked to have former air raid shelters (where Gestapo and Nazi party had operated at the end of the war) painted with antifascist themes by local artists.[71]

In all the cases I have mentioned, it was crucial to activists that, once a memorial had been agreed upon in principle, they continued to have a voice in the design and content of the site. The most radical interpretation of this idea was implemented at the Ahlem concentration camp near Hanover. Here, the involvement of citizens was placed at the center of the design process: "regular residents" were called upon to find historical traces, interview witnesses, develop design ideas, and make models of these designs.[72] More commonly, memorial activists made sure that their associations were consulted or even formally represented in committees that governed the design and construction procedure of a site they had initiated. In Stuttgart, one of the main concerns of the *Initiative Hotel*

---

[69] Lupu, 'Memory Vanished, Absent, and Confined'; Tomberger, *Das Gegendenkmal*, Young, *The texture of memory.*
[70] Goldman, 'Marking Absence.'   [71] Buggeln and Marszolek, 'Concrete Memory.'
[72] Anschütz and Heike, *"Wir wollten Gefühle sichtbar werden lassen."*

Silber was how to be integrated permanently into the governing structures of the planned site – so that their demands about what should be displayed in the permanent exhibition could not be ignored. Even after a site was completed, initiatives usually remained closely associated, often working on temporary exhibits, offering guided tours, or even transforming themselves into "Friends of" associations with fundraising responsibilities. I examine more closely this interlinking of civic and state activity in Chapter 7.

With all these initiatives springing up and facing similar obstacles, the wish to exchange ideas and support one another was quickly apparent. Through personal contacts, groups unsystematically collaborated from early on and saw this as crucial to their development.[73] This informal networking gradually became more institutionalized through the establishment of a Movement newsletter (*Gedenkstättenrundbrief*), workshops (*Gedenkstättenseminare*) and a coordinating office (*Gedenkstättenreferat*). A few individuals, organizations and memorial sites played a critical role in the shaping of many local and specialized groupings into a nationwide Movement with communicative structures and at least a nascent common identity. These included the *Aktion Sühnezeichen/Friedensdienste* (ASF – Action Reconciliation/Service for Peace) in Berlin with Thomas Lutz, the *Initiative Dokumentationsstätte Neuengamme* in Hamburg and Detlef Garbe, and the Memorial in Dachau under the leadership of Barbara Distel. Very rapidly, these "organs" of the Movement were widely utilized and distributed.

In June 1981, the Neuengamme Initiative submitted an application to the executive committee of the ASF "to initiate the nationwide coordination of those groups and organizations working on the shaping and creation of documentation and memorial sites."[74] The application also noted the particular suitability of ASF for such a task given its long years of experience in memory work since the 1960s. Attached to the application was a list of merely ten initiatives. Thomas Lutz, who has run the coordinating office almost from the outset, recalls that

> when a whole range of new memorials was created at the beginning of the 1980s, they needed an organization that could coordinate. First, they asked the Federal Agency for Civic Education – but that was all too bureaucratic and did not really take off. They did not want go with the Association of Persecuted Social Democrats or the Association of the Persecuted of the Nazi Regime (VVN), because they were too politically one-sided. So they asked the Action Reconciliation, which had an important coordinating and balancing function within the peace movement at the time.[75]

---

[73] Behrens, Ciupke, and Reichling, "'. . . und im nachhinein ist man überrascht'"
[74] Garbe, 'Von den "vergessenen KZs"' p. 76.
[75] See Interviews, Thomas Lutz.

The first meeting of the network took place on the 17th and 18th of October 1981 in a church community center in Hamburg-Eimsbüttel (which incidentally was a center of the History Movement). The short notice with which this meeting was put together speaks to the as yet unbureaucratic functioning of the network, as did its "do-it-yourself" nature: the invitation for the meeting reminded participants to bring their sleeping bags. The second gathering took place in Dachau in May 1982, was three days long, and received some financial support from the *Bundeszentrale für politische Bildung* (Federal Agency for Political Education). In 1983, the network was bolstered by the formal creation of the coordinating post at ASF, which was initially run by Thomas Vogel. His first letter to the network – the first *Gedenkstättenrundbrief* – was sent on May 24, 1983 and was a modest three pages in length. In it, Vogel refers to Detlef Garbe's new edited volume on the "forgotten concentration camps," arguing that the book "shows the many hopeful signs that have been set in many locations, so that our past of blood and ashes will not be forgotten, but rather the 'traces will be secured' and we can learn from history."[76] The language employed here very echoes that of the History Movement.

The third meeting in October 1983 in Hannover already showed definite signs that the Memorial Site Movement was becoming more established. Hanover's mayor officially welcomed the activists and opened an exhibit about concentration camps in Hanover to the public. Their meeting in November 1984 was held at the memorial *Alte Synagoge* (Old Synagogue) in Essen, which had been made into a memorial and documentation center to the victims of Nazism in 1980. Gunnar Richter (now Director of the Memorial Breitenau, at the site of a Nazi camp run by the Gestapo) took a photo that shows key members of the Movement, as well as panels with information about various memorial initiatives (Figure 3.5). It confirms the important role of these seminars as venues for sharing information and exchanging ideas.

From now on, Movement activists met regularly, usually combining lectures, discussion, and at least one memorial site visit, with much informal merriment in the evenings. In 1985, when activists met at the site of what would become the Topography of Terror in Berlin, the seminar had become international (Figure 3.6). Representatives from memorials in nine countries were in attendance.[77] In 1987, the activists traveled to Auschwitz for their annual gathering. By 1991, the seminar

---

[76] *Rundbrief* Nr.1 der Gedenkstätteninitiativen, available at www.gedenkstaettenforum.de /fileadmin/forum/Rundbriefe/001–010/Rundbrief_1.pdf.

[77] Gunnar Richter, email communication 12 September 2016.

Figure 3.5. Memorial seminar, with participants from across West Germany, Essen 1984.[78]

had expanded to five days in duration with attendees from all over Germany, Israel, the United States, and beyond.[79] In 2014, the sixtieth such meeting took place in Bad Urach near Stuttgart attracting forty-six attendees.[80]

Thus, from the early days of the Memorial Site Movement, activists drew inspiration and support from one another through networking. Thomas Lutz has called this "competition with solidarity," arguing that the existence of many sites commemorating Nazi terror make up a key strength of German memory work: "without this competition, with such limited funds and few people who work here, we would not have been able to collect material, to conserve, to conduct educational work at these memorial sites at such a level of sophistication. And when you are based in such a peripheral location, it is of course important that you know about each other."[81]

The Memorial Site Movement, like the History Movement, was made up of people who had been shocked by the refusal of the parent generation to confront the Nazi past, but who wanted to work in more concrete terms

[78] Gunnar Richter, Archive Gedenkstätte Breitenau.
[79] Garbe, 'Von den "vergessenen KZs'" p. 78.
[80] communication with *Landeszentrale für politische Bildung Baden-Württemberg*, October 21, 2014.
[81] See Interviews, Thomas Lutz.

Figure 3.6. Activists of the Memorial Site Movement visit the future site of the Topography of Terror in Berlin as part of the first international memorial seminar, October 1985.[82]

than the student activists of the 1960s.[83] As many of my interview partners stressed, most of the locations with authentic connections to the Nazi regime of persecution were transformed by citizen activism into important commemorative sites during the 1980s. Those involved were crucially politicized through their local efforts, their networking with others, and the resistance they faced from local politicians, bureaucrats and publics. The sense of struggle against the mainstream drive to "forget" is formative for the Memorial Site Movement.[84] And yet, early on, we also see that there is a considerable amount of support from selected local and national officials for the process of working through the past. Thus, while the image of a worthy fight for memory against the establishment is accurate in many instances, it is just as important to recognize the

[82] Thomas Lutz, Stiftung Topographie des Terrors (holding the megaphone is Heinz Schilling).
[83] Garbe, 'Von den "vergessenen KZs."'
[84] See Interviews, Thomas Lutz, Norbert Kampe, Detlef Garbe.

function of this imagery for the Movement. For the mobilization and coherence of Movement participants, the idea that "the state" was refusing its responsibility to commemorate was – and remains – crucial. The case of the Topography of Terror, which is not only a key site that emerged from the Movement but has been pivotal for the networking of activists, shows that the relationship between civic memory activists and the state is more complex. My account of the campaign that resulted in the Topography serves to illustrate the patterns of memory activism that I have already outlined.

Topography of Terror: From Memory Activism to Institution

The Topography of Terror memorial is today regularly listed as one of the most important memory sites in Germany, alongside the Memorial to the Murdered Jews of Europe, the Memorial to German Resistance, and the Jewish Museum – all of which are within walking distance of one another. The permanent building of the *Topo* (as memory politics insiders call it) opened in the spring of 2010 after a contentious process that lasted almost thirty years. Given the size, location, and official sponsorship of the memorial, it is hard to believe that in the early 1980s, the site had been all but forgotten and marginalized as a mound of rubble adjacent to the Berlin Wall (a remnant of which is still present along the length of the memorial site). The story of how it was transformed is an instructive case study in how the Memorial Site Movement has made its way into the institutional structure of the state.

The "Gestapo Terrain": A Place of Terror in the Heart of Berlin

A collection of buildings surrounding and including the Prinz-Albrecht-Palais together composed the headquarters of the SS-state, housing the Nazi Party leadership, the SS, and the secret police (Gestapo), among other agencies. By 1939, seven thousand bureaucrats worked there, and the complex was the most feared address in Berlin.[85] Here, political prisoners were held, interrogated, and tortured – including such personalities as Martin Niemöller, Kurt Schumacher, and Ernst Thälmann. Resistors such as those of the *Rote Kapelle* and those of the July 20, 1944, plot were imprisoned in the Gestapo jail. In other parts of the complex, reports about mass executions were received,

---

[85] Young, *The Texture of Memory: Holocaust Memorials and Meaning.*

battalions assigned, and key decisions made about the Holocaust.[86] The site epitomizes the centrality of covert and open terror against political opponents in the Nazi regime, as well as showing that there was a small minority who attempted to safeguard their political and moral integrity by resisting and who often paid with their lives.[87] This locale is therefore well suited to commemorate two themes of utmost importance to the Memorial Site Movement: the identity and actions of perpetrators at the heart of German society and the importance of personal responsibility. As a shorthand, the entire complex of buildings became known in the 1980s as the "Gestapo Terrain" or "Prinz-Albrecht-Terrain."

As a pivotal center of Nazi power, the area was targeted by Allied bombing raids, though not all the buildings in the complex were entirely destroyed. In fact, one of them, the former Museum of Anthropology, was not dynamited until 1963.[88] During the 1950s, the drive to modernize led West Berlin authorities to raze large areas of the city, including parts of the remaining Terrain, and to plan a large road and a helicopter landing zone. In 1961, the Berlin Wall was built immediately adjacent, and so these plans were shelved.[89] James Young notes that "as a result, the past role of this site in Nazi crimes was overwhelmed by its present role in the East-West conflict: memory itself had been divided and conquered by the new powers of the land. What had once been the heart of the city remained desolate and devastated, a buffer and possible flashpoint between the East and West."[90] The Terrain was used as a practice area for student drivers and to store building debris.[91]

During the West Berlin government's attempts to radically revamp parts of the city in the 1970s – against which the squatters movement actively protested – plans to raze the area and build a new road were revitalized. The matter of the Gestapo ruins was first raised in 1978 in the context of the *Tunix-Kongress* [Do-Nothing-Congress], which is regarded as an inaugural event of the new left social movements and alternative scene.[92] During a guided tour of the area, architectural historian Dieter Hoffmann-Axthelm was one of the first to protest the neglect of the site and to demand a confrontation with history. The planners of the International Exhibition of Construction and Design (IBA), which was strongly influenced by new ideas about design

---

[86] Hausmann, *Duell mit der Verdrängung?*, Sander and Bucholtz, 'Das 'Hausgefängnis' der Gestapo-Zentrale.'
[87] Sander and Bucholtz, 'Das 'Hausgefängnis' der Gestapo-Zentrale.'
[88] Young, *The texture of memory*.   [89] Rürup, 'Topographie des Terrors.'
[90] Young, *The texture of memory* pp. 84–85.   [91] Till, *The New Berlin*.
[92] '30 Jahre Tunix-Kongress. Gegenmodell Deutschland,' *die tageszeitung*, 25 January 2008.

and memorialization, subsequently sought to protect the area from further destruction. In 1981, the district authorities in Kreuzberg erected a sign referring to the "torture chambers of the Gestapo," thus first marking the location.[93] This wording was very much in line with the lingering trend to focus on commemorating the victims, rather than asking about the perpetrators.[94] In the same spirit, local Social Democrats demanded a memorial to those imprisoned in the Gestapo jail, ignoring the additional historical importance of the place as one where crimes of genocide were planned. Also in 1981, the highly touted exhibition on Prussia was opened in the refurbished Gropius-Bau (the only building in the complex left standing), suggesting questions about nearby history.[95] This shows that there was already some awareness about the site before memory activism started in earnest – in line with the familiar pattern as I have argued.

In 1982, then-Mayor of Berlin, Richard von Weizsäcker, announced a public competition for a memorial design that was to include not only a monument, but a park and a playground. Probably because of these contradictory guidelines, the winning design did not satisfy any of the stakeholders. The proposal was to seal the area in cast iron, showing historical documents related to the locale, interspersed with trees. "The raised lettering on these otherwise smooth plates would literally cause visitors 'to stumble over their own history.' This would be an iron-floored forest, a cold landscape, sealed against the possibility of anything ever growing here again."[96] The main critique of the design among History Movement activists was that it neither invited participation and reflection on the past, nor problematized the postwar silence about the site.[97] Shortly after announcing the winners in 1984, the new Mayor Eberhard Diepgen revoked the decision and ordered a phase of rethinking.[98]

The beginnings of the debate surrounding the Gestapo site are thus closely connected to the more general process of rethinking urban development and memorialization in Berlin. In hindsight, it is not surprising that the various parties involved were unable to agree on a commemorative solution in the midst of this fluid situation. This was also the time when activists came together to found the Active Museum as a designated force to make the Gestapo site into a new kind of memory space.[99]

---

[93] Lutz, 'Von der Bürgerinitiative zur Stiftung.'   [94] Haß, *Gestaltetes Gedenken.*
[95] Rürup, 'Topographie des Terrors.'   [96] Young, *The texture of memory* p. 87.
[97] Rürup, 'Topographie des Terrors.'   [98] Hausmann, *Duell mit der Verdrängung?*
[99] See Interviews, Stefanie Endlich.

An Active Museum

The "Aktives Museum Faschismus und Widerstand in Berlin e.V." was created in the aftermath of the January 1983 events organized to commemorate the Nazi ascendance to power with which the Berlin History Workshop had been very involved. Sabine Weißler, who was with the Active Museum from the beginning, explains that there were two main purposes for the group: the preservation of the materials collected for the 1983 projects and political activism concerning the Gestapo terrain.[100] The latter quickly became the Active Museum's primary focus of activity and made it a gathering pool for various new (and old) left organizations and initiatives.

The Active Museum's philosophy, identity, and development place it squarely in the Memorial Site Movement and displays many links to the History Movement as well. Long-time activists acknowledge its commitment to local and everyday history, an emancipatory understanding of historical research, and a political purpose for memorialization.[101] The Active Museum was founded in June 1983 by over a dozen groups, including the Berlin Cultural Council, the New Society for Fine Arts (*Neue Gesellschaft für Bildende Kunst*), the ASF, the VVN, the League for Human Rights, and the Berlin History Workshop. Like many of the other initiatives I have mentioned, it was at first a coalition of interested parties before developing an identity in its own right. In time, many individuals joined, so that today, Active Museum consists more of active individuals than of organizational members. They immediately worked to bring the idea of a focus on perpetrators to the memorial competition underway and succeeded in having the competition guidelines amended to include the idea of a participatory museum. Furthermore, this museum was seen as a counterpart to the Museum for German History, which authorities envisioned in the Gropius Building and that was suspected of providing only an official and sanitized version of history.[102]

During long nights of discussion at official events and in living rooms and bars, the members of the group developed a conceptual framework for the "active museum" they wanted in lieu of a traditional memorial. In the public announcement about founding of the group, it was argued that "this city needs an institution, which undertakes as an 'active museum' the constructive confrontation of the recent German past of 1933–1945, as

[100] See Interviews, Sabine Weißler.
[101] See Interviews, Gerhard Schoenberner, Christine Fischer-Defoy; Thomas Lindenberger, Martin Becher in *Aktives Museum Mitgliederrundbrief* No.49 July 2003.
[102] *Berliner Geschichtswerkstatt Rundbrief 4/1983* pp. 9–10.

Figure 3.7. Installation intended to show all the purposes of a future Active Museum, 1989.[103]

well of the neofascist tendencies of the present."[104] The active museum was to be a hybrid of information center, history workshop, location for political education, library and archive, and space for self-directed historical research. The various purposes of such a museum – transmitting, educating, remembering, learning, marking, commemorating, researching, encountering, and designing – were depicted in a protest installation put up by the activists in 1989 (Figure 3.7). In short, the vision was for an institution that would provide a base for the for alternative history and memory initiatives. As Christine Fischer-Defoy, founding member and chair of Active Museum for the last decade, told me, "our idea was that for such a necessary, critical, independent, emancipatory engagement, one needs a house or institution, where people can work, where there is material, where there are people to help you to put together an exhibition."[105] Thus, the Active Museum's purpose was not just to create a memorializing

---

[103] Monika Rummler, Aktives Museum Faschismus und Widerstand in Berlin e.V.
[104] *Aktives Museum Mitgliederrundbrief* No.49 July 2003 p. 4.
[105] See Interviews, Christine Fischer-Defoy.

space with the goal of public remembrance, but rather to influence collective consciousness.[106] The methods to attain this goal – project-based work, critical research, and personal involvement, rather than traditional memorialization – were typical of the overall Movement.

The Active Museum's rejection of monumental designs and grand mnemonic statements was again poignantly expressed during a public dispute with another contender for the Gestapo space. In 1988, *Perspektive Berlin*, a Social Democratic-leaning citizens' initiative led by the prominent television producer Lea Rosh, called for a Holocaust memorial to be built there, essentially ignoring the focus on perpetrators which had been at the center of debate thus far.[107] Rosh's aggressive style angered many and her call to build a monument "big like the crime"[108] or "as big as the Springer building"[109] (the close-by high-rise of the Springer newspaper empire, much reviled by the left) was deemed to be entirely inappropriate by the Active Museum. The incompatibility of the Memorial Site Movement's and the *Perspective Berlin's* aesthetic and political objectives resulted in a bitter competition – complete with accusations of anti-Semitism. This dispute was cut short by the fall of the Wall and the resultant availability of an alternative location for what is today the Memorial to the Murdered Jews of Europe.

From 1983 onward, the Active Museum was the most consistent driving force in the discussion over the Gestapo Terrain. In addition, a group called *Initiative zum Umgang mit dem Gestapo-Gelände* (Initiative on the Treatment of the Gestapo Terrain) intermittently became an important actor, though it by and large united the same combination of activists and at times enveloped the Active Museum until the "Initiative" was dissolved in the late 1980s. During the activist high point of the Movement in the mid-1980s, it seems that the organizational form of the Movement was not of primary importance. Activists from various groups of the new left almost unquestionably participated in the Active Museum[110] and so its membership was large but also fluctuating. Nevertheless, these two loose formations appeared in the public sphere as the voice of critical citizens[111] and were the primary backers of what eventually became the Topography of Terror Foundation.[112] Events and meetings organized on account of the Gestapo Terrain turned into

---

[106] Haß, *Gestaltetes Gedenken.*
[107] Lutz, 'Von der Bürgerinitiative zur Stiftung', See Interviews, Gerhard Schoenberner
[108] Koshar, *From monuments to traces* p. 264.
[109] See Interviews, Reinhard Rürup
[110] See Interviews, Gisela Wenzel, Udo Gößwald, Andreas Ludwig.
[111] See Interviews, Reinhard Rürup.
[112] See Interviews, Stefanie Endlich.

networking and rallying opportunities for memory initiatives and other politically sympathetic groups in Berlin.

The work of the Active Museum involved creating publicity and raising public consciousness about the Gestapo Terrain and about Germany as a "society of perpetrators" (*Tätergesellschaft*). This was done by organizing public debates, publishing brochures about the site, lobbying politicians, and staging publicity-effective protests. The most high profile of actions was a symbolic dig on the Gestapo Terrain, held on May 5, 1985 (see cover image of this book). The invitation to this event stated:

> With the support of the antifascist member organizations of the Active Museum we want to take a clear stand on the meaning of May 8 and to demand for the future that on these grounds of the terror headquarters of German fascism, a "thinking-site" [*Denk-Stätte*] is finally created. It is to convey the experiences and lessons of history and so make sure that fascism and war can never again originate on German soil. Support us! Join us! NO GRASS CAN BE ALLOWED TO GROW OVER THIS![113]

Through the pressure and publicity created by the activists, the city felt compelled to undertake a genuine archeological investigation. To the surprise of many, in 1986, they unearthed the basement foundations of several buildings, including cell fragments of the Gestapo prison. It was now clear that the authorities had to react in some way, especially given that the 750th anniversary celebrations of Berlin were fast approaching in 1987. The Active Museum shifted from publicizing the site's significance to seeking to influence the process by which the Terrain was safeguarded, marked, and interpreted. The fear was that in light of the 1987 festivities, the city would try to take control, shut out the citizens' initiatives, and come up with an administrative solution that would function to end debate, rather than to make memorialization into a continuous undertaking.[114] A collective decision-making procedure was demanded:

> A central thinking site [*Denkstätte*] of European caliber is called for here, with a documentation and exhibit center (Active Museum). We need to talk about this. After a forty-year process of forgetting and repression, neither politicians nor administrative branches nor individuals are competent to preserve and interpret the remaining traces of the center of state terror.[115]

In the early phase, the activists had felt that they were pitched against authorities that were resistant to an honest reckoning with history, and thus cultivated an oppositional self-image. This was manifested for example during the preparations for the symbolic dig in 1985 in letter to

---

[113] Rürup, 'Topographie des Terrors' p. 212.
[114] See Interviews, Christine Fischer-Defoy.
[115] Rürup, 'Topographie des Terrors' p. 214.

members noting that: "we should establish a list of people who will be able to participate in our action on May 5. Since the action is only barely legal, each participant should think carefully about who they want to inform about this."[116] Matthias Haß argues that the activists remained attached to the ideological divide that had still been a reality during the 1982/83 design competition when authorities were passive and unwilling to act, while civil society groups were taking charge and proposing design solutions. State actors' conduct then was decried by the activists as another instance of their unwillingness to address the past.

The Active Museum continued to cling to an oppositional identity, however, even when parts of the Berlin government opened up to the idea of a memorial site and began to see activist projects as an asset for the city rather than a threat. By 1987, the city had actually begun addressing the issue of the Gestapo site by removing trash and weeds from the site and building a protective roof over the ruins.[117] By this time, in part due to the successes of both the Memorial Site and the History Movements, the authorities' approach to the Nazi past had changed, but the initiatives had difficulty adapting.[118] Members and supporters of the both Movements were becoming increasingly embedded in institutional memory politics. Many were working on the official 750-year exhibit or in local government or museums. At the same time, key decision-makers on the governmental side had grown sympathetic to the groups' demands and adopted many of them. The stark division between progressive civil society and "the establishment" was over. Indeed, in a meeting between Cultural Senator Volker Hassemer, other government officials, and the "Initiative on the Treatment of the Gestapo Terrain," all were able to agree on crucial next steps such as clearing and preserving the ruins and documenting the history of the site. Despite this, at subsequent hearings, the activists restated their basic opposition and remained distrustful of the state's motivations. Since they could no longer utilize previous arguments about what should be done with the Terrain – because the state concurred – they fell back on general statements that "the time was not ripe" for action or even rejected any attempt at designing the site.[119] The *process* of memorialization and insistence on civil society's moral high ground had become a goal in and of itself, at least for some vocal activists.[120]

Haß contends that due to their static reading of power relations, the activists in effect maneuvered themselves out of an opportunity to

---

[116] Internal letter to members of *Aktives Museum*, March 28, 1985, Aktives Museum archives.
[117] Hausmann, *Duell mit der Verdrängung?*   [118] Haß, *Gestaltetes Gedenken* p. 182.
[119] Ibid. p. 183.   [120] Ibid. p. 185.

participate directly in the political decision-making about the Gestapo site. Since the institutionalization of memory was regarded as incompatible with critical citizen engagement, the initiatives could not at this point accept any state action or recognize officials who were genuinely invested in an honest reckoning with the past. As a result, the state sometimes excluded them from decisions and processes.[121]

The city decided to commission a temporary installation called "Topography of Terror" as an addendum to the "Berlin, Berlin" exhibit in the Gropius Building that was the centerpiece of the 1987 anniversary. The historian Reinhard Rürup, who was one of two scientific directors of the large exhibit, by default became responsible for the Gestapo site.[122] There was much mistrust between these curators and the activists because: 1. Rürup embodied the state, 2. the activists feared that the Nazi past would be sidelined by the larger show, and 3. they thought irreversible facts were to be created through the Topography exhibit.[123] According to Rürup, he and his collaborators took care not to make any design decisions for the future.[124]

As it turned out however, the 1987 exhibit did much to determine the future of the Terrain. The display was integrated in the bare ruins of the Prinz Albrecht buildings and dealt with the prior history of the area, as well as the power structures of the Nazi regime, the actions of Nazi perpetrators who resided there, and the identity of their victims. The exhibit also addressed the history of postwar forgetting, indicating again the considerable influence of the larger Movements. The documentary and nonjudgmental style was also in line with the Movement's commitment to information provision and meant that the diverse set of victims' representatives – from conservative to Communist – lauded the display. In fact, the exhibit was such a success that it was rapidly clear that it would be extended beyond the originally planned six months and that a permanent solution had to be found. Almost 300,000 visitors came and the catalog sold twenty-eight thousand copies during the first year. The press response was overwhelmingly positive.[125]

In the absence of a clear concept for the future, officials agreed to regard the Topography as a "provisional arrangement of indefinite duration" until something better could be agreed upon. For Rürup, who stayed with the project, this amounted to a firm commitment to safeguard the site.[126] Activists, however, continued to be suspicious of the government's intentions and of any existing forms of institutionalization.

[121] Ibid. p.183.   [122] See Interviews, Reinhard Rürup.
[123] Endlich, 'Gestapo-Gelände' p. 7.   [124] Rürup, 'Topographie des Terrors.'
[125] Endlich, 'Gestapo-Gelände' p. 8.   [126] See Interviews, Reinhard Rürup.

As Leonie Baumann, at the time head of the Active Museum, wrote in 1990:

> The remaining problem is that of administrative responsibility [*Trägerschaft*]. The association "Active Museum" concluded as a result of its search that in our bourgeois democracy, there is apparently no model that would be appropriate as an umbrella organization. In light of the bureaucratic mechanisms that were operative in the Nazi terror apparatus on the Gestapo Terrain, such a model should work according to principles such as: greatest possible autonomy; no delegation of responsibility; no hierarchy in decision-making structures; opportunities for intensive substantive processes of discussion so that results continuously improve in quality in the absence of time pressure; decisions under extensive consultation of the public. Such an administrative arrangement would first have to be invented and could probably never expect funding from any side since those who provide the money always unquestionably demand decision-making power. No matter which form is being discussed, the danger [exists] of increasing bureaucratization and shifting of responsibility – away from initiatives and those organizations that have been concerned with the Gestapo Terrain in the past years – toward advisory committees that hold responsibility due to their official but not substantive connection to the Terrain. Intervention [of the initiatives] will remain necessary.[127]

The end of the Cold War meant renewed activity on the Gestapo Terrain. Suddenly this area was once more located at the center of the city and included not only ruins of the Nazi past but also one of the few stretches of Wall that was not immediately torn down. It was quickly clear that the site would be close to centers of political and economic power of what was to become the new German capital. In 1992, the Topography of Terror Foundation was founded, at first as an entity dependent on the Berlin authorities (in 1995 it was converted to an independent foundation). Also in 1992, a new design competition for the site (now officially referred to as Topography of Terror) was inaugurated and won in 1993 by the star architect Peter Zumthor. Building work began in 1995 but it soon became clear that the project was badly over budget and the design almost impossible to implement. Amid a serious financial crisis in 1996, the Berlin parliament ordered the work halted – a move that was protested vigorously by activists in Germany and observers abroad and consequently revoked.[128] Despite the complexity of implementation, Topography leaders noted as late as 2001 the importance of making a major architectural statement in order not to fall short next to the Jewish Museum designed by Daniel Libeskind and the Holocaust Memorial by Peter Eisenman: "In view of the

---

[127] Baumann 'Vorwort.'
[128] Rürup, 'Topographie des Terrors', Lutz, 'Von der Bürgerinitiative zur Stiftung.'

complementary character of the three institutions, the Topography of Terror should not lag behind the rightly exciting constructions of these other two architects in the aesthetic quality of its building."[129] This statement indicates the shift from a citizen-driven project to an institution invested in state representation. While many of the demands of the Active Museum had been met – a documentary exhibition, the focus on perpetrators, the educational mission – the Foundation was nevertheless concerned to inhabit a prominent position in the new Berlin memory landscape and to an international audience. Movement principles had thus been (at least partially) elevated to serve the *raison d'état*.

The Zumthor design proved both practically and financially impossible to build. The period of 2000 to 2004 was marked by the wrangling between city and federal politicians and administrators, Topography leaders, intellectuals, and activists over the feasibility of the building.[130] The Active Museum demanded that the moratorium on construction be lifted, at one point even climbing up on a crane to make their point (Figure 3.8). In August 2001, the German Center for Tourism (*Deutsche Zentrale für Tourismus*) published a poll suggesting that the image of Berlin in Israel and the United States was damaged through the debate about the Holocaust memorial and the Topography.[131] Finally, after the bankruptcy of the main construction contractor and conflicts over financing, the Zumthor fragments were demolished and a third design competition announced in 2005.[132]

In the authorities' guidelines for the competition, the influence of the Memorial Site Movement's influence is evident. For instance, official Topography documents argue that what is needed on the Gestapo site was not a conventional memorial, but a "thinking or learning place" for which there were virtually no existing models. "It will therefore be necessary to blaze new paths to address this challenge."[133] Andreas Nachama, long-time Director of the Foundation, emphasizes that the comparison between the Topography and sites such as Yad Vashem in Jerusalem and the US Holocaust Memorial Museum are misguided. In contrast to these victim-centered spaces, what distinguishes the Topography of Terror is its focus on perpetrators and the existence of authentic traces.[134] The Foundation further declared that the design of such a site could

---

[129] Rürup and Camphausen in *Stiftungsbericht Topographie des Terrors* April 1999 – March 2001, p. 6.

[130] 'Die Baukrise' *Stiftungsbericht Topographie des Terrors* April 2001 – March 2003.

[131] *Stiftungsbericht Topographie des Terrors* April 2001 – March 2003 p .85.

[132] Stiftung Topographie des Terrors *Realisierungswettbewerb* p. 20.

[133] Rürup 'Abschlussbericht der Fachkommission 1990' in Stifung Topographie des Terrors *Realisierungswettbewerb* pp.14–15.

[134] Ibid. p. 7.

Figure 3.8. Activists of the Active Museum on top of a construction crane at the Topography of Terror site. The banner reads "End the halt to construction now!" 2004.[135]

---

[135] Niels Leiser.

not be done through sculptural means, but only with the aid of architecture that neither evades historical traces nor overwhelms them. Everything that alters the overall impression of the Terrain was to be avoided.[136] The new building was to hold not only exhibits, but meetings rooms, a library, an archive and the administrative quarters of the Foundation. As such, at least the envisioned facilities suggested that the Active Museum's ideals of public participation, reflexivity of the exhibit, the rejection of monumentalism, and a commitment to authenticity were still present in the Topography Foundation.

The winning design was chosen due to its successful implementation of competition guidelines to "develop a new documentation center, that is appropriate to the national and international significance of this historic locale in the center of the capital but that simultaneously does not overwhelm this 'site of perpetrators.'"[137] In the press, the new building was commended for its understated aesthetic and its focus on documentation.[138]

The story of the Active Museum is a remarkable demonstration of the impact of the citizens' initiatives on the German memory landscape. Though the Memorial Site Movement is no longer as motivated by the need to struggle against official resistance and has lost some of its grassroots identity, many of the smaller sites still rely heavily on volunteer work. In fact, many could not remain open without these activists. For instance, almost half of the NS memorial sites in North Rhine-Westphalia have no paid staff.[139] Thus, while the Movement has lost some its drive, most of the memorial sites and institutions that emerged from it are uniquely infused with civic culture. An examination of the Topography of Terror as an institution makes this clear.

Becoming an Institution

Despite activists' weariness of state intentions and Matthias Haß's somewhat negative assessment of the initiatives' actions in the late 1980s, there is a more nuanced reading of the relationship between civil society and state. Though Haß is correct to point to an attachment to old ideological patterns, a part of the activist community has been able to both reinvent itself as a reaction to the new situation and profoundly influence the institution

---

[136] Stifung Topographie des Terrors *Realisierungswettbewerb.*

[137] www.topographie.de/historischer-ort/nach-1945/das-dokumentationszentrum/

[138] For instance: 'Historiker Herbert würdigt "Topographie des Terrors"' *Deutschlandradio Kultur* May 6, 2010.

[139] Behrens, Ciupke, and Reichling, "'. . . und im nachhinein ist man überrascht,'" www.ns-gedenkstaetten.de/nrw.html.

that was founded to administer the Gestapo Terrain. In particular, the Active Museum successfully established itself as a more general actor in Berlin memory politics, especially after 1989. The Active Museum has curated numerous independent exhibitions and became extremely active in commemorating Nazi resisters through plaques. Further, it worked to publicize the renaming of streets in East Berlin, in some cases safeguarding those named after resistance fighters, and in general problematized the issue of street names as a part of the decentralized memory landscape.

By the early 1990s, Active Museum member Sabine Weißler was in the local parliament for the Green Party and through her position helped the group acquire a permanent source of funding from the city. Since then, the group has been able to cover office rent, some staff costs (up to two permanent positions) and a newsletter, giving it a certain amount of security and continuity.[140] The Active Museum in these ways became a routinized player in Berlin politics, has professionalized its operation in terms of exhibit standards and public image, and was increasingly seen as an acceptable partner for authorities. Christine Fischer-Defoy, one of the most committed leaders of the group, in fact married the Berlin cultural senator (1991–1996) Ulrich Roloff-Momin.[141] Today, the Active Museum has its offices and archive in the building of the Memorial to German Resistance (GDW) and cooperates often with the GDW and other resident groups.[142]

The creation of the Topography Foundation in 1992 had brought up the question of the continued existence of the Active Museum. Its already expanded set of activities did provide a new (if less dramatic and visible) purpose. According to Fischer-Defoy, these self-directed projects allowed the Active Museum to implement the principles that did not find their way into the official memorial institution.[143] Nevertheless, the bitterness and unwillingness to compromise that Haß identified was displayed by some members and meant a serious crisis for the group. According to founding member and former leader of the Active Museum Gerhard Schoenberner, some activists had harbored the illusion that they would be able to run the newly created organization.[144] The longer the Topography of Terror Foundation existed, the more established it was as a player in local and federal memorial politics. This was increasingly recognized by other stakeholders and by the media, shifting clout and public visibility away from the citizens' initiatives. During this time,

---

[140] See Interviews, Christine Fischer-Defoy and Thomas Lutz.
[141] Roloff-Momin, *Zuletzt: Kultur.*
[142] See Interviews, Christine Fischer-Defoy and Johannes Tuchel.
[143] See Interviews, Christine Fischer-Defoy.
[144] See Interviews, Gerhard Schoenberner.

Foundation leaders made plain that they had the exclusive authority to speak for the Topography.[145]

Since this period of institutional flux in the early 1990s (including the 1994 decision of the federal government to finance 50 percent of the Topography budget), a workable institutional structure has been established for the Foundation. Its current leaders stress the formal integration of civil society advocates into the structure, as well as the continuing philosophical commitment of the "Topo" to Movement principles. According to Thomas Lutz, a former activist and long-time leader of the *Gedenkstätten-Referat*, the legal framework – a public foundation – means that administrative representatives must always hold a majority of votes in the governing bodies of the Foundation. However, the balance of power within Topography committees is 4:3 – the highest ratio of civil society representatives that is legally allowed. These members are provided by the Active Museum, though their specific involvement is not laid down in the rules.[146] In many other public memorial foundations, for instance those in charge of concentration camp memorials in other parts of Germany, the ratio is 9:1, meaning the sole civic member is easily outvoted.

In practice, activist members in Topography committees often end up representing the entire organization to the public or other institutions. For Lutz, this means not only actual power within the Topography but also a different atmosphere among its staff and representatives.[147] Topography Director Andreas Nachama acknowledges that when it comes to financial questions, the federal and Berlin representatives have the last say but argues that this power is offset by the civic initiatives and experts present in the Foundation's governing council.[148] Topography leaders no longer regard the Active Museum as a competing entity. Nachama argues that the involvement of activists is an intentional "interlinking through individuals" and calls the group a "sister organization."[149] Lutz regards the Active Museum a "association of supporters" [*Förderverein*] that can take action on behalf of the Topography when problems arise.[150] In other words, the Topography can in this way benefit from civil society strategies that are not open to a state institution. Fischer-Defoy, however, insists on the Active Museum's independence and critical stance toward the Foundation.

Topography staff and civic activists proudly emphasize the influence of the Active Museum in particular and initiatives in general in the

---

[145] See Interviews, Reinhard Rürup.
[146] See Interviews, Thomas Lutz and Reinhard Rürup.
[147] See Interviews, Thomas Lutz.
[148] See Interviews, Andreas Nachama.
[149] See Interviews, Andreas Nachama.
[150] See Interviews, Thomas Lutz.

development and nature of the Foundation. Lutz believes the Topography to be "by far the most political, the most politicized museum ... that has a great influence on the other memorials."[151] Outside observers cite especially the work of the *Gedenkstättenreferat* as an example of civil society driven work from within an institution. When the ASF ran out of funds for the *Gedenkstättenreferat*, it migrated to the Topography where it has considerably greater means at its disposal.[152] It works to coordinate memorial institutions and Memory Site Movement groups in Germany and internationally, organizes workshops, publishes a newsletter for the memorial community, and runs a well-frequented website.[153] In the press coverage on the occasion of the new Topography of Terror building, the importance of citizen initiatives was highlighted, indicating that these groups have made their way into the official narrative of the institution. For Topography staff, references to these civic origins provide a sense of grounding in society and the reassurance that they have not become the type of state representatives that some of them fought against in the early 1980s. For the activists, the public recognition of their contribution is crucial to reinforcing their own role in memory politics and to their self-image of having achieved some level of success – despite continuing frustration with the institutional arrangements. In sum, the relationship between state and civil society in the arena of the Topography today is complex and not easily painted in black and white. Neither side is maliciously exploiting or dominating the other – I would argue that the players involved genuinely respect and value each other. But neither does either side neglect its interests in self-preservation and image-cultivation.

Since the mid-2000s, the Topography of Terror Foundation has expanded its range of activities, functioning both as an umbrella for various memorial spaces aside from the Gestapo Terrain, and as a host to debates about commemoration. The complex relationship with civil society has remained. However, because its institutional clout and responsibility has been amplified, it is increasingly seen by activists as a regular and unwieldy state institution – notwithstanding Topography staff's self-understanding as a civically driven organization.

Officially, the function of the Foundation is to convey historical knowledge about the Nazi regime and its crimes, as well as evoke an active confrontation with this past (and its silencing after 1945). It is also tasked with providing counsel to Berlin authorities, collecting relevant materials in its archive and library, being present in national and international

---

[151] See Interviews, Thomas Lutz.
[152] See Interviews, Christian Staffa and Stefanie Endlich.
[153] www.gedenkstaettenforum.de/.

forums, and helping to coordinate the German memorial community. As an institution in the German capital, it is explicitly identified as an entity whose meaning reaches beyond the local context and is representative of the Federal Republic's approach to the past.[154]

In recent years, this mandate has been interpreted more expansively, indicating a certain drive to claim a broader influence on the memorial scene. In March 1999, the Foundation erected an information column at the Rosenstrasse, where women had in 1943 courageously protested the deportation of their Jewish husbands. Since then, more information panels have been inaugurated, for instance at the site of a synagogue in Berlin-Wilmersdorf and in Berlin-Steglitz at the location of an SS administrative building where the concentration camps had been overseen.[155] Furthermore, the Topography has actively intervened in ongoing memorial debates, such as that over a more appropriate memorial marking the site where the Nazi program of "euthanasia" was planned. This *T4 Aktion* named after the villa in the Tiergartenstrasse No.4 was first commemorated there through pressure from the Berlin History Workshop and others in the mid-1980s, but the resulting memorial was not very prominent in the Berlin cityscape. In 2007, the Topography initiated a series of Roundtables among victim representatives, civic activists, experts, and officials in order to publicize the dearth of memory and come up with a plan for action. In 2009, the Berlin Senate Administration for City Development integrated the site into a "cultural master plan" for the area and announced a design competition.[156] In March 2013, the "Topo" also supported efforts by ASF and many prominent individuals to create a monument commemorating the millions of victims of Nazi *Lebensraum* policy, particularly Soviet POWs. They called for a Roundtable with experts and engaged institutions in order to develop a concept for a memorial that should stand in direct relationship to the four other large memory sites in the vicinity.[157] Through these activities, the Foundation has worked to network and organize disparate societal actors in order to promote memorialization and has thus functioned as a mediator between civil society and the state. At the same time, however, this has amounted to an augmentation of power of the Topography as a player in memory politics – a position that is viewed critically by civil society activists. This dynamic was especially evident in the process of commemorating the history of Nazi forced labor in Berlin.

[154] Stiftung Topographie des Terrors *Realisierungswettbewerb* p. 14.
[155] www.topographie.de/topographie-des-terrors/ausstellungen/gedenk-und-mahnorte/.
[156] www.sigrid-falkenstein.de/euthanasie/runder_tisch.htm.
[157] www.gedenkorte-tiergarten.de/.

In 1993, the Berlin History Workshop together with the *Bund der Antifaschisten* (BdA – Union of Anti-Fascists) in Berlin-Treptow first alerted the public to the existence of the "forgotten camp" in Berlin-Niederschöneweide, a neighborhood in the southeastern part of the city. This complex is the only remaining intact former labor camp of over three thousand erected by the Nazis in Berlin. Though the site received protected status in 1995, it was not until 2004 that the city voted to create an official memorial there.[158] In the interim, civil society activists pressured authorities to take action to create a documentation center. Furthermore, the *Arbeitskreis Berliner Regionalmuseen* (ABR – Working Group of Berlin Regional Museums) developed both individual exhibits on particular neighborhoods and a joint display on forced labor in Berlin. This was a significant move to publicize the topic, as well as to support the work of already existing initiatives.[159] The Berlin History Workshop (as well as some smaller groups) put together an independent archive on forced labor in Berlin and established contact and organized visits with former forced laborers. In 2001, they helped found an association specifically to agitate for a documentation center.[160] This *Förderverein* (support association), and especially its head Cord Pagenstecher, became the driving force behind the documentation center. In 2001, the Berlin parliament officially recognized the efforts of the History Workshop and the *Förderverein*.[161] In April 2005, the Topography of Terror took over administrative leadership for the documentation center and it was opened to the public in summer 2006.

In this way, the Topography was made home to another memorial that would not have existed without civil society activism. According to longtime observer of Berlin memory politics and Active Museum supporter Stefanie Endlich,

> Without the [Berlin History Workshop], the Topography would never have been asked, would not have been interested as an institution, to administer this memorial "Forced Labor Camp Schöneweide." ... As such, civic engagement flowed directly into the Topography. The Topography would never have become involved with this site of its own accord, but because there where people inside and outside the Topography who pushed from below, we now have this memorial.[162]

In other words, though there were Topography staff who continued to recognize and ally with initiative demands, the innovative drive clearly

---

[158] http://topographie.minuskel.de/fileadmin/schoeneweide/flyer/flyer_en.pdf.
[159] See Interviews, Bernt Roder.
[160] www.zwangsarbeit-in-berlin.de/schoeneweide/foerderverein.htm, Wenzel and Martin, 'NS-Zwangsarbeiterlager Berlin-Schöneweide.'
[161] Ibid.   [162] See Interviews, Stefanie Endlich.

came from outside the institution. Though the activists were pleased with their success in realizing the memorial, they were frustrated by the way in which the decision-making process about the site was handled once the Topography was in charge. Lutz acknowledged this conflict and explained it through disappointed expectations on the part of the activists:

> There are always problems when you transition from a large initiative to a small institution because ... when the small institution comes, the initiative disintegrates to some extent because the assumption is: we now have someone to take care of this. Since the institutional stance is in the end different from the civic one, ... such expectations simply cannot be met by an institution.[163]

The activists' account of the dispute was more specific and involved frustration over being excluded from the formal decision-making about Schöneweide. Gisela Wenzel and Angela Martin, both long-time activists in the Berlin History Workshop, argued that the Topography sneakily withdrew voting rights in the governing council of the development documentation center from the Workshop and *Förderverein*. After they protested, they were granted guest status, which was interpreted as an image-saving but essentially meaningless concession. The initiatives had become a mere veneer to feign civic connectivity.[164] Moreover, the activists were dissatisfied that they were denied employment opportunities in the new memorial. Pagenstecher in particular, who had been so instrumental in making the memorial happen, should in their eyes have been a serious contender for the position of Director. Instead, a woman unconnected to the struggle to achieve the site got the job.[165] Gisela Wenzel told me that "when a movement initiates something that then becomes institutionally relevant, then I believe those people who have been engaged should also have the opportunity to work there professionally. These institutions should open up and not merely take these ideas and then pursue only their own corporative interests."[166]

These activists' discontent, then, is not only an outcome of professional ambitions – though these may at times play a role. Rather, the participation of individuals with a well-established civic background are thought to make for different kinds of institutions, ones that continue to implement Movement principles and maintain an open institutional structure for activists to participate in. These are probably the kinds of expectations that Lutz regards as unrealistic. Furthermore, the presence of former activists in institutions is itself no guarantee of grounding in civil society contexts. Memorial staff tend to become professionally immersed in

---

[163] See Interviews, Thomas Lutz.
[164] Wenzel and Martin, 'NS-Zwangsarbeiterlager Berlin-Schöneweide' p. 7.
[165] Ibid. p. 7.   [166] See Interviews, Gisela Wenzel.

institutional frameworks, so that their grounding in civil society weakens as their identification with the institution increases.[167]

In sum, the success of the Memorial Site Movement and other civic initiatives in advocating and creating memorial institutions is not without ambivalence. On the one hand, the Topography of Terror, the Documentation Center on Forced Labor, and similar memory sites would not have existed without the sustained pressure of these activists. Through their influence on public debates and through the participation of some of their members in these new institutions, key principles and topics have found their way to the center of the German commemorative landscape. On the other hand, the lack of direct influence on institutions, the incomplete implementation of principles, as well as the perceived consolidation of power on the part of these expanding institutions is frustrating to activists. The more resigned civil society becomes to their loss of clout, the less innovative and widely supported memory initiatives are likely to become.

The story of the Active Museum and the Topography of Terror is an especially instructive instance of the institutionalization of memory through civil society activism. Since this story unfolded over the entire lifetime of the Memorial Site Movement and into the present, it has allowed me to examine the larger development and impact of the Movement even after its decline. Moreover, the Topography memorial holds special significance due to its location in the new German (and formerly Nazi) capital for our understanding of German and Berlin memory politics.

From Civic Sites to Memorials of Nationwide Importance

The 1990s and 2000s were times of intensive and high-profile memorialization activities, especially in Berlin where the fall of the Wall had freed up central and historically significant real estate, and the new capital status of Berlin necessitated a new approach to national commemoration. In 1993, the *Neue Wache* was inaugurated as a result of the Kohl government's long-standing efforts to create a traditional national memorial – under the protest of left-wing parties and members of the History and Memorial Site Movements.[168] The *Neue Wache* was controversial both because of its previous usage by Nazis and the GDR for

---

[167] See Interviews, Christian Staffa.

[168] Büchten and Frey, 'Im Irrgarten deutscher Geschichte', Kirsch, '"Hier geht es um den Kern."'

purposes of state representation and because Kohl insisted on an inscription that did not distinguish between the victims of German crimes and those who had otherwise perished as a result of the war – including German soldiers. As Siobhan Kattago writes, "In the Neue Wache, German guilt is displaced by creating an imagined community of victims and by blurring the building's original military function with national honor and sacrificial loss."[169] It has been widely reported that Kohl struck a personal bargain with Ignatz Bubis in which Bubis agreed to the *Neue Wache* and Kohl promised to install the Holocaust Memorial just a few hundred meters away, next to the Brandenburg Gate.[170] The selection of the memorial design and the building of the Memorial to the Murdered Jews of Europe occupied the headlines until after its inauguration in 2005. By the mid-2000s, the official landscape concerning the Nazi past was comprehensive and well supported by the federal state.

This is reflected in the development of the memorial sites outside of Berlin as well. Since the mid-1990s, the concentration camp memorials in particular have become part and parcel of the official symbolic politics. As Detlef Garbe pointed out, during the fiftieth anniversary of the end of the Second World War, the federal President spoke at Bergen-Belsen, the President of the German parliament at Ravensbrück, and the foreign minister at Sachsenhausen. Moreover, almost all the heads of the state governments were present at a memorial site that day, including Edmund Stoiber of Bavaria who took part in an event hosted by the survivors' group, Comité International de Dachau.[171] With the elevation of many sites to "Memorials of Nation-Wide Importance" (*Gedenkstätten von gesamtstaatlicher Bedeutung*) – meaning that they receive federal funding – the centrality of the memorials to Nazi terror has continued to grow since the 1990s. As Historian Jan-Holger Kirsch writes,

> At the governmental level, the awareness also grew that the field of "history politics" could and had to be an integral component of state representation. Here, an ambivalent "nationalization of negative remembrance" was manifested: the reckoning with National Socialism – that was previously undertaken by particular societal groups and was for a long time not accepted by a majority and often critical of the state – was now elevated to a governmental obligation. Through the new position of the culture minister, the federal concept for memorial sites [*Bundesgedenkstättenkonzeption*] and other activities, these history politics were strengthened after the change of government in 1998; this can be seen as a consistent continuation of the Kohl era.[172]

---

[169] Kattago, *Ambiguous Memory* p. 133.
[170] Jeismann, 'Mahnmal Mitte', Leggewie and Meyer, *"Ein Ort, an den man gerne geht."*
[171] Garbe, 'Von den "vergessenen KZs"' p. 80.
[172] Kirsch, '"Hier geht es um den Kern"' pp. 44–45.

Even though such projects as the Neue Wache and the Memorial to the Murdered Jews of Europe (Holocaust Memorial, for short) have been promoted from above, it is important to recognize the role played by civic initiatives here – both as critics and sometimes as supporters. When the inscription of the Neue Wache Memorial became public, memory activists protested until an additional plaque listing all the victims groups was added to the site. In similar ways, Memorial Site initiatives have accompanied mainstream memorial projects, in addition to their own, since the 1980s. As Horst Seferens explains:

> In the late Seventies and Eighties in the Federal Republic, a decentralized network of memorials at the locations of National Socialist crimes was created through civic engagement. It was motivated by the intention to conserve and to mark the relics of the crime scenes and to provide information about the victims, crimes and perpetrators. At the center of these efforts was an educational interest to create consciousness for the fact that these crimes took place locally and emerged from the midst of society. This often led to conflicts and raised resistance from citizens, local politicians, and municipal authorities. At the same time, the activists of the history workshops and the regional memorial site initiatives eyed the grand projects of centralized, state commemoration . . . with great suspicion. The fear was that the exact opposite of concrete memory work would take place, namely the emotional and unspecific summoning of a large community of the fallen and the victims of the concentration camps.[173]

These suspicions continued to shape the memorial debates of the 1990s and 2000s. Though the Memorial to the Murdered Jews of Europe had been initiated by civic groups (first "Perpektive Berlin" and later the "Förderkreis Denkmal für die ermordeten Juden Europas"), its adoption as an official federal project made it the focus of critique by Memorial Site activists. The two groups (both led by publicist Lea Rosh) were not integrated into the Memorial Site Movement – indeed, they clashed with this Movement when it came to determining the location and the design of the Memorial, for which Rosh had first envisaged the Prinz-Albrecht-Terrain. The most important points of critique for the Memorial Site activists were that the Memorial to the Murdered Jews of Europe was not at an authentic location and might detract attention from the decentralized landscape of Nazi terror for which the Movement had fought so vigorously. Moreover, the exclusive focus on Jewish victims was criticized for sidelining the "forgotten victims" of the Holocaust. In the course of the debate about the Holocaust Memorial, however, the nation-wide working group of the *Gedenkstätten* ultimately endorsed the site as a "sign that the memory of the crimes of National Socialism would remain

---

[173] Seferens, 'Zwei Jahrzehnte Diskussion' p. 83.

a crucial component of identity in the united Germany."[174] Many individual Memorial Site representatives remain skeptical, but acknowledge the important symbolic value of the Holocaust Memorial, as well as of the Memorial to the Homosexuals Persecuted under the National Socialist Regime and the Sinti and Roma Memorial. Both of these had been promoted by what might be called "interest groups" – the Federation of Lesbians and Gays in Germany (LSVD) and the Central Council of Sinti and Roma in Germany. In the case of the gay victims memorial in particular, the initiative "Remember the Homosexual Victims of National Socialism" had modeled itself and maintained many connections to the Memorial Site Movement.[175] In Chapter 7, I discuss in depth the ways in which civic initiatives and the resultant memorials have developed and become intertwined in what I call "hybrid institutions."

Conclusion

In concluding this chapter, it is clear that the memory of National Socialism in Germany and in particular the landscape of physical traces of Nazi terror has been crucially shaped by civic engagement. The most significant locations – many of which are today officially funded "Memorials of Nation-Wide Importance" – were the focus of activism by the victims' organizations of the first hour (sometimes with the temporary assistance of Allied authorities). The survivors tried to keep the sites of Nazi persecution in the spotlight for decades under the difficult conditions of a society more interested in remembering war veterans and expellees and relegating the Nazi past to general pronouncements about "the hard years of dictatorship." A few key locations were used by the federal state – Bergen-Belsen and the Memorial to German Resistance in Berlin especially – but most sites were subjected to widespread oblivion. While the victims' groups' efforts made important contributions to safeguarding the sites and forcing local authorities into at least minimal commemoration, they were unable to fundamentally alter (West) German remembrance politics. This situation of course corresponded to the refusal of most of society during the 1950s to 1970s to confront the Nazi past that was epitomized by the lack of judicial prosecution and generalized amnesty enjoyed by Nazi perpetrators.

A genuine shift in civic memory activism occurred in the early 1980s. Alongside and closely related to the History Movement, citizen initiatives emerged all over the country, determined to mark and inform the public about specific sites of Nazi terror. Though these local groups were

[174] Ibid. p. 84.   [175] See Interviews, Eberhard Zastrau.

idiosyncratic in that they reacted to local conditions and struck up unique local alliances, they followed similar patterns: their initial mobilization and protest relied on already existing (if limited) knowledge of the indigenous structure of National Socialism. They often began by doing the groundwork of commemoration: historical research, interviewing witnesses, identifying traces. They often reacted to municipal or commercial plans to alter the site in question. They engaged in protest actions (sit-ins, rallies, collections of signatures on the street, etc.) typical of other "new social movements." They also lobbied officials and managed to find allies within local governments and bureaucracies. Despite these allies, the image of activists struggling against the resistance of the "establishment" to remember was (and is) crucial to the identity of the Memorial Site Movement. And to be sure, often this struggle was very real indeed: their memory work became memory protest because it was still contentious in German society to demand a detailed confrontation with the legacies of the Holocaust.

The many groups that composed the Memorial Site Movement were closely aligned in terms of their demands as well. The honoring of victims was one goal, but more important was the promotion of public awareness about the sites and perpetrators of Nazi atrocities. In this emphasis and in the aesthetic ideas espoused by the activists, they distinguished themselves from the victims' organizations that were more concerned with traditional mourning and with grasping the suffering as a cautionary tale for the future. The old and new activists frequently clashed over these issues though they usually became allies once the culture clash had been overcome. Key for the Memorial Site Movement was that the Nazi past was not merely regarded as a "lesson" for future generations; it entailed the responsibility to work for a critical society and "deep" democratization.

By 1981, the scattered initiatives began exchanging ideas and supporting one another. Within a few years, a decentralized but nevertheless coherent and well-organized network had been established with regular communications and meetings. It is this interlinking that makes the hundreds of local groups into a nationwide Movement with a clear identity and with the power to influence national memorial debates. To this day, the activists of the 1980s are highly involved both in local sites and in federally funded ones. The case of the Active Museum and the resulting Topography of Terror poignantly illustrates not only the indispensable role played by the Memorial Site Movement in the creation of key monuments to Nazi terror, but also the ways in which the Movement shaped the institutional landscape of memorialization. Moreover, it demonstrates how the critical memory of the Nazi past – previously marginal and yet pivotal to the deepening of German democracy – moved into the mainstream of the federal state's memorialization agenda.

The civic origin of sites such as the Topography of Terror provides these institutions with a unique character, but also with complex dilemmas. These must be kept in mind when assessing the contribution made by civil society to sites of Nazi terror from 1945 to the present. Many of the large and now official memorials underwent several phases of civic mobilization, with victims' groups succeeding in an initial marking of the site, and the activists of the 1980s then elevating them to large institutions with staff and educational agenda. In sum, the leftist activists of the 1980s certainly stood on the shoulders of survivor activists and benefited from a general shift in German political culture. Nevertheless, the Memorial Site Movement should be credited with a profound transformation of the reckoning with the Nazi past. In the next chapter, I analyze the History Movement, which was closely related and intertwined with the Memorial Site Movement, but pursued a broader goal of reworking history writ-large from a grassroots perspective.

4   Dig Where You Stand: The History Movement and Grassroots Memorialization

Every year since 1987, activists of the Berlin History Workshop have gathered in the chill of winter to symbolically rename a small bridge in Berlin's central *Tiergarten* district after Rosa Luxemburg, the revolutionary murdered by right-wing forces in January 1919. The bridge spans the canal where Luxemburg's body was found after she was killed. Every year, they hung a sign. Every year, the police removed it (Figure 4.1).

Simultaneously, the activists of the *Berliner Geschichtswerkstatt* lobbied the Berlin legislature persistently to rename the bridge, along with numerous streets. Many of these street names had their origin during the Nazi period.[1] The action was spearheaded by the Berlin History Workshop's *Dampfergruppe* (steamship group), which began to offer biweekly boat tours with an alternative take on city history in 1984. The boat trips have changed significantly over the years, especially since it became possible to ride through East Berlin. They were designed to point out sites of local interest with a focus on topics such as women's history, "rebellious Berlin," "the forties," and more.[2] These tours, as well as the group's efforts to recast Berlin's streetscape, illustrate the activists' concern with highlighting how Germany's authoritarian pasts are manifested locally, on a small scale. This strategy is typical for the History Movement. Through detail-oriented and politically motivated work, activists focused on sites of memory in everyday life rather than large memory sites popular among most tourists. This *Geschichtsbewegung* helped to reinvent attitudes, landscapes, and institutions of commemoration in a way that transformed memory politics in the Federal Republic.

Persistent activism focused on many small changes was an effective strategy. In January 2013, the Workshop could finally celebrate their success with the official renaming of the Rosa-Luxemburg-Bridge. A group of about fifteen – by now aged – activists, gathered to read

---

[1] The project resulted in a book: Berliner Geschichtswerkstatt e.V., 'Sackgassen.'
[2] See www.berliner-geschichtswerkstatt.de/dampfer/termine.htm.

Figure 4.1. Policemen remove the sign put up by the Berlin History Workshop from a bridge in Berlin-Tiergarten, 1987.[3]

from Luxemburg's writings and pinned red carnations to the frozen iron barriers along the canal (Figure 4.2).

The History and the Memorial Site Movements, though distinct, are closely intertwined, with some of the individual members and subsidiary groups straddling the two. With the emergence of these Movements in the early 1980s, public remembrance experienced an unprecedented shift in West Germany. While civil society had been active in initiating memorials since 1945, what happened now was different in quantity, quality, and long-term impact. Commemoration was being refashioned "from the ground up," by many and diverse groups researching local history. Crucially, after years of struggle, these grassroots activists were no longer marginalized by the state – and they came to be among the most important actors in German memory politics. This was the case despite the fact that the History Movement did not see the creation of memorials as one of its primary goals.

Thus, as I argue throughout this book, the interaction and intertwining of civic society and the state is once again the terrain on which public memory is contested. And even though the members of the History Movement rallied around the need to push critical memory work *against* the resistance of the

[3] Peter Homann, 1987.

Figure 4.2. Members of the Berlin History Workshop celebrate the
official naming of the Rosa-Luxemburg-Bridge on January 1, 2013.
The small memorial with flowers is visible in the foreground.[4]

state, official authorities relatively rapidly embraced many of their efforts.
Over the course of the 1980s and despite the Movement's oppositional
identity, history workshops and alternative archives all over West Germany
strongly influenced existing and newly created memorial institutions and
even became part of them as their leaders and staff. As the example of the
Rosa-Luxemburg-Bridge illustrates, the impact of the History Movement
was manifested most commonly through persistent, piecemeal, and small-
scale challenges to the status quo that were significant cumulatively, rather
than manifested in high-profile memorialization actions.

In this chapter, I provide for the first time a comprehensive academic
analysis of the *Geschichtsbewegung*. Though its members wrote some
accounts during the 1980s to self-reflect on their actions, there have
been few published attempts to assess the collective impact and importance of this decentralized Movement. I examine the political opportunities that made possible the success of these history initiatives, as well as
the identity and motivations of the activists, the organizational tools used,
and their collective action repertoires. I conclude with a discussion of how

[4] Jenny Wüstenberg, 2013.

the activists framed their work in terms of the struggle for democracy and a clear vision for how memory activism could shape progressive social change.

Introducing the *Geschichtsbewegung*

Despite the fact that, during the 1980s, history workshops sprung up all over West Germany and West Berlin, the *Geschichtsbewegung* is not widely known as such. This may be because of its relatively quiet approach when compared to the noisier peace or environmental movements. The History Movement emerged as a varied collection of initiatives focused on researching, exhibiting, and commemorating history – especially of the Nazi period, of workers' lives, of the struggles of ordinary people. Though they were locally grounded, the activists were also well networked across the Federal Republic. They were united by a common commitment to an engaged and political – and clearly left-wing – perspective on history. Their motto was "dig where you stand:" it was a call to scrutinize and publicize the meaning of the past in one's own social and geographic environment and to make the findings relevant to current political decisions and struggles. Though the activists' main objective was not to build monuments, but rather to create opportunities for ordinary people to critically discuss history,[5] their interest in local groundedness meant that they became crucial initiators of memorial sites. The History Movement, together with the Memorial Site Movement, shaped Germany's memory landscape, as well as the institutional infrastructure of public memory during the 1980s – and continued to do so in the years that followed.

The term *Geschichtsbewegung* was apparently coined in a 1983 article in the *Spiegel* magazine, indicating that, early on, there was a perception that a coherent social movement was at play.[6] According to Thomas Lindenberger, one of the founders of the Berlin History Workshop, the movement label was readily accepted by the activists, even though they had as yet not discussed it themselves in those terms. Their own inclination was to identify with the many *Bürgerinitiativen* (citizens' initiatives) in the "alternative scene," which was made up of myriad autonomous groups that were highly networked but without an organizational core.[7] The History Movement, though it was much smaller and less visible than the better-known of the new social movements (NSMs), can be placed

[5] See Interviews, Thomas Lindenberger.
[6] Reprinted as Spiegel, "'Ein kräftiger Schub für die Vergangenheit.'"
[7] Vandamme, *Basisdemokratie als zivile Intervention*, See Interviews, Thomas Lindenberger.

squarely in that same tradition.[8] The distinction between old and new left should not be viewed as a hard and fast one, but the NSMs did have a different style of politics, emphasizing grassroots mobilization, internally democratic structures, decentralized forms of organization, a rejection of political dogmatism, a varied collective action repertoire, and a focus on local concerns and communities.

The *Geschichtsbewegung* not only had similar principles and organizational forms as the other NSMs, but was not always neatly separable from the environmental, peace, and women's movements. The History Movement thrived as part of this larger movement "scene" and served as a collective archivist and historian of its sister struggles. The Movement, then, took the form of a network of locally autonomous and diverse groups, which kept in touch through a range of forums, including annual meetings, a newsletter, and more informal channels. The primary focus of attention for these memory activists always remained local history, but, according to long-time Hamburg activist Beate Meyer, "we did feel that we are part of a large movement, but we also felt that within this movement, everybody had their issue in their small location."[9]

Despite the aversion against formality and the priority of the local in the History Movement, a federal organization was initiated in 1981 and its founding completed in 1983. *Geschichtswerkstatt e.V.* soon had a membership of forty local initiatives and over three hundred dues-paying individuals. Adelheid von Saldern estimates that by the mid-1980s, about seventy local and regional history workshops had been created,[10] not all of which were members of the federal association. By 1992, the *Frankfurter Rundschau* newspaper wrote that there were about 120 history workshops in the FRG.[11]

The history initiatives ranged from small collections of activists in rural settings to larger workshops such as those in Marburg, Konstanz, or Hanover. Hamburg alone at one point had eighteen workshops based in different neighborhoods. A few workshops were cross-regional in their ambitions, but most had a local center of gravity. Some were focused on particular issues, others investigated "history from below" in all its facets. A central concern was the history of National Socialism in its local manifestations, although according to Maximilian Strnad, the Holocaust moved to the center of attention only in the later 1980s.[12]

---

[8] Sperner, *Die neue Geschichtsbewegung*, Haß, *Gestaltetes Gedenken*, Ullrich, 'Wie alles anfing', see Interviews, Gisela Wenzel.
[9] See Interviews, Beate Meyer.
[10] von Saldern, 'Stadtgedächtnis und Geschichtswerkstätten' p. 55.
[11] '"Barfuß-Historiker" ohne Boden,' '"Barfuß-Historiker" ohne Boden.'
[12] Strnad, '"Grabe, wo Du stehst."'

Workshops went into great detail, often letting contemporary concerns guide research interests. For instance, due to Solingen's strong labor tradition, the *Geschichtswerkstatt* there examined the plight of foreign workers during 1942–1945 and later branched out into a local account of immigration. At the peak of the peace movement, an exhibition about "War and Peace in Solingen" was developed.[13] Wuppertal activists focused on "guest workers" and Marbach on deserters from the Wehrmacht.[14] While the Marburg workshop started out studying the squatters' movement, as well as a local brewery that had been demolished under protests, Marburg's Nazi past was a constant concern.[15] The *Geschichtswerkstatt Arbeiten und Leben in Pasing e.V.* was founded in response to the closing of a household goods factory and documented work and life in that Munich neighborhood, drawing vocal criticism from local conservatives.[16] The History Workshop in Tübingen created a permanent archive for local Jewish history.[17] Many of the archives founded by the History Movement remain open today.

The activists' interests betrayed their leftist affinities: they investigated the history of progressive struggles – from early workers' movements, Communist parties, the student movement, to the antinuclear movement. And they aimed to understand the lives of "regular people" – those ordinarily left out of mainstream accounts. History activists were proponents of an undogmatic brand of leftist politics, though some of their training in Marxism shines through in their writings. For example, the general declaration of principles of *Geschichtswerkstatt e.V.* stated the goal of understanding the "everyday reality of the classes."[18] Marxist language was even more pronounced in early documents on the creation of a workshop in Berlin, citing as justification for the founding:

- that the history of those who have (so far) been overcome in class struggles is usually suppressed and falsified by the victors, but is often also repressed by the vanquished ...
- that historical knowledge and historical consciousness, and the working through of experiences of struggle is crucial and useful – also and especially during times of roll-back or stagnation – for the maintenance of leftist identity.

---

[13] Putsch, 'Die Solinger Geschichtswerkstatt.'
[14] See Interviews, Thomas Lindenberger.
[15] Roth, 'Notizen zu einem Jubiläum', Freisberg and Werther, 'Was wir wollten, was wir taten.'
[16] Strnad, 'Grabe, wo Du stehst' p. 175.
[17] www.geschichtswerkstatt-tuebingen.de/index.php?article_id=2.
[18] *Geschichtswerkstatt* 4, August 1984.

- that it is crucial especially in Germany and especially in Berlin to demonstrate, re-create, and continue the continuity of left-wing movements and progressive traditions, which was interrupted (or partly eradicated) through Hitlerite fascism and the postwar period.
- that we would feel awfully isolated and limited if we didn't regard ourselves as the continuers of struggles that began long before our birth, and if we also didn't see ourselves as preparers of the struggles that will happen after our death ...[19]

In spite of this initial rhetoric, a culture of undogmatic leftism, as well as pragmatism when it came to possible partners and sources of funding, prevailed in most history workshops.[20] As Thomas Lindenberger wrote,

We always took our political interests as the point of departure and acted accordingly – at times somewhat recklessly disregarding our theoretical and political differences ... And so our quite diverse political pasts, that in times of left-wing factionalism and organizational struggles might have prevented any cooperation, have not bothered us in the least, on the contrary.[21]

As was the norm within NSMs, decision-making took place as much – if not more so – in the informal scene locations, as in more formal movement organizations.[22] As Berlin History Workshop activist Andreas Ludwig told me, projects were usually assigned through *Kneipenkontakte* [pub contacts].[23] Many of the activists identified with the *Sponti*-scene, rejecting stringent organization and theoretical debates in favor of spontaneous political action.

The collective action repertoire included cooperative historical research that resulted in the creation of independent archives, exhibits, and publications; public meetings and rallies; lobbying and petitioning; reaching out to local media and otherwise creating publicity; and staging symbolic actions in public. The common denominator for the local groups was a commitment to grassroots historical research and a striving for autonomous activism within a framework of broadly left-wing values. In other words, the belief in the need for local independence and politicized memory work was what gave an otherwise hodgepodge Movement its unity.

The memory activists came together in response to what they regarded as unacceptable public representation and political usage of the past by the "establishment" and to create a "counter public" where memory would be part of a peaceful struggle for political change. They sought to directly

---

[19] Diethart Kerbs 'Vorlage zum Gespräch im Mehringhof am 18.VII.1980' July 17, 1980, personal archive Thomas Lindenberger.

[20] See Interviews, Thomas Lindenberger.   [21] Lindenberger, 'Werkstattgeflüster' p. 24.

[22] Haunss and Leach, 'Social movement scenes' p. 83.

[23] See Interviews, Andreas Ludwig.

challenge elites, authorities, and cultural codes through collective action. Notwithstanding their diversity, the activists recognized their commonalities in goals and methods, and stated their adherence to them explicitly in meetings and written resolutions. The History Movement consistently pursued its activities throughout the 1980s in sustained interactions with local, regional, and federal authorities, as well as other actors. Collective action peaked surrounding key events, such as anniversaries. Though the Movement's willingness to cooperate with and receive support from the state increased with time, the principled distrust of the state was one of its defining features. As I argue in Chapter 7, even when activists had become regular employees of the state, they largely maintained their self-image as an extra-institutional force.

Participants in the History Movement spent most of their time digging in archives, interviewing "witnesses," cobbling together exhibitions, and debating the issues at endless meetings: *doing memory work*. Public protests against mainstream history policy or for a particular memorial also happened routinely, though they were not the primary occupation of the Movement. And, as the workshops became more established players, they also devoted much time to traditional lobbying behavior. Despite this often unobtrusive demeanor, the Movement's work routinely became contentious. Because the activists were concerned with the representation of the past in public space, they inevitably had to confront the authorities at every level. In order to attach an information panel to an existing memorial or to construct a new memorial, the state had to be engaged and, for most of the 1980s, the activists overwhelmingly encountered resistance from it. Thus, although the History Movement's repertoire was mostly quieter and less visible than those of other new social movements, it was no less contentious in nature: the everyday actions of the *Geschichtsbewegung* challenged the status quo of memory politics in West Germany. In this sense, the History Movement conforms to the classical notion of a social movement as a challenge to state power and a bottom-up push for more democratic values in (memory) politics. But as the Movement evolved, its relationship with the state became more complex. The History Movement – akin to the Memorial Site Movement – clearly shows that memory politics were not composed simply of civil society actors clashing categorically with the state. The relationships were in tension but multifaceted and changing through persistent engagement and interaction.

Making Grassroots Memory Work Possible

The memory activists did not see themselves or their interpretation of history represented in established venues in politics or the historical profession in the early 1980s. This perceived lack of access shaped both their strategies and their objectives. The activists saw the need to construct a "counter-public." With this *Gegenöffentlichkeit*, they sought to prevent "the 'stealing of history' [*Geschichtsklau*] by universities, state apparatuses, parties, unions, companies and established intellectuals by researching and discussing our own past."[24] History and memory were regarded as a field of politics and policy that could not be left to mainstream actors. While other NSMs encountered aggressive police tactics during their protests, the History Movement did not have to fear repressive measures to prevent their mostly "intellectual" activities. Nevertheless, the activists' impression that they faced massive conservative *cultural* resistance was important to their self-image as rebels and helped them recruit members. They regarded history as "dangerous" to the establishment.[25]

While the highest levels of mnemonic policy-making were not directly accessible to the memory activists, the federal system meant that the Movement could target local authorities with their collective action. Sidney Tarrow refers to this practice as "venue shopping:"[26] protesters identify those access points in the political system that are most vulnerable to movement activity. Consequently, the History Movement, while still debating national issues internally, focused its energy on a diverse set of local struggles. In this way, it successfully created scores of local exhibits and memorials, while it may have had a much lesser impact if it had concentrated solely on the national level. At the same time, the embeddedness of the History Movement in the wider scene of the new left and the extraparliamentary opposition (APO) meant that those actors who gradually entered conventional politics (especially through the emergent Green Party), carried their concerns into – at first local – institutions. As Adelheid von Saldern argues, history workshops fought against conservative interpretations of the past and claimed cultural definitional power for themselves. With time, more and more local administrators and archivists would be convinced of their arguments.[27]

Early on, the activists' impressions were mostly accurate: at the beginning of the 1980s, state authorities were for the most part resistant to publicly commemorating the German (and particularly the Nazi) past in ways that explicitly acknowledged the identity of perpetrators and their racist motives for violence. In the first half of the decade, a direct confrontation with the Nazi past by state actors was the exception, taking

[24] Lindenberger, 'Werkstattgeflüster' p. 27.
[25] 'BGW Entwurf für ein programmatisches Selbstverständnis (Statut August 1981)' personal archives Gisela Wenzel.
[26] Tarrow, *Power in Movement* p. 209.   [27] von Saldern, 'Schwere Geburten' p. 13.

place only in a few larger cities, and there only haltingly. Cities that had
experienced bombings, such as Hamburg, commemorated primarily their
own victims and left little room for German misdeeds. The traditional
historical associations (*Geschichtsvereine*) usually did not study the Nazi
period, arguing that not enough time had passed to allow for an objective
analysis.[28] Von Saldern writes:

> As in federal memory culture, there was a general disavowal of Nazi atro-
> cities in city memory politics, but little information was provided about
> what specifically took place in concrete locations. "In 1933, dark clouds
> descended on our beloved home town" – this was how the Nazi period was
> designated, then one quickly moved on to the time of postwar
> reconstruction... At city anniversary celebrations, the Nazi dictatorship
> was also brushed aside. Neither the exclusion of Jews and other persecuted
> fellow citizens was commemorated nor the responsibility of local authorities
> and societies reflected upon. It was especially difficult to affect change in
> these celebrations because their purpose was to create or strengthen local
> identity that was not to be tarnished by the dark stains of Nazism.[29]

In the course of the decade, as progressives moved into institutions,
history workshops became more influential, and memory culture writ-
large changed. The resistance faced by local initiatives to commemorate
German crimes was encountered with diminishing frequency, but resistance nevertheless still existed. For example, as Norbert Haase reports, in
the summer of 1989, efforts to put up a plaque commemorating the
sentencing and execution of conscientious objectors at a local courthouse
in Berlin were met with stiff opposition from the judicial authorities.[30]

w?>Despite the delay and sometimes prevention of memorial initiatives by reluctant authorities, such blockage in hindsight presented an
opportunity for the activists. The official refusal to commemorate and
acknowledge the culpabilities of the past allowed the Movement to
repeatedly point to the current manifestations of an unreformed memory
culture and to link their calls for commemoration to contemporary politics. In other words, they were often able to connect a local conflict over
a comparatively small matter such as a memorial plaque to the larger
question of a "democratic mode of remembrance." They argued that
because the government was unwilling to act, their own unconventional
actions were indispensable. Furthermore, the more the authorities
stalled, the easier it was for the Movement to convince sympathetic
audiences of the legitimacy of its nonmainstream collective action tactics.

Aside from the opportunities afforded the History Movement by the
political system writ-large, the activists benefited from a range of cultural

---

[28] von Saldern, 'Stadtgedächtnis und Geschichtswerkstätten.'   [29] Ibid. pp. 60–61.
[30] Haase, 'Berlin-Charlottenburg.'

openings that were specific to their focus on history and memory. First, and most generally, generational change facilitated the reckoning with the past. On the one hand, those who had adult memories of the Nazi period and could be accused of direct participation in the regime were retreating from positions of influence so that the public discussion of their past no longer had the same political explosiveness. On the other hand, with the waning of the generation of Holocaust survivors, there was recognition of the need to determine how the past would be dealt with in the absence of direct witnesses. In other words, the gradual shift from "communicative" to "cultural memory" set off a struggle over the meaning of German history in which both conservatives and the left participated.[31]

Another generational shift took place within left-wing politics that also facilitated the rise of the History Movement. Student radicalism (and its legends) continued to attract young adults in the 1970s and 1980s, particularly to large university cities such as Berlin and Frankfurt. However, many of the new cohort were disappointed by the factionalist squabbles and ideological stasis. Marxist and structuralist theory seminars, which had been established in the wake of 1968, were abstract and did not speak to students interested in more practical approaches.[32] A sizable portion of the left was now interested "not in analyses of capitalism and grand societal schemes, but rather in small alternatives and concrete life-altering praxis. 'Small is beautiful' was the buzz word."[33] It was this critique that underscored the shift of political activity from the university to the local neighborhood and the cultural field.[34]

The History Movement applied this kind of ideological restraint to their topics of scholarly inquiry, again reacting to the previous generation of leftist politics. There was much dissatisfaction with what was perceived as the stalled process of memory work. The 1968ers had failed to truly listen to the witnesses of the Nazi period – both on the side of victims and perpetrators or bystanders – and had arrogantly declared the lessons to be learned, rather than trying to understand the complex situations in which historical decisions were made.[35] It seems that for the history activists, many of whom were the grandchildren of those who had been in positions of responsibility during the Nazi era, it was easier than for the 1968ers to ask nonaccusatory questions – and the grandparents talked more willingly.[36] The history activists consequently did much more than their

---

[31] Müller, 'Introduction: the power of memory' p. 14.
[32] See Interviews, Martin Düspohl.
[33] Martin, 'Bewegung! Stillstand. Aufbruch?', p. 12.
[34] Düspohl, '20 Jahre Berliner Geschichtswerkstatt.'
[35] See Interviews, Eva Brücker.
[36] Spiegel, 'Ein kräftiger Schub für die Vergangenheit.'

predecessors to illuminate the everyday reality of fascism.[37] In sum, the generational shift within the left provided the opportunity for a new approach to the past – one that was less ideological and more open to dialogue across the political spectrum. This openness enabled the History Movement to influence a broader section of society and find allies outside of its political base.

Second, history activists took advantage of key events that crystallized their issues and provided opportunities for publicity and funding. In the wider public sphere, such events included national controversies such as those surrounding the creation of a war memorial in Bonn or President Reagan and Chancellor Kohl's visit to Bitburg. At the local level, important anniversaries often provided the impetus for action. Many history workshops were founded in response to a lack of activities on the part of local authorities in preparation for the fiftieth anniversary of the Nazi seizure of power in 1983.[38] Mobilization also occurred when activists realized that their perspective on the past, particularly on the local history of 1933–1945, was being sidelined in town anniversary celebrations. For example, activists came together in Augsburg to create a "counterhistory book" and alternative city tour on the occasion of the city's 2000th anniversary.[39] The history workshop in Düsseldorf was also founded in the context of that city's 700th anniversary.[40] And in West Berlin, the Berlin History Workshop had the highest number of participants and resources in the run-up to the 750th-year festivities in 1987. These events not only brought the workshops an interested audience, they also showed state actors that there was a public demand to address even difficult periods of history. This meant that though the History Movement continued to be viewed (and see itself) as the mnemonic opposition, the authorities also began to see their potential as part of the local cultural and tourist industry. History projects therefore increasingly attracted funding from municipal and regional institutions.

A third cultural opportunity was presented by the general rise in interest in history and a boom in exhibitions and publishing on historical subjects. The fact that people outside of the Movement showed an interest in all matters historical, and increasingly in the Nazi past in particular, reinforced the drive of the activists and made their work seem all the more important. At the local level, the "memory boom" meant that there were partners in established institutions who were interested in supporting historical projects. These provided some level of material support and

---

[37] Szejnmann, 'Die Bedeutung der Regionalgeschichte' p. 86.
[38] Lindenberger and Wildt, 'Radikale Pluralität ' p. 400.
[39] Forster, 'Antworten lesender Augsburger'.
[40] www.geschichtswerkstatt-duesseldorf.de/unserverein/index.html.

allies for particular undertakings. The local manifestations of the Nazi regime and other "pasts" were beginning to be examined in schools, labor unions, local party organizations, and municipal governments that made memory part of their cultural and social activities.[41] The activities taking place in the organizational and institutional fields form the context for the *independent* initiatives that composed the History Movement. The independent activists regularly cooperated with partners in unions,[42] the Social Democratic Party, or local administrations or were active in both arenas.[43] For the Memorial Site Movement, the same actors were crucial allies in their efforts to mark places of Nazi terror, and so they were generally more open to "reaching across the aisle." History workshops, by contrast, harbored a certain skepticism vis-à-vis these projects due to their affiliation with mainstream politics. The dominant sentiment was that the *Geschichtsbewegung* was "new" in the sense of offering a novel take on the study of history. As the innovators, it was important for the activists to distinguish themselves from the establishment and to guard against cooptation – no matter how compatible their interests were at times. Moreover, Social Democrats in particular were viewed skeptically by workshoppers as jealously guarding their left-wing terrain and colluding with mainstream historians who rejected grassroots initiatives.[44] As Bernhard Müller, member of the Berlin History Workshop, wrote in a report about a seminar organized by a Social Democratic foundation:

> On the one hand, the SPD of course feels that it is about to miss the train once again, and is stumbling immensely while attempting to jump on at the last moment. On the other hand, while the party has noticed the work accomplished by history workshops, and peace, women's and other alternative groups, it cannot – in its famously sluggish nature, establish a real connection to them, let alone genuine cooperation.[45]

A key "mobilizing structure" for the History Movement was the larger environment of new left social movements and its social infrastructure of neighborhoods, shops, printing presses, publishing houses, self-help groups, and more. Especially important for the history workshops (and sometimes synonymous with them) were the "alternative" or "free" archives. A guide to "alternative archives" in six countries, which was published in 1990 but was based on a meeting in 1985, listed 239 organizations mostly in West Germany – many of them workshops, but also women's, gay rights, environmental, peace, anarchist, and other

[41] Strnad, 'Grabe, wo Du stehst' p. 173.   [42] Scharrer, *Macht Geschichte von unten.*
[43] See Interviews, Eva Brücker and Andreas Ludwig.
[44] See Interviews, Thomas Lindenberger.
[45] Müller, 'Die Sozialdemokraten entdecken' p. 12.

groups that were engaged in "emancipatory" archival work.[46] The most recent estimate puts the number of still existing independent archives in the Federal Republic at one hundred, with the majority founded in the early 1980s. Archiving took place parallel to political activism and in order to safeguard not only the documents of the movements, but their political identity, from state control.[47] As Sonja Miltenberger recalls, archival work was also the stimulus for in-depth discussions about language and conceptual frameworks within history workshops.[48]

Sebastian Haunss and Darcy Leach argue that social movement scenes can provide a foundation for several movements, creating links between them and loyalties that extend beyond any particular struggle. Members of a scene share basic convictions and directly engage in it, but their participation is a part-time activity and can wax and wane depending on the cycles of mobilization of various movements.[49] From this perspective, it makes sense that History Movement activists were commonly also active in other movements and brought those concerns into their research activities. Such interpersonal and cross-movement connections were crucial and offered a mobilization pool, sites of experimentation with alternative forms of organization and self-governance, and a source of collective identity and solidarity.[50] The History Movement's integration into a larger scene is one reason that makes it difficult to estimate the exact number of its members, as the boundaries of activism were relatively fluid and constantly in flux. Haunss and Leach add that scenes serve as "culture-carriers for movement traditions, norms and history. Scene locations such as movement archives, book stores and movie-houses can do this in a very concrete and explicit way, acting as the institutional memory of the movement."[51]

The history workshops consciously sought to be "culture-carriers," recording not only the history of sister movements, but also preserving norms through praxis. Haunss and Leach stress that scenes must be grounded in locations – such as bars, parks, info-shops, collectivist projects, living communities (WGs), and whole neighborhoods. In West Berlin, for example, the "alternative scene" was concentrated in the Kreuzberg, Schöneberg, and Wedding neighborhoods. It was also closely identified with the *Spontis*[52] and the *Autonomen*,[53] as well as the

---

[46] Zeitgeschichte/Amsterdam, 'Reader der 'anderen' Archive.'
[47] Bacia and Wenzel, *Bewegung bewahren* p.10, see also Hüttner, *Archive von unten.*
[48] See Interviews, Sonja Miltenberger
[49] Haunss and Leach, 'Social movement scenes' p. 73.   [50] Ibid.   [51] Ibid. p. 81.
[52] The Spontis were a largely unorganized segment of the leftist scene that rejected dogmatic Marxism.
[53] The Autonomen are a movement closely associated with anarchism.

squatters' movement and its struggle against the city's radical urban renewal politics of the time. Local history workshops were intimately involved in the squatters' drive to preserve historic neighborhoods and communities.[54]

The new left was careful to publicize and promote its decentralized structure, by publishing records of active groups. Alternative city guides (*Stattbücher*) were put out in several cities, including in Stuttgart (since 1979), Karlsruhe (1980), Heidelberg/Mannheim (1982), and others.[55] According to the third edition of the Berlin *Stattbuch*, it contained everything that "moved in emancipatory fashion" and sought to network those initiatives that were otherwise suspicious of any organizational structure. The introduction outlines the goal of the *Stattbuch*: "We want to trace the web that we are all knitting – we who still have 'raisins in our heads,' who work for our ideals together, cooperatively, without profit, and autonomously."[56] The *Stattbuch* itself was cited as an example of a successful exercise in left-wing independence: edited by an alternative publisher, printed and bound by collectives, and distributed primarily through left-wing bookshops. In other words, the *Stattbücher* and similar projects were aimed at organizing the scene without threatening its autonomy.

As is evident from my account so far, the movement scene existed mostly in urban settings. However, as Detlef Siegfried has argued, the new left did not bypass the countryside entirely. In fact, particularly young people took note of urban developments and sought to develop a counterculture, as well as a "provincial pride" in small towns and villages.[57] Further, some pivotal battles of NSMs were fought in the countryside, particularly against nuclear facilities, with urban activists at times present.[58] And, there was a significant group of former urbanites ("*Aussteiger*") who – idealizing the "simple life" – founded collective farms, wineries, or meeting spaces in rural locations in order to escape the grind of the city.

The History Movement, then, was made possible by a complex set of political and cultural opportunities – some of which were specific to it, some of which were taken advantage of by a wider range of new social movements at the time. It is important to stress that the Memorial Site

---

[54] See Interviews, Gisela Wenzel, Eva Brücker, Thomas Lindenberger, and Martin Düspohl. This milieu is also evident in an initial contact list of the Workshop: 'Vorschlag für einen Verteiler für unseren Aufruf ... ' (November 25,1981), personal archive Thomas Lindenberger.

[55] Based on a search in the online catalog of the *Deutsche Nationalbibliothek*.

[56] Arbeitsgruppe Stattbuch 3 Berlin, 'Stattbuch 3.'

[57] Siegfried, 'Urbane Revolten, befreite Zonen' p. 355.   [58] Ibid.

Movement emerged and thrived under these same conditions. These openings had direct implications for the organizational forms and strategies both Movements utilized.

Organizing the Struggle for Critical Memory

Some history workshops were founded by members of universities (often historians) who then attracted a wider circle of activists – this was the case for example in Siegen, Darmstadt, Göttingen, Freiburg, and Konstanz (where it was called *Arbeitskreis Regionalgeschichte Bodensee*).[59] But the usual path of mobilization was more spontaneous. Most local workshops were founded by participants in ad hoc research or exhibition projects who then decided to establish a more routinized effort at memory work. These projects emerged from an existing left-wing scene from which those who were already historically sensitized came together. The first history workshop in Hamburg, the *Stadtteilarchiv Ottensen* (Neighborhood Archive Ottensen), was created in 1980 in the context of an exhibit on the everyday life of the neighborhood in the Museum Altona.[60] Another Hamburg group, the *Geschichtswerkstatt Barmbek* (History Workshop Barmbek), resulted from a working group for an exhibit on the area's history from 1945–1949.[61] In 1988, in the wake of the creation of the concentration camp memorial in Fuhlsbüttel, Nazi victims, historians, and regular citizens founded the *Willy-Bredel-Society,* dedicated to researching the history of the Hamburg workers' movement, the antifascist resistance, and the history of surrounding suburbs.[62] The *Archiv der Münchner Arbeiterbewegung e.V.* (Archive of the Munich Workers' Movement) was founded in 1987 after an exhibit when participants decided that there were documents needing to be safeguarded and more work was to be done.[63] In Cologne, some of the activists who had protested against the 1987 census stayed together to examine the local history of "regular people," such as workers, farmers, and artisans. The *Werkstatt für Ortsgeschichte Köln-Brück e.V.* (Workshop for Local History Köln-Brück) was officially founded in 1988.[64]

In some larger cities, multiple initiatives existed and they cooperated with each other to exchange ideas, secure funding, and reinforce their

---

[59] See Interviews, Thomas Lindenberger; www.geschichtswerkstatt-siegen.de/; www.darmstaedter-geschichtswerkstatt.de/ber-uns/; www.geschichtswerkstatt-goettingen.de/; www.geschichte.uni-freiburg.de/studierende/fuer_alle_studierenden/werkzeugkasten/ak_regionalgeschichte.html.

[60] Böge, 'Treffpunkt, Meinungsumschlagplatz,' www.stadtteilarchiv-ottensen.de/pages/stadtteilarchiv.php.

[61] Ibid.   [62] www.bredelgesellschaft.de/schoeps/wbg.htm

[63] Ledig, 'Geschichte von unten.'   [64] www.gw-koeln-brueck.de/index.php?menid=1.

movement identity. In West Berlin in 1983, the government authorized the leftist *Kulturrat* (Cultural Council) to distribute funds to various initiatives preparing the fiftieth anniversary of the Nazi takeover of power. Since 1985, a regular meeting of all the Hamburg history workshops (fluctuating between twelve and eighteen in number) has taken place. Through joint intensive lobbying efforts, especially by key workshops such as Eimsbüttel, Barmbek, and Ottensen, the Hamburg workshops in 1988/89 acquired a regular budget for themselves from the city government. In social democratic Hamburg, support for "culture from below" was strong, and so the memory activists found quite a bit of backing within the city government early on. Institutional funding remained stable until the early 2000s, when a conservative government attempted to make drastic cuts. In response, the workshops have founded both a citywide association and a foundation, in order to strengthen their bargaining and fund-raising ability.[65]

The initial impulse of history workshop participants was not to found organizations – it was to undertake historical research in an independent and innovative fashion. In fact, in line with the widespread conviction of new left movements at the time, the activists were often reluctant to organize formally and favored decentralization and spontaneity. Nevertheless, most initiatives eventually adopted an official form, registering with the authorities as nonprofit associations in order to be able to receive state funding and tax-deductible donations. It meant they had to formalize their organizational structure and objectives in statutes, and elect representatives.[66] This ambivalent relationship with the state is a common theme that recurs throughout the history of memory activism in Germany.

This notwithstanding, many activists remained attached to a self-image of subversiveness that seemed incompatible with the petit-bourgeois image of the association (*Verein*). Even in hindsight, a rebellious identity was still present, as the following reflection on the work of the Marburg history workshop indicates: "I want to assure you that our actions were more mischievous than my summary suggests. Since I cannot detail everything here, I will confine myself to allusions: trucks and memorial transports, night-watches, contravening commemorations on opposite ends of the Schülerpark, the Marburg Jäger [a veterans' organization] on one side, and we on the other."[67] The history workshops continued to

---

[65] See Interviews, Beate Meyer and Ulrike Hoppe; Meyer, 'Zwischen Anspruch und Wirklichkeit', www.stiftung-hamburger-geschichtswerkstaetten.de/.

[66] Vandamme, *Basisdemokratie als zivile Intervention* p. 48.

[67] Roth, 'Notizen zu einem Jubiläum' p. 14.

grapple with the problem of how to square organizational necessities with their oppositional identity for the duration of their activity.

Who were the people deciding to spend so much of their free time researching and debating history? As the various stories behind the foundation of local workshops show, the range of personalities taking part in the History Movement was wide. They included long-time residents who enjoyed deepening their connection to the neighborhood and older people who sought company (leading to discussions among younger activists about their responsibilities as quasi-social workers).[68] Other participants were part of the wartime generation (victims and bystanders alike) who sought to transmit their experiences through the emerging initiatives. Some were "1968ers" who were searching for a new outlet for their political energies. The majority of history activists, however, were of a younger cohort and almost all had or were working on university degrees. Thomas Lutz, who was active in both the History and Memorial Site Movements and is now a leading figure in the Topography of Terror Foundation, assesses the role of this cohort as follows:

> the 1968ers were not the ones who built the memorials [*Gedenkstätten*]...
> My impression is this: the 1968ers were very important in opening this
> society, in lifting the taboo surrounding the subject of National Socialism,
> so to speak... And only when people realized, there's only so far we can go
> with this, and when the History Movement emerged – the "dig where you
> stand" Movement... – that was when one started working in concrete
> locations, doing "on the ground" research.[69]

According to 1985 estimates, 40 percent of history workshop members were employed in academia, 20 percent were unemployed, and the rest was made up of teachers, others in social professions, and members of the media.[70] Many had turned to projects outside the walls of academia due to frustrated expectations in the aftermath of the student movement. Detlef Siegfried argues (through an examination of the biographies of key members of the Movement) that a collective process of deradicalization underpinned the workshops. Many activists – mostly born during the 1950s – had been active in far left and Leninist organizations but then moderated their stance as they were wrapping up their studies in the early 1980s. This group included figures such as Hannes Heer, Ulla Lachauer, Dorothee Wierling, and Michael Zimmermann – all of whom later became prominent historians.[71]

---

[68] Kinter, Kock, and Thiele, *Spuren suchen* p. 62.   [69] See Interviews, Thomas Lutz.
[70] Frei, 'Geschichtswerkstätten.'
[71] Siegfried, 'Die Rückkehr des Subjekts'; von Plato, 'Ambivalenter Etablierungsprozess.'

While some History Movement members continued to work in academia simultaneously, others consciously left the ivory tower in order to work in a less competitive and more cooperative environment. For its duration, the Movement had a fraught relationship with the mainstream historical discipline.[72]

However, it seems apart from lofty ideals of a new democratic history, another driving force of the History Movement was the search for an occupation for under- or unemployed university graduates, especially historians and teachers.[73] After the university boom of the 1960s and 1970s, students in the 1980s were faced with considerable uncertainty and many took the matter into their own hands by creating jobs for themselves. These could either be combined with the common short-term contracts in museums or universities or turned into full-time employment.[74] As Roger Fletcher argued in one of the few early reports on the Movement in English:

> With no academic jobs to go to, or even to aspire to, a large unemployed academic proletariat has begun to make its presence felt in West Germany... Free of the traditional patron-client relationship within German universities and enjoying far greater independence and flexibility than their more fortunate or 'successful' academic colleagues, these hapless professional underdogs have flocked to the history workshop festivals and have provided the new history movement with much of its initiative, enthusiasm, and mass base.[75]

Once the Movement had taken off and its value was recognized by local governments, they provided the workshops with subsidized positions (ABM or *Arbeitsbeschaffungsmassnahmen*) and thus indirectly financed the Movement.[76] With this, individual aspirations to create employment out of activism became more realistic. Martin Düspohl, now Director of the Kreuzberg Museum in Berlin, is a good example of someone who created his own job through the Movement. "The Eighties were the decade of history, the life of a strange orientation towards the past, which paradoxically provided us personally with perspectives and let us appear extremely progressive."[77] Local authorities indeed quickly saw the added value of the history workshops as providers of cultural offerings and as part of the tourist industry. Many of the protagonists of the Movement found permanent employment in memorial institutions, local cultural administration, and in *Heimatmuseen* (homeland or local museums) in particular.

---

[72] See Interviews, Thomas Lindenberger.   [73] Sperner, *Die neue Geschichtsbewegung.*
[74] Schildt, 'Zur Einleitung.'
[75] Fletcher, 'Review: History from Below Comes to Germany' p. 560.
[76] Schildt, 'Zur Einleitung.'   [77] Düspohl, '20 Jahre Berliner Geschichtswerkstatt ' p. 49.

Figure 4.3. "History workshops of all regions – unite!"[78]

This, in turn, increased the willingness of institutions to support the History Movement.

Notwithstanding their ambivalence vis-à-vis organization in general, the official federal union of history workshops was established quite early on, formally connecting the myriad of local initiatives. An image that was circulating in the Movement around that time repurposed Marx's famous call to action: "History Workshops of all regions – unite!" It encapsulated not only the drive to create a national organization, but also the History Movement's unapologetic commitment to left-wing traditions (Figure 4.3). Early in the 1980s, a group of historians had looked for a way to create a journal for new approaches to history. In order not to impose such a project from above, it was determined first to enhance the substructure of local initiatives and progressive historians.[79] After some initial skepticism, the grassroots activists were persuaded, partly through "targeted ensnarement" and strategic distribution of sleeping quarters in order to enhance personal links, as Thomas Lindenberger fondly remembers. The federal association *Geschichtswerkstatt e. V.* was founded in 1982 and 1983 in the course of two meetings in Göttingen and Bochum, with other activists, including from Bremen, Berlin, and Cologne.[80]

[78] VSA: Verlag Hamburg (in Kinter, Kock, and Thiele, Spuren suchen p. 57).
[79] Frei, 'Die Zukunft liegt in der Vergangenheit '.
[80] Berliner Geschichtswerkstatt e.V. *Rundbrief* 4/1983, Sperner, *Die neue Geschichtsbewegung*, See Interviews, Lindenberger.

Along with it, a journal called *Geschichtswerkstatt* was created which was published three times a year, with editorial control rotating among local groups, so as to prevent centralizing tendencies. This journal was used not only to report on the historical research undertaken by the initiatives, but to record their meetings, to network with sympathetic groups, and to carry out contentious debates.

These writings exemplify the discursive culture among the workshoppers, in which the nature of the communication was often more important than the content of their research or even its public representation. In *Geschichtswerkstatt*, the writing style is extremely informal, with authors often using only first names to refer to each other, colloquial terms, and polemics. This is a manifestation of the self-image of the movement as alternative, informal, antiestablishment, nondogmatic, and close to "real life." Similarly, participants in events organized by the history activists noted the pleasant (though lively) discussions in contradistinction to the cutthroat atmosphere in conventional academic venues.[81] Those most active members of the Movement invested much time, energy, and passion into their projects and organizations, but they also expected the work to be fun.

The best illustration of the History Movement's unique combination of scholarly seriousness, political motivation, and penchant for having a good time were the annual meetings in the form of history festivals – the other main forum of communication for the Movement. The idea for a festival had been developed during the foundation of the federal association, and was intended to be clearly distinct from existing forums, as Lindenberger remembers: "Let's just call it history festival, so that this whole spectrum can show itself, without admittance requirements according to academic rituals, but rather as open and everyone could propose workshops."[82] It first took place in May 1984 in Berlin with seven hundred participants and in subsequent years, with between four- to five hundred each in Hamburg (1985), Dortmund (1986) and Hanover (1988). A report about the second festival was titled *Tango & Theoriearbeit* (tango and theoretical work), encapsulating the aspiration of the meeting to merge substance with fun[83] and to shake up the routine of academic historiography.[84] Festival-goers were usually housed by local activists, an arrangement which surely contributed to the establishment of cross-regional connections and friendship networks. During these *Geschichtsfeste*, cooperative projects were conceived, methods and theories discussed, and local struggles supported.[85] The larger purpose of the

---

[81] *Geschichtswerkstatt* 4, August 1984 p. 42, See Interviews, Sonja Miltenberger.
[82] See Interviews, Thomas Lindenberger.   [83] Frei, '2. Geschichtsfest.'
[84] Heer and Ullrich, 'Einleitung.'
[85] Böge, 'Zur Einleitung', Frei, 'Die Zukunft liegt in der Vergangenheit.'

festivals was summarized by the 1984 organizers as follows. "With the history festival, we want to increase our presence in the wider public arena: it will show what the work of history initiatives has produced thus far and it will demonstrate our determination to contribute in a critical manner to the political culture of our society."[86]

Festivals featured a series of workshops run by activists on topics ranging from everyday life during fascism, postwar history, the early modern period, colonialism, and social politics, to methodological and didactic issues such as how to represent history using theater, film, exhibitions, or guided tours. The workshop form was adopted in order to break down the division between the "knowing" expert speaker and "unknowing" listener. Further, the activists visited local projects and took part in alternative tours. Initiatives presented their work and publications at a "marketplace." And a series of evening and cultural events were organized which were open to the public and aimed at recruiting people to the cause.[87] The festivals also offered the opportunity to debate pressing issues facing the Movement, such as its relationship to the historical profession, the impact of accepting funds from the state, or the need for professionalization. Looking back, two protagonists of the movement argued that the term *Geschichtsfest* was an expression of the euphoria of the early period: "this was, after all, not in reference to the very serious topics we studied, but rather to the communicative style to which we aspired."[88]

This communicative style was also evident at the local level. Beate Meyer goes so far as to elevate an "integrationist debate culture" to the status of a trademark for the *Galerie Morgenland*, a history workshop in Hamburg-Eimsbüttel.[89] In order to ensure the strengthening of such forms of interaction, the activists espoused strategies familiar to new social movements and applied them to memory work specifically. The concept of a temporally limited "project" (rather than any kind of permanent institution) was common in the alternative scene as a way of organizing autonomy, collective ownership, self-determination, and a manageable size conducive to direct democratic principles. The goal was to involve all participants in all steps of a process, to overcome the separation of work and leisure, and of "head" and "hand."[90] Reality was of course not this simple. Siegfried writes,

---

[86] *MOZ – Moderne Zeiten* 4 (Sondernummer April 1984).

[87] *Geschichtswerkstatt* 2, December 1983, *Geschichtswerkstatt* 7, September 1985.

[88] Gerstenberger and Schmidt, 'Von den Festen', p. 9.

[89] Meyer, 'Zwischen Anspruch und Wirklichkeit' p.52; see also film *Galerie Morgenland/ Geschichtswerkstatt Eimsbüttel* By Lars Ole (2004).

[90] Siegfried, 'Die Rückkehr des Subjekts', Olk, Reim, and Schmithals, 'Qualitative Studie.'

Not only because of its result, but also due to the intensity of the subjective experience, the approach of "history from below" as a cooperative endeavor was seen as superior to individualized work. In contrast to these assumptions, practical experiences showed that project work often reproduced the unequal vantage points of participants. Informal hierarchies, self-exploitation, and organizational chaos were some negative side-effects of an – in many ways innovative – work and life style.[91]

The workshoppers also applied such cooperative and emancipatory principles to their research activities. Crucial was the use of oral history methods as a way of including and taking seriously the protagonists of history themselves. The history of everyday life and oral history did have some important advocates within academia, most importantly Alf Lüdtke, Lutz Niethammer, Ulrich Borsdorf, and a few others.[92] Niethammer's 1980 book *Lebenserfahrung und kollektives Gedächtnis* (*Life Experience and Collective Memory*) was particularly influential and was closely reviewed by the activists.[93]

The trend in official memory politics toward wide-angle lenses was in some sense mirrored in the historical profession. Though historical work on the origins and development of Nazism and the Holocaust was continuing to become more serious and sophisticated during this time, the dominance of the "Bielefeld School" of social history, led by social democratic-leaning historians Hans-Ulrich Wehler and Jürgen Kocka, focused on large-scale processes such as modernization and industrialization. Wehler famously derided the history workshops as romantics who produced only "greenish soap bubbles" (*grünlich schimmernde Seifenblasen*), referring to the History Movement's affinity with the new Green Party.[94] The workshoppers matched these polemics and argued that history was too important to be left to the historians.[95] For Thomas Lindenberger and Michael Wildt, the "history workshops contribute to grasping history as 'public science,' to liberate them from the isolation of academic institutions and the self-limitation of conventional 'homeland' researchers (*Heimatforscher*), and to integrate them into political and cultural controversies."[96] At the *Historikertag* (the national convention of historians) in 1984, there was an open confrontation between historians of everyday life and the "establishment" personified by Wehler.[97]

---

[91] Siegfried, 'Die Rückkehr des Subjekts' p. 130.
[92] Kierdorf and Hassler, *Denkmale des Industriezeitalters*.
[93] Niethammer, 'Lebenserfahrung und kollektives Gedächtnis', See Interviews, Thomas Lindenberger.
[94] Schöttler, 'Die Geschichtswerkstatt e.V.' p. 422.   [95] See Interviews, Reinhard Rürup.
[96] Lindenberger and Wildt, 'Radikale Pluralität ' p. 394.
[97] van Laak, 'Alltagsgeschichte' p. 50.

Despite this bad blood, the division between history workshops and academia should not be overdrawn. A growing group of professional historians were engaging in *Alltagsgeschichte*[98] and particularly in university towns there were instances of close cooperation between history workshops and academics.[99] It is difficult to determine in hindsight whether particular impulses originated in the Movement or in the universities. However, it is clear that there was significant cross-fertilization. Both workshoppers and historians assign the *Geschichtsbewegung* the pivotal part of politicizing local research and honing in on the Nazi period as the most important focus of study.[100] In the arena of official history politics too, there were points of contact with the approach championed by the workshops. In fact, the history competition created by President Gustav Heinemann employed an everyday history approach beginning in the mid-1970s.[101] In sum, the division between grassroots and mainstream advocates of history was never black and white.

Such nuanced hindsight notwithstanding, history activists criticized academic historians for being removed from reality, writing unintelligibly, and supporting the "ruling circumstances" while feigning objectivity: "the history workshops are not interested in a theoretical 'rational and disciplined' historiography, which is removed from current affairs, supposedly objective and neutral, and detailed to a fault, but which in the end loses its way."[102] Historical departments were also seen by some activists as "bastions of social democratic court historiography"[103] and inherently suspicious. More practically, the many students in the Movement sought alternatives to the stagnant departments and to complement their academic experience through grassroots history work.[104]

History workshops were among the pioneers of oral history and other innovative approaches. This was humorously depicted in a contemporaneous Movement publication in the form of a multitasking "alternative historian" (Figure 4.4). The work of interviewing "real people," including bystanders and perpetrators, was an indispensable motivator for the activists. According to Eva Brücker, it was *"the* foundation without which we would not have developed as we did."[105] The reliance on spoken

---

[98] For more on the "history of everyday life:" Davis, Lindenberger, and Wildt, 'Einleitung', Lange, 'Politische Alltagsgeschichte.'

[99] Lindenberger and Wildt, 'Radikale Pluralität ' p. 410.

[100] See Interviews Udo Gößwald and Reinhard Rürup.

[101] Reinhard Rürup, who later led the Topography of Terror foundation, was crucially involved with this. See Interviews, Reinhard Rürup, Siegfried, 'Subversiver Alltag ', Siegfried, 'Die Rückkehr des Subjekts.'

[102] *Geschichtswerkstatt* 7, September 1985.   [103] Schildt, 'Zur Einleitung.'

[104] See Interviews, Eva Brücker and Andreas Ludwig.

[105] See Interviews, Eva Brücker.

Figure 4.4. The alternative historian, as depicted in a History Movement publication.[106]

evidence and materials other than text was evident in exhibitions assembled by history workshops, where visitors could listen to audiotapes – a practice that is now commonplace in German museums.[107] The workshops also

[106] VSA: Verlag Hamburg (in Kinter, Kock, and Thiele, *Spuren suchen* p. 71).
[107] Zimmermann, 'Haben Geschichtswerkstätten Zukunft?', See Interviews, Gisela Wenzel.

used other nontextual materials, such as photo albums, resumés, jokes, and artifacts of all kinds.[108] In line with the focus on everyday life and political engagement, another signature research strategy was the investigation in great detail of particular localities or issues. From these specific cases, insights were then drawn into the larger functioning of political structures or national meaning. Volker Böge calls this the "micrological method."[109]

Intimately connected to new research methods were new forms of representation, which were intended to include the audience in an ongoing dialogue about the past and present, rather than view them as passive recipients of information. Activists organized guided tours and boat rides, games, theater, bike and canoe trips, and more.[110] In addition to specific research results, alternative city guides were published, but also more specific volumes, particularly on the locations of Nazi terror and resistance to it.

One of the most ambitious projects in this arena was the series of *Heimatgeschichtliche Wegweiser* (Homeland History Guides), organized regionally and published by the *Studienkreis Deutscher Widerstand* (Association for Studying German Resistance).[111] The activists understood guided tours not merely as a way of providing information to new audiences. The goal was for participants to develop a relationship with the topography of history and to take part in an active process of reflection and memory making – rather than merely passively absorbing what a guide told them. Members of *Geschichte für alle e.V.* (History for All) – a group offering tours of Nürnberg, Fürth, and Erlangen in Bavaria – argued that bus tours were a form of television, where tourists have no contact with reality and on top of that contributed to pollution and problems in public transportation.[112] Their goal was to explain historical connections through concrete local and regional history and in the context of social and everyday life history. They wanted to distinguish themselves methodologically from the conventional, rejecting the idea of "leading" people, and instead encouraging a conversation among participants, asking questions, and including witnesses in the tours.

Here, the influence of the History Movement on the Memorial Site Movement and thereby on many memorial institutions is plain. This approach also often meant that guides did not pretend to be politically neutral and inserted their own views into the presentation.[113]

---

[108] Heer and Ullrich, 'Einleitung.'   [109] Böge, 'Zur Einleitung.'
[110] For many examples, see Paul and Schoßig, 'Die andere geschichte.'
[111] www.studienkreis-widerstand-1933-45.de/index.html.
[112] Schmidt and Windsheimer, 'Geschichtskultur' p. 7.   [113] Ibid. p. 6.

"The critical approach of our work consists of not presenting history for its own sake but that we draw comparisons across cultures and across time and offer interpretations. In this sense, our work always relates to the present and can result in active interventions in local politics."[114] At the same time, however, these alternative providers realized that they increasingly faced competition by regular touristic companies reacting to the rising demand for "gentle" tourism."[115]

In addition to vibrant exchanges within the History Movement, the initiatives had some international role models to draw on, underlining its internationalist spirit even while focusing on local history. As a result, the activists made regular references to movements in other countries and took inspiration from them. Most important in this regard were England, France, and Sweden.[116] In the mid-1960s, Ruskin College at Oxford University (a working class and union college) saw the emergence of history workshops that debated the political nature of history and truth and operated in a clear socialist tradition.[117] The ideas of ordinary peoples' history and the involvement of workers in the writing of their own story were established.[118] In France, there was no cohesive history workshop movement, but various initiatives such as the *Action culturelle* (a movement for local culture and democratization),[119] the *Association faire de l'histoire*,[120] and the *écomusées* that had emerged in the early 1970s and were focused on ecologically integrating nature, human populations, and regional culture.[121]

Even more influential was the Swedish "Dig where you stand" movement, triggered by a 1978 book by Sven Lindqvist, which demonstrated how to research personal and occupational history, using the example of the Swedish cement industry.[122] This book at first circulated in an improvised translation among activists and Lindqvist was invited to speak to German history workshops.[123] The translator of the later officially published German volume, Manfred Dammeyer, writes in the afterword that the Swedish movement consisted of around ten thousand study groups that produced exhibitions, books, and even museums of labor history.[124] The motto "dig where you stand," which was also adopted by the Movement in West

---

[114] Ibid. p. 5.   [115] Ibid. p. 5.

[116] See Interviews, Thomas Lindenberger, "'Grabe wo du stehst.'"

[117] Samuel, 'Das britische Modell.'

[118] Ullrich, 'Wie alles anfing', Schildt, 'Zur Einleitung.'

[119] Sperner, *Die neue Geschichtsbewegung.*   [120] *Geschichtswerkstatt* 20, March 1990.

[121] Kierdorf and Hassler, *Denkmale des Industriezeitalters*, Fédération des écomusées et des musées de société http://fems.asso.fr/index2.html.

[122] Lindqvist, *Grabe wo du stehst.*   [123] See Interviews, Thomas Lindenberger.

[124] Manfred Dammeyer in Lindqvist, *Grabe wo du stehst.*

Germany, refers to the call to unearth the past in your own location – whether geographical or social – and to uncover the wealth of experiences and resources available in order to understand how current circumstances came about. According to Dammeyer, "this is aimed not only at discovering alternatives to conventional history writing, but demands a concrete political engagement for the future. The future began yesterday. History lives on."[125]

The German History Movement differed from its international counterparts in that it was much larger and that it focused to a much greater extent on the negative periods in its history rather than mainly on leftist struggles. As Reinhard Rürup, a historian deeply involved in memorial institutions, told me:

> In Germany, the focus of the history workshops was not the history of the workers' movement, or industrialization. Instead one concentrated strongly on the Nazi period ... such citizens' initiatives are always also protest movements and in Germany, the way to rub against the grain was to address the treatment of the history of National Socialism and its "forgetting" in particular locations.[126]

The History Movement depended on the commitment of its members. The core activists of each group devoted a great deal of time and energy to the cause, sometimes working full-time without pay. My interviewees report deriving much satisfaction and joy from their efforts. They experienced recognition from the like-minded, and – equally satisfying – opposition from the "establishment." Activists also contributed material and financial means, often using private materials to make exhibits possible. Furthermore, most local initiatives collected membership dues, their amount usually dependent on the income of each member. The early exhibitions and publications were relatively basic and improvised (as in Figure 4.5), which gave them a nonacademic flair. Not all history workshops had their own premises – and those that did had to be creative to keep them going. Beate Meyer, who was instrumental in shaping the early years of the Geschichtswerkstatt Hamburg-Eimsbüttel remembers how rundown the office – a former milk shop – was at the outset.

> The rooms at *Galerie Morgenland* were really trashy back then. We had a few mattresses that I covered with red fabric and we bought some fold-up chairs at Ikea ... Other than my salary, we had no money, not even for paper. If we had an event, I brought in some paper, wrote on it with a marker and stuck it in the window ... Susanne Lohmeyer [another activist] cheaply bought a used database program from a travel agent and we used this to systematize our archive ... Once, we did an event about food in Hamburg. It was not possible

---

[125] Manfred Dammeyer in ibid. p. 333.
[126] See Interviews, Reinhard Rürup.

Figure 4.5. Activists of the Berlin History Workshop assembling the exhibit "Rote Insel," April 1989.[127]

to use the lights and the stove at the same time, so we made eel soup and did our literary reading with candlelight.[128]

At times when activist momentum stalled, however, enthusiasm would sometimes wane, with individual workshoppers becoming increasingly frustrated as the burden of an unfinished project weighed on them. This happened during a project on "Everyday Life during the Second World War" undertaken by the History Workshop Solingen where after initial eagerness only a small group carried out the bulk of the work. Archival work became a lonely affair and there was little time for those kinds of exchanges that were supposed to make history workshop research unique and stimulating. As one activist put it, "we began our work with the intention of practicing new forms of cooperation through the investigation of the history of subjugated and dependent peoples – and now isolation, pressure, and lack of passion ruled the day.[129]

---

[127] Detlev Davids for the Berliner Geschichtswerkstatt.
[128] See Interviews, Beate Meyer.
[129] Putsch, 'Die Solinger Geschichtswerkstatt' pp. 270–71.

As initial passion decreased, workshops began searching for other funding sources. They applied for ABM positions and sought funding for particular projects from local administrations. Foundations and sympathetic organizations (especially unions and churches) were also asked to provide funding or at least material support such as exhibition spaces. It was much more difficult to acquire regularized funding from local governments. The Berlin History Workshop tried repeatedly and unsuccessfully; the consortium of Hamburg history workshops were eventually granted a regular budget. In 2003, the cultural senator in Hamburg attempted to cut this budget entirely and only a vigorous media and lobbying campaign managed to prevent an outright cut and turn it into a 25 percent reduction.[130]

The activities and tactics of the History Movement were diverse, but can be analyzed in terms of two different modes of mobilization. *Memory work* took place relatively quietly, with little publicity beyond the internal communications within movement organizations and their immediate social environments. Workshoppers held meetings, networked with potential grantgivers, and identified partners for particular projects; organized discussion forums, partly with the goal of attracting "witnesses" and other lay participants; engaged in informal lobbying; conducted archival and interview research; collected materials for exhibitions and archival storage; presented the findings to the public in the form of exhibitions, city tours, publications, plays and more; and shared their work within the Movement through the newsletter, at festivals or workshops.

Thus, during this mode of action, most of the activists' time and energy was devoted to practical labor – engaging with the traces of the past and interpreting them. However, the History Movement laid great emphasis on making this work a social and interactive experience, so that it was crucial to any potential development of "social capital." In the *Galerie Morgenland* (Hamburg-Eimsbüttel) a popular event was called "Mrs. Barbara is expecting guests" and offered 1950s-era cuisine along with lectures and performances on the same period. The objective here was not only to present information in a creative way, but to build personal relationships of memory-making in the neighborhood.[131] As in other new social movements, the "path was the goal" – and the path here was historical research and presentation.

Many of the groups that were part of the History Movement never moved beyond the memory work phase, and thus did not employ protest

---

[130] See Interviews, Ulrike Hoppe and Beate Meyer; www.geschichtswerkstatt-barmbek.de /ueberuns.html.

[131] Meyer, 'Zwischen Anspruch und Wirklichkeit.'

tactics as such. Nevertheless, they regarded their activity as contentious because the content and methodology of their research challenged established historical narratives – both in the historical profession and in public life. The feat of reinterpreting history and influencing public knowledge about it in itself challenged societal forces – particularly conservative governments and interest groups that held a stake in supporting the mnemonic status quo. The right kind of history was seen as "dangerous" to the establishment[132] and activists explicitly aimed to provide related social movements with ammunition. The Marburg History Workshop for instance developed an "antimilitaristic walking tour," and investigated the participation of a local military unit in a host of historical crimes going back to the defeat of the Paris Commune of 1871, in order to supply historically grounded arguments to the peace and anti-NATO movement.[133]

It was in the course of such actions that many initiatives entered the second mode of operation – *memory protest* – when the History Movement clashed directly with state actors, changed its collective action repertoire, and became instrumental in the creation of built memorials (as opposed to more temporary outputs). The line between memory "work" and "protest" was in practice not clear-cut and was not necessarily recognized or acknowledged by activists. In addition to ongoing networking, research, and representation actions of the memory work mode, the protest phase also included: collecting signatures on the street, lobbying, and creating publicity through the media; public information booths and publicity-effective exhibitions; symbolic (protest) actions, often provocative and without permit; disrupting mainstream commemorative ceremonies; the (formally illegal) placement of monuments and commemorative symbols; repurposing or critiquing existing memorials through art or graffiti (Figure 4.6); and the organization of public rallies.

"Memory protest" meant intervening more directly in local memory politics, either on issues already being debated or in order to trigger discussion and political action in the first place. At times, such interventions were only indirectly related to "memory work" under way, but adapted lessons learned from history to current political events. In other instances, the activists brought their own research into wider view. History workshops were, for example, directly responsible for putting the topic of forced labor under the Nazis on the agenda, by publicizing the names of implicated companies, organizing meetings, and convening activists and

---

[132] 'BGW Entwurf für ein programmatisches Selbstverständnis, Statut' August 1981, Archive Berliner Geschichtswerkstatt.
[133] Freisberg and Werther, 'Was wir wollten, was wir taten' p. 16.

Figure 4.6. Graffiti on a military memorial in Marburg: "Being a soldier is a shameful profession – N.Tolstoy."[134]

victims to memorialize locations of forced labor.[135] The *Alexander-Seitz-Geschichtswerkstatt* in Marbach worked over many years to transform the ways in which the National Day of Mourning (*Volkstrauertag*) was commemorated, using "irritation and provocation" as key tools.[136]

Most examples of memory protest, however, resulted from local processes of memory work. Activists either identified locations during their research where historical events of critical importance had taken place or collectively developed interpretations of the past – in the course of meetings, guided tours, or exhibition planning. They then determined that it was not sufficient merely to continue the piecemeal labor of public education but that more aggressive tactics were called for. They sought to increase public awareness by explicitly politicizing history in an unconventional manner. In other words, the activists *shifted from a focus on producing contentious content to publicizing that content through contentious means.*

The target for the History Movement during memory protests were the local (and sometimes national) public spheres, as well as official

---

[134] Michael Heiny, Geschichtswerkstatt Marburg

[135] Freisberg and Werther, 'Was wir wollten, was wir taten', Wenzel, '"Grabe, wo du stehst."'

[136] von Saldern, 'Stadtgedächtnis und Geschichtswerkstätten' p. 63.

Figure 4.7. Opening of the Berlin History Workshop's Mobile Museum exhibit "Von Krenz zu Kohl," summer 1990 at the Alexanderplatz Berlin.[137]

authorities whom they wanted to pressure to commemorate a given issue in public space. History Movement tactics included creating publicity through media outreach, information booths on the street or at events, and utilizing exhibitions in order to attract attention to the larger memory concern. The Berlin History Workshop used its "Mobile Museum" bus (Figure 4.7) to attract press coverage of its advocacy for a memorial to the victims of the Nazi policy of euthanasia, among other causes. Symbolic "happenings," which were highly creative and could be carried out by a limited number of committed supporters, were another strong suit of the History Movement. The annual ritual of renaming the Rosa-Luxemburg-Bridge is a good example of this.

The Marburg History Workshop organized a series of contentious actions to foster the critical remembrance of Germany's military in creative ways.[138] This included repeatedly disrupting commemorative ceremonies of the Marburger Jäger, a local military regiment, which (as Workshop research brought to light) had been involved in war crimes

[137] Detlev Davids for the Berliner Geschichtswerkstatt.
[138] Freisberg and Werther, 'Was wir wollten, was wir taten' p. 16.

Figure 4.8. Activists of the Marburg History Workshop protest during a commemoration of the Marburger Jäger, September 1989.[139]

during the world wars. Despite this history, veterans and the Bundeswehr (German armed forces) continued to honor the regiment at the Jäger Memorial, which had been inaugurated in 1923.[140] On antiwar day, September 1, 1989, the Workshop symbolically unveiled and placed (without a permit) a "Memorial to the Unknown Deserter" in the Schülerpark, opposite the Jäger Memorial. The Jäger monument had also been spray-painted with an antimilitary quote by Tolstoy (see Figure 4.9). On September 2, activists stood with signs in silent protest next to Bundeswehr soldiers during the Jäger remembrance ceremony, which was attended by veterans wearing Nazi-era medals (Figure 4.8). One of the participants, Michael Heiny, noted that these actions were "perceived as an extreme provocation: we had desecrated the Jäger Memorial." A few days later, the city of Marburg removed the Workshop's deserter memorial. To this the activists reacted by staging a kind of memorial service, complete with a wreath and an improvised grave marker that read "Here stood for 4 days a memorial for deserters

---

[139] Michael Heiny, Marburger Geschichtswerkstatt.
[140] Friedrich and others, 'Zur Geschichte und Nachgeschichte' p. 97, Michael Heiny, email communication 9 September 2016.

from Marburg – removed by the city of Marburg" (Figure 5.5 in the next chapter).[141]

These actions by the Marburg History Workshop fed into larger efforts by a coalition of organizations – many of them part of the new left peace movement – to oppose the politics and culture of militarism in German society. Memory activism was a crucial component of this and so the History Movement was able to organize events that drew participants from the wider alternative scene.

The main goal of the *Geschichtsbewegung* was not memorialization – but memorial sites were often the result of local historical research and contentious debates about the meaning of the past for current politics. The sites that were initiated by history workshops in coalition with local partners – often intertwined with initiatives of the Memorial Site Movement – reflected both Movements' emphasis on historical specificity, authenticity, antimonumentalism, and the importance of using memorials to trigger critical reflection about past and present (Chapter 5).

For the History Movement, the goal was not merely to mark the sites that were identified as important, but rather to make the debate about these locations relevant to the transformation of German memory culture. In order to achieve this, it was critical not simply to kick off a memorialization procedure, but to continue to influence the public debate and to become an essential partner in the decision-making process about design, placing, purpose and institutional oversight of the monument. The activists' objective was to make *their* approval an indispensable component of the legitimacy of the commemoration. In other words, they sought to wrest definitional power away from state authorities in matters concerning public memory. To be successful, the history workshoppers needed to strategically frame their concerns within larger contexts. Often they did this by staging political confrontations with the government that explicitly tied higher normative values of democracy to their preferred form of memorialization. They positioned themselves as the civil society check on state actors that did not reflect democratic principles in its memory politics.

Investigating the Past to Shape the Future

The history activists were very much aware of the importance of gaining definitional power over memory. They cited conservative historian Michael Stürmer's pungent observation, "In a land without history…, those who fill memory, who define terminology and interpret the past, will

---

[141] Michael Heiny, email communication September 9, 2016.

win the future" to argue that the field of memory could not be left to the right and that the movement had to go on the offensive.[142] Thus, while the practice of the *Geschichtsbewegung* may have seemed parochial, its political objectives in fact aimed higher. The Movement framed its memory work as devoted to the progressive shaping of the future, and particularly as indispensable to the reinvention of a democratic political culture. In pursuing this goal, the workshoppers explicitly distinguished themselves from what they viewed as the conventional representation of the past that was identified as part of a serious democratic deficit.

Though the Movement by definition organized around the meaning of history, its political identity was explicitly future-oriented. "Those who do not understand their past, cannot sensibly plan for the future."[143] Indeed, the need to shape a better tomorrow by understanding power dynamics of the past justified their memory work. As Eva Sperner explained in 1985,

> The reemergence of fascist tendencies and neoconservative ideas necessitate the search for political alternatives and realizable concepts for a livable future. On this path, the "digging for our own roots" in history has the function of uncovering the causes and contexts of today's dreadful situation, to regain old solutions or interrogate their relevance to the present, and to find new answers by reviving previous democratic traditions, discovering models for political action, and/or creating livable and manageable units.[144]

The objective of shaping present and future through a collective effort to understand the past – and of thereby intervening in current politics – was exemplified in the founding of a history initiative under the umbrella of the already existing *Galerie Morgenland* (a community art and meeting place begun in 1978) in Hamburg-Eimsbüttel. As historian Volker Böge recounts:

> With this transformation from a "gallery" to a "neighborhood cultural center with local archive," new ground was broken. The history work was – precisely according to the principles of the "new history movement" – integrated into the radical-democratic political education work that was already being practiced; the "Morgenland" as a locale where – with the means of culture and art, as well as political debate and self-reflection – the concrete utopia of "tomorrow's land" ["Landes Morgen"] was being constructed, was given a deep historical dimension by making it into a history workshop. In order to build the "land tomorrow," the memory of the "land yesterday" is needed . . . Even more: history workshop was future workshop.[145]

[142] Berliner Geschichtswerkstatt e.V., 'Alltagskultur, Subjektivität und Geschichte.'
[143] *Geschichtswerkstatt* 7, September 1985 p. 42.
[144] Sperner, *Die neue Geschichtsbewegung* p. 5.
[145] Böge, 'Treffpunkt, Meinungsumschlagplatz ' pp.27–28.

The History Movement insisted that writing and representing history was not done for its own sake, but rather with the purpose of becoming politically engaged, developing insights for present-day struggles, and motivating people to think politically.[146] As Hannes Heer and Volker Ullrich wrote at the time, "history from below means uncovering the propaganda of the victors by developing our own interpretations and representation and thereby creating insight into historical processes and their results, recognizing people's ability to resist and change, and thus supporting their own identity and rebellious potential."[147] This "active memory work" was regarded as "unthinkable without societal analysis which is present-oriented."[148]

In these quotes, the perception of a conservative siege shines through. According to Peter Schöttler writing in 1984, the History Movement in Germany emerged "in a period of *roll back* and of the conservative 'Wende.'"[149] To some extent this perception was exaggerated: the Movement often did find advocates and allies within local administrations, and even on the national stage there were those – such as President Richard von Weizsäcker – who were pushing for a more critical approach to the past. However, there was also real and adamant resistance to efforts at commemorating uncomfortable episodes – and this emboldened the activists to continue their work. To mention just one typical example, the *Arbeitskreis Regionalgeschichte Neustadt* (Working Group Regional History Neustadt) began agitating for a plaque in remembrance of a synagogue destroyed by the Nazis in 1981. In 1985, the sign was finally put up, though in a concession to city officials, the activists put up with a milder text than originally demanded.[150] Such conflicts played out in similar ways all over the country.

At the federal level too, the Movement perceived resistance to the kind of memory approach it advocated. On numerous occasions, activists undertook interventions in the state's memory projects during public events and in the streets. An important example of the Movement's arguments (but also of the complexity of state actors' position) was the debate surrounding the planned German Historical Museum (DHM) in Berlin, which the activists regarded as part of the federal government's revisionist and nationalist history politics. Kohl had said, during an announcement of the Berlin museum, that though 1933–1945 was a major period of German history, the Federal Republic was not defined by it and also had positive episodes to represent. Kohl promised

---

[146] Lindenberger, 'Werkstattgeflüster.'   [147] Heer and Ullrich, 'Einleitung' p. 28.
[148] Paul and Schoßig, 'Geschichte und Heimat' p. 20.
[149] Schöttler, 'Die Geschichtswerkstatt e.V.' p. 423 (emphasis in the German original).
[150] von Saldern, 'Stadtgedächtnis und Geschichtswerkstätten' p. 63.

265 million deutsche marks for this purpose.[151] On the occasion of the 750th anniversary of Berlin in 1987, the Chancellor and the Mayor of Berlin Eberhard Diepgen laid a symbolic block precisely where today the Chancellor's Office is located. History workshop activists, Social Democrats, and Greens protested and organized a rally. For several weeks, this block was thought to be in danger of being damaged or abducted and received round-the-clock police protection.[152] Apparently, the left believed that Kohl's "governmental historians" had conspired to exclude the opposition from the planning process[153] and that consequently the museum would epitomize the top-down and nationalistic version of the past against which the history initiatives righteously fought. The executive committee of the *Geschichtswerkstatt e. V.* passed a resolution against the DHM and related projects in 1986, entitled "Against the planned historical reprocessing plants of the government."[154] This reference to the concurrent contention over nuclear waste indicates both the importance the activists attached to the DHM and the status that they sought for their Movement in the wider political landscape. The resolution decries the government's museum plans as whitewashing, wasteful, and aimed at reestablishing a national identity as a distraction from looming crises, while preventing "mourning work" (*Trauerarbeit*). It notes the role of history in legitimating the state and gaining cultural hegemony, and categorically rejects a static interpretation of history. The declaration states that the History Movement rejects a central national museum because "we must go lower, into the 'provinces,' try to understand everyday and regional life." The document further disparages attempts by Social Democrats or progressive historians to reform the DHM by involving the parliament and independent initiatives in the conception. In fact, the first director of the DHM, Christoph Stölzl, actively courted the Berlin History Workshop, visiting the shop several times in order to persuade activists to agree to a formal cooperation. This was rejected by the Workshop and interpreted as an attempt to improve the DHM image through a Movement "seal of approval."[155] The fact that such an inclusion was proposed suggested to them the immense impact that the History Movement had already had but also the patronizing attitude of the "officials" in response to the changing "bourgeois public sphere." The establishment was seen as feigning a consensus about history so that societal alternatives do not emerge as

---

[151] 'Die Nation als Austellungstück' *Geschichtswerkstatt* 11, November 1989.
[152] 'Der Stein des Anstoßes' and see interviews, Sabine Weißler.
[153] Wolfrum, *Geschichtspolitik in der Bundesrepublik* p. 337.
[154] 'Wider die geplanten historischen.'   [155] See Interviews, Thomas Lindenberger.

realizable possibilities.[156] In a special issue on the topic, the *Geschichtswerkstatt* called the museum concept "pluralistic to the point of being void of identity [*pluralistisch bis zur Profillosigkeit*]."[157] The history workshops were not merely against these particular museum plans, but programmatically opposed to a state-driven and centralized version of history. In the end, unification prevented Kohl's original plans from going ahead. Instead, the DHM officially opened in June 2006 in the former location of the GDR equivalent near the Brandenburg Gate. And interestingly, Movement activists have been among DHM employees and project staff. Thus, despite their principled rejection of state museums, their approach to history has been integrated into this largest of official institutions, taking advantage of openings partially demanded by the Movement early on.

In 1993, members of the History Movement used similar arguments when protesting against the rededication of the *Neue Wache*, a memorial close to the Brandenburg Gate, which had already served a similar function in the GDR. They succeeded in forcing the government to add a separate (small) plaque differentiating between the dead.[158] It is noteworthy that in its publications, the History Movement routinely lamented the conservative climate and the lack of progressive culture and solidarity – paradoxically at the same time that alternative initiatives and lifestyles were flourishing everywhere. Although the reality of a conservative onslaught was overblown in some ways, the perception of being the progressive force fighting against the odds aided mobilization and motivation. Activist Sabine Weißler told me that this perception of conservatism became a rallying point for the Movement and in turn helped make the desire for collective work and solidarity a reality at least in the limited context of history festivals and similar events.[159] The Movement's chosen role as the democratic alternative to mainstream policy in the memory field, thus, was crucial to its members' identity and self-confidence. Gisela Wenzel of the Berlin workshop went so far as to compare this oppositional stance to conditions in the GDR: "There was the official view of history of the GDR, then that of the East German opposition with its critical impulse, then there was our established official view of history, and that of the new History Movement. These are all very different approaches and they all met [after 1989]."[160]

[156] 'Wider die geplanten historischen, ' p. 6.
[157] 'Die Nation als Austellungstück' *Geschichtswerkstatt* 11, November 1989 p. 11.
[158] Büchten and Frey, 'Im Irrgarten deutscher Geschichte.'
[159] See Interviews, Sabine Weißler.   [160] See Interviews, Gisela Wenzel.

Democracy was the key concept used by workshoppers to frame and motivate their actions, but also as a way to reject more ideological brands of leftism. Thomas Lindenberger recounts that:

> It was motivating to see ourselves as part of, if you like, democratization strategies. The sense was, if urban planning is being democratized, if citizen initiatives are intervening in all kinds of urban planning projects and direct democracy is being demanded in all kinds of big decisions, why not also democratize the confrontation with the past and why not infuse historical reckoning into democratic processes? This notion of creating more critical public engagement, as an expansion of democracy, so to speak – this existed at a basic level in the Movement. It also meant that our political direction was relatively unspecified. This was in line with the mood of the moment. The 1980s was the time when all the left-radical party-political projects, which had touted a clear goal, had been exhausted. It was clear: the next person to come with such a suggestion would be finished; not more of these proposals! And this openness was useful and so we argued that we need a critical examination of history in order to promote democratic conditions in the present. This is something we can try, without knowing exactly where the journey ends. More democracy cannot hurt, we thought, and there was a certain optimism.[161]

Democracy was also particularly important because it was directly resonant to the wider public. The activists tapped into democracy as an existing value in society, in what might be called "frame alignment."[162] In a narrow sense, the History Movement wanted to turn historical research into a democratic enterprise. As a 1985 manual for history activists states: "The new History Movement aims not only to popularize historical writings and education, but to fundamentally democratize historical research, including the process of working through history. The division of labor between experts and lay people should be eliminated and historical research deprofessionalized."[163] By including everyone who was touched by a particular historical episode, writing and displaying history was conceived of as a democratic act.[164] This basic principle was reinforced by a general aversion against centralized control, an effort to maintain the autonomy of local initiatives, and the call for "nonprofessional historians" to work alongside progressive academics – to "overcome the tension between mental and physical labor (Hand- und Kopfarbeit)."[165] The goal was a cooperative practice built on solidarity

---

[161] See Interviews, Thomas Lindenberger.
[162] Tarrow, *Power in Movement* p. 110.
[163] Kinter, Kock, and Thiele, *Spuren suchen* p. 23.
[164] Frei, 'Die Zukunft liegt in der Vergangenheit' p. 5 and Wenzel, '"Die zwölf Jahre werden Euch begleiten ... "' p. 55.
[165] Sperner, *Die neue Geschichtsbewegung* p. 22.

that could potentially transform interpersonal relations and organiza-tional forms more broadly.[166]

Democracy was also supposed to be reflected in the memory spaces the Movement helped to create. The activists distrusted traditional rituals of commemoration and frequently criticized monumental memory, citing as their crucial achievements "uncovering repressed memory and dislodging statues."[167] As I argue in the next chapter, the memorials resulting from Movement activity typically combined grassroots history work, decentra-lized memory, the preservation of authentic spaces and the rejection of grand monumental schemes.

However, the frame of democracy was tapped into for more than the goal of changing the ways in which historical research was conducted and represented. The critical reflection upon the past was to show that society writ-large could be transformed through democratic action.[168] The late Michael Zimmermann argued that some history activists still harbored a faint hope for revolution,[169] but this social transformation was to happen through a painstaking process of democratic debate and self-guided education in many decentralized locations. For this reason, the *processes* of memory-making were regarded as much more important than *results* in the form of an exhibition or a memorial.[170] Across the board, history workshops explicitly framed their work as critical to developing democratic values and concrete democratic practices. Activists in Marbach stated as their goal to promote democratic consciousness and autonomous activities and to write history in a way that can be understood by as many people as possible.[171] Providers of alternative city tours in Bavaria argued that their work "does not exploit public interest in history as a vehicle of certain political interests, the objective is instead to con-tribute long-term to a culture of democratic contention, to our ability for dialogue in our society."[172] The founding declaration of the History Workshop Augsburg notes: "With our history work, we want to encou-rage people to intervene in current social and political struggles, and so to make a contribution to an active democracy."[173]

The History Movement was concerned with the plight of ordinary people, the voiceless, and oppressed. The goal was not only to study those groups that were usually left out of mainstream historical narrative,

[166] Kinter, Kock, and Thiele, *Spuren suchen* p. 24.
[167] Lachauer, 'Geschichte wird gemacht.'   [168] 'Die Geschichtswerkstatt e.V.' pp. 3–6.
[169] Zimmermann, 'Haben Geschichtswerkstätten Zukunft?'
[170] Spielmann, *Denk – Mal – Prozesse.*
[171] von Saldern, 'Stadtgedächtnis und Geschichtswerkstätten' p. 58.
[172] Schmidt and Windsheimer, 'Geschichtskultur' p. 8.
[173] Forster, 'Antworten lesender Augsburger' p. 43.

but to engage them and help them develop a new collective memory by defining their own history.[174]

> We consciously choose the perspective of those concerned [*die Betroffenen*], the excluded, the oppressed. We are not neutral in writing our history – grassroots history – we want to encourage ourselves and others, to claim our/their history, in order to draw from this experience a political consciousness which will allow us to shape our future. This is why it is the ultimate goal of the history workshops to study the history of the people and to present it in an intelligible manner.[175]

In other words, the intention was to make lay people into subjects as opposed to objects of historical work and to effect the audience's emancipation rather than its instruction from above.[176] For example, the activists in Hamburg-Barmbek felt that running a workshop meant constructing local conceptions of the past jointly with neighborhood residents.[177] While the history activists genuinely tried to implement this credo by opening their projects to neighborhoods and inviting interview partners to participate directly,[178] the extent to which older people from outside the left-wing scene participated was apparently limited. Because the appearance at a history workshop event of a "witness" [*Zeitzeuge*] was somewhat of a special occasion, there seems to have been a certain uncritical reverence for them among some of the activists. In particular, the generation of "red grandfathers" – socialist and communist militants from the pre-1945 era – were suddenly in high demand.[179] Aware of this problem, Siegfried Heimann of the Berlin History Workshop early on warned of putting the authentic witness on a pedestal without verifying his or her claims through other sources.[180] One movement publication depicted comic drawings that mocked the workshoppers' fascination with working-class living conditions (Figure 4.9).

While the ground covered by the activists brought much genuinely new material into focus, they were also at times overly captivated by the life of the "little guy," as evident in the following passage:

> Mostly unexplored territories came into view as part of this "journey of discovery into our own people [Volk]." How did they dress, eat, and make love? ... Now [the historians] no longer shirked from descending into the depths of everyday habits and practices. Province and village, neighborhood

---

[174] Böge, 'Zur Einleitung', Zimmermann, 'Haben Geschichtswerkstätten Zukunft?', 'Die Geschichtswerkstatt e.V. ' pp. 3–6.

[175] *Geschichtswerkstatt* 7, September 1985 p. 43.   [176] Jaspert, 'Vorwort.'

[177] www.geschichtswerkstatt-barmbek.de/Werkstatt.htm.

[178] Kinter, Kock, and Thiele, *Spuren suchen* p.49.   [179] Szodrzynski, 'Einleitung.'

[180] Heimann, 'Wie der Popanz "Zeitzeuge."'

Figure 4.9. "How do you feel in such organically grown structures?"[181]

and street, company and workshop, kitchen and launderette, schnapps casino and county fair – these were the locations that were no longer safe from curiosity.[182]

Wulf Kansteiner argues that "some everyday history projects glorified modest resistance efforts. On other occasions, the search for identity and role models led to valorizations of stories and artifacts from the past without providing any critical conceptual framework to explain their significance (or insignificance)."[183] The Movement's objective of evoking *Betroffenheit* or empathy with historical actors stood in direct

---

[181] VSA: Verlag Hamburg, original drawn by Till Schröder, printed in Kinter, Kock, and Thiele, *Spuren suchen* p. 48.
[182] Ullrich, 'Vorwort' p. 7.   [183] Kansteiner, 'Losing the War' pp. 122–123.

contradiction to the idea of an objective historiography and was therefore strongly criticized by academic historians.[184] At times, their distaste for the activists was expressed in quite polemical terms.

Mainstreaming Movement Memory

The History Movement presented its actions in terms of the need to engage the past in order to shape a more democratic future and to seize definitional power over memory from the conservative mainstream. In order to democratize society from below, memory work had to be undertaken in particular ways: the focus was on everyday life, ordinary people, and an empathetic understanding of historical decision-making. The value of historical research and representation was evaluated chiefly on the basis of its ability to call into question contemporary power relations. As one handbook put it: "Because a representation of history that is directed against the ideological scaffolding of societal power structures – what is it worth, if in the process of investigating such power structures, similar modes of action creep back in?"[185]

In fact, power mechanism of the mainstream did make their way into the History Movement. With the booming interest in history in German society, the success of the Movement in influencing memory politics, and an increasingly responsive academia, government, and media, activists gradually realized that they were no longer "the opposition." Writing in *Geschichtswerkstatt*, two activists saw the "danger that the history workshop movement morphs into an executor of the history-crazed Zeitgeist."[186] For the self-image of the Movement, this was extremely difficult to swallow, because its passion and motivation was derived precisely from its antiestablishment identity. The public interest in history and the achievements of the workshops were a double-edged sword: their brand of memory work had become influential, but success carried with it the danger of "corruption."

For the cohesion and motivation of the Movement, its success in initiating memorials and influencing official institutions was a problem. As Detlef Siegfried contends, "When previously marginal topics moved to the center of public debate, they unfortunately 'no longer had avant garde character;' when workshops were supported by public monies, they were no longer autonomous; when members of history workshops made a name for themselves as historians, they were part of the

---

[184] von Saldern, 'Stadtgedächtnis und Geschichtswerkstätten' p. 59.
[185] Kinter, Kock, and Thiele, *Spuren suchen* p. 34.
[186] Ulmer and Weber *Geschichtswerkstatt*, August 18, 1989.

establishment."[187] Key questions caused conflicts among activists: How to achieve a high quality of historical work while still maintaining a grassroots identity? How to engage with the state without being co-opted by it? These concerns had been present from the outset of the Movement, but became more acute when initial enthusiasm had waned and the initiatives were faced with the need to justify and shape their own existence.

One persistent conflict, consequently, revolved around the need for professionalization, which some members of the Movement promoted while others rejected it as selling-out. The disagreement derived from the stated goal of the History Movement to practice "history from below." While participants certainly tried to attract nonacademics to their projects, their success was limited[188] and so the contention was less between academics and "ordinary people" than between those who had academic aspirations and those who were more inclined to work in cultural institutions or politics.[189] Personal rivalries no doubt played a role as well. According to Andreas Ludwig, the professionals quickly had the upper hand,[190] though the quarrel simmered on until the early 1990s. Emblematic of this larger conflict was the struggle for control over the Movement's journal *Geschichtswerkstatt*, which ultimately resulted in the creation of *WerkstattGeschichte* by the professionalist faction including Thomas Lindenberger, Peter Schöttler, Eva Brücker, Michael Wildt and others. *Geschichtswerkstatt* remained an organ of the Movement for a while longer, before being discontinued as the Movement declined.[191]

Those who denounced the drive for higher theoretical and methodological standards argued that such a development would further widen the gap between researchers and population, decrease the openness of projects, and endanger the autonomy of the workshops. They saw the danger of a "creeping integration into bourgeois culture"[192] and the transformation of the history workshop into a *Kaderschmiede* [cadre training unit][193] for the historical profession. Professionalism was suspect by nature because of its association with the mainstream institutional and

---

[187] Siegfried, 'Subversiver Alltag' pp. 104–105.   [188] See Interviews, Gisela Wenzel.
[189] 'Protokoll des Treffens am 7.7.1990 in Essen' *Geschichtswerkstatt*, July 21, 1990, See Interviews, Thomas Lindenberger.
[190] See Interviews, Andreas Ludwig.
[191] The *Zeitschriftenstreit* (journal dispute) has received quite a bit of attention: See Interviews, Thomas Lindenberger, Eva Brücker; *Berliner Geschichtswerkstatt e.V. Rundbrief* 2/1992 Frei, 'Die Geschichtswerkstätten in der Krise', '"Barfuß-Historiker" ohne Boden,' Hüttner, *Archive von unten*, Wildt, 'WerkstattGeschichte,' Wildt, 'Die große Geschichtswerkstattschlacht.'
[192] *Geschichtswerkstatt* 13, September 1987 p. 76.
[193] Müller, 'Zur Beteiligung der BGW.'

political culture that stood in contradistinction to the Movement's culture of spontaneity and antielitism. The other side contended that the improvement of historical research, theoretical sophistication, and representation in the form of exhibitions was indispensable. At a time when history workshops were becoming increasingly influential in the realms of education, memorial institutions, and local cultural offerings, they could no longer pretend that only their own stringent principles mattered.

At the local level, the dilemma of professionalism and a rising demand for historical "products" often caused bitter disagreements among the activists or forced them to take on roles with which they were not entirely comfortable. Reinhold Forster, of the *Geschichtswerkstatt Augsburg,* reports that, after a decline in activist participation, the workshop sought more city funding and consciously professionalized. This necessitated devoting more time and energy to lobbying, to the detriment of substantive historical work which in turn caused conflicts between "quasi-professionals" (those unpaid activists who devoted most of their time to the project) and participants who were less involved but nevertheless wanted a say in how the workshop was run. By the time a particular large project was completed, the activists had become estranged and somewhat discredited in the eyes of the city as a partner.[194] When the *Geschichtswerkstatt Augsburg* was asked to examine the history of now-vacant US barracks, it had to essentially operate as a subcontractor and distribute work to external individuals or organizations. Problems ensued: unpaid activists had to guide and oversee paid employees and when these did not meet standards, the activists themselves had to complete the work. "Because in the end, the *Geschichtswerkstatt* as an association was the guarantor of the reliability and quality of the expertise."[195] Essentially, the Geschichtswerkstatt brand needed to be protected.

The other pressing problem experienced by the workshops was that of how to handle their relationship with state actors and whether to regard state support negatively as cooptation or positively as cooperation. This tension and the complex agency of civil society groups in memory politics are at the center of this book. The History Movement consistently sought both to resist the state and also win its approval through its practice of memory politics. This dilemma of memory formation and democratic praxis was on frequent display in the everyday life of memory activists in the 1980s and 1990s.

For example, an internal conflict in the *Geschichtswerkstatt e. V.* during the discussion about the German Historical Museum (DHM) is illustrative: despite the resolution passed against the museum, the member

---

[194] Forster, 'Antworten lesender Augsburger' p. 44.   [195] Ibid. p. 45.

organization *Arbeitskreis Regionalgeschichte Bodensee* in Konstanz wanted to organize a seminar together with DHM staff in 1989. Since the federal executive committee had categorically rejected the museum, it was argued that its members should not legitimate the DHM by cooperating with it. The action of the Konstanz *Arbeitskreis* thus violated stated principle and was denounced. This episode shows that at this point, the Movement was in the midst of internal conflict over how to maintain their oppositional stance and identity in the face of more frequent cooperation with the authorities. This dilemma had arisen even in the early 1980s, but became much more pressing during the latter part of the decade when the growing popularity of the workshops' approach to history made more state cooperation and funding available.

The specter of state cooptation was raised regularly when funding from the state was being sought or received. The *Geschichtswerkstättler* did not come easily to accepting government financing, even in the limited form of staff subsidies (ABM). The idea of taking money from the state rattled the core of the activists' identity as an antiestablishment movement that was "dangerous" to the dominant version of history. As Bernhard Müller noted in reference to the Berlin history workshop's participation in Berlin's 750th Anniversary, though the ABM positions were helpful, they meant implicitly accepting the state's objectionable policy on unemployment. Members were afraid of (self-)censorship and of losing their critical edge through outside funding.[196] On the other hand, the *Geschichtswerkstatt e.V.*, as early as 1984, noted its financial limitations and began considering how to expand the budget by increasing membership dues, fundraising, or asking the federal government for support.[197] Some activists believed that, though the state's policy of celebrating grand anniversaries and museums was to be rejected, only the participation in such projects "promises a large gulp from the bottle of state subsidies."[198] For Andreas Ludwig, the resolution of this *Staatsknete-Debatte* (state dough debate) was relatively straight-forward: "of course we should take money from the state – what we are doing is a public responsibility, so in a way we saw ourselves as the rightful recipients of taxes."[199]

An alternative to governmental funding was the creation of a for-profit branch of history workshops,[200] offering guided tours or contracting out historical research expertise. Such solutions were common, but also caused rifts among Movement adherents about the upholding of original principles and the adequate use of profits. Furthermore, it subjected the

---

[196] Müller, 'Zur Beteiligung der BGW.'   [197] *Geschichtswerkstatt* 4, August 1984.
[198] *Geschichtswerkstatt* 14, April 1988, pp. 8–9.   [199] See Interviews, Andreas Ludwig.
[200] Wildt, 'WerkstattGeschichte' p. 36.

initiatives to more direct competition from other historical service providers and hence pressure to professionalize. In any case, both efforts to secure funding and the debates that ensued within the History Movement used up much energy and contributed to the Movement's decline.

Activists in the History Movement – just like those of the Memorial Site Movement – meanwhile became part of the state-funded institutions that they had criticized and helped to transform. The History Movement's approach, including the focus on the "microstructures" of historical circumstances, the use of oral histories, the decentralized and antimonumental nature of memorials, has been mainstreamed (see Chapter 5). History Movement principles have been adopted by research institutes and memorial institutions in large part because many former workshoppers have made "the long march through the institutions:" they are today staff members of memory foundations, professors, and even museum directors. In other words, "the new history culture has shifted from a critical minority position on the fringes to the center of society."[201]

The individual professional and collective institutional successes of the History Movement paradoxically contributed to its decline, but so did the larger circumstances. The problems of state cooptation and professionalization came to a head right around the time that the discourse about history and memory underwent a shift more generally due to the end of the Cold War. A "new past" (the GDR) was placed on the mnemonic agenda. In Berlin in particular, the political and institutional arena of operations for the initiatives changed suddenly, requiring them (and everyone else) to find their footing. In the immediate aftermath of the opening of the Wall, there were some attempts to cooperate with East German colleagues, as well as some projects about GDR history. These, however, were few and far between. The Movement was unable to discover a new innovative focus that could have sustained its identity and mobilizing power.

By the early 1990s, the history workshops were no longer radical in either their message or their methodology, although the activists' oppositional self-image lasted longer. Nevertheless, many history workshops remain operative to this day and some continue to play important roles in their local contexts. These organizations, however, no longer make up a larger social movement, nor do they all cultivate the traditions and memory of the History Movement.[202] They have become part of a larger field of organizations that conduct memory work.

[201] Wenzel, "'Grabe, wo du stehst.'"
[202] In a 2009 promotional film on the Hamburg history workshops, the Movement is not referenced at all. www.stiftung-hamburger-geschichtswerkstaetten.de/.

Indeed, many new history initiatives were founded since 1990 – some citing their debt to the Movement explicitly. For example the History Workshop Oberhausen was founded in 1994, but notes on its website that it was inspired by the "history workshop movement of the Eighties" to organize publications, exhibitions, and events to encourage debates about forgotten history. This workshop's topics include women's, Jewish, and working class history.[203] Also founded in 1994, the *Frauengeschichtswerkstatt* (Women's History Workshop) in Memmingen is devoted particularly to researching the history of Jewish women in that town.[204] The History Workshop in Bochum was founded in late 2007, but is concerned specifically with the history of new social movements during the 1970s and 1980s.[205]

Today, the label "history workshop" has been appropriated by various kinds of actors: academics, local authorities, unions, and participants in classes at adult education centers (*Volkshochschulen*). Original Movement members regard this dissemination of their approach with a mixture of amused skepticism and pride, though Geschichtswerkstatt no longer always denotes critical memory work.[206] Some newer history workshops focus on local history without the critical lens characteristic of the History Movement, though they often adopt the principles of oral history and *Alltagsgeschichte*. For example, the History Workshop Neuhausen was founded in 1992 and simply states as its mission to research the history of the Munich neighborhoods Neuhausen, Nymphenburg, and Gern and to enable contacts between people interested in history.[207] Similar uncritical approaches are found in the Hachenburg workshop (founded 2008).[208] Other initiatives were founded in the mid-1990s in eastern Germany. The History Workshop Rostock seeks to provide a link between academic research and lay historians.[209] The workshop in Jena is specifically concerned with working through the history of the GDR dictatorship and resistance to it. In this instance, the critical impulse of the History Movement may have been applied to the examination of the GDR past.[210] Lindenberger believes that members of the GDR opposition in particular were well positioned to understand and adopt History Movement principles and techniques because dissident practice bore

---

[203] www.geschichtswerkstatt-oberhausen.de/default.asp?nc=535&id=2.
[204] Hinske-Gengnagel, 'Die eigene Vergangenheit finden.'
[205] www.bo-alternativ.de/geschichtswerkstatt/.
[206] See Interviews, Thomas Lindenberger.
[207] www.geschichtswerkstatt-neuhausen.de/.
[208] www.geschichtswerkstatt-hachenburg.de/.
[209] www.geschichtswerkstatt-rostock.de/seiten/start.php.
[210] www.geschichtswerkstatt-jena.de/index.php?id=02.

a kind of family resemblance with the political culture of the West German workshops.[211]

Those older workshops that were part of the original Movement have undergone a transformation. Though the topics covered may not have changed dramatically, the contentious internal debates during the 1980s effectively led most workshops to become more professionalized, accept state funding, and even become providers of historical "services" or subcontractors of a sort. Joachim Szodrzynski, a member of a pioneer workshop in Hamburg, argues that, "in its quotidian practice, the *Galerie Morgenland* today understands itself as a provider and multiplier of materials and research results, which can be utilized by interested persons inside and outside the neighborhood in the absence of bureaucratic hurdles or institutional barriers."[212] The history workshop in Barmbek "has long been seen and used as a service entity. Consultancy and information, archive use, production of photographs, lectures or guided tours to order – all this can be summed up under the heading 'history service.'"[213] Many other workshops advertise their service component on the websites or function as administrative umbrellas for projects funded by local authorities, as is the case for the Berlin History Workshop.[214] Thus, while the *network* of history workshops has disintegrated and the contacts among activists in various cities have dried up, most individual workshops remain, usually with reduced membership, and continue their work. Nevertheless, the faithful continue to regard their work as indispensable to democratic political culture and have not lost their identity as critical memory "Movement."[215]

The History Movement – through both its painstaking memory work and its protest activity – profoundly altered the ways in which the past was confronted in West Germany. This fact is broadly acknowledged – for instance, the *Frankfurter Rundschau* in 1992 noted the Movement's achievement of "working through the legacy of fascism right down to the smallest neighborhood."[216] More broadly, Detlef Siegfried contends that the history workshops had "massively participated in the discourse of historical self-assurance of society; in other words had communicated history – into the depths of society, as part of a larger nonparliamentary movement, that was formative for the political culture of the Federal Republic."[217]

---

[211] See Interviews, Thomas Lindenberger.   [212] Szodrzynski, 'Altern in Würde' p. 251.

[213] www.geschichtswerkstatt-barmbek.de/Geschichte.htm.

[214] Wüstenberg, 'Vom alternativen Laden zum Dienstleistungsbetrieb'

[215] See Interviews, Jürgen Karwelat, Andreas Bräutigam and Sonja Miltenberger.

[216] '"Barfuß-Historiker" ohne Boden', '"Barfuß-Historiker" ohne Boden.'

[217] Siegfried, 'Subversiver Alltag' p. 103.

Despite the Movement's decline since the 1990s and the difficulty of recruiting new, younger activists,[218] its influence continues to be felt in memorial institutions throughout the Federal Republic. Because of this, the processes and mnemonic principles that developed through civic engagement since the 1980s must be taken into consideration by new generations of activists, including those seeking to commemorate political repression in the GDR (Chapter 6). The study of the History Movement shows how grassroots actors have taken advantage of the new political opportunities of the 1980s and have consequently transformed memory policies and cultures. The *Geschichtsbewegung* shared many of its conditions for success, its motivations, and even its participants with its sister movement, the *Gedenkstättenbewegung*. In the next chapter, I analyze the memorial aesthetic espoused by these two Movements in order to underline their lasting impact on the German landscape of remembrance.

---

[218] See Interviews, Susanne Lohmeyer.

5 Memorial Aesthetics and the Memory Movements of the 1980s

Despite its relatively short period of existence at the end of the Second World War, the concentration camp Ahlem in Hanover, a satellite camp of the Neuengamme camp, was a place of unimaginable suffering. Ahlem was created in late 1944 and housed a total of 1,500 inmates until the end of the war, before being liberated by American troops, the young Henry Kissinger among them. The prisoners, mostly Polish Jews, were forced to work in cold and wet conditions and under constant threat of violence, to prepare an asphalt mine for industrial use. Over half of them did not survive.[1] Other than a small memorial plaque that had been put up after the war, the Ahlem concentration camp had been mostly forgotten until a local resident issued a call for remembrance in 1979. Nothing much changed until the mid-1980s, when the local chapter of the *Vereinigung der Verfolgten des Naziregimes/Bund der Antifaschisten* (Union of the Persecuted of the Nazi Regime/Association of Antifascists – VVN/BdA) put up a wooden marker and the local Protestant church began holding regular remembrance services. In the wake of this increased public attention, a group of local residents founded the *Arbeitskreis Bürger gestalten ein Mahnmal* (Working Group Citizens Design a Memorial) in early 1987.

From the outset, the goal was an open-ended and participatory process leading to a monument that would commemorate the suffering at Ahlem.[2] Supported by the city administration, a core group of citizens met once or twice a week for seven years.[3] They began by holding public seminars on the history of the site and undertaking visits to other concentration camps. They consulted with artists, students, memorial activists from elsewhere, and some survivors of the Ahlem camp. They rejected initial figurative memorial proposals in favor of a design that focused on emotional experience and recalled prisoners' work in the asphalt mine. Then they methodically experimented with different materials during art workshops that

[1] www.erinnerungundzukunft.de/?id=91.
[2] Anschütz and Heike, *"Wir wollten Gefühle sichtbar werden lassen"* pp. 64–65; 'Das Interesse für das Projekt.'
[3] Anschütz and Heike, *"Wir wollten Gefühle sichtbar werden lassen"* p. 73

Figure 5.1. Members of *Bürger gestalten ein Mahnmal* work on asphalt panels for the memorial in Hanover-Ahlem in 1988.[4]

included art students and complete novices. They debated their reactions to both historical research and artistic expression.

Through heated discussions, they eventually settled on a memorial design and then decided on how to place it in the landscape after visiting the site as a group. They organized a space for artistic production and together produced the 750 asphalt panels (Figure 5.1) that are a central component of the memorial. They guided the construction of the memorial and organized its inauguration in February 1994. They continue to maintain it and hold educational events to this day. In 2005, for example, the association together with a local school put together a book of memory for the victims of Ahlem, copies of which have been donated to Yad Vashem, the US Holocaust Memorial Museum, and the Berlin Jewish Museum.[5] *Bürger gestalten ein Mahnmal* was hailed by the mayor of Hanover as "a formidable example of civic engagement, for engagement for the strengthening of democracy."[6] Group participants spoke of the emotional meaning the memorial design process had for their own

[4] Ruth Gröne.
[5] Renate Bauschke, See Interviews, email communication September 1, 2016.
[6] Anschütz and Heike, *"Wir wollten Gefühle sichtbar werden lassen"* p. 79.

confrontation with the Holocaust and of the pride they felt for having been part of it.

The Ahlem concentration camp memorial is unusual because a citizens' initiative drove and even controlled every step on the path to memorial creation – including the artistic ones. However, the ideas put forward in this project are emblematic of the way in which the Memorial Site and History Movements have conceived of the role of memorials, both in terms of the process that led to its inauguration and its aesthetic design. To be sure, these Movements were not alone in advocating for a different kind of public memory, one that was decentralized, authentic, self-reflective, and differentiated. Individual artists (sometimes active within these Movements) were at the forefront of arguing for a novel approach to commemoration and some local governments were supportive of new design ideas. In this chapter, I explain how those grassroots activists of the 1980s and 1990s who sought to transform German society's confrontation with the Nazi past took advantage of and drove forward this set of important aesthetic principles. And I argue that they have since become so widely applied and accepted that they have profoundly altered the German memorial landscape.

The monument as an aesthetic form has existed since antiquity, but has become especially relevant since the nineteenth century when the state sought to integrate the rising bourgeoisie through the fostering of national identity. Various regimes of the twentieth century appropriated the memorial as a way to unite disparate groups and classes behind state-supporting ideas and war efforts. Through this usage, the memorial came to be established (and mistrusted) as an undemocratic device, as an instrument of the powerful and particularly of the state. In this sense, as Christoph Heinrich notes "the opposition, as long as it is the opposition, does not build memorials."[7] The political purpose of memorials is reflected in their monumental aesthetics: they are meant to appear large, imposing, and powerful in design and establish a vision of permanent political order. The materials are selected accordingly: stone and bronze dominate while timber and paint are rare. The repertoire of forms is also usually monumental, with large, simple, and symmetrical designs being the norm. The goal of such memorials was to fixate a particular interpretation of the past and harness its meaning for the political community of the future.[8]

With the cataclysms of the two world wars, this function of the monument was gradually called into question, though design ideas did not undergo radical changes until later. Traditional monuments to heroes

---

[7] Heinrich, *Strategien des Erinnerns* p. 12.   [8] Ibid.

or grand feats were built more rarely. In the immediate aftermath of the Second World War, most German memorials focused on remembering and honoring the dead – with the causes of their demise referred to only indirectly as "injustice," "rule of terror," or "dark times."[9] At the center of such a *"Mahnmal"* (memorial that warns or admonishes), were usually victims of war, broadly understood to include all Germans. Aesthetically, these memorials frequently employed Christian iconography or universal figures of human suffering and mourning or replicated traditional war memorials, using such forms as obelisks, reliefs, or gravestones.[10] Accordingly, these sites were often located away from public view – in cemeteries, rather than public squares. Explicit memorials for Holocaust victims were rare and erected almost exclusively by the victims themselves during this time,[11] but even these used similar design forms. Meanwhile, surviving synagogues and sites of Nazi terror were rotting or even being torn down.[12]

As the reverence for German "victims" became politically problematic in the 1960s and 1970s, and the Holocaust was discussed more, two developments occurred. First, public remembrance began to focus primarily on Jewish victims. Yet the causes of their deaths and the identity of the perpetrators still remained obscure in the monuments. The iconography of Holocaust memorials of the time was quite conventional, employing many of the same forms and materials as earlier war monuments. These sites were mostly initiated by non-Jews (a fact betrayed by the inexpert and sometimes insensitive use of Jewish symbols).[13]

Second, there was criticism of the memorial as such, questioning whether it could be an acceptable form of portraying the past for collective identification. This was a discussion taking place in the international scene of art and design. For instance, Claes Oldenburg's sculpture of a clothes pin fourteen meters in height seemed to ridicule the whole idea of monumental objects in public space.[14] In West Germany, the Nazi obsession with monumental architecture and sculpture made such critiques of monumentality all the more resonant. In leftist circles, the notion was linked with a basic distrust of the state. The monument was rejected because it suggested a "harmony between the governing and

---

[9] Haß, 'Mahnmaltexte 1945 bis 1988.'
[10] Hausmann, *Duell mit der Verdrängung?*, Heinrich, *Strategien des Erinnerns*, Haß, 'Mahnmaltexte 1945 bis 1988.'
[11] Marcuse, Schimmelfennig, and Spielmann, *Steine des Anstoßes.*
[12] Hausmann, *Duell mit der Verdrängung?*
[13] Haß, 'Mahnmaltexte 1945 bis 1988', Hausmann, *Duell mit der Verdrängung?*
[14] Heinrich, *Strategien des Erinnerns* p. 20.

governed"[15] that had become unacceptable in the wake of popularly supported fascism. During this time then, public and physical memorialization did not seem the appropriate form of social action to confront the past.

The state-driven history politics of the 1980s that was manifested in the "museum-boom" were therefore met with much suspicion on the left. At the time, Harold Marcuse wrote that "since memorials mainly epitomize ruling societal norms, we commemorate in the Federal Republic of Germany mainly acts of bourgeois and military resistance, soldiers and bombing victims. This remembrance corresponds to the self-image of the Federal Republic."[16] The Memorial Site and History Movements, instead of rejecting the memorial outright, made this distrust fruitful by seeking to recast the memorial as an impulse for critical debate. In other words, rather than understanding a monument as the attempt to crystallize an interpretation of the past for the collective, it was to evoke a process of communication between memory and the local public, as well as amongst visitors. A memorial should provoke, shock, call into question established wisdom, and change the urban environment.[17]

Memorial Principles of the 1980s Memory Movements

Both the Memorial Site and the History Movements were locally grounded and made up of a diverse set of initiatives. Their publications do not succinctly state specific memorial principles common to all groups in one or both Movements. Furthermore, the dominant ideas that animated memorial projects were popular among leftist activists more broadly and not exclusive to the Movements. However, the concept of using memorials as a form of political confrontation is a clear theme in the monuments that emerged out of their civic actions. In hindsight at least, there appears to be a considerable level of consistency in the Movement aesthetic of the 1980s. This aesthetic includes a decentralized structure for the memory landscape; an emphasis on authenticity; the rejection of monumentality; and specificity and diversity in the content of commemoration.

A Decentralized Landscape

The Memorial Site and History Movements were instrumental not only in rethinking the concept of the individual memorial, but in offering a new

---

[15] Ibid. p. 19.   [16] Marcuse, Schimmelfennig, and Spielmann, *Steine des Anstoßes* p. 4.
[17] Heinrich, *Strategien des Erinnerns* p. 163.

perspective on how memory is situated in urban and rural environments and what should be viewed as part of the memory landscape. Rudy Koshar argues that,

> Citizens' initiatives, labor unions and the SPD, and history workshops not only "produced" new monuments, rather they transformed the meaning of the memory landscape to include a whole new array of objects. Because many groups wanted to explore what was close to home or what could be understood "from below" rather than from the point of view of the powerful, a new array of buildings, streets, and spaces came into view as the successful framing strategy took hold ... The memory landscape was no longer defined by a cluster of cathedrals, castles, and city halls, but was a wider and more complex assemblage of historical traces scattered throughout a city, village, or natural setting.[18]

The idea of "decentralized" memorials united several meanings. As Koshar indicates, memorial spaces were reconceived and redistributed across an existing (but socially constructed) historical topography – emerging from historical events, rather than artificially created in centrally located squares. Commemoration was to be determined by the contention over the past, rather than by what could unite the community or be useful to the state. Further, memory was to be found where life took place, in everyday spaces, so that it could be experienced as part of life, rather than in specialized (and sometimes hard-to-find) locations. Finally, memorials were ideally to be initiated from the midst of society – from below – rather than mandated from above by a central authority. All of these ideas were conceived in contradistinction to the mainstream memory politics of the 1980s, and even more so in opposition to the traditional purposes of a memorial. Christine Fischer-Defoy, one of the key leaders of the Active Museum, argued in the early 1990s that the many plaques that one can see on a stroll through Berlin are the counterparts to the monumental *Neue Wache* memorial, which had just been inaugurated. She called memorial plaques "footnotes to history," that allow us to see individuality, as opposed to a central memorial in which all this is lost. She advocated *Denkorte* (locations for thinking) as opposed to *Gedenkzentralen* (centers for remembrance).[19] These ideas are reflected both in the creation process and the design of the majority of monuments that resulted from civic initiatives.

From 1985 to 1988, a West Berlin bank sponsored a program (*Berliner Gedenktafelprogramm*) to put up a total of 211 memorial plaques recalling the lives of figures from different periods of history. They were uniformly designed and made of white porcelain. A commission decided who was to

---

[18] Koshar, *From monuments to traces* p. 239.
[19] Christine Fischer-Defoy in Schönfeld, *Gedenktafeln in West-Berlin.*

be included.[20] There were protests against this centrally controlled process, and several alternative initiatives for plaques were started partly in response. The most comprehensive was the *Kreuzberg antifaschistisches Gedenktafelprogramm* (Antifascist Commemorative Plaque Program), which sought to commemorate exclusively victims of Nazi persecution and resisters. For each plaque, a different artist was commissioned in order to underline the individuality of the victims as well as the rich cultural life that had been destroyed by the Nazis. For the activists, the memorial itself was only the end point of a "decentralized memory process" which integrated local residents, property owners, and memorial initiators and sought to make commemoration into a more lasting societal experience.[21]

Opposition to existing memorial plans also triggered action by the Bavarian history workshop *Interessengemeinschaft Geschichte Geretsried*. In 1988, the group discovered a report during archival work, indicating that Geretsried had been on the route of a death march from the Dachau concentration camp in April 1945 – something the town had thus far denied.[22] The workshop conducted intensive research, published documentation, and sought to place markers along the route of the death march. The mayor of Geretsried rejected the idea, arguing that expellees had played a more important role in the town, and then proposed a joint memorial chapel for expellees and victims of the death march. Rejecting such indiscriminate commemoration, the *Interessengemeinschaft* (with the support of the Green Party) persuaded the local parliament to provide forty thousand deutsche marks for the creation of the memorial, which was inaugurated in November of 1992.[23]

The memorial surrounding the Bayrischer Platz in Berlin-Schöneberg is another good example of the idea of decentralized memory. Initiated by the Berlin History Workshop, conceived by artists Renata Stih and Frieder Schnock, and guided to completion by the local cultural administration, this memorial is composed of about eighty panels attached to street signs. One side of each panel shows the date and text of a law disenfranchising and endangering the local Jewish population in the 1930s and 1940s (as in Figure 5.2). On the other side is a pictogram that relates to the text as well as to the placement of the panel. In this way, each image and regulation is set in context with today's everyday life. The central square, which had originally been intended as the site of (a more traditional) memorial, holds only maps of 1933 and 1993,

[20] Jordan, *Structures of Memory* p. 46, Schönfeld, *Gedenktafeln in West-Berlin.*
[21] Schönfeld, *Gedenktafeln in West-Berlin* p. 22.
[22] Wagner, 'Mahnmal für Todesmarsch aufgestellt.'
[23] Ibid., www.a-wagner-online.de/todesmarsch/.

Figure 5.2. One of the signs of the Memorial around Bayrischer Platz in Berlin: "Postal workers married to Jewish women are forced into retirement, 8 June 1937."[24]

indicating the location of the panels. These maps were also distributed on the street and placed in local mailboxes. The intention of the artists was to link the commemoration of life, in what had been a vibrant neighborhood formerly referred to as "Jewish Switzerland," to current life and so make memory more real to residents and visitors alike.[25]

The most well-known and by now most extensive decentralized memorial is the *Stolpersteine* (stumbling blocks). This memorial is composed of thousands of brass-plated blocks in over five hundred towns in Germany and elsewhere placed on sidewalks in front of private homes and business. Each block bears the name and states the fate of a victim of Nazism that once lived at that address. This simple and powerful concept distributes the monument to the victims of the Holocaust into the streets of everyday life in which the crimes were committed. Gunter Demnig, the artist behind the project, was active in the peace movement of the 1970s and

---

[24] Jenny Wüstenberg, 2006.
[25] See Interviews, Renata Stih and Frieder Schnock, and Bodo Förster.

1980s. In 1993, he made a public impression by marking the path of deportation of Sinti and Roma in Cologne with a self-built marking device.[26]

Shortly thereafter, Demnig began making the stumbling blocks, recalling each individual Holocaust victim with an individual memorial in their former neighborhoods. Each stone is sponsored by a different group that tries to unearth as much information as possible about the life of the person memorialized. The findings are usually published in some form and presented at the memorial inauguration ceremony.[27] While the stumbling block project took off after the heyday of the Memorial Site and History Movements, it is clearly conceived in the spirit of locating memory in everyday life and recognizing the individuality of victims as opposed to commemorating "in bulk." These small memorials create a profound impression in formerly Jewish neighborhoods where nearly every street has a reminder of the local realities of the Nazi past. History workshops and other civic groups continue to be frequent initiators of individual stones and of coordinating efforts in cities where stumbling blocks are in high demand (see Figure 5.3).[28]

Today, the decentralized nature of Germany's memory landscape is no longer a subject of struggle on the part of grassroots initiatives. On the contrary, it has found its place alongside the large representative monuments (such as the Memorial to the Murdered Jews of Europe), historical icons (such as the Brandenburg Gate), and museums (such as the German Historical Museum) as a key defining feature of the state's approach to the past. State representatives emphasize the uniqueness and democratic credentials of this landscape. Gabriele Camphausen, an official in the federal agency overseeing the Stasi files, put it like this:

> In general, we in the Federal Republic do not have a centrally organized memory culture, but a de-centrally grown one. Because of this we also have a high degree of local, regional grounding. The "working through" of history is usually bound to very concrete historical sites [Schauplätze]. I believe that this is a very important approach: this way, one can show "grand" history in the "small" ..., one can show the historical framework at a concrete historical location, with the help of concrete historical events, with concrete biographies ... Of course Berlin, as the capital of the "Reich," and as the current capital, inevitably has a special collection of important historical places and therefore we clearly have concentration of "memory work" in this city. But I think that, when you look at the other Länder, at the regions – the large number of Gedenkstätten, of initiatives, of documentation

---

[26] Horst, 'Stolpersteine – auch in Bielefeld' p.260, brochure 'Ein Strich durchs Vergessen' December 1996.

[27] Neue Gesellschaft für Bildende Kunst e.V., 'Stolpersteine'; Redies, 'Zehn Jahre Stolpersteine'; Lohmeyer, 'Stolpersteine in Hamburg-Eimsbüttel.'

[28] See Interviews, Edeltraut Frankenstein, Jupp Klegraf, Susanne Lohmeyer.

Figure 5.3. A Stolperstein before its placement in the offices of the Berlin citizens' initiative *Bürgerverein Luisenstadt e. V.*[29]

sites – this number shows clearly how branched out and how grounded our memory culture is.[30]

Similarly, Uwe Neumärker, the Managing Director of the federal foundation that runs the (very much central) Memorial to the Murdered Jews of Europe argues that

> this country has an aversion against central spaces or "wreath-dumping-locations" [*Kranzabwurfstellen*]. There seems to be a sensibility and an understanding at the state level [*Staatsverständnis*] that rejects hegemonialization . . .. This was different in the GDR, and this is different in the United States, France, Russia. Almost all countries seem to work differently in this regard.[31]

Authenticity

The important concept of authenticity in memorial aesthetics is closely connected to the Memorial Site and History Movements' insistence on

[29] Jenny Wüstenberg, 2005.   [30] See Interviews, Gabriele Camphausen.
[31] See Interviews, Uwe Neumärker.

finding the physical evidence of what is left of local history. The monuments therefore reflect the high value placed on undergoing a collective process of discovery and then securing the traces of history (*Spurensuche* and *Spurensicherung*). For Koshar, "the paradigmatic expression of the German memory landscape was now a topography of traces."[32] Another element that informed the ideal of authenticity was the connection between memory and the special resonance of grounding memorials in the spaces of history. This meant not only locating a memorial at a site of an historical event but also relating the design to that location aesthetically, rather than merely placing a "plop-sculpture" that could stand anywhere without drastically altering its meaning.[33]

The notion of the memory landscape as a "topography of traces" implies that memory is "naturally" present in that environment and that it needs to be made visible to become part of the culture of remembrance. However, the authenticity of a site is socially constructed. As Jennifer Jordan argues, "people may feel a chill down the back of their necks, or deeply saddened by a given site, but ... this troubling atmosphere or powerful feeling frequently emanates, not from the site itself, but from the social activity poured into the place and reminding those of us with no firsthand experience of the events what exactly happened here."[34] Most "authentic" locations – that is, places where a potentially meaningful historical event occurred – never actually become memorials.[35] The 1980s Movements worked hard to stress authenticity as an important principle of memorialization – by choosing appropriate sites for their memorial markers, by promoting the idea of their authenticity, and by pushing to highlight any extant traces of the past (however slight). Authenticity was regarded as crucial not only to the effect of a site on its audience, but also on the long-term effect of memory on society. "Because a political culture that is not anchored in every individual place is in the long run not sufficiently 'grounded' and hence structurally endangered. The history workshops contributed to this grounding in the form of direct-democratic [*basisdemokratischer*] public history."[36]

According to Brigitte Hausmann's survey, 70 percent of memorials inaugurated during the 1980s mark "authentic" places of historical events, such as camps, residences of persecuted persons, or synagogues.[37] By this measure, most of the memorials I discussed in the previous section qualify as authentic. There are others, however, in which authentic traces are more evident or where, when such traces have been

---

[32] Koshar, *From monuments to traces* p. 228.   [33] Heinrich, *Strategien des Erinnerns* p. 21.
[34] Jordan, *Structures of Memory* p. 175.   [35] Ibid. p. 15.
[36] von Saldern, 'Stadtgedächtnis und Geschichtswerkstätten' p. 68.
[37] Hausmann, *Duell mit der Verdrängung?*

slight or removed from public view, the memorial design tries to substitute for authentic traces.

The obvious locations to mention here are the former concentration camps. Many original elements were lost through postwar reuse of the camps for new kinds of prisoners, displaced persons, or expellees. Since the 1980s, the emphasis in memorials at these locations has been on preserving existing structures – but usually not rebuilding them, because that would no longer be authentic. These original elements are supplemented by straightforward historical exhibits.

The most important authentic site is arguably the Topography of Terror memorial in central Berlin, the location of the former Gestapo headquarters in addition to other administrative centers of Nazi terror. As I detailed in Chapter 3, this site was rediscovered in the late 1970s after being actively repressed since the war. In 1986, in response to the activism of the Active Museum group, the archeological remains of headquarters were unearthed, including some of the cells where Gestapo victims had languished. Integrated in these structures was an outdoor exhibit about not only the location and victims, but also crucially the perpetrators. Moreover, the exhibit addresses the history of willful forgetting of the postwar period as part of the memory of this locale. The new (and first permanent) building for the Topography was opened in May 2010 after much conflict. It is an unassuming structure set back from the outdoor exhibit that is built around the ruins of the original buildings. It is designed not to overpower the authenticity emanating from the site.

Among the numerous locations of destroyed synagogues that have been made into memorials by history initiatives since the 1980s, one is particularly illuminating. In the West Berlin district of Steglitz, the building of the former synagogue still existed adjacent to a central square. In 1987, a citizen's initiative called *Initiative Haus Wolfenstein* was formed in order to create an authentic memorial. In addition to a commemorative wall listing local victims, a "living memorial" was to be built, named after the former head of the synagogue, where public events and debates would be held, and cultural life could once again flourish. According to its long-time leader Friedrich Hossbach, this initiative was in close contact with the Berlin History Workshop and consciously followed the principles of "dig where you stand."[38] Though the building was classified and safeguarded as an historical structure, its owner could not be persuaded to turn it into a memorial. Though he had it renovated, he built a large residential building in front of it, thereby denying public access and visibility. The history initiative then shifted tactics and advocated

---

[38] See Interviews, Friedrich Hossbach

Figure 5.4. The Mirror Wall Memorial in Berlin-Steglitz.[39]

a memorial to be built on the adjacent public square. The local government, controlled by conservatives, resisted. With the help of local Social
Democrats and Greens, the activists publicized their efforts, reaching
a national and an international audience through the media. In order to
prevent more negative publicity, the Berlin authorities took over and
mandated the memorial against the opposition of the Steglitz
government.[40] In the course of a general refurbishment of the square,
the "Mirror Wall" memorial was placed in its middle (Figure 5.4).
It consists of a large wall decked out in mirrors, so that the visitor sees
herself while she reads about the history the site, as well as the names of
hundreds of Steglitz Jews that were deported.[41] Not only the mirror
effect, but also the Wall's location in the square (often in the midst of
a market) suggests the intention of placing memory in the context of real
life – while linking it to the authentic location of the synagogue close by.

A different kind of site has also become a regular tourist attraction in
Berlin: the Blindenwerkstatt Otto Weidt. This memorial is a set of rooms

[39] Jenny Wüstenberg, 2006.   [40] See Interviews, Sabine Weissler.
[41] Seferens, *Ein deutscher Denkmalstreit.*

in Berlin-Mitte where Weidt, a maker of brushes, hid and tried to save his Jewish employees, some of whom were blind. Located in what is now the tourist attraction of "Hackesche Höfe" – a series of connected buildings and courtyards in the heart of Berlin – under the GDR regime the building had become dilapidated and forgotten. Inge Deutschkron, who had been hidden by Weidt, was the lone voice calling for remembrance, but was not heard until the Wall fell. After that a group of students and artists worked with her to devise an exhibit called "Blind Trust: Hidden at Hackescher Markt, 1941–1943."[42] The popular exhibit stayed on and was taken under the auspices of the Berlin Jewish Museum. After a major refurbishment of the building – which was threatening to collapse – the site was officially reopened in 2006 and became an annex of the Memorial to German Resistance. With this institutional affiliation came an extensive research effort, examining not only the deeds of Otto Weidt and his helpers, but also of other "silent heroes" of the Nazi era.[43] Aside from the interesting story of how it became a memorial, the *Blindenwerkstatt* is a good example of the attempt to preserve an aura of authenticity. Even after the building was renovated and thus became consistent with the touristy and high-end shopping of the Hackesche Höfe, the Weidt rooms themselves were left to look old and run down, with bare floorboards and bare walls.[44] The room where one family was hidden until their betrayal remains "in its original form."[45] As Jennifer Jordan contends "one of the elements of the exhibition's longevity is its powerful claim to authenticity, to having a direct connection to compelling historical events."[46]

Authenticity has become a commonplace term in German memory discourses. Memorial officials readily stress the authenticity of sites even and especially when they resulted from state-driven efforts – such as the *Gedenkstätte Deutscher Widerstand* (Memorial to German Resistance) or the Memorial House of the Wannsee Conference.[47] The importance of this concept was apparent even in the debates surrounding the creation of a decidedly inauthentic memorial – the Memorial to the Murdered Jews of Europe. Most of the members of and sympathizers with the Memorial Site and History Movements whom I interviewed were vocal opponents of this memorial. Eberhard Diepgen, the Mayor of Berlin from 1984 to 1989 and 1991 to 2001,though usually at odds with the Movements, has adopted its emphasis on authenticity and was also strongly opposed to the Memorial to the Murdered Jews of Europe.

---

[42] Jordan, *Structures of Memory* p. 3.
[43] 'Das Versteck im Schatten der Gestapo' *Die Welt*, December 5, 2006.
[44] Jordan, *Structures of Memory*.   [45] www.museum-blindenwerkstatt.de/de/ausstellung/.
[46] Jordan, *Structures of Memory* p. 6.
[47] See Interviews, Norbert Kampe, among others.

The basic consideration is that in our culture – I use this term explicitly – in our "culture of remembrance" in Berlin we want to go to places where something actually happened. And where we have the unmitigated connection to people who lived in this city, with this city, to foreground the remembrance of their fate. This is why the ramp at the Grunewald station [from where deportations took place] developed. In the middle of the city – the city lives with this memory – think of the memorial at the Levetzowstrasse. Controversial, after reunification, the Mirror Wall. And there are a multitude of places in the city, where something happened, including the synagogue in Mitte, the remembrance of the women [at Rosenstrasse], the cemeteries. All this was created one by one, at the places where something happened. This was my very firm position. Incidentally, this is part of my critique of the location of the Holocaust memorial.[48]

Those who were not opposed to it linked the Holocaust memorial to the authentic landscape, as Rainer Klemke, of the Berlin Senate for culture, did:

[The Memorial to the Murdered Jews of Europe] is a symbol that has been set in stone – with all its size and centrality. And through the addition of the "Place of Information" exactly this is being achieved: it is not supposed to replace the Gedenkstätten, but rather it is supposed to function as a flag post to say: if you are interested in this topic, you can get some basic information here and then we will guide you from here to the Topo [Topography of Terror], to the House of the Wannsee Conference, to Sachsenhausen, and to all the authentic places. And exactly this is the reason why we – in contrast to other countries – do not need a Holocaust Museum. You have to show something in a museum if you can't show the original. We have the original places. And that is why we are compelled to go to these original places for our remembrance.[49]

Peter Fischer of the Central Council of Jews echoes this rejection of a Holocaust Museum – an idea that was pursued for some time and found a few prominent supporters – and underscores that these historic sites are "indispensable because as historical material witnesses they radiate their own trustworthiness [Glaubwürdigkeit], as they in general develop a very special effectiveness as spaces of remembrance."[50]

Antimonumentality and Reflexivity

Another important theme of the civic memorialization activity of the 1980s was a new understanding of what a memorial is meant to accomplish in the public realm. The activists rejected the traditional function of offering an unequivocal interpretation of the past's meaning for the

---

[48] See Interviews, Eberhard Diepgen.
[49] See Interviews, Rainer Klemke.
[50] See Interviews, Peter Fischer.

present – and with it the monumental aesthetic that embodies this idea. Further, there were varying attempts at transforming the monument from a unidirectional medium, to a dialogic one. The audience was intended to partake in an active process of thinking about the past, as well as about the individual and political significance of remembrance itself. In other words, public memory should be self-reflexive, interrogating processes of commemoration as much as history itself. Thus, "this 'history from below' movement, that was driven mostly by the second and third generation, also showed the 'second guilt' of repression and forgetting."[51]

Most memorials resulting from these Movements have a participatory element, particularly in the sense of being developed through a collective process of research and decision-making. Moreover, some monuments are explicitly participatory in their aesthetic or continuing function. The original plans for an "Active Museum" on the site of the former Gestapo headquarters are the most prominent instance.

> Our idea was that for such a necessary, critical, autonomous, emancipatory reckoning with the past, you need a house or institution, in which people can work, where there is material, where people are available to help you for instance put together an exhibition ... We hoped to create a place with a library, work spaces, seminar rooms, workshops – with everything you might need to enable people – be they individuals, neighborhood initiatives, school groups, association or whatever – to investigate a portion of this history themselves, to document it and to make something out of it.[52]

Some of these ideas have found their way into the current Topography of Terror, but activists had more radical implementations in mind. In a recent project undertaken by the History Workshop Bayreuth, the memorial itself was put together through public participation. The artist Horst Hoheisel had come up with the idea of *Denk-Steine* (thinking-stones): "he asked himself whether a memorial marker could be made without a political mandate, with the participation of many people, 'democratically from below.' A memorial by citizens for former citizens."[53] In May 2001, the *Geschichtswerkstatt* approached six schools in Bayreuth and had students pick a name from a list of deported Jews – usually a person to whom they had some kind of connection in terms of their birthday, name, or address. Each student conducted research on that individual and wrote their name on a stone. At a public event in 2003, these stones were placed in a case together and are now displayed in a local museum, along with documentation about the project and

---

[51] Hausmann, *Duell mit der Verdrängung?* p. 8.
[52] See Interviews, Christine Fischer-Defoy.
[53] Hamel, 'Denk-Steine setzen' p. 65.

comments from participants.[54] The *Stolperstein*-project works in a very similar manner: each stumbling block is created through the engagement and research of a group of people. The result is not merely memorialization, but participation and documentation.

A memorial form that has been much discussed is that of the "countermonument." Though none of the most prominent countermonuments were directly initiated by history workshops, civic initiatives were often involved on the sidelines and some of the artists are closely affiliated with the Movements.[55] Ideally, according to Noam Lupu, "countermonuments would be memorial spaces conceived to challenge the very premise of the monument – to be ephemeral rather than permanent, to deconstruct rather than displace memory, to be antiredemptive. They would reimpose memorial agency and active involvement on the German public."[56]

In October of 1986, the Monument against Fascism, War and Violence, designed by the artist couple Jochen Gerz and Esther Shalev-Gerz was inaugurated in Hamburg-Harburg. Initiated in 1979 by the local SPD and supported by the *Vereinigung der Verfolgten des Naziregimes* (VVN – Union of the Persecuted of the Nazi Regime), the memorial was originally intended to recall working class suffering and resistance under the Nazis in a central square in the former industrial suburb.[57] Over the course of its creation, however, it became a much more critical and engaging monument. The Gerzes insisted on placing the memorial in a busy shopping area, so that it would be in the midst of bustling life. At its inauguration, the monument was a column of twelve meters in height and one square meter wide, made of hollow aluminum and plated with a soft layer of lead. The explanatory plaque invited passersby to engrave their names in opposition to fascism in seven languages. Whenever all reachable space on the column was full, it was lowered 140 centimeters into the ground. After the eighth lowering in 1993, it had disappeared entirely and only the information sign remained.[58]

Though the column referenced traditional memorial forms, the Harburg monument was intended both as a questioning of monumentalism and as a call to action in the present. By letting the column sink away, the artists sought to emphasize that "in the long run, nothing but we ourselves can stand up against injustice."[59] The monument was

[54] Ibid.   [55] Tomberger, *Das Gegendenkmal.*
[56] Lupu, 'Memory Vanished, Absent, and Confined' p. 131.
[57] Hausmann, *Duell mit der Verdrängung?*
[58] Lupu, 'Memory Vanished, Absent, and Confined.'
[59] Tomberger, *Das Gegendenkmal.*

a personal admonition to visitors to add their names and thus state their commitment to act against racism and remember fascism. Each sinking was accompanied by a ceremony, press reports, and cultural events organized by the city, so that the debate and publicity was prolonged much beyond a conventional marker. Interestingly, the more people signed the column, the faster it was lowered in the ground, bringing nearer the time when citizens could no longer rely on a physical artifact to aide their commemoration.

Jochen Gerz, together with his art students, also implemented similar memorial principles a little later. They secretly marked 2,146 cobblestones in Saarbrücken with the names of all known Jewish cemeteries in Germany. They then replaced the stones with the engravings facing down. Key to this "Memorial Against Racism" was again publicity – and the inability of local authorities to stop the project without losing face. The square where the memorial is located has meanwhile been renamed the "Square of the Invisible Monument,"[60] indicating that the negative memorial form has found its way into the city's official commemorative culture.

The newly designed Aschrott Fountain in the center of Kassel is another well-known countermonument. The original fountain was built in 1908 by the Jewish industrialist Sigmund Aschrott and destroyed by the Nazis in 1939 as a "Jews' Fountain." During the 1960s, the city put up another fountain, exemplifying the contemporary culture of forgetting. In 1984, the *Verein zur Rettung historischer Denkmäler in Kassel e.V.* (Association for the Rescue of Historical Monuments in Kassel) proposed that the fountain be restored in some manner and its history recalled.[61] Horst Hoheisel (a Kassel resident) won the design competition. His solution was neither to restore nor to rebuild the fountain. Instead, he poured the shape of the original obelisk form in concrete and lowered it into the ground as a negative form. At the surface only a rosette shape can be seen into which water runs. Only from close proximity can a visitor see the obelisk underground.[62] Hoheisel describes his memorial's purpose as follows:

> It brings home to the viewer the extent of the deep wound inflicted at the heart of Kassel on April 9, 1939, right in front of the City Hall – a wound that will never heal, a wound not to be paved or glossed over. It sparked numerous public debates even while it was being built, evoking great interest among Kassel's residents. This interest in the Aschrottbrunnen continues today, intriguing especially young people, who are curious to know more about the darkest period to their city's

[60] Hausmann, *Duell mit der Verdrängung?*   [61] Young, *The texture of memory* p. 43.
[62] Tomberger, *Das Gegendenkmal.*

history, now rescued from oblivion. For it is a memorial in the deepest sense of the word, a stimulant to memory, a flint to fire debate. And although it is a "negative form" and, as such, sunk deep into the ground, it has remained a stumbling block for those who would prefer it not to be there.[63]

A final example of a countermonument aimed to unsettle its audience is Norbert Rademacher's memorial at the former subcamp to the Sachsenhausen concentration camp at the Sonnenallee in Berlin-Neukölln. Rademacher's monument, inaugurated in 1994, is a light installation that is triggered by visitors. Text fragments are first beamed into trees and then slowly descend to be more visible on the pavement, before fading away. The effect varies depending on the season, weather, and time of day, making a memorial in constant flux. Rademacher invited school children to study the location and its history, and add their own texts to his.[64] This memorial highlights the ever-changing nature of remembrance, as well as speaking individually to passersby and encouraging participation.

Countermonuments, then, call into question the medium of the monument itself, while addressing not only the distant past, but also reflecting on postwar confrontation with Nazism and making it relevant for the future. Rudy Koshar contends that:

> Whether because of their transience and immateriality or their breaking down of barriers between the monument and usually passive spectators, the countermonuments questioned traditional forms of commemoration and used historical time itself to emphasize the temporality of history and memory. Memory changes constantly, the countermonuments pointed out; monuments should do all they can to symbolize this transience and actively involve the viewer in the process of seeking out such fleeting traces.[65]

By inviting reflection and participation, all these memorials stress that even "authentic" sites are not meaningful by themselves: we must actively remember in order for them to become so. This emphasis on the importance of the actions and discourses of today has also been present in recent large and representative memorial projects. Most poignantly, it was pointed out repeatedly during the conflict over the Memorial to the Murdered Jews of Europe in Berlin that such a monument must not function as endpoint of the discussion or even of memory. Numerous commentators argued that the debate itself was a much more lively memorial than a physical one could ever be.[66] Andreas Eberhardt, the managing director of the association *Gegen Vergessen, Für Demokratie*

---

[63] www.hoheisel-knitz.net/index (original in English).
[64] Young, *The texture of memory* p. 41.   [65] Koshar, *From monuments to traces* p. 267.
[66] Heimrod, Schlusche, and Seferens, 'Der Denkmalstreit.'

(Against Forgetting, For Democracy), argued in this context: "In general, it is laudatory that the state has managed to make negative memory into one of its main components. Into a part of its national identity. For this reason, I believe that the fifteen years of debate were almost better than the memorial itself and it would be my wish that, now that the memorial is complete, the debate continues."[67] Such contributions indicate how deeply the rejection of monumentality and the critical understanding of the memorial have impacted German memory culture.

The significance of reflection and public participation was also stressed by members of the History Movement during the process of dealing with monuments erected by the GDR regime. For example, the Berlin Senate established a ten-person commission after 1990 to evaluate what to do with East Berlin memorials, most of which reflected the conventional state-socialist ideology of antifascism and had the corresponding aesthetic. The Active Museum, which has made East Berlin memorials and street names one of its main foci of action, argued that rather than remove memorials, they should be used to provoke a public confrontation with the GDR (as well as the Nazi) past. Rather than erasing the remnants of the regime, memorials should be reinterpreted.[68]

This was the approach taken with a small – but prominently placed – memorial stone dedicated to the Communist resistance group around Herbert Baum. The stone is located in the Lustgarten, close to the Brandenburg Gate, and marks the site where Baum and his comrades set fire to an anti-Soviet exhibition staged by the Nazis in 1942 and distributed anti-Nazi flyers. The Nazis reacted with a wave of arrests of Jews and many of the Baum group were executed shortly afterwards.[69] The original stone was inaugurated in 1981 and is inconspicuous in design and inscription, citing merely the steadfastness of the young Communists in Baum's group and pledging "everlasting friendship with the Soviet Union." It does not directly refer to either the act of resistance or the death of individuals, who were Jewish, as its consequence.[70] In 2001, the memorial plaque commission of Berlin-Mitte placed two Plexiglas plaques over the stone, adding information about the large and loose grouping and naming key members.[71] The original inscription remains visible underneath, underlining memory's complex layers of interpretation (Figure 5.4).

Another instance of officially dealing with the GDR memory legacy through an antimonumental aesthetic is evident in the memorial recalling

---

[67] See Interviews, Andreas Eberhardt.
[68] Jordan, *Structures of Memory* p. 55.   [69] Endlich, *Wege zur Erinnerung* p. 254.
[70] Jordan, *Structures of Memory* p. 74.
[71] Endlich, *Wege zur Erinnerung*, Jordan, *Structures of Memory*.

Figure 5.5. Memorial to the Baum resistance group, with Plexiglas addition, Berliner Lustgarten.[72]

the burning of books by the Nazis on May 10, 1933, on what is now called Bebelplatz in the center of Berlin. After the event had not been commemorated for decades, Heinz Knobloch, one of the few "memory activists" in the GDR,[73] initiated a plaque there in 1983. In 1987, official plans for a larger memorial were drawn up and a traditional figure of a socialist fighter against fascism was even purchased in Spring 1990. However, these aesthetics were deemed inappropriate after unification and in 1993, a new memorial competition was announced.[74] The winning design by Micha Ullmann was a conceptual monument made up of an underground room with empty bookshelves that could hold twenty thousand books. This "Library" was inaugurated in 1995 and is visible through a glass window in the ground. It is a "negative space" in which "loss and presence come together" and evoke reflection. Though the memorial is barely visible from the street, it has achieved great resonance with the public and is the location of regular readings, events, and artistic installations.[75]

---

[72] Jenny Wüstenberg, 2006.   [73] Endlich, *Wege zur Erinnerung* p. 242.
[74] Jordan, *Structures of Memory* p. 102.   [75] Endlich, *Wege zur Erinnerung* p. 243.

Specificity and Diversity

A final important theme in the memorials of the Memorial Site and History Movements is the specificity of information about the past provided on them and the diversity of groups remembered. In particular, the memory initiatives focused with great energy on recalling the perpetrators of the Holocaust and pioneered the remembrance of victim groups such as the Sinti and Roma and the deserters from the Wehrmacht.[76] With the growing temporal distance from 1945, memorial markers were increasingly initiated not by victims' organizations, but by those who are descendants of the perpetrator society.[77] This legacy was openly addressed by the history workshops and reflected in the memorials. In this context, the Topography of Terror and the House of the Wannsee Conference are the most prominent examples.

At the same time during the 1980s, several groups of "forgotten victims" found their public voice and founded organizations that called for restitution and symbolic recognition: the Central Council of Sinti and Roma was founded in 1979, the association of former forced laborers in 1986, the association for those who suffered under the policy of "euthanasia" in 1987, and the Union of Victims of Nazi Military Justice in 1990.[78] The Memorial Site and History Movements, together with the growing pressure from various victims organizations, then, succeeded in diversifying public memory and transforming "the cityscape into a place of learning and instruction"[79] by providing extensive information to new generations that did not remember from first (or even second) hand knowledge. Ulrike Haß, in her study of the changing nature of memorial texts, summarizes the character of 1980s memorials as follows:

> Memorial texts often result from local and quotidian search for traces [*Spurensuche*] which begins in the 80s and through which individual persons and groups become memorializable. In contrast to the cemetery silence and in a deeper sense mute memory of the 60s and 70s, the hunger for knowledge of the new generation [*Nachgeborenen*] now leads to a novel language in memorial texts that prioritizes the need for information. From this point forward, the placing of much more extensive panels is being pursued by various initiatives which explicitly focus on so far forgotten victims (Sinti and Roma, homosexuals, victims of "Euthanasia" and medical experiments). The relationship of the texts to their locality becomes very important: the more informative the texts, the less do cemeteries appear as the proper place for them.[80]

[76] von Saldern, 'Stadtgedächtnis und Geschichtswerkstätten' p. 67.
[77] Schönfeld, *Gedenktafeln in West-Berlin* p. 23.
[78] Hausmann, *Duell mit der Verdrängung?*   [79] Jordan, *Structures of Memory* p. 45.
[80] Haß, 'Mahnmaltexte 1945 bis 1988' p. 141.

The primary purpose of the memorialization efforts of these Movements was not the declaration of moral or political lessons. The purpose was rather to elicit a reaction from visitors, encouraging them to think and discuss, and ultimately, to become politically engaged in a way that linked historical meaning to discrimination in the present.

Many of the memorials I have discussed in this or other chapters could serve as examples of the focus on perpetrators, "forgotten victims," or specificity in information provision. Here I want to concentrate on a set of memorials that was championed primarily by the History Movement in close cooperation with elements of the peace movement: those commemorating the deserters from the Wehrmacht. Starting in the mid-1980s, initiatives were launched in the context of peace movement activists emboldened and enraged by the stationing of American missiles in Europe. In approximately forty West German cities, memory activists began investigating the treatment of soldiers who had deserted from the Nazi army.[81] It is estimated that Nazi courts passed down over twenty thousand death sentences against deserters, about fifteen thousand of which were carried out. In neither the FRG nor the GDR were these individuals recognized as participants in the resistance, nor did survivors receive a victims' pension. The stigma attached to desertion remained strong.[82]

In Marburg in 1988, the history workshop was instrumental in pushing for a memorial as part of local peace groups' protest against the posturing of veterans' organization and their celebration of military culture (see Chapter 4). A memorial was made by the stonemason Joe Kley (himself a conscientious objector) and unveiled for the first time on September 1, 1989 (antiwar day) – and then repeatedly as part of antimilitarist protests.[83] Because the placement of the memorial had been unauthorized, the city of Marburg removed it, prompting further protest from the Workshop (Figure 5.6). According to Roland Müller of the *Marburger Geschichtswerkstatt*, the main purpose of the sculpture was to trigger public debate and evoke dissonance in Marburg's presentation of the past.[84] The Marburg workshop was also active in organizing coordinating meetings among the various West German groups advocating for deserter memory.[85]

[81] Bonner Friedensplenum Arbeitskreis "Von der Fahne", 'Für die unbekannten Deserteure.'

[82] Landeshauptstadt Potsdam, 'Das Denkmal des unbekannten Deserteurs.'

[83] Michael Heiny, Marburger Geschichtswerkstatt, email communication September 9, 2016.

[84] www.geschichtswerkstatt-marburg.de/ddenkmal/index.htm.

[85] Kristian Golla, Bonner Friedensplenum, email communication May 19, 2009.

Figure 5.6. Activists of the Marburg History Workshop protest
the removal of their monument to the unknown deserter,
September 1989.[86]

The *Bonner Friedensplenum* (Bonn Forum for Peace) was founded in
1988 as part of the local peace movement, though it was of broader
significance due to its location in the (then) capital. Triggered by the
erection of the first deserter memorial in Bremen three years earlier, the
Bonn group also sought to memorialize the fate of deserters. The original
goal was to dedicate a permanent memorial on the Friedensplatz in Bonn
(also on antiwar day in 1989) and for the city to cover all expenses.
A resolution passed by the Forum stated:

> With this "think-monument" [*Denk-Mal*] for the "unknown deserter," we
> want to instigate thinking and open dialogue about deserters and their deci-
> sion to desert. Deserters embark on their path in desperation and high
> personal risk. We believe that their continued stigmatization is untenable
> and demand an official amnesty and rehabilitation for all deserters, as well
> as reparations for their families. Our "Denk-Mal" initiative in the federal
> capital sees itself as representative of similar initiatives that have been created
> in about forty cities of the Federal Republic in order to work through a long-
> repressed chapter of German military history, to liberate the deserters from
> the stain of "treason," and instead to honor them as an anti-militarist warning
> for the future. (*Bonner Friedensplenum*, version passed May 10, 1989)[87]

[86] Michael Heiny, Marburger Geschichtswerkstatt.
[87] Bonner Friedensplenum Arbeitskreis "Von der Fahne," 'Für die unbekannten
Deserteure' p. 4.

The CDU mayor rejected the proposal, underlining the fact that, at this time, memorial projects of the History Movement tended to receive support mainly from Social Democrats and Greens. Meanwhile, the initiative was able to collect enough donations to purchase a marble slab from which the Turkish artist Mehmet Aksoy crafted a large sculpture pro bono.[88] The memorial received support from over a thousand citizens and numerous prominent individuals and was accompanied by theater and book projects, as well as other public events. The authorities did allow the memorial to be unveiled repeatedly as part of demonstrations, making it a prop in antiwar rallies. For a time, the sculpture had a nomadic existence, but its life was far from over: the revolution of 1989 gave it the unexpected chance to be permanently installed. In the eastern city of Potsdam, a new association called "Friends of Refusers of Military Service" [Wehrdiensttotalverweigerer] now wanted to erect the sculpture. In August 1990 (shortly before unification and new elections), the Neues Forum proposed this to the city parliament and the memorial was agreed to with a large majority. This decision was an interesting testament to the links between the West and East German peace movements and the way in which they were able to take advantage of the small window of opportunity during the transitional period in 1990. On September 1, 1990, the Aksoy monument was brought from Bonn and put up in Potsdam. At the inauguration ceremony, the well-known East German dissident singer Wolf Biermann performed (Figure 5.7).[89] The city of Potsdam is now responsible for the memorial's upkeep and protection. It has become a place for rallies, but it has also been damaged by detractors. In 1998, the Bundestag passed an amnesty bill for deserters and since then, there have been more efforts at local commemoration, for example in Stuttgart.[90]

These memory sites recalling the plight of Wehrmacht deserters hold a special place in the left-wing politics with which most memory initiatives of this period were affiliated. They also exemplify the means and alliances through which the workshops brought new aspects of the Nazi past into the public sphere and thereby diversified the memorial landscape. Furthermore, their activism was pivotal in integrating specific information about perpetrators, victims, and historical events into memorial design.

---

[88] Ibid.

[89] Landeshauptstadt Potsdam, 'Das Denkmal des unbekannten Deserteurs' p. 5.

[90] Initiative Deserteur Denkmal für Stuttgart, 'Stuttgart braucht ein Denkmal.'

Figure 5.7. Singer Wolf Biermann performs at the inauguration of the deserter memorial in Potsdam in 1990. The banner reads: "This sculpture is to be the only German soldier that moves East ever again."[91]

Conclusion

The two "memory booms" of the 1980s (one initiated by official institutions and the other as a countermovement) together profoundly transformed West Germany's memory landscape in a way that continued to shape memory politics and institutions after the fall of the Wall. While there was certainly overlap and cross-fertilization between these two booms, they tended to be driven by different actors with different motivations and different design principles. On the one hand, government agencies, conservative politicians, and members of the "establishment" sought to create large and representative museums and memorials (Chapter 2). They were to reflect the "longue-durée" of German history and emphasize its potential for positive identification. On the other hand stood leftist politicians, artists, and citizens' initiatives – above all those of the Memorial Site and History Movements. These activists concentrated

---

[91] Kristian Golla, Bonner Friedensplenum/Netzwerk Friedenskooperative.

their energy on the Nazi period and promoted a critical, self-reflexive, and overtly political approach to the past. This stance was mirrored in the design ideas the Movements put forward.

The aesthetic of these activists (and of others who endorsed the same purpose for public memory) has influenced the German memorial land-scape to the point that this aesthetic is today no longer marginal or oppositional. It has made its way into the main memorial institutions of the state. In the early 1980s, however, the principles of decentralism, authenticity, self-reflection, and mnemonic diversity were still radical and highly politicized. At every turn, the activists had to contend with local and federal authorities, and often popular discontent, in their efforts to erect memorial markers. This gave their work and their aesthetic vision a particular political salience. Over the course of the decade, as demand for critical memory grew (especially in urban centers), local governments realized that the history initiatives were addressing a real and sizable public need.

As a result, the work of the Movements and affiliated artists became increasingly valued and funded to enhance the local touristic infrastruc-ture – to devise exhibits, memorials, city tours and more. Different groups developed various topical specialties,[92] determined by the interests of their members and by the history of the locale. At the same time, this meant at times the commercialization of their activity – it was seen by municipalities as a way to attract visitors – and some workshops sought to use this to their advantage. In 1989, Thomas Lindenberger and Michael Wildt, of the History Movement, wrote:

> In contrast to the early times four or five years ago, the history workshops no longer hover free, but poor, in the space of municipal and cultural politics. Instead, they are well on their way to conquering a passable material position in the budgets of history-conscious towns and states [Länder] – even in problematic competition to other projects such as women's crisis centers. Especially those initiatives that were able to sail in the winds of big round numbers (750 years Berlin, 1200 years Singen, 800 years Hamburg harbor etc.) know that critical history work of civically-minded [bürgernahen] initia-tives is now an indispensable part of state-sponsored anniversaries.[93]

In other words, the initiatives fulfilled a public demand that became increasingly crucial for state actors to address – but that they could not themselves fulfill precisely because of their official identity. Critical mem-ory had to come from "below" to be taken seriously. Sometime in the later

---

[92] van Laak, 'Alltagsgeschichte' p. 52.
[93] Lindenberger and Wildt, 'Radikale Pluralität ' p. 409, see also Wüstenberg, 'Vom alternativen Laden zum Dienstleistungsbetrieb.'

1980s, the "official" and the "grassroots" drives to remake the memory landscape merged and became more accepting of each other. For example, a significant official recognition for the History Movement came when the notion of a "history of everyday life" found its way into the House of History in Bonn.[94] Activists found jobs in historical institutions or funded their memory work through municipal grants.

During the 1980s, a complex and diverse memory landscape was thus created and transformed, and it laid the foundations for the memory political and design decisions of the 1990s and 2000s. It certainly included large and conventional memorials and museums that seemed to speak to a rediscovered national self-confidence and more traditional functions of memory in the service of national identity. However, the Memorial Site and History Movements and their allies were instrumental in making these large mnemonic spaces more nuanced and sensitive to the traumas of German history. Furthermore, without the Movements, countless reflexive, contemplative, self-critical, and antimonumental memory sites would not exist to compose the decentralized memory landscape. These are the elements that make German arena of memorials arguably unique in international comparison.

The memorial principles I have discussed can today be seen to form part of a consensus in Germany on what palatable public memory should look like – a consensus that has shaped not only memorialization of the Nazi past since 1989, but also that of other "pasts." The reasons for the broad implementation and acceptance of these design concepts lie both in the successful activism of civil society and in the gradual institutionalization of those ideas. In the next chapter, I analyze a new generation of memory activists – those focused on the GDR past – and the ways in which they have dealt with the norms and institutional arrangements that were shaped so profoundly during the 1980s in West Germany.

---

[94] van Laak, 'Alltagsgeschichte' p. 54.

6   A Part of History That Continues to Smolder: Remembering East Germany from Below

In the usually quiet offices of the Brandenburg Agency for Political Education, dozens of memory activists, academics, and memorial staff gathered on May 22, 2013. Some were holding protest signs, others distributing flyers. There were not enough seats to accommodate everyone who was there to attend the launch of a book about the *Memorial at Leistikowstrasse* Potsdam – the site of a brutal former prison of Soviet counterintelligence services.[1] The event featured a panel discussion with its editor, historian Wolfgang Benz, as well as the head of the *Leistikowstrasse Memorial* Ines Reich, executive director of the governmental *Stiftung Aufarbeitung* Anna Kaminsky, and former Gulag prisoner and civic activist Horst Schüler.

The book presented the history of the site and the process that led to the creation of the memorial, as well as linking it to similar conflicts over other places of GDR memory. In the previous five years, the debate over the Memorial at *Leistikowstrasse* was among the most contentious in East German memory politics – revealing deep divisions between various memory activists. For many months, critics of the memorial – including former prisoners – had vocally protested the design and presentation of the history of the prison and attacked the leadership of the institution for insensitivity to their concerns. For their part, the historians running the memorial gave very little ground and defended their approach as reflective of objective historiographical methods. This highly charged controversy (profiled later in this chapter) exemplifies some the central tensions between East and West German memory activists, including how to memorialize sites of both NS and SED crimes and how to manage institutional versus activist approaches to commemoration.

The heated debate was at the center of the book launch event. Some activists argued passionately that the book wrongly characterized their

---

[1] Benz, 'Ein Kampf um Deutungshoheit.' 'Die Auseinandersetzung um die Gedenk- und Begegnungsstätte Leistikowstraße in Potsdam' May 22, 2013, *Brandenburgische Landeszentrale für Politische Bildung* (event attended by the author).

engagement and that they were not offered an opportunity to represent their side of the conflict. In the book's introduction, Benz rejected the memory activists' basic approach: "Rallies on the street, causing commotion in the media or political compromise which values emotions above factual accounts and finds pawns to sacrifice in order to placate, will only harm the necessary memory work."[2] However, the majority of the book's chapters also do not attempt to offer a balanced analysis. Several focus on (partially existent) right-wing tendencies of various GDR victims group and thereby summarily implicate the *Leistikow*-activists. Several of the authors are former staff members of the Brandenburg Memorial Foundation or the Center for Anti-Semitism Research, both of which have reputation for being part of the "memory establishment" and are mistrusted by the GDR civic groups. At the event, activists gave impassioned testimony about the site and their vision of a true memorial, but left without winning concessions for future compromises. The emotion that animated the book launch – and the protests against the Memorial leadership that preceded it – indicate that the contention over the *Leisikowstrasse* has touched a nerve for GDR memory activists. It is illustrative of their profound discontent with current memorial policy, which they have voiced through repeated contentious action. The largest of these was the rally and human chain held in protest of the new permanent exhibition in 2012 (Figures 6.1 and 6.2).

Over the past twenty-five years, GDR memory has moved to the center of concern for government and funding agencies. This was driven chiefly by civil society, but in the context of a rapidly developing institutional landscape of memory that was strongly shaped by earlier generations of memory activists. What the event in May 2013 suggests is that the struggles between civil society and the state concerning the appropriate interpretation of this "second dictatorship" for Germany continue to this day. This contention – over meaning, content, and strategies of remembering East Germany – is crucial to understanding not only the dynamics of this specific arena of memory activism, but also the more general transformation of the relationship between state actors and mnemonic civil society since 1989.

In comparison with their eastern neighbors, also grappling with a state-socialist past, East Germans have had a relatively good vantage point from which to address the history and memory of the GDR. They were faced in 1989 with a state that was not only willing to support remembrance initiatives, but had developed a high level of competency in memory policy-making – unmatched by any other government on the planet. Not only did

---

[2] Benz, 'Probleme mit der Erinnerung' p. 15.

Figure 6.1. Protesters at Leistikowstrasse 1 form a human chain on the occasion of the opening of the new permanent exhibit, April 18, 2012.[3]

unification mean the availability of considerable funding that could be invested in memorial sites, education policies, and publicity – West Germans also willingly shared the lessons learned from coming to terms with the National Socialist past and provided an experienced set of memorial experts. As a consequence, "the pace of the process after 1989/ 90 was far more rapid and the study of the SED dictatorship much more intense. The intention was to avoid any repetition of the mistakes that had resulted from the foot-dragging that followed the demise of the National Socialist regime."[4] The legacy of dealing with the Nazi past, and especially the memorial professionals who grew up with this legacy in the West, have profoundly influenced the GDR memorial landscape. In turn, the memory politics surrounding the remembrance of the GDR have transformed pre-1989 memorial institutions by challenging the dominance of the Nazi past in the memorial culture of the Federal Republic. Nevertheless, the meeting of the various memory activists and the merging of government memorial institutions during the unification process also brought with it bitter conflicts.

[3] Christian Albroscheit.   [4] Camphausen, 'Constructing Remembrance.'

Figure 6.2. A protester wearing his prison camp jacket at the same rally, holding a UOKG sign, April 18, 2012.[5]

One of the chapters in the controversial book edited by Benz helps to explain why – despite generous support and attention for GDR memory projects – the activists continue to protest today. It includes a transcript of

[5] Christian Albroscheit.

a conversation between Winfried Meyer (a historian and former staff of the concentration camp memorial at Sachsenhausen) and Roland Brauckmann (a political prisoner during the GDR and currently staff member at the Human Rights Center/Memorial in Cottbus). In this exchange, Brauckmann argues that both the Cottbus Memorial and the *Leistikowstrasse* can draw on the engagement of former prisoners, but that they are treated very differently in these locations. In Brauckmann's view, the victims should be in charge of the place of where they suffered, rather than merely contributing to research about the site. They should feel welcome and respected. This is an argument that is *not* based on the importance of historical facts and scientific detachment, but on the need to respect and value victims as a matter of principle. For Brauckmann, "this partisanship [for human rights] is largely missing in the Leistikowstrasse exhibition. There everything is dissected with the coldness of a surgeon ... and shown in virtually empty rooms. Empathy does not appear. This is not enough to inspire current generations with our democratic alternative."[6] It is thus not enough to *represent* the plight and perspective of victims; they also need to be *actively involved*, even if this means that the message radiating from memorials cannot be officially controlled. From the standpoint of the activists, their participation must extend beyond the memorials themselves to *the rules that govern* those memorials. For memorial professionals such as Meyer, by contrast, these rules are not really up for debate:

> Brauckmann: We are talking here about a part of history that continues to smolder ... The disputed issue is: How do we interact with the living witnesses? Are they merely our lifeless research objects or are they allowed to actively participate in the representation and interpretation of their history?
> Meyer: They are of course allowed to participate in the representation of this history within a regulated system. And we can only be thankful to them if they do this. And with their own personal history, they are not only allowed to participate, they are allowed to and should narrate it.
> Brauckmann: This "regulated system" is another point of critique in the memorial politics at Leistikowstrasse. Before the concept of the current exhibition was pushed through, the witnesses were able to speak freely, without researchers at their side who interrupted them. Now a witness is often accompanied by a researcher or staff member, whose job it is to make sure that the witness does not "talk nonsense," to put it simply. And so these people, who were courageous and resisted in a repressive system, now feel bossed around, guided and personally humiliated. These rules should therefore first be jointly discussed.[7]

[6] Meyer and Brauckmann, 'Geschichtspolitik und Ausstellungsdidaktik' p. 233.
[7] Ibid. p. 234.

One of my central objectives is to analyze the ways in which mnemonic civic activists have been integrated in (and excluded from) the making of memorial policy in unified Germany through the construction of a governing framework. The key point in this chapter is that civil society pivotally shaped the process of GDR commemoration – but from the beginning in a highly institutionalized setting. This story is not a straightforward one. The GDR memory activists are not a cohesive group, but rather a collection of diverse actors, with varied backgrounds and political cultures. They often disagree about concrete goals of memorialization, though they are united by their motivation to integrate the experience of East Germans into the mainstream of memory of the Federal Republic. Using an analytical framework derived from social movement theory, I analyze the GDR *Aufarbeitungsszene* (memory scene), including victims' groups, former dissidents, for-profit initiatives, and "pragmatic activists." I pay attention to the framing of their actions in terms of democracy and the need for recognition. I also examine the strategies for memorial creation used by these various groups, including historical research, lobbying, occupation of sites, and protest activity. Throughout, I point to similarities and differences of GDR memory activism to the History and Memorial Site Movements. I go on to examine how the efforts of memory initiatives have become institutionalized, as well as the kinds of memorial sites that have emerged from civil society activity. Finally, I use the case study of the conflict over the Memorial *Leistikowstrasse* in order to illustrate the complex relationship between civic activists and victim groups with state actors.

Memory During the Transition from Old to New Federal Republic

After unification in 1990, there was a wide spectrum of efforts – generously funded and staffed – to work through the memory of the dictatorship of the *Sozialistische Einheitspartei* (SED – Socialist Unity Party) of East Germany and especially the legacy of the Secret Police: the Stasi. Thomas Großbölting argues there was a strong will on the part of the "political class," to undertake this work.[8] James McAdams suggests that no other state so rapidly and so thoroughly undertook steps to confront the past.[9] Indeed, there were immediate measures of transitional justice, in the form of trials against the GDR leadership and border guards.

---

[8] Faulenbach, 'Diktaturerfahrungen und demokratische Erinnerungskultur ', Großbölting, 'Die DDR im vereinten Deutschland.'

[9] McAdams, *Judging the Past.*

Restitution procedures were put in place. On the day of unification, October 3, 1990, the Stasi Records Agency began its work under the leadership of Joachim Gauck. Officially named the "Federal Commissioner for the Records of the State Security Service of the former German Democratic Republic" (BStU), this agency had over three thousand staff at its highpoint in the mid-1990s, and thousands of citizens were given access to Stasi records. Both the main office in Berlin and the dozen satellite offices were and continue to be involved in the creation of local memorial spaces, such as the "Memorial to Victims of Dictatorship" in Frankfurt an der Oder. In Berlin, the BStU maintains a permanent exhibition about the Stasi in its former headquarters at Normannenstrasse.[10] From 1992 to 1994, the first *Enquete Commission* for "Working Through the History and Legacies of the SED Dictatorship" underwent a participatory process of collecting memories and interpretations of the GDR from across the political and societal spectrum, producing thirty-six thousand pages of material in 31 volumes.[11] The Commission was parliamentary in nature and applied proportional representation to the selection of speakers. Victims' groups and other civic representatives were heard at length.[12] Moreover, ample time and extensive documentation was provided to all the participants, so that the Commission itself arguably contributed to the process of reconciliation. The second *Enquete Commission* "Overcoming the Legacies of the SED-Dictatorship in the Process of German Unification" (1995–1998) continued this process, but laid more emphasis on the active shaping of German memory culture writ-large, and on the future of the memorial landscape in particular.[13] Importantly, the Commission's final report included the first state regulatory policy on memorial sites, defining them as "places of remembrance and political education rather than state-dictated ritual, thereby signaling a departure from commemorative practices in the GDR."[14] This second *Enquete* also laid down principles for federal funding eligibility, including that sites must be of national or even international significance and must demonstrate a clear museological and pedagogical concept. At first, this funding mechanism was restricted to Berlin and the new *Länder* (federal states), though in 1998 the Social Democratic-Green coalition government extended funding to Western federal states as well. Another crucial result of the second *Enquete* was the creation in 1998 of the *Stiftung Aufarbeitung*

[10] www.bstu.bund.de/SharedDocs/Ausstellungen/Region-Berlin/.
[11] www.bundesstiftung-aufarbeitung.de/pressemitteilungen.
[12] Bundestag, 'Formen und Ziele der Auseinandersetzung.'
[13] Rudnick, *Die andere Hälfte der Erinnerung* p. 73.
[14] Pearce, 'An Unequal Balance?' p. 176.

(Foundation for Working Through the Past). Its mandate is to promote the "comprehensive examination of causes, history, and consequences of the dictatorship in the Soviet Zone and the GDR, to accompany the process of German unification, and to take part in the reckoning with dictatorships in the international arena." While the *Stiftung* organizes public events, promotes networking among stakeholders, maintains an archive, and has put together exhibits of its own, its primary function is to distribute government funding to memorials, museums, independent archives, victims' organizations and other civic partners.[15] On average, the foundation finances 150 new projects annually; by 2013, it had paid out almost 37 million euros for memorial projects and related research undertakings.[16] From the outset, then, GDR memory activists were obliged to navigate – but also profited from – a whole set of institutional support and funding mechanisms. Their main task vis-à-vis state actors was not primarily to prevent official "forgetting" – as had been the case for the memory movements of the 1980s – but to influence the ways in which government support was allocated.

Notwithstanding the crucial role of state actors, it must be stressed that civil society groups were pivotal in the creation of GDR memorial sites almost without exception. Their role was encouraged in part by the very fluid situation in the aftermath of the fall of the Wall. State cultural institutions at this time were in a great state of reorganization, particularly in Berlin, where two bureaucracies – along with large museums, libraries, concert houses, and more – had to be merged. These enormous tasks had to be accomplished with insufficient numbers of staff and rapidly changing chains of authority. The fate of specific memorial sites and memory policy writ-large were not necessarily at the top of the agenda. This state of flux created a challenging environment for civic groups – but it also allowed them a lot of freedom to shape particular memory realms in a way that was difficult for other actors to undo at a later date.

The complexity of public memory is reflected in the memorial campaigns that emerged in the first years after 1989, which were not exclusively about the dual legacy of dictatorship. Perhaps most impressive in terms of civic mobilization was the initiative to rebuild the Frauenkirche, a church in the city of Dresden that had been destroyed by Allied bombing in 1945. The synagogue there (burnt down in 1938) was rebuilt only later. Thus, it seems initially the majority of Dresdeners wanted to be confronted neither with the Nazi nor with the GDR past.

[15] www.bundesstiftung-aufarbeitung.de/die-stiftung-1074.html.
[16] 'Tätigkeitsbericht 2013' *Bundesstiftung zur Aufarbeitung der SED-Diktatur*, March 31, 2014.

"Postreunification Dresden thus aim[ed] to establish a distinct counter-movement to the previous political situation, with most inhabitants seeing their future in the pre-National Socialist past."[17] In a related development, many towns in the Eastern Länder rededicated their anti-fascist memorials after 1989. These memorials, which had been part and parcel of the state socialist narrative, were made into monuments to "the victims of war and violent dictatorship" – a phrase that conveniently encompasses Nazi and SED dictatorships, as well as all manners of war casualties, without reflecting on questions of responsibility or instrumentalization of memory. This impulse was akin to commemorative practices in the early decades of the old Federal Republic.[18]

In the course of debates about particular places – and especially about those sites with a "double past," which had witnessed injustices both before and after 1945 – civil society in Eastern Germany also became more active in commemorating the Nazi past. For example, citizen initiatives formed to preserve the former Nazi missile development plant in Peenemünde, the "Kraft durch Freude" resort on the Baltic sea, various satellites of the Ravensbrück and Neuengamme concentration camps, an execution site of deserters from the Nazi army in Anklam, and a former prisoner of war camp in Mühlenberg, where Soviet POWs had suffered.[19] However, the more recent memory of life in East Germany dominated memorial politics and was driven by a diverse set of civic activists.

The GDR Memorial Scene

Despite the rapid and decisive actions taken by state representatives after 1990 to confront the past – above all the BStU, the *Enquete Commissions* and the *Stiftung Aufarbeitung* – civil society groups were the ones pushing for the creation of the majority of concrete memorial sites. Parliamentary debates and federal funding initiatives did not mitigate the feeling that they were left to their own devices in the struggle against local forgetting. The early 2000s, however, saw a major shift in public attitudes toward the GDR past. One reason for this may have been, as Gabrielle Camphausen suggests, that a certain temporal distance needed to be acquired before locals and tourists could develop interest in visiting sites that recall East Germany as a historical era. Until then, the dominant sentiment – in

---

[17] Vees-Gulani, 'The Politics of New Beginnings' p. 36.
[18] Scheer, *Der Umgang mit den Denkmälern*; Leo, 'Unscharfe Konturen' pp. 27–33.
[19] Wagner, 'The Evolution of Memorial Sites', Weigelt, 'Chronik der Initiativgruppe Lager Mühlberg.'

Berlin and other border towns especially – had been to do away with the despised symbols of confinement and repression.[20]

Around the beginning of the new millennium, then, three developments coincided. First, there was increased interest in the GDR past among the general public, manifested in rising visitor numbers at existing memorials and in the many documentaries, movies, and publications that came out during this period. Second, the federal-level policies and funding bodies that had been put in place became more routinized and established so that civic initiatives had consistent government partners to address. Third, the many local efforts at memorial creation became more visible through effective networking, availability of funding, and public demand. Who were these memory activists and how were they mobilized into action since 1989?

The History and the Memorial Site Movements that I have described in the previous chapters were composed of many disparate groups and focused on local memory work. Nevertheless, they were well networked and displayed a relatively consistent identity. By contrast, the activists engaged in the commemoration of the GDR past cannot be called a coherent social movement. They are recruited from groups that are not only dispersed and focused on various kinds of memorial sites, but are fundamentally different in terms of their political beliefs, socialization, and style. However, there are clearly three main types of activists involved: victims' associations made up primarily of former political prisoners including those incarcerated during the Soviet occupation period and the early years of the GDR; former dissidents who were especially active in the final decade before 1989; and what I call "pragmatists": individuals – often West Germans – who did not suffer directly under the East German regime, but who founded civic organizations out of a general drive to create awareness. In addition, there are a considerable number of initiatives that combine genuine interest in the GDR past with the recognition that there is money to be made in the lucrative tourist industry. These for-profit organizations must also be taken into account. Of course, these are "ideal types" that in practice often overlap significantly. An individual memory activist may identify both as political prisoner of the 1960s and as dissident of the 1980s, for example. Moreover, many groups assemble activists from these different "branches." Nevertheless, these distinctions are useful in order to understand some of the contention within civic groups and vis-à-vis state institutions.

---

[20] See Interviews, Gabrielle Camphausen.

The various types of activists may not be one movement, but they are all part of what has been called the *Aufarbeitungsszene* (memorial scene). It is crucial to recognize that, due to the initial government-driven efforts to work through the past and the institutions that were created early on, this scene encompassed both civic and state actors from the beginning. Thus, the intermeshing of civil society and state spheres that developed gradually in the cases of the History and Memorial Site Movements, existed from the get-go in the GDR realm. This preexisting infrastructure and the competence in both government and civil society institutions to engage in hybrid civic/state activities is a product of the movements of the 1980s.

The GDR victims' associations, dissidents and other civic groups are constantly engaged in exchanges with representatives of BStU, *Stiftung Aufarbeitung,* state ministries, and state-run memorials. The exchanges happen through regular meetings, listservs, interlinking of websites and so forth. Each year, the calendar is filled with conferences and meetings at which many of the same organizations and individuals congregate. One such routine opportunity is presented by the annual conference of the *Landesbeauftragten für die Unterlagen des Staatssicherheitsdienstes der ehemaligen DDR* (State Representatives for the Files of the Secret Police of the Former GDR – LStU) and the *Stiftung Aufarbeitung.* Horst Schüler, a former Gulag prisoner and memory activist, has called these meetings "the highlight of the year for victims' organizations."[21] At the local level, there are also regular forums. For example, the LStU in Brandenburg, led by Ulrike Poppe, organizes about four annual gatherings with representatives of political prisoners and other victims in order to understand their concerns and to support the creation of links amongst them.[22] In Berlin, the *Arbeitskreis 2* (AK2 – Working Group 2) was created by the city government to bring together institutions and initiatives working on GDR memory in parallel with an equivalent *Arbeitskreis 1* for the memory of the Nazi era. Participants stress the importance of building personal relationships in this way.[23] Despite these regular opportunities for networking, many of which have been actively promoted by state agencies, there remain distinct differences between various types of activists – differences that make for a complicated dynamic in the *Aufarbeitungsszene.*

[21] Kongress der LStU and Stiftung zur Aufarbeitung der SED- Diktatur, 'Über Grenzen und Zeiten' p. 37.
[22] See Interviews, Ulrike Poppe.
[23] See Interviews, Rainer Klemke and Gabriele Camphausen.

Victims' Organizations

Arguably the most important and vocal set of GDR memory advocates is made up of associations and memorial initiatives that self-identify as victims of the East German regime: former political prisoners, relatives of those killed while trying to overcome the border, those evicted from their homes due to collectivization measures. These groups vary greatly in terms of their membership and their focus of action. They can be distinguished by whether they were founded before 1989 in West Germany or after 1989 in the East. Further, their work is focused on different levels of the political system, so that over the years, a certain hierarchy, but also complementarity, has developed.

The largest and most visible organization at the federal level is the *Union der Opferverbände Kommunistischer Gewaltherrschaft* (UOKG – Union of Victims' Associations of Communist Dictatorship). This group was founded in 1992 as an umbrella organization for the already existing and many emerging victims' initiatives. According to several observers, this founding was promoted by the Federal Ministry of the Interior, which foresaw problems in dealing with many disparate groupings. Gerhard Finn of this Ministry argued that it would be impossible to handle the many anticipated applications for funding and a mountain of accounting paperwork. He initiated a meeting in December 1990 of victim groups in Königswinter near Bonn, out of which first a loose alliance and then eventually the UOKG emerged.[24] In other words, from the beginning, state actors helped to shape the framework within which these civic groups were organized. Today, the UOKG has over thirty member groups that together account for two million individual members.[25] The majority of these are part of the Federation of Expellees (BdV). Though there may be strength in numbers, the inclusion of the memory of expulsion in the UOKG's mandates may also decrease the organization's effectiveness when it comes to addressing the human rights violations of the GDR regime.

The UOKG seeks to represent its members primarily through publicity – its leaders are often consulted by journalists and government agencies as the most important voice of SED victims. Furthermore, the UOKG works to bundle and screen for quality the applications of its members for state funding. The UOKG has also been utilized by the state in the reverse direction, as a link to civic groups. For instance, the *Stiftung Aufarbeitung* and the Interior Ministry tasked it with distributing funds, derived from a commemorative postal stamp, to smaller victim groups.

[24] Siegmund, *Opfer ohne Lobby?* p.83, see Interviews, Hugo Diederich.
[25] www.uokg.de/cms/index.

In its publications and public statements, the UOKG contends that its work receives recognition by the public and the government and stresses its arbitration function: "We continue to see ourselves as a mediator between state institutions and the associations – only through the joint efforts of all organizations active in political education can we work effectively against the Zeitgeist of GDR nostalgia."[26] The UOKG engages in a broad set of activities, including providing assistance to victims, lobbying for pension payments, and publicizing the actions of former members of the GDR regime. In addition, they are directly involved in a host of memorialization initiatives. They regularly organize commemorative events, often in cooperation with smaller associations. The UOKG also directly participates in key memorials, such as the former Stasi remand prison in Berlin-Hohenschönhausen and the former headquarters of the Stasi in the Normannenstrasse in Berlin, where they maintain offices. Most recently, the UOKG has spearheaded a campaign to build a central memorial to the victims of communism in Berlin. Launched in 2013, the campaign had received funding from the federal cultural ministry (BKM) and is supported by the *Stiftung Aufarbeitung*. Both institutions welcome the public debate about the victims of communism in the Federal Republic.[27] In order to enhance publicity, the UOKG has created an independent website for the *Initiative Mahnmal* (Memorial Initiative), put out brochures and flyers, and organized public events. The mandate of the proposed memorial is sweeping: it is to recall all victims of Communist rule, from political prisoners, Gulag inmates, victims of forced collectivization, all the way to expellees. The organizers write: "For all these victims, we strive for a memorial that can contribute to the development of a democratic historical consciousness, especially among our younger fellow citizens."[28] So far, this initiative has not progressed considerably and has not received much public attention.

Though every victim biography varies, there are some characteristics that appear to be common among this group of memory activists. Rainer Wagner, a former head of the UOKG whom I interviewed, is quite a typical example. Wagner was first arrested in 1967 and was incarcerated for fourteen months for attempting to flee from the GDR. After his release, he tried to escape again and experienced more prison and surveillance, while leading an oppositional church group. In 1983, the FRG government "bought him out" of the East, partly for health reasons. He

[26] Konferenz der LStU, 'Vom Wert der Freiheit' p. 173.
[27] See Interviews, Anna Kaminsky; www.initiative-mahnmal.de/index.php/ueber-die-initiative.
[28] www.initiative-mahnmal.de/attachments/article/71/Flyer%20Initiative%20Mahnmal.pdf.

was then a member of memorial organizations in the West and from 2002 onward became very active in political prisoner associations. Wagner – like many others I have met or interviewed from this *Aufarbeitungsszene* – combines two key traits. First, he has a pragmatic approach to memory politics and obviously understands the political realities. He seeks to present himself and his organization as professional and reasonable to other actors in this arena. Second, his own legacy of suffering is also evident in the way he speaks about the topic. He stresses the need for justice and recognition for the victims and explains the emotional meaning of memorial spaces. Memory politics are clearly personal for Wagner, and it is this authenticity that made him an acceptable leader to the UOKG membership.[29] Horst Schüler and Dieter Dombrowski, two other UOKG chairs, were incarcerated in the Soviet forced labor camp Workuta and in GDR prisons, respectively.

Another influential organization, the *Vereinigung Opfer des Stalinismus* (VOS – Association Victims of Stalinism) was temporarily a member of UOKG, but has since decided to withdraw to maintain a higher level of autonomy. The VOS was founded in 1950 (see Chapter 2) in West Germany, mostly by former inmates of Soviet Special Camps, and quickly had local branches in all the Western *Bundesländer*. During the first decades of its life, VOS organized practical assistance to newly arrived GDR victims and provided them with a forum to share their experiences. The VOS enjoyed considerable patronage by Bonn political elites, even hosting former Chancellor Konrad Adenauer at one of its gatherings in 1960.[30] In 1998, the regular funding by the federal government was terminated and the group rapidly saw its access to the halls of political power decline. Hugo Diederich, VOS managing director, speculates that the important position held by VOS previously, was attributable to its anti-Communist stance in the context of the Cold War.[31] Despite this, the VOS experienced a strong rise in membership immediately after the fall of the Wall. In 1991 alone, 1,811 people joined and today VOS still has 1300 members.[32] In addition to its main Berlin office, the VOS now has fifteen local branches, many of which are driving forces in local memorial initiatives and remembrance events. In a sense then, the VOS underwent a transformation from a group that was closely intertwined with political elites to one that is closer to the grassroots.

[29] See Interviews, Rainer Wagner.
[30] Richter, 'Aus der Geschichte der VOS' p. 99.
[31] See Interviews, Hugo Diederich.
[32] Stiehl, 'Die VOS 50 Jahre', email communication with Hugo Diederich, September 1, 2016.

Today, the self-described activities of VOS include being a forum for victims – particularly through its newsletter *Freiheitsglocke* (Freedom Bell), lobbying for financial compensation, and working through political channels to prevent the development of extremism – particular on the left. Both the UOKG and the VOS have had to defend themselves against accusations of right-wing tendencies. As a result, their leaders routinely stress their principled rejection of left and right radicalism. Moreover, they regularly make statements underlining the singularity of the Holocaust and their rejection of competition between SED and NS victims.[33] At the same time, they continue to demand that GDR victims receive the same level of recognition and pension payments as victims of National Socialism.[34] Moreover, due to racist utterances of some of its leaders, the group has been accused of being on the radical right. Despite this, the VOS is often included in key memorial events and receives funding from the *Stiftung Aufarbeitung*. Nevertheless, these activists have a sense that they are not always heard by official institutions and must struggle for their position. As VOS executive director Hugo Diederich told me: "in the old days, the Mayor of Berlin would come to [our commemorative ceremony at] Steinplatz. We were much more visible then, were regarded as a kind of instrument of power for politics, one could say: this is human proof that injustice is happening in the Communist system, these people were in camps. That is not necessary any more today."[35]

Founded in January 1990, a second organization that seeks to be panregional in nature is the *Bund Stalinistisch Verfolgter* (BSV – Federation of Those Persecuted by Stalinism).[36] This group is seen by the VOS as a sister organization and a merger has been discussed more than once, but not as yet broadly implemented.[37] Similar to the VOS, the BSV keeps in touch with its members through its joint newsletter with the UOKG – the *Stacheldraht* (Barbed Wire) – and is composed of local branches, albeit only in the Eastern *Länder*. In terms of its goals and strategies, VOS and BSV are nearly indistinguishable.

Though these panregional organizations participate in the creation of memorials, more specific groupings have collectively been the most important memorial initiator, gradually transforming the landscape of

---

[33] Detlef Stein, UOKG in Konferenz der LStU, 'Vom Wert der Freiheit.'

[34] See Interviews, Hugo Diederich and Rainer Wagner, Angelika Barbe of the UOKG in: Kongress der LStU and Stiftung zur Aufarbeitung der SED- Diktatur, 'Über Grenzen und Zeiten.'

[35] See Interviews, Hugo Diederich.   [36] Siegmund, *Opfer ohne Lobby?* p. 66.

[37] Stiehl, 'Die VOS 50 Jahre'; Sachsen-Anhalt is an exception where VOS and BSV have been united. See Interviews, Annegret Stephan.

GDR memory. Unable to congregate during GDR times, former Special Camp inmates and political prisoners have now established organizations specifically focused on particular memory sites – usually those where they or family members had suffered. Between March 1990 and September 1992, associations of former inmates in the *Speziallager* of Buchenwald, Fünfeichen, Jamlitz, Ketschendorf, Mühlberg, and Sachsenhausen were founded, each with between two hundred and 550 members. In addition, there are organizations for inmates of Soviet camps on non-German soil, such as the *Lagergemeinschaft Gulag/Workuta* (Camp Community Gulag/Workuta), which has been quite vocal.[38] Many more local initiatives exist to commemorate specific prisons and Stasi facilities all across East Germany. For example, the *Bautzen Komitee* was founded in March 1990, in the aftermath of successful protests for the release of the remaining political prisoners of the notorious Bautzen prison. Bautzen had been a prison during the Nazi, the Soviet, and the GDR periods and thus has a complex history to work through. From the beginning, the Komitee demanded not only a rehabilitation of prisoners but the creation of a memorial. By early 1992, the prison had been closed and the memorial opened in 1994.[39] Though all three periods are addressed in the exhibition, the clear emphasis is on the GDR period.[40] Former prisoners meet annually at the Bautzen forum and remain actively involved in the memorial's activities, though it is run by the Memorial Foundation of the state of Saxony.

Next to and often closely allied with initiatives for particular sites, are smaller civic groups that pursue a general purpose of advocating for the memory of human rights abuses in the GDR. Among them is the *Vereinigung 17. Juni,* which was founded in the aftermath of the 1953 uprising by some of the surviving protesters who had fled to the West. Since those early years, the group has been involved not only in the anniversary ceremonies of that event, but has supported the creation of memorial markers, for instance for victims of the Berlin Wall.[41] Today the *Vereinigung 17. Juni* is driven primarily by a few individuals including Carl-Wolfgang Holzapfel and his partner, both former political prisoners. There are even more obscure groups with very few members, which nevertheless sometimes make a splash. The best example is that of Jürgen Litfin and his Berlin Wall watchtower memorial to his brother Günter, who was the first to be shot at the Berlin Wall in 1961. In the

---

[38] Siegmund, *Opfer ohne Lobby?* p. 77.
[39] Hattig and others, *Geschichte des Speziallagers Bautzen*, Hattig and others, *Stasigefängnis Bautzen II.*
[40] Thomas, 'Coming to Terms with the Stasi.'
[41] See Interviews, Carl-Wolfgang Holzapfel.

post-1989 chaos, Litfin encountered a former border guard who happened to have retained a key to one of the Wall watchtowers. The guard
disappeared, but in 2003 Litfin transformed the site into a memorial to his
brother. Today, this is one of the few remaining border towers and also
a reminder of the fluid post-wall situation that enabled the creation of
memorials through civic initiative. Such spontaneous action is no longer
possible. Despite Litfin's bitterness about the lack of support he has
received over the years, his tower was integrated into the Berlin Wall
Concept in 2006 and has received state funding.[42]

Less recognized than Litfin's, have been the ad hoc memorial activities
of such figures as Gustav Rust and Rainer Schubert. Rust, a former
political prisoner, has for years set up his own makeshift memorial in
the central Berlin tourist zone between Reichstag and Brandenburg Gate,
calling for the recognition of victims of communism (while spouting anti-
Semitic slurs).[43] Less provocatively, Schubert founded the *Aufarbeitungs-
Initiative* (Initiative for Working Through the Past) in 1998 and has
supported various memorial initiatives. In 2004, Schubert was one of
those activists who chained themselves to the cross-memorial at
Checkpoint Charlie in order to prevent its demolition.[44] While these
actors are not central to the *Aufarbeitungsszene*, they are nevertheless
important, because they are an energetic but unpredictable factor for
GDR memory leaders. Their actions are often radical and not compatible
with the mainstream and state-funded memory community, but their
visibility means that they cannot be ignored entirely.

Dissidents

The second key category of memory activists is made up of former
members of the *DDR Bürgerbewegung* (GDR citizens' movement).
Younger than members of victims' organizations on average, these
individuals had typically become engaged in political opposition groups
during the 1980s and have been instrumental in shaping the transitional
period of 1989/1990. Former dissidents have become pivotal actors both
as members of state institutions and as civic memory activists – or they
have shifted between the two. Blurring the lines between state and civic
spheres, these activists occupy a hybrid position in memory politics that

---

[42] http://gedenkstaetteguenterlitfin.de/gedenkstaette/geschichte, See Interviews, Jürgen Litfin.
[43] See Interviews, Gustav Rust, Berg and Goetz 'Protest am Reichstag.' As of 2016, Rust
was still engaged in this problematic memory protest near Brandenburg Gate.
[44] See Interviews, Rainer Schubert.

was unheard of a generation before. But this is now common and illustrates the complex interactivity between the two sectors.

One important path from dissidence to post-1989 memory activism was the occupation of Stasi facilities and the safeguarding of secret police files in the transitional period. Some of the participants in this revolutionary action had been involved in oppositional work for years; for others, this was the first time they became active. For all, the experience of "taking over" and asserting their democratic rights was formative. In the Thuringian town of Erfurt, for instance, members of the opposition movement took over the local Stasi remand prison at Andreasstrasse on December 4, 1989. Over the years, over five thousand political prisoners had been held here.[45] The *Bürgerkomittee* (Citizens' Committee) Erfurt3, which formed in the course of the revolution, continues to be involved in this site that opened officially in late 2013. For instance, former civic occupiers offer guided tours and their publications are sold there. Moreover, the joint history of political repression and resistance is present in the memorial's design: not only has the former prison been made accessible, the visitor center is housed in a "revolutionary cube" that depicts the events of 1989 through illustrations in the style of a graphic novel.[46]

The headquarters of the Stasi (Haus 1 at Normannenstrasse) in Berlin were also occupied – on January 15, 1990 – and immediately plans were made to turn the building into a memorial to both state oppression and resistance. Though the initial expectation was for the site to become an official, state-run memorial, it has remained in the hands of the association *Antistalinistische Aktion* (ASTAK – Anti-Stalinist Action). This group emerged out of the occupying citizens committee *Bürgerkomitee 15. Januar* that opened the Haus 1 to the public in mid-1990 and put together the first exhibits.[47]

The most well-known case of a Stasi-building-turned-memorial is the Museum "Runde Ecke" (Museum Round Corner) in Leipzig, the center of citizen protests in 1989. The Bürgerkomitee Leipzig (Citizens' Committee Leipzig) was founded spontaneously during the occupation of the local secret police headquarters on December 4th, 1989. The Committee safeguarded the documents until they were handed over to the official authority in charge of the Stasi files (BStU). The same opposition group put together the first exhibition "Stasi – Power and Banality" in August 1990 and became the initiator and

---

[45] www.stiftung-ettersberg.de/en/andreasstrasse/, Maser, 'Der lange Weg in die Andreasstraße.'
[46] Maser, Veen, and Voit, 'Haft Diktatur Revolution.'
[47] See Interviews, Jörg Drieselmann; www.stasimuseum.de/geschichte.htm.

responsible party (Träger) for the Museum Runde Ecke.[48] From the beginning, this group collected Stasi materials and files from Leipzig and elsewhere, conducted historical research, and designed their exhibitions. Today, the Museum has a professional inventory of over thirty thousand Stasi-related objects and is visited by about eighty thousand people annually.[49] The long-time leader of the Museum, Tobias Hollitzer, is typical of dissident memory activists. Hollitzer had become active in various opposition groups during the mid-1980s. Since 1990, he has held various professional positions related to working through the GDR past, including for the Leipzig LStU office. Despite its growth in size and its increasing professionalization, the Runde Ecke was led by Hollitzer and the Bürgerkomitee through unpaid civic engagement until 2007. Hollitzer then became its official (and remunerated) director and continued the work of planning exhibits, caring for the collection, creating publicity, fundraising and more. While he remained a civic activist then, and crucially drove forward the development of the Runde Ecke, Hollitzer was also head of the steering committee of the state of Saxony's memorial foundation – straddling the civic and state sectors.[50]

These examples from Erfurt, Berlin, and Leipzig illustrate vividly two points about the memory activism of former dissidents. First, it is crucial to understand the important legacy of (and sometimes myths about) civic protests of 1989/1990 in the creation of many memorials, the function of these buildings during the transition period, and the civic identity of the memorial initiators (and often now leaders). Another case in point here is the former Stasi prison in downtown Potsdam's Lindenstrasse. After the revolution, this building was used by several opposition groups, including the Neues Forum, Demokratie Jetzt, Gruppe Argus, and the social democratic party, among others. These groups demanded early on that the site be converted into a memorial. When the Fördergemeinschaft Lindenstrasse 54 was created in 1995, many of those actors from the transitional period were among its founding members.[51] Second, many former oppositionists have acquired a kind of hybrid identity as both civic advocates and as employees of state institutions for memory work. Rüdiger worked for the Potsdam branch of the BStU from 1990 onward and before retirement as its director. Meanwhile she was active not only

---

[48] www.runde-ecke-leipzig.de/index. Carola Rudnick argues that the role of the citizens' committees in the dismantling of Stasi facilities has been exaggerated and that this "myth" has been integrated into the foundational narratives of sites such as the Normannenstrasse and Runde Ecke (Rudnick, *Die andere Hälfte der Erinnerung*).

[49] 'Tobias Hollitzer wechselt.'

[50] www.chronikderwende.de/lexikon/biografien/biographie_jsp/key=hollitzer_tobias.html.

[51] See Interviews, Claus Peter Ladner and Gisela Rüdiger.

for the Lindenstrasse, but also in efforts to make the former Soviet prison at Leistikowstrasse into a memorial. Maria Nooke, prominent in the opposition movement in the Brandenburg town of Forst, became a leader in the official Wall Memorial at Bernauer Strasse in Berlin that was also pushed forward by civic activism right after 1989.[52] Well-known dissident Ulrike Poppe likewise engaged in hybrid activities. In 2006, she participated in the "Sabrow Commission" tasked by the federal government with coming up with a comprehensive plan for GDR remembrance. She then became the first *Beauftragte für Aufarbeitung* (Commissioner for Historical Reckoning) in Brandenburg. However, she also continued her civic engagement, for instance when she participated in a civic initiative in the Berlin neighborhood of Prenzlauer Berg that resulted in a memorial in East Berlin recalling the victims of a local Soviet secret service prison "Haus 3."[53]

In relation to dissident memory activism, it is crucial to address the role played by the federal and state authorities for the secret police files, the *Bundesbeauftragte* and *Landesbeauftragte der Stasiunterlagenbehörde* (BStU and LStU). These institutions are directly connected to the protests and building occupations of 1989/90; they had been demanded by opposition leaders and enshrined in the unification treaty.[54] In fact, the BStU was at first located at Normannenstrasse. All three leaders of the BStU thus far have been prominent oppositionists: Joachim Gauck, Marianne Birthler, and Roland Jahn. At the state level too, the positions are held by former dissidents such as Poppe in Brandenburg, Martin Gutzeit in Berlin, Christian Dietrich in Thuringia, Anne Drescher in Mecklenburg-Vorpommern, and Lutz Rathenow in Saxony. These individuals' history equips them with irreplaceable personal relationships from oppositional times through which they can cooperate across institutional and state boundaries. Moreover, despite their status as state officials, these dissidents can often create trust with older generations of activists through their joint experience of imprisonment in the GDR.[55] However, there is also a marked rift between the dissidents of the 1980s and the victims of Stalinism. The reason for this are partly generational, partly to do with the divergent experiences and sense of suffering felt by political prisoners who were incarcerated when conditions were more dramatic than in the later decades of the GDR. Moreover, dissidents are sometimes accused by victim groups of having wanted to reform the GDR, rather than get rid of

---

[52] Camphausen and Fischer, 'Die bürgerschaftliche Durchsetzung der Gedenkstätte an der Bernauer Straße,' see Interviews, Maria Nooke and Manfred Fischer.
[53] See Interviews, Ulrike Poppe and Bernt Roder.
[54] See Interviews, Gabriele Camphausen.
[55] See Interviews, Ulrike Poppe.

it as a criminal system. Nevertheless, the BStU and LStU – and the dissidents who are their leaders – act as mediators between civic groups and state institutions while they themselves participate in both spheres.

This hybrid institution has also been involved in the creation of numerous memory sites. The BStU has opened an exhibit about the history and methods of the Stasi, which was initially located in downtown Berlin near Checkpoint Charlie. Moreover, the BStU, sometimes in cooperation with an LStU or civic groups, has put together over twenty exhibitions on specific Stasi-related topics that can be borrowed and displayed by memorial or educational organizations free of charge. Many LStU or local branches of the BStU in East German towns have designed permanent exhibits about local Stasi activities. And there are even some memorials that are run by the BStU. For example, the BStU together with the city government runs the Memorial and Documentation Center Frankfurt (Oder), which recalls the "victims of political violent dictatorship 1930–45 /1945–89." The memorial had been initiated during the transitional period in 1990, developed in cooperation with victims' groups, and opened to the public in 1994.[56]

Pragmatics

The third important type of memory activists is an even more diverse group without a common identity. They are nevertheless an important component of the *Aufarbeitungsszene* as they provide memorial initiatives with experience, personal reputation, and level-headed intervention. These individuals were usually not themselves directly affected by the GDR regime and are often from West Germany. They are important allies for East German victim representatives or dissidents in arguing for the indispensable nature of the GDR legacy for pan-German history and for democratic governance writ-large.

A good example of a pragmatic memory activist is Claus Peter Ladner, a West German judge in an administrative court, who had come to Potsdam in the early 1990s to help rebuild the East German justice system. In the context of rehabilitation cases, he met some of the former civic occupiers of the former Stasi remand prison at Lindenstrasse and they decided to become active, founding an association of twenty-one members.[57] This *Fördergemeinschaft Lindenstrasse 54* was instrumental in creating an official memorial here against the initial resistance of the city. Today, the site recalls both its use by the Nazis (as a court where the

[56] www.museum-viadrina.de/.   [57] See Interviews, Claus Peter Ladner.

policy of forced sterilization and euthanasia was put into practice) and the Stasi.

Harald Fiss, another pragmatic, was the bureaucrat responsible in 1989/1990 for the *Notaufnahmelager* (refugee camp) in Berlin-Marienfelde, one of two facilities where refugees from the GDR were processed by the West German government before they could become residents in the FRG. Thus, Fiss was tasked with organizing the transformation of a place that was emblematic of what the German separation had meant for thousands of affected individuals. During the 1990s, Marienfelde took in those ethnic Germans arriving primarily from the former Soviet Union (*Aussiedler*), as well as asylum seekers. At the same time, Fiss was acutely aware that the traces of an important piece of German history were being lost and he wrote to the Berlin authorities about the need to safeguard Marienfelde as a memory site. Though the responsible senator was supportive, the city's priorities lay elsewhere. Fiss put together the first small exhibition as part of his professional duties, but during its opening laid out lists for interested people to sign up and become part of the association for the Marienfelde Refugee Center Museum (*Erinnerungsstätte Notaufnahme-Lager Marienfelde e.V.*). Its members all had a personal connection to the site – either having been themselves a refugee or having worked for the Allied authorities – and could thus contribute critical knowledge.[58] This civic organization, just like the one founded by Ladner, was then able to apply for public funds to develop the site.

Peter Boeger, is a West Berlin expert for document preservation, and is now in a leadership position at the BStU's education and research division. When he moved to Klein-Machnow on the outskirts of Berlin, he became involved in an existing citizens' initiative that aimed to preserve "Checkpoint Bravo," one of the largest crossing points between East and West on the Autobahn. As most Easterners were not allowed to traverse the border, this site is especially important for the many West Germans who recall waiting in line for hours and worrying about being searched. At the time, the association "Checkpoint Bravo e.V." was rocked by partisan conflicts, which Boeger's pragmatic approach, focused on the preservation and development of Checkpoint Bravo, was able to overcome. Today, the "Erinnerungs- und Begegnungsstätte Grenzkontrollpunkt Dreilinden-Drewitz" (Memorial and Meeting Site Border Crossing Dreilinden-Drewitz) is a popular spot, particularly for motorists and cyclists following the Berlin Wall

[58] See Interviews, Harald Fiss.

Cycling Path. It continues to be run by the association, albeit with public funds from Berlin, Brandenburg and the *Stiftung Aufarbeitung*.[59]

What characterizes these and other memory activists as pragmatic in their approach is, first, that their motivation for civic engagement derives not from personal investment in the GDR past, but from a more generalized belief in the importance of addressing past injustice in the service of democracy. This means that they are often more flexible in their demands and more willing to cooperate with diverse partners, including with memory advocates on the Nazi past. They have less need than victims of the East German regime to defend their position within the hierarchy of meaning in the Federal Republic. Second, their pragmatism is manifested in their willingness to contemplate giving up control over the memorial sites they helped initiate, in order to secure a sustainable future for them.

Victims' representatives in particular tend to be suspicious of too much institutional control. In my many interviews with such memory activists, there was a strong sense that those civic campaigners who initiated a memorial should not cede the capacity to make sure it stays on the "right path." Thus, they have generally rejected attempts to create umbrella organizations to streamline governance of various memory sites and have insisted that they remain a strong voice when a site became part of a state foundation. By contrast, when asked about plans for the future of their memorial, the pragmatics spoke (unprompted) about the difficulty of keeping a civically run memorial going in the face of aging association members and fundraising problems. They saw the most obvious solution in transferring responsibility for their site directly to government institutions or becoming part of state structures. Thus, Harald Fiss welcomed plans to create the *Stiftung Berliner Mauer* (Berlin Wall Foundation) and this was an attractive partner for Peter Boeger as well. Volker Römer, head of *Gegen das Vergessen e.V.* (Against Forgetting), the association that initiated and runs the only Western German GDR museum in Pforzheim, has approached the state museum of Baden-Württemberg about the possibility of their taking over the museum. He told me: "a civic museum is nice, but if another constellation were to develop, I would deem the continued existence of the museum as more important than its civic aspect. But the situation will not change – it will remain civic." The state government has turned Römer's proposal down.[60] Such flexibility on the part of "pragmatics" mean they are important mediators between the pre- and post-1989 memory factions,

[59] See Interviews, Peter Boeger, www.checkpoint-bravo.de/foerderer.htm, Boeger and Dollmann, *FREUNDwärts, FEINDwärts*.

[60] See Interviews, Harald Fiss, Peter Boeger, Volker Römer, and Birgit Kipfer.

as they have gained civic credibility through their engagement for GDR memory, but often have a similar political cultural background as many in the Nazi past memory community.

For-Profits

A final type of actor is the for-profit memory initiative. These are, by definition, not driven primarily by the principled belief in the importance of memory for society, but by the profit motive. Nevertheless, they form an important part of the GDR memorial landscape and some of them self-identify as civil society. Moreover, for-profit memorial enterprises focus our attention on the importance of memory for an expanding tourist industry. Memory entrepreneurs recognized the lucrative potential of the crumbling GDR right after the fall of the Berlin Wall. Vendors of pieces of the Wall, tours with a Trabi (the old East German car), or the "Story of Berlin" multimedia show quickly became part of the touristic lineup. As Sibylle Frank has argued, this vibrant "heritage-industry" stood in contrast to the official, more reserved, approach that derided such initiatives as commercial, populist, or Disney-like.[61] Despite the fact that most civic memory activists and institutional officials rejected for-profits as unscientific and inauthentic, they did recognize that these entrepreneurs were meeting an existing demand. Indeed, one of the first post-1989 memorial markers – a double row of cobblestones marking the location of the Wall – was developed by the city of Berlin in cooperation with the tourism development company *Berlin Partner*.[62]

The two most prominent instances of for-profit memorial initiatives show clearly how this type of institution has influenced the *Aufarbeitungsszene*. The first is the DDR Museum (GDR Museum) that opened in 2006 in the heart of the Berlin tourist zone next to the cathedral and the museum island (Figure 6.3). The Museum is located in commercial space and relatively small – a visit can easily be fit into a busy tourist's schedule. As its founder, Peter Kenzelmann, told me, the GDR museum receives no public funding; it is a commercial enterprise that seeks to make a profit through satisfied customers. Though the exhibit was designed with the help of Stefan Wolle, a well-known historian of the GDR, it is distinguished from public museums by the high level of interactivity offered to visitors. Most of the items displayed can be touched and handled. Visitors can sit in a Trabi (the typical East

---

[61] Frank, 'Der Mauer um die Wette gedenken.'
[62] See Interviews, Eberhard Diepgen (at the time the company was called *Partners for Berlin*).

Figure 6.3. DDR Museum in central Berlin.[63]

German car). There is an interactive game about the GDR for guests to play, a version of which can be purchased in the Museum's shop. Here, tourists can also acquire GDR quiz cards with interesting, but also funny questions. A few years after the Museum's opening, its owners added an

---

[63] Jenny Wüstenberg, 2007.

"authentic" GDR restaurant next door, with some of the items on the menu crossed out due to ostensible shortages.[64] The *DDR Museum* has both been criticized as trivializing the East German dictatorship and lauded for providing information about the GDR to visitors who may not otherwise have sought it out. In any case, its makers are unapologetic about their business model, which attracts over half a million people annually.[65]

A more complex case is that of the *Museum Haus am Checkpoint Charlie*. This private Museum grew out of the civic initiative *Arbeitsgemeinschaft 13. August* (Working Group 13th of August), started by one man, Rainer Hildebrandt, who opened it in reaction to the building of the Berlin Wall in 1961. Initially, it was located in a two-bedroom apartment at Bernauer Strasse where the Wall cut through the middle of a neighborhood. The high-level of interest quickly made that space too small and Hildebrandt moved the Museum to Checkpoint Charlie – the border crossing point of the Allied forces and famous locale of the tank confrontation in 1961 – where it remains to this day. Hildebrandt's initiative from the outset was meant as a protest against the Wall and repression in the GDR, and it was a hub for those who sought to help people escape from the East. The Museum collected many authentic items related to escapes from the GDR and enjoyed a high level of respect.[66] After 1989, Checkpoint Charlie became one of the locations most frequented by Berlin tourists and the city added not only the double-row of cobble stones, but installed large photo portraits of an American and a Soviet soldier symbolically facing each other.[67] Later, when the real estate that used to be the death strip remained in dispute, the city added a temporary exhibit on a fence, as well as a "black box" with an exhibit about the Cold War. It also allowed the erection of a large panorama by the artist Yadegar Asisi, which depicts a fictional but realistic view from the Western side of the Wall. Checkpoint Charlie today presents tourists with a bizarre set of offerings related to the GDR and beyond – from a Trabi museum to an exhibition about Currywurst (a Berlin specialty). The *Museum Haus am Checkpoint Charlie* also continued to expand, adding more space within its building and including in its already somewhat hodgepodge exhibition examples of human rights violations and activists from all over the world. In 2000, Hildebrandt erected a replica of the old guard house and the famous sign "You are now leaving the American Sector" outside.

[64] See Interviews, Peter Kenzelmann; www.ddr-museum.de/en
[65] www.ddr-museum.de/en/blog/museum-news/we-are-delighted-about-the-attendance-record-504564-people-visited-the-ddr-museum-in-2012.
[66] www.mauermuseum.de/index.php/en/about-us, See Interviews, Alexandra Hildebrandt.
[67] Frank, 'Der Mauer um die Wette gedenken.'

Particularly after the death of Rainer Hildebrandt in 2004, the Museum under the leadership of his wife Alexandra developed a unique and independent approach to GDR memory that was controversial in the *Aufarbeitungsszene*.

Most notoriously, Alexandra Hildebrandt in 2004 rented a piece of land that was still undeveloped in the former death strip at Checkpoint Charlie and erected over a thousand black wooden crosses, each ostensibly commemorating one victim of the German-German border. During the time of its existence, this installation became the primary GDR memorial site of the city, attracting thousands of visitors who could not easily distinguish between this private action and an officially sanctioned monument. In summer 2005, after a prolonged dispute with the landowners who did not want to extend Hildebrandt's lease, the crosses were bulldozed (with the approval of the Berlin government). Memory activists, including from the UOKG and the *Aufarbeitungsinitiative*, tried to prevent the demolition by chaining themselves to the crosses (see Chapter 1). Afterward, the Museum collected thousands of signatures demanding the memorial's rebuilding. Also in 2005, Hildebrandt successfully applied to put up building-sized posters recalling the anti-regime uprising in the GDR on what is now the Finance Ministry, and which in 1953 had been a central location of the demonstrations in Berlin. The official memorial at this site had been criticized by Hildebrandt and victims' groups for being not visible or clear enough in its message. Hildebrandt left up the posters long after her permission had expired and they were only taken down after a court order.[68]

Hildebrandt's actions in 2004–2005 and her abrasive style made her the object of much scorn among other memory advocates in the city. Most mainstream politicians and memorial officials criticized the cross installation as overly emotional and not historically accurate: the exact number of Wall dead remained a matter of dispute and there had in fact only been a few (albeit dramatic) escape attempts at Checkpoint Charlie itself. Nevertheless, critics acknowledged the important role these disputes had played in pressuring the Berlin authorities into taking action.[69] As head of the *Stiftung Aufarbeitung*, Anna Kaminsky put it: Hildebrandt "with her guerilla memory – you can think of this what you will – but she managed to plainly demonstrate that something had to happen in this city."[70] The direct outcome was a process that led to the

---

[68] Wüstenberg, 'Transforming Berlin's Memory.'
[69] Klemke, 'Das Gesamtkonzept Berliner Mauer', See Interviews, Günter Nooke, Thomas Flierl 'Speech to the Expert Conference on Wall Remembrance', Martin-Gropius-Bau, Berlin, February 2, 2005.
[70] See Interviews, Anna Kaminsky.

city's Berlin Wall Concept in which all existing sites – both civic and state in origin – were connected, the Bernauer Strasse memorial was expanded considerably and a comprehensive plan for funding and development was agreed upon in 2006.[71] The Berlin Concept was integrated into the federal government's memorial concept.

Meanwhile, an international group of prominent historians and politicians founded an association with the goal of creating a Museum on the Cold War at Checkpoint Charlie, aiming to focus on the international dimensions of the conflict. The Berlin government was initially supportive, but deemed a realization difficult in practice and perhaps not politically expedient in the face of demands for a more emotional remembrance of individual suffering caused by the Wall.[72] The project has not been abandoned, but seems to be dormant at present. The *Museum Haus am Checkpoint Charlie* and numerous victim groups rejected the Museum outright as drawing an unacceptable equation between the Soviet and Western systems of governance and their roles in the Cold War. Meanwhile, Alexandra Hildebrandt undid her organization's status as an association and became a private entity. This "privatization" notwithstanding, Hildebrandt stressed the civic nature of her actions (and the lack of appreciation shown by the powers-that-be):

> If we build a memorial on the street, with our own strength, without applying for tax funds, that is wonderful, you have to be happy and grateful, and thank us for this. This is not private remembrance, this is public … There is civic engagement, but there is no private remembrance. There is civic engagement and there are monuments built by the state.[73]

Another reading of the nature of the *Museum Haus am Checkpoint Charlie* – shared by many in the *Aufarbeitungsszene* – is that it is first and foremost a highly profitable enterprise – by some estimates making millions of euros every year. It is plain that the high number of visitors (an estimated 850,000 in 2008) to Museum coupled with an entry fee of €12.50 per person translates into considerable revenue.[74] Moreover, Hildebrandt's unwillingness for regular cooperation with other GDR memorial sites in the city suggests that a coherent landscape of

---

[71] 'Gesamtkonzept zur Erinnerung an die Berliner Mauer. Dokumentation, Information und Gedenken,' June 12, 2006, www.berlin.de/imperia/md/content/senwfk/pdf-dateien/mauerdialog/asv2006616_1.pdf?start&ts=1171978112&file=asv2006616_1.pdf.

[72] See 'Debatte für ein Museum des Kalten Krieges' *Zeithistorische Forschungen – Studies in Contemporary History* 5 (2008) and http://markus-meckel.de/engagement/museum-kalter-krieg/.

[73] See Interviews, Alexandra Hildebrandt.

[74] www.berlin.de/rbmskzl/aktuelles/pressemitteilungen/2009/pressemitteilung.54980.php; www.mauermuseum.de/index.php/en/opening-times-a-tickets.

commemoration is not her primary motivation. Nevertheless, though the *Haus am Checkpoint Charlie* is a for-profit enterprise, its civic origin and self-perception, as well as its notable public impact, have made it into an important factor in GDR memorial politics writ-large. What its role will be in the future, as the mnemonic institutional framework solidifies and relationships within the *Aufarbeitungsszene* are regularized, remains to be seen.

Framing GDR Memory Activism

The interaction of victims' representatives, dissidents, pragmatic activists and for-profit enterprises – in addition to state representatives from BStU, LStU, *Stiftung Aufarbeitung* and other regional and federal institutions – makes for a complex "scene" of GDR memory actors. From its inception in 1989, state and civil society in the *Aufarbeitungsszene* were not neatly separated but intricately intertwined through personal connections, individuals who straddle dividing lines, and crosscutting funding and institutional structures. What unites all of these diverse actors is their high level of personal investment in the cause of remembering the East German regime and society, its victims, and its resistors. This investment is manifested in many hours spent working for their initiatives – often wholly unpaid, but around-the-clock – and to the detriment of other aspects of their lives. Most of these individuals – though certainly not all – have both the financial and temporal resources to allow them such a self-effacing level of engagement; many of them are pensioners.[75] Some of the activists I have mentioned display deep emotional links to the memorial sites they promote and feel a natural connection to their fellow activists. Many of my interview partners clearly use their activism as a way of coming to terms with their own experiences of incarceration and trauma. This emotionality can result in difficulties in the negotiation with "memory professionals" who have other priorities, such as the presentation of the past in historically contextualized terms and its professional implementation. For this reason, the "pragmatics" – who have civic credentials but are less personally affected – often act as useful mediators between victims and state actors. These pragmatic civic campaigners are also highly motivated, but they are driven primarily by principled beliefs about the crucial function of memory for present-day democracy.

Another uniting factor for all these activists is a kind of productive competition among the different memorial sites. As Jörg Drieselmann,

---

[75] See Interviews, Siegfried Reiprich and Hugo Diederich.

head of the *Antistalinistische Aktion* (ASTAK), the group that runs the
Stasi Museum at Normannenstrasse, explained:

> We have all been friends for many, many years. This is good prerequisite for
> keeping egotism and competition in check. I also believe that my Museum
> is the best and the greatest, and the most beautiful that exists. That is of
> course important and necessary. You have to stand behind your own
> institution with self-confidence, because that's what keeps it alive. If I feel
> that we are not doing well, I cannot keep it alive. This is good. And we work
> hard every day to do a good job. But it does not cross my mind that the
> others are not doing a good job. They are also good and undoubtedly the
> biggest and most beautiful – of course. And if it is the case that the others are
> also the biggest, best and most beautiful, and we are also friendly with each
> other, then cooperation comes easy.[76]

Personal memories and solidarity among those active in GDR memory are
key for maintaining activist motivation. The need for action is also explained
in more fundamental terms. Two important collective action frames are
deployed. First, the activists stress the meaning of the GDR past for present-
day democracy in unified Germany. Second, they demand recognition of the
suffering and the accomplishments of resistors in East Germany.

Representative of the argument that public remembrance is indispensable to a lively democracy is a statement made by Tom Sello of the
Robert Havemann Archive, which holds the largest collection of materials
of the GDR opposition movement:

> One of the few positive aspects [of the GDR] is that there were always
> people, right after the war, before the creation of the state, and despite the
> construction of the Wall, until the end, who did not bend, who tried to resist
> dictatorship, who attempted – sometimes not even in a political sense, but
> merely as humans, to maintain a "straight spine," who undertook indivi-
> dual action. And I think that this is something that is worth remembering in
> a positive way. And on the flip side, we repeatedly need to point out that
> democracy is not given by God; that it cannot be taken for granted; that you
> have to be vigilant and that every individual's behavior counts.[77]

This notion – that the past holds important lessons for present and future
citizens of the democratic state – has been put forward in similar ways by
the memory activists of the History and Memorial Site Movements.
By using this line of argument, GDR memory advocates are therefore
also linking to a well-established discourse and claiming recognition
alongside the Nazi past. As the oppositionist Rainer Eppelmann said
succinctly: "Central is not merely historical knowledge, but more

[76] See Interviews, Jörg Drieselmann.
[77] See Interviews, Tom Sello.

importantly and especially the sensitization for the dangers and threats to our current democracy and a call to actively participate in society."[78] The frame of democratic values is used not only to underline the crucial nature of remembrance, but also to criticize and to distinguish oneself vis-à-vis other actors. Delegates to the annual conference of the LStU repeatedly stress that the attending associations are undertaking crucial work for democracy, that they are often left to their own devices in these efforts, and that a democratic political culture must give pride of place to victims of history.[79] "A democratic society based on human rights has the responsibility to foreground the fate of the persecuted."[80] Thus, in 2001 the LStU of the state of Mecklenburg-Western Pomerania Jörn Mothes said:

> With this conference we want to send a signal: for a morality of remem-
> brance, which does not exclude questions of guilt and responsibility; for
> a morality of remembrance, in which resistance is held up as a value of
> freedom and is not denigrated and where conformity is not rewarded again.
> We want to send signals at a time when memory work is a task of "those left
> behind;" at a time when associations and initiatives feel only weak reso-
> nance in politics and society; at a time when the history of injustice does not
> appear much in schools. We want to send signals against a cheap reconci-
> liation that is based on a covering-up of conflicts and psychological repres-
> sion, rather than on a genuine working through of the past.[81]

The second collective action frame used by GDR memory activists is evident in this quote as well. These campaigners demand recognition for the suffering experienced and sacrifices made in the service of democracy during dictatorial times. They also want their efforts to bring this history to light and make it usable in the present so that it can be acknowledged. Though difficult to define precisely, the importance of recognition becomes clear in activists' statements about their own accomplishments or key events in the commemorative calendar. Victims' representatives in particular are clearly proud to be invited to official events and also of their informal relationships with key political figures. The issue of recognition becomes even more poignant, however, when activists feel they are being slighted or their concerns dismissed. My interview partners cited many such examples. Lack of recognition manifested in lack of funding for their initiatives, failure of state representatives to show up for meetings, insuf-ficient pension payments for victims of the GDR regime, and so forth. It is

---

[78] Eppelmann, Krüger, and Meckel, 'Zum Geleit' p. 8.
[79] Der LStU Freistaat Thüringen, 'Von der Überwindung kommunistischer Diktaturen' p. 14.
[80] Meyer and Brauckmann, 'Geschichtspolitik und Ausstellungsdidaktik' p. 222.
[81] Der LStU Mecklenburg-Vorpommern, 'Demokratie braucht Erinnerung' p. 10.

difficult to assess each instance objectively; what is plain is that there is a pervasive sense among GDR memory activists that they are struggling against strong societal and state resistance to adequate remembrance. This impression certainly motivates the activists – just as the activists of the History and Memorial Site Movements were propelled into action by their sense of struggling against a resistant establishment.

In what can be called "frame alignment," GDR memory activists demand recognition by drawing direct connections to the memory of the Nazi dictatorship and the Holocaust. On the one hand, this is done through the use of language that is commonly associated with the Nazi past. For example, the Soviet special camps – and sometimes even the GDR as a whole – are problematically referred to as concentration camps ("KZs"). Moreover, memory initiatives' names sometimes refer to earlier efforts: the "Bautzen Komitee" links to the "Buchenwald Komitee" that was the most famous association of concentration camp inmates in the GDR.[82] Another common trope is the use of the phrase "against forgetting" ("Gegen Vergessen") that recalls an early rallying cry of Nazi victims. The association that runs the GDR Museum in Pforzheim, for example, is called "Gegen das Vergessen e.V." On the other hand, the connection to the Nazi past is made explicitly and even provocatively in order to underline what many GDR activists see as a double standard in remembrance. To cite just one typical example, Angelika Barbe of the UOKG argues in relation to the Sachsenhausen memorial site, which was used both as a concentration camp by the Nazis and as a special camp by the Soviet secret police (NKVD), that

> As long as the memorial stone for the victims of the Communist KZ, the so-called internment camps or special camps, as long as there is no such stone next to those for the other victims, the victims of the Communist dictatorship are not first class victims, but recognized only as second class victims – this is unacceptable ... The point is that victims of the first and second German dictatorship must be given a level playing field. And as long as our people only get alms, they are seen as second class victims – this is unacceptable.[83]

Key here is not whether or not the division into different classes of victims is accurate, but rather that, for many memory activists, German society and state have not provided them with the level of recognition that they deserve. According to trauma expert Stefan Trobisch-Lütge, individual reckoning with the past cannot be successful until the victim senses societal recognition: they need to acquire the feeling that their suffering

---

[82] Rudnick, 'Wenn Häftlinge und Historiker streiten' p.202
[83] Angelika Barbe in: Kongress der LStU and Stiftung Aufarbeitung, 'Über Grenzen und Zeiten' pp. 75–76.

has not only been acknowledged but has not been in vain, in other words, that resistance against injustice pays, at least in the long run.[84] Recognition is often demanded in the form of material compensation. This is partly because many GDR victims, in contrast with former members of the Stasi, live in precarious economic circumstances due to curtailed careers and ruined health. In addition, however, memorials and victims' participation in their creation and operation is key. As former dissident Ulrike Poppe (now LStU of Brandenburg) explains,

> The former prisoners want to be included in the memorials' work as witnesses and conceptual advisors. Maybe we are also in need of rituals that can express mourning: mourning those comrades who have died, mourning one's own lost years of life, mourning the loss of confidence in the world (*Weltvertrauen*) and, connected with this, the joy and lightness, by which life before incarceration had been characterized.[85]

Thus, the significance of memorials for GDR memory activists goes beyond the publicizing of the past and educating the public. Their continued engagement with sites of memory fulfills an important function of remembrance and of individual coming to terms – a function that cannot be accomplished when "memory professionals" take over a site and run it under the auspices of state institutions. This dilemma and the conflicting concerns of victims, historians, and memorial officials explain a lot about the conflicts over GDR memorial sites in recent years. The demand for recognition and the inability of some key sites to meet this demand to the satisfaction of activists is also grounded in the social relationships between the various civic, state, and hybrid actors that have developed since before the end of the East German regime. I analyze this dynamic more concretely below through specific cases, most importantly that of the Memorial *Leistikowstrasse* in Potsdam.

Activist Strategies

The tools employed by GDR memory activists vary considerably based on the character of the initiative, the site, as well as the local context with which they were confronted. Nevertheless, a set of common strategies can be identified – some of which recall those used by the History and the Memory Site Movements. As with the West German movements of the 1980s, the civic initiatives commemorating the East German past merge "memory work," focused on the local reckoning with dictatorial legacies, with "memory protest," which arises in response to political and societal

---

[84] cited in Poppe, 'Gesellschaftliche Aufarbeitung' pp. 87, 95.   [85] Ibid. p. 96.

obstacles. Again, these two categories cannot be neatly divided, as often protest was necessary in order to make memory work possible. Also, as with earlier initiatives, the making of exhibits or the holding of remembrance events was regarded as a highly contentious activity. Memory work, then, has involved historical research, conducting oral history interviews, collecting files and artifacts, designing exhibitions, and organizing guided tours, lectures, and commemorative occasions. Often these activities were both historical and political work.

The safeguarding of historical evidence took on an especially crucial role from the beginning when Stasi facilities were taken over by the GDR opposition committees. Groups formed that aimed to systematically preserve files and publicize their contents in order to expose the criminality of the East German government apparatus. Thus, archival work and the making of public exhibits had a highly political meaning and resulted in the creation of more permanent civic initiatives and institutions. Good examples of this are the exhibits and eventually memory sites that emerged in Leipzig (Runde Ecke), Magdeburg (Moritzplatz), and Berlin (Stasi Museum Normannenstrasse), where civic groups or rudimentary memorial organizations opened exhibits in the former Stasi buildings as early as Fall 1990.[86] Memory activists also began collecting independently of such emblematic locations: in 1989, Klaus Knabe in Pforzheim began what was at first a private collection of artifacts that in 1998 became the local GDR museum and has been run by a civic association since 2000.[87] Andreas Ludwig, a former activist of the Berlin History Workshop, gathered items of everyday GDR life after the fall of the Wall and opened the "Documentation Center of Everyday Culture of the GDR" in Eisenhüttenstadt in 1993.[88] The Library in Honor of the Victims of Communism in Berlin (*Gedenkbibliothek zu Ehren der Opfer des Kommunismus in Berlin*) assembled books that were formerly prohibited in the GDR and continues to organize lectures and readings.[89] The Robert-Havemann-Society in Berlin, which emerged out of dissident archival collections, has maintained its recognition as the key archive of the East German opposition. Though the safeguarding of opposition materials is its primary raison d'être and its staff seeks to expand the collection particularly with respect to evidence from resistance during the 1950s and 1960s, the group has also become active as a memorial

---

[86] www.runde-ecke-leipzig.de/index, Stephan, Puhle, and Bohse, 'Vorwort'; See Interviews, Jörg Drieselmann, Annegret Stephan.
[87] See Interviews, Volker Römer.
[88] See Interviews, Andreas Ludwig, www.alltagskultur-ddr.de/.
[89] See Interviews, Thomas Dahnert and Tom Sello; www.gedenkbibliothek.de/.

creator.[90] In 2009, the Society placed eighteen columns throughout Berlin, marking key sites of the *Bürgerbewegung* and installed an open-air exhibit about the revolution at Alexanderplatz. Similarly, the *Thüringer Archiv für Zeitgeschichte "Matthias Domaschk"* (ThürAZ – Thuringian Archive for Contemporary History) in Jena is a civically driven archive of the local opposition movement whose members have devised exhibitions and been involved in local memorial debates, including about the city's Memorial to the Victims of Communist Dictatorship.[91]

At other sites, civic groups have created publicity and public interest by offering guided tours and commemorative events before any state institution did. As early as 1991, the *Grenzturmverein* (Border Tower Association) started working to maintain a watchtower at Kühlungsborn where many tried to flee across the Baltic Sea, offering tours and building an archive.[92] At the largest of former GDR prisons, former political prisoners and others formed the *Verein Menschenrechtszentrum Cottbus e.V* (Association Human Rights Center Cottbus) in 2007. For three years, operating from a dilapidated building adjacent to the prison, members worked with witnesses and school groups to educate them about the injustices of the GDR prison system. In 2011, through a grant provided by the federal and local governments, the group was able to purchase the prison buildings. The association is now in the unique position of being owner and manager of this memorial site, giving it full control and little to state institutions. The Verein has designed a permanent exhibition explaining the history of the site since 1933. Though the exhibit is sophisticated, it also includes some artistic elements that one might not find in a state-run site. For example, one of the reconstructed prison cells is populated by sculptures that indicated how crowded it had been (Figure 6.4). The fence in front of the memorial's entrance features numerous posters inquiring after the whereabouts of children who had been taken away from oppositional parents by the GDR regime. Clearly, advocacy for ongoing concerns of the victims is front and center in Cottbus. The *Cottbus Menschenrechtszentrum* also places emphasis on the current struggle for human rights and has devised innovative ways of creating publicity. For instance, in Summer 2014, it hosted an open-air production of Beethoven's opera *Fidelio*, using the prison building as a prop.[93]

The creation of publicity about the significance of a site of memory through stressing its importance to victims and for educational purposes

[90] See Interviews, Tom Sello, Kongress der LStU and Stiftung Aufarbeitung, 'Über Grenzen und Zeiten,' www.havemann-gesellschaft.de/index.php?id=497.
[91] www.thueraz.de/.   [92] www.polmem-mv.de/index.
[93] www.menschenrechtszentrum-cottbus.de/, see Interviews, Hugo Diederich.

Figure 6.4. Art installation to show how tight quarters were in prison cells, Cottbus Human Rights Center.[94]

was a key tool for GDR memory activists. Annegret Stephan, the founding director of the memorial at Moritzplatz in Magdeburg, recounts how numerous former inmates, many of whom had never spoken about their experiences, came to the site from the beginning. For them, it was an

[94] Jenny Wüstenberg, 2014.

important first step in working through their own past. Staff worked to win their trust, help with applications for rehabilitation, and to provide a safe space for memory work.[95]

Another tool was the tactical placement of monuments in order to mark a site as worthy of commemoration and to make it more difficult for state officials to grant it a non-mnemonic purpose. The most famous example of this is Hildebrandt's erection of the cross installation at Checkpoint Charlie, which I have already described. Less well-known, but ultimately more effective, were a series of actions undertaken by activists of the Memorial Lindenstrasse in Potsdam. In 1991, when the future use of the site was still uncertain, the group attached a large bronze plaque (paid for by donations) to the building, declaring it to be a satellite of the City Museum – before this was officially the case. Claus Peter Ladner, the head of the *Fördergemeinschaft Lindenstrasse 54*, referred to this move as a clever "case of trickery." In 1995, the association succeeded in getting the courtyard of the site cleared of debris by donating a large sculpture to the city. The donation came with a requirement that the city had to maintain the sculpture and the site upon which it was located. What this meant in the first instance was that by accepting the donation the city was agreeing to clear up the site. This ingenious strategy was implemented at a time when there were plans to convert the former remand prison into an office building. The monument had both a protective function for the character of the site and created publicity, especially during its inauguration. The *Fördergemeinschaft* used this tactic again when it erected a sculpture near the Glienicker Bridge (a crossing point where Eastern and Western agents had been exchanged and recently made famous by the movie "Bridge of Spies"), in order to force the authorities to clean up the surroundings and make it more attractive to visitors.[96]

The occupation of memory sites and the "irregular" placement of monuments already straddle the dividing line between memory work and protest. However, GDR activists have also employed protest tactics explicitly. For instance, Carl-Wolfgang Holzapfel of the *Vereinigung 17. Juni* undertook a nine-day hunger strike in 2005 in order to call attention to the demand to rename the square next to the federal Ministry of Finance after the 1953 uprising.[97] Activists of the *Verein Freiheit e. V.* (Association Freedom) and others demanded the creation of a memorial at the former remand prison at Andreasstrasse in Erfurt, keeping up protests over

---

[95] Stephan, "'Ich hatte gedacht'" See Interviews, Annegret Stephan.

[96] See Interviews, Claus Peter Ladner; Hannes Wittenberg in: Kongress der LStU and Stiftung Aufarbeitung, 'Über Grenzen und Zeiten.'

[97] See Interviews, Carl-Wolfgang Holzapfel.

several years. In 2010, they occupied the building for over a month, with one activist undertaking a hunger strike, demanding a more rapid and decisive development of the site. According to Hugo Diederich of the VOS, this pressure successfully led to the granting of 5.6. million euros to refurbish the building and turn it into a memorial.[98]

Another example of memory protest that was effective in getting media attention was the chaining of activists to the crosses at Checkpoint Charlie in 2005. Such contentious methods were employed primarily when activists felt the need to raise public awareness with regard to sites that they believed were not being adequately commemorated by "the establishment" and when more low-key efforts such as lobbying had proved insufficient. The fact that such dramatic actions were the exception rather than the rule in GDR activists' repertoire offers an interesting contrast to the frequency of memory protests a decade or two earlier. As I argue in the next chapter, this is largely because those earlier activists had by now become part of the main memorial institutions and created a relatively accommodating climate for civil society in general – notwithstanding the disputes that occurred between new and old activists.

Some GDR memory activists have been wary of formally registering their initiatives with the German authorities as "associations" (*Eintragung als Verein*). This hesitation may be based on a fundamental suspicion of the state and the requirements for a high-level of transparency about a Verein's finances and membership. Unlike for the left-wing activists of the 1980s, for whom the reasons for suspicion lay in their principled rejection of "petit bourgeois bureaucratic control," for the GDR activists the recent experience of a dictatorial state is likely more relevant.

Despite such considerations, most activists rapidly determined that having official status is an overall advantage. As Claus Peter Ladner of the *Fördergemeinschaft Lindenstrasse 54 e.V.* explained, the group's position as a Verein enabled it to submit funding grants for which individuals or the city government would not have been eligible.[99] Moreover, designation as a registered citizens' initiative makes activists identifiable to other actors as interlocutors on a particular site or topic. Local governments have also voiced the need to have reliable civic partners who are able to take on responsibility. Herbert Wagner told me that as the post-1989 mayor of Dresden, he was already engaged in plans to transform the city's Stasi remand prison at Bautzener Strasse into a memorial, and that he therefore prevented the sale of the complex.

[98] See Interviews, Hugo Diederich.
[99] See Interviews, Claus Peter Ladner.

However, the city was in need of a legal entity to run the future memorial. Wagner promoted the foundation of an association. Today, he is himself the head of the resulting group *Erkenntnis durch Erinnerung e. V.* (Insight through Remembrance).[100] In Berlin too, the Senate administration aided the foundation of the *Verein Berliner Mauer* made up of those individuals who had pushed for the memorial at Bernauer Strasse from the very beginning. "They helped with the foundation of the association, for them it was important to have a legal counterpart, not just various people, but a tangible counterpart."[101]

Another strategy used by activists that is heavily shaped by state institutions is their efforts to network with similar groups: to coordinate meetings and exhibits, to learn from each other, or even to organize protests. In large part, this takes place informally, through personal connections – often ones that date back to the pre-1989 era in opposition or exile. But government actors have also done much to facilitate or fund such exchanges and have thereby helped mold the structures through which activists communicate.

Representative of the accomplishments, but also difficulties of such state-guided networking, is the experience of the Berlin-Brandenburg working groups (*Arbeitskreise* – AKs) 1 and 2, which assemble institutions working on the Nazi and GDR pasts, respectively. Rainer Klemke, who was long the leader of the department on memorials in the Berlin Senate administration (*Gedenkstätten-Referent*), inaugurated these working groups at the beginning of his tenure. He also initiated a joint "Forum on Contemporary History" where educational and methodological questions pertaining to sites recalling both before and after 1945 events could be discussed. In my interview with him, he was markedly proud of this accomplishment, saying: "the working groups are my children! I invented them! That was my first official act as Gedenkstätten-Referent; I said we must create an institutional environment for joint debate."[102]

Thus, the formal organization of memory initiatives was driven both by activists and encouraged by the institutional environment in which they operated. Networking forums and state-funded foundations in the field of remembrance have therefore become a mediating vehicle between state and civil society – and ones in which actors from both "realms" participate.

---

[100] See Interviews, Herbert Wagner.
[101] See Interviews, Manfred Fischer.
[102] See Interviews, Rainer Klemke.

Institutionalizing GDR Memory

While memory initiatives have become increasingly active at local sites of the GDR past, institutional structures and funding mechanisms have simultaneously become more refined. Together, these form the *Aufarbeitungsszene* in which civic and state actors are not always neatly distinguishable. With civic initiatives growing in strength and numbers, there was a shift in the official approach. As Andrew Beattie argues, while there was an initial emphasis on direct intervention through the Gauck authority and other entities, increasingly government actors preferred funding external memorial projects, though there remained a preference for sites recalling repression rather than opposition or everyday life. Beattie suggests that "the state was increasingly concerned to (appear to) stay at arms length from the development of policies even for state-mandated memory."[103] This reluctance to get involved overtly was especially evident in Berlin where by the early 2000s, voices calling for more visible commemoration of the Berlin Wall were growing louder – driven by controversial projects like the cross installation at Checkpoint Charlie. The dilemma for government decision-makers, therefore, was that they needed to take action without being accused of wanting to take charge of the many civic memory spaces that had emerged. As Norbert Lammert, President of the German Federal Parliament, wrote in 2009:

> Memory culture therefore implies a – for cultural politics somewhat unusual – direct responsibility on the part of the state. One of the few topics and fields of action in culture where politics cannot limit itself to the creation of a framework, is memory culture. Here, the state with its institutions is an important and indispensable actor, albeit only one among several. The state may neither claim a monopoly on information nor interpretive primacy (Deutungshoheit). In a democratic and pluralistic society, national memory can neither be formulated officially nor regulated through a bureaucracy.[104]

The solution pursued by the BKM of the red-green coalition government in 2005 was to delegate pressing questions about the future nature of GDR commemoration to an expert commission, led by the prominent historian Martin Sabrow. The goal of the Commission was to develop a model for a decentrally organized group of sites and organizations for working through the SED dictatorship. The Sabrow Commission was made up of well-known individuals: historians, former dissidents, and memorial professionals who deliberated and conducted site visits for about a year before presenting the results in May 2006. The Commission

---

[103] Beattie, 'The Politics of Remembering the GDR' p. 31.
[104] Lammert, 'Bikini-Verkäufer am FKK-Strand?' p. 33.

proposed to organize the existing memory sites through the categories of "rule, society, and opposition," "surveillance and repression," and "separation and border" in order to clarify the field of remembrance, while maintaining its openness, plurality, and autonomy.[105] Sabrow stresses that the objective was not a unified view of the past.

> The decentralized structure of the existing memory landscape has been by and large successful. This should be maintained in recognition of the historical achievement of the civic memory initiatives that helped to shape them, but also because of their proximity to citizens and in order to safeguard regional working relationships if possible. The creation of a panregional, centralized structure for memory work would be counterproductive and would be more likely to endanger institutional initiative than to produce synergy effects.[106]

In addition, the report emphasized the need to develop networks among sites and improve efficiency so as to use public monies wisely, and to increase the professionalism of memorial staff. One of the most hotly debated aspects of the Sabrow document was its call to emphasize (and fund) more strongly the quotidian aspects of life in a dictatorship, in order to understand how the dictatorial system intersected with ordinary life in complex ways. For the Commission, this was a crucial remedy against nostalgia about the GDR. Sabrow hoped to shift away from the primary emphasis of state-funded memory on suffering and repression.[107] Well-known GDR dissidents such as Joachim Gauck and Richard Schröder welcomed the support for everyday memory institutions.[108] Many in the *Aufarbeitungsszene* however – particularly victims' groups and those working for sites recalling Stasi repression – were extremely critical of the Sabrow Commission's results. They argued that attention to everyday life would detract from educating the public about the dictatorial and unjust nature of the East German regime. Critics also argued that the role of the Soviet Union and the fundamental depravity of Communist ideology were being sidelined. The "Wall Concept" of the city of Berlin, which was being debated at the same time, received similarly harsh reviews. One member of the Sabrow Commission, oppositionist Freya Klier, did not sign off on the report and issued a dissenting opinion welcomed by victim groups. She stated that she did not see the GDR as a bygone system, which could be historicized and memorialized. She argued that "since the end of the GDR, I see the continuing functioning of the former nomenclature. Their networks have not disintegrated but

---

[105] Sabrow and others 'Wohin treibt die DDR-Erinnerung?'
[106] Sabrow, 'Die DDR im aktuellen Gedächtnis.'
[107] Beattie, 'The Politics of Remembering the GDR.'
[108] Gauck and Schröder in Sabrow and others 'Wohin treibt die DDR-Erinnerung?' pp. 79/85.

rather become more strategically intricate." She also contended that memorials should offer a graphic depiction of state repression in order to help younger generations understand the depths of human nature and that this would be an effective tool for democracy education.[109] Despite such internal critics, the Sabrow Commission was also accused of not being representative of all GDR victims and seeking to impose memory culture from above. The *Bürgerbüro Berlin*, a group that provides counsel to victims, protested that victims' organizations were not formally represented on the Commission.[110] It was also suspected of being assembled based on political calculations. As Jörg Drieselmann put it:

> No politician is so crazy as to instate a commission without knowing in advance what the result of its work will be ... So if I know today what result a commission should produce, then I will influence the work of the commission by selecting its members accordingly ... This is how it must have worked with the Sabrow Commission as well. Professor Sabrow, Klaus-Dieter Henkel of Dresden University – with these I have two people in the Commission upon whom I can rely as Cultural Minister Weiss ... Then I can even invite one or two people, not dangerous ones, but decorative ones, like Tina Krone of the Havemann Society or Freya Klier ... The outcome of the Commission is bad. It's disastrous. But this outcome was to be expected because of how the Commission was composed.[111]

Martin Sabrow himself is adamant that at no point during the Commission's work did government actors attempt to influence the outcomes – and that he would not have tolerated such interventions. The representatives of civil society inside and outside the Commission, had no qualms about "saying what they want and how they want to implement this."[112] Sabrow expressed a fundamental skepticism about the role of civil society in memory politics: "I think that the danger for history culture comes less from the state as from the uncontrolled and wild growth of civil society actors. One should not disencourage this – of course this is a very good thing – but one should field regulatory instruments through which a plurality of opinions can be articulated and so that one group cannot implement its own interpretation due to its political power."[113] This kind of doubt about the trustworthiness of autonomous mnemonic civic groups – especially those that had not been "tamed" through institutional mechanisms – was voiced to me by several of the leading figures of established memorial culture. Their sense was that while the contribution of civic initiatives was important and valuable,

[109] Klier in ibid. pp. 44–5.   [110] Bürgerbüro Berlin 'Presseerklärung' May 15, 2006.
[111] See Interviews, Jörg Drieselmann.
[112] See Interviews, Martin Sabrow.
[113] See Interviews, Martin Sabrow.

the actual decision-making could not be left up to them. The standards of memorialization needed to be set by the professionals.

The Sabrow report had the important function of invigorating a national debate about the nature of GDR memory, but its recommendations were not implemented directly. Before its work was even presented, the red-green coalition government, which had instated it, was voted out of office in fall 2005 and replaced by a coalition of Conservatives and Social Democrats. Angela Merkel installed Bernd Neumann as her new Cultural Minister and Hermann Schäfer, the founding director of the House of the History of the Federal Republic in Bonn, as his deputy. Their approach to governing German memorial culture was different in procedure, but similar in terms of its emphasis on "state-mandated" memory (with only indirect state involvement), though some direct intervention was also proposed. After the uproar over the Sabrow Commission had abated, the BKM quietly drafted a "Continuation of the Federal Memorial Concept." This was to expand existing legal regulation on federal funding and standards for "Memorials of Nation-Wide Importance" (*Gedenkstätten von gesamtstaatlicher Bedeutung*). Thus, rather than aiming to draw up an entirely new structure for GDR sites, Neumann sought a more comprehensive path. The process that resulted in this new document was less public and contentious, despite the fact that it adopted many of Sabrow's recommendations. In summer 2007, the draft was circulated quietly among memorial leaders with a request for comments – a method that was welcomed by Drieselmann and others from the GDR memory scene.

The bill, which passed in June 2008, created four categories of GDR memory (division and border; surveillance and repression; society and everyday life; resistance and opposition), thus allowing for an enhanced focus on everyday life as envisaged by Sabrow. Two official projects noted in the Bill have meanwhile been implemented by the House of the History of the Federal Republic: the "Palace of Tears" (*Tränenpalast*), which examines the meaning of the border for ordinary Germans, and an exhibit about everyday life – both centrally located in Berlin.[114] In addition, the federal government pledged its support for the Berlin Wall Concept, as well as the Berlin Wall Foundation (which, as we recall, began as a civic association). The most vital innovation of the bill concerned not GDR memory, but the permanent funding of four Nazi concentration camp memorials. Of the total memorial budget of 35 million euros, two-thirds were allotted for pre-1945 and one-third for post-1945 remembrance.

---

[114] www.hdg.de/berlin/traenenpalast/, www.hdg.de/berlin/museum-in-der-kulturbrauerei/.

A carefully worded introductory section drew a clear distinction between the two regimes and reemphasized the unrivalled centrality of the memory of the Nazi past for German society, but the two pasts were nevertheless regarded as part of the same imperative for a democratic collective memory.[115]

Almost a decade has passed since this pivotal bill and many more sites of memory – small and larger, civic and state-run – have been created since. The new edition of the guide to GDR memory sites published by the *Stiftung Aufarbeitung* lists over nine hundred sites on over six hundred pages.[116] However, several prominent commemorative projects have run into trouble. Initiatives in Berlin and Leipzig for unity and freedom memorials, both of which had already undergone memorial design competitions and extensive debate, have faced considerable obstacles. In Leipzig, the project appears to have failed entirely.[117] The long-stalled Memorial to the Victims of Communism, which is pursued primarily by the UOKG, recently received a boost when conservatives and social democrats in the Bundestag called on the government to implement this idea.[118] But its realization remains an open question. The barriers encountered by initiatives to build "centralized" memorials may be an indication of the continuing strength of a now mainstream memorial culture that favors decentralization.

Two decades after the collapse of the GDR regime and after years of controversial debate, the institutional structure for shaping the remembrance of life and dictatorship in East Germany has solidified. This does not mean that there are no longer disputes about specific sites of memory, nor that civic advocates are always satisfied with the level of support and recognition received from state and society. However, the institutional interlocutors, the standards for funding, and the organization of the landscape of memory is relatively clear and settled. As I have argued, state actors have actively created forums for communication and the structures of organization within which memory activists operate – and these often benefit from this established support system. Civic actors and those (former) activists who have moved into state institutions have strongly shaped the process of institutional creation: they were involved

---

[115] Deutscher Bundestag 'Fortschreibung der Gedenkstättenkonzeption des Bundes. Verantwortung wahrnehmen, Aufarbeitung verstärken, Gedenken vertiefen' Drucksache 16/9875, June 19, 2008.

[116] Kaminsky and Gleinig, 'Orte des Erinnerns' The first edition of 2004 lists 356 monuments: Kaminsky and Gleinig, 'Vorwort.'

[117] Endlich, 'Projekte für ein Freiheits- und Einheitsdenkmal'; 'Neue Initiative.'

[118] Deutscher Bundestag 'Antrag der Fraktionen der CDU/CSU und SPD. 25 Jahre Deutsche Einheit – Leistungen wördigen, Herausforderungen angehen' Drucksache 18/6188, September 29, 2015.

in negotiating the results of the Sabrow Commission and the 2008 bill, and they continuously lobbied for funding and recognition for the memorials they helped bring to life. Thus, the institutional structures that now exist incorporate many civic demands and integrate spaces and procedures put in place by activists.

The contemporary memorial landscape is also diverse in terms of which aspects of the GDR it commemorates. Thus, as Andrew Beattie put it, the German government certainly "has not imposed a univocal memory regime."[119] But if it did not *impose the content of memory*, it did work to establish – in cooperation with many civic advocates – *a framework and standards* for public remembrance that must be taken into account by memory activists – and that sometimes excludes them from the realm of what is legitimate and worthy of support. This framework was not established surreptitiously by state actors to "trick" civil society into compliance. Instead, the framework was the outcome of the many debates and institutional innovations that happened since 1989, and since the mid-2000s in particular. Most of the governmental actors involved no doubt genuinely believed in the cause of establishing a sophisticated and democratically accountable memorial landscape. However, finding the balance between officially supporting important memory causes and not stifling civic autonomy and initiative is difficult. As long-time participant and observer of the Berlin memorial scene Günter Schlusche argued,

> The state of course does not just intervene with money, rather it attempts to guide developments in civic memory culture. There are now state-level funding programs and, parallel to this, also federal programs for crucial memory spaces or memory political issues – but these only come into play when the projects have reached a certain level of maturity. And this sequence is sometimes problematic, because of course if the federal government funds, it must nevertheless not exert pressure or censorship. This is a very delicate field. That's why when the state or federal governments finance memorials, there must always be awareness that the state should not steer but it should play a supportive role – even when it sometimes comes too late or supports the wrong project. But the state should never play first fiddle. This role must always remain with civil society. And this important balance must always found anew, it does not happen automatically.[120]

Again, Lindenberger's notion of an indirect exercise of state power through the construction of governing frameworks rings true. This soft pressure from the state enforces boundaries around the process and limits what outcomes can be achieved through state-supported memory institutions. By these means, the normative values of democracy held by

[119] Beattie, 'The Politics of Remembering the GDR' p. 34.
[120] See Interviews, Günter Schlusche.

established memorial institutions shape and constrain the full picture of the German memorial landscape. But these values reflect the ideal of democracy held by the leadership – the network of professionals in the state institutions and civil society groups, some of whom occupy key positions in both. Tensions arise when individuals or organizations clash with these democratic values and demand representations of the past that challenge normative views about the primacy of Holocaust memory, liberal ideals of social tolerance, or a resistance to German nationalism. For the memory culture to be democratically representative, it must find ways to engage with and give a voice to these views (without necessarily condoning the normative values adopted by controversial memory activists). And yet the current structure tends rather to marginalize these groups by defining their methods as unprofessional. A clear example of this kind of tension appeared in the creation of *Leistikowstrasse* Memorial.

Leistikowstrasse No.1: From Secret City to Official Memorial

After the Potsdam Conference of the Allies in 1945, one Potsdam neighborhood – over one hundred properties – was turned into the "Military City Number 7." Residents were evicted and the area turned into a no-go zone, accessible only to the Soviet military. The villa at *Leistikowstrasse* 1 had been owned by the Protestant church and housed a Protestant women's charitable organization (*Evangelisch-Kirchlicher Hilfsverein*). The building was seized and turned into the central remand prison of Soviet Counterintelligence SMERSH (which became part of the KGB in 1954), with thirty-six barren cells and measures to prevent any communication to the outside world. During the early 1950s, up to twelve hundred German and Soviet prisoners were held at *Leistikowstrasse*; later, mainly Soviet military personnel were incarcerated here. Conditions were extremely harsh. Inmates were interrogated, tortured, and unable to contact their families; some were shot on prison grounds. For many, it was the first stop in a long journey through the Gulag system. Others were sent to trial and shot in Moscow.[121]

Given the secrecy long surrounding the "Military City," the difficulty of identifying former prisoners today, and the continued unattainability of most Soviet files, historical research about the site has been challenging. What is clear is that *Leistikowstrasse* 1 epitomizes the brutality of Stalinism in Germany: it is the only Soviet remand prison that has been preserved in

---

[121] www.gedenkstaette-leistikowstrasse.de/inhalt_en/index.html.

its original form – including many prisoners' inscriptions on cell walls – not only in Germany, but probably in all of East-Central Europe.[122] From the mid-1980s onward, the building was used as a storage facility and after the withdrawal of Soviet troops, it was returned to its owner, the *Evangelisch-Kirchlicher Hilfsverein*. In April 1995, the formerly secret terrain was made accessible to the public again. Since then, the *Leistikowstrasse* has been the focal point of intense memory activism by former prisoners, concerned citizens, and existing groups such as *Amnesty International* and *Memorial Germany* (which supports the work of the Russian civil society group *Memorial* concerned with uncovering Soviet abuses).

In 2003, a formal association, the *Gedenk- und Begegnungsstätte Ehemaliges KGB-Gefängnis Potsdam e.V*, was founded to encourage the creation of a memorial site. In 2004, *Leistikowstrasse* 1 was placed under protective conservation status. The building was renovated and a small visitor center erected before the site was opened in a limited way in 2009. In April 2012, a new permanent exhibition was inaugurated and regular visitor service began under the auspices of a memorial foundation that is financed by the *Land Brandenburg* and the federal government. The *Hilfsverein* contributed the building, grounds, and visitor center, and funding also came from the European Union and other sources. The role played by civil society activists in the safeguarding and creation of this memorial site is superficially part of its official narrative. These origins are mentioned briefly in the official catalog[123] and during events held at *Leistikowstrasse*. On May 16, 2014, for example, the Memorial administration organized a commemorative wreath laying (Figure 6.5), followed by a panel discussion entitled "Preserving Memory, Organizing Encounters. Civic Renewal and Civic Engagement at the Leistikowstrasse Prison." Here, selected activists reminisced about the early days when they gathered every Sunday to open the building to visitors and worked to find witnesses.[124] Not part of the official story, however, are the bitter conflicts that accompanied the Memorial's development and that are emblematic of the clash between different generations of memory campaigners, as well as with institutional structures.

Starting in the mid-1990s, a group of ad hoc civic activists began working to prevent the destruction of the former prison and to publicize its existence.

---

[122] www.memorial.de/index.php?id=35.
[123] Reich and Schultz, 'Sowjetisches Untersuchungsgefängnis' p. 213.
[124] 'Erinnerung bewahren, Begegnungen schaffen. Ziviler Neubeginn und bürgerschaftliches Engagement am Gefängnisstandort Leistikowstraße', Kranzniederlegung und Podiumsgespräch, May 16, 2014.

Figure 6.5. Commemorative ceremony at Leistikowstrasse, May 16, 2014.[125]

They included former members of the local *Neues Forum* (a key opposition group in the final days of the GDR) who were also involved in the Memorial at *Lindenstrasse*; members of *Amnesty International* who for a while maintained offices in *Leistikowstrasse*; and *Memorial Germany*. One of the activists, Gisela Rüdiger, contends that "without the creation of this civic group, this would not have become a memorial" – and many of my interview partners concur.[126] The memory activists set up a volunteering schedule to open up the site to visitors on weekends (when it was not too cold in the unheated building) and organized information events with former inmates, funded by cash donations. Under the leadership of *Memorial Germany*, the first exhibit about the history of the site was created in 1997, entitled "From Potsdam to Workuta," and shown (in revised versions) in the building until 2005. This work also entailed an interview project with twenty-eight German and Russian former prisoners, results of which were published in an accompaniment to the exhibit.[127] Similar to memory activists at many other venues of repression in the GDR, the civic advocates for *Leistikowstrasse* laid claim to

[125] Jenny Wüstenberg.
[126] See Interviews, Gisela Rüdiger, Anna Kaminsky, and Ulrike Poppe.
[127] Winters, 'Der Streit um die Leistikowstraße,' Fein and others, *Von Potsdam nach Workuta*.

the site by engaging in memorialization (offering tours, conducting oral history interviews, curating an exhibit), drawing public attention, and even "occupying" it for use as offices.

During this first phase, two developments took place. On the one hand, while the city of Potsdam and the state of Brandenburg were initially not involved with the site, there was a gradual realization on the part of state actors that they needed to take action. On the other hand, activists, who were loosely organized as the *Initiativgruppe Leistikowstrasse 1*, recognized that their efficacy depended on the more formal and regularized organization of civic efforts. In 1999, two members of *Memorial* founded the "Working Group Memorial and Meeting Site Former KGB-Prison," which became a formally registered association in 2003 (*Gedenk- und Bildungsstätte Ehemaliges KGB-Gefängnis Potsdam e.V.* or merely *Gedenkstätten-Verein Leistikowstrasse*).[128] Association-status allowed activists to collect tax-deductible donations and to appear as a clear voice vis-à-vis press and government. The association was at first headed up by the director of the Memorial at *Berlin-Hohenschönhausen*, Hubertus Knabe, who is seen by many former political prisoners as a key defender of their interests. Knabe has become well-known for his many fiery and controversial interventions in memory politics. Most notably, he has argued repeatedly that the power of Stasi operatives continues into the present and that the GDR's repressive past is being minimized by the German political establishment.[129] *Memorial* and the *Gedenkstätten-Verein* continued to organize tours and events there and increasingly received support from state actors, including Brandenburg's then-Minister for Science, Research and Kultur, Johanna Wanka (since 2013 the Federal Minister for Education and Research).

It is thus not surprising that these civic groups assumed that they would continue to play a central role in the Memorial when the decision was taken to restore the building and add a visitors' center. However, when work on the site was completed in late 2008, a legally nonautonomous foundation *Stiftung Gedenk- und Begegnungstätte Leistikowstraße Potsdam* was established under the umbrella of the Brandenburg Memorial Foundation (*Stiftung Brandenburgische Gedenkstätten*). Its governing committee (Kuratorium) consists of representatives of the *Hilfsverein* as owner, the head of the Brandenburg Memorial Foundation (Günter Morsch), the BKM representing the federal level, and the state of Brandenburg. This committee holds power over all

---

[128] Winters, 'Der Streit um die Leistikowstraße' p. 40.
[129] Jones, *The Media of Testimony*; Knabe, 'Das Aufarbeitungskombinat'; Knabe, *Die Täter sind unter uns*.

fundamental questions concerning the *Leistikowstrasse* Memorial, including the guiding principles of its work, the appointment of leadership and the leader's competences. Since 2009, the director of the *Leistikowstrasse* has been Ines Reich, a historian who formerly worked with Morsch at the Brandenburg Memorial Foundation and was responsible there for the exhibit on the Soviet Special Camp at Sachsenhausen. Reich and the *Kuratorium* are aided by the *Beirat* (an expert committee) of up to ten members, including representatives of the civic groups involved (*Gedenkstätten-Verein* and *Memorial*), a former prisoner, as well as Anna Kaminsky of the *Stiftung Aufarbeitung*, Maria Nooke of the Berlin Wall Foundation, Ulrike Poppe (former dissident and LStU of Brandenburg), and historian Martin Sabrow.[130] Thus the *Beirat* is made up primarily of prominent personalities who are respected by most victims' groups as vocal advocates of adequate remembrance of repression in the GDR – and it is a veritable powerhouse of the GDR "memory scene."

However, the activists who had been instrumental in the development of the Memorial *Leistikowstrasse* up to this point were dissatisfied with the new situation on two fronts. First, they were not formally integrated into the governance mechanisms of the site where before they had been its central driving force. Second, the individuals involved – most importantly Günter Morsch (and Ines Reich, who was seen as guilty by association) and Hubertus Knabe – were already implicated in the ongoing conflict over the meaning and representation of the two German dictatorships and thus brought a lot of baggage with them. Morsch and Knabe can be regarded as figureheads of two opposing sides of this conflict and both are mistrusted by the other side. To the memory activists at *Leistikowstrasse*, Morsch represents the "establishment" of the remembrance landscape that leads the large memorials to the Nazi past. Some of these are professional historians by training and self-identification; others rose through the ranks and identify with the Memorial Site Movement of the 1980s and 90s. Thus, a personality such as Morsch speaks with a lot of authority acquired through professional experience, institutional clout, and support from the established memorials of the old Federal Republic. But he also comes with the baggage of having been a main protagonist of earlier disputes about sites with a dual dictatorial past. Gisela Rüdiger, of the *Gedenkstätten-Verein Leistikowstrasse*, encapsulated the mistrust directed at Morsch:

---

[130] Winters, 'Der Streit um die Leistikowstraße.'

We had seen that there were problems at Sachsenhausen between the leadership of the foundation and the association of those affected after 1945. The director of the foundation Morsch is well-known for – well! How should I put it? – he once said, that he had the impression that there are efforts to "upgrade" the victims of Soviet special camps and to "downgrade" the victims of National Socialist concentration camps. And that he feared that the goal is to achieve a balance in terms of the suffering of the victim groups.[131]

Gisela Kneist, a victim of the Sachsenhausen Soviet special camp and a vocal activist of the *Arbeitsgemeinschaft Lager Sachsenhausen* (Working Group Sachsenhausen Camp), argues that Morsch presents those who suffered in the Soviet camp as "second class victims."[132] While these misgivings may initially have been unfairly extended to Ines Reich, her interaction with activists and former prisoners seemed to confirm their concerns. According to the *Gedenkstätten-Verein*, the association was no longer allowed to conduct guided tours or hold events at the Memorial, and their publications were not made available there. During an interim period before the inauguration of the permanent exhibition, the Memorial was open only on weekends. The association unsuccessfully tried to persuade Reich to let them offer tours on weekdays and present parts of the existing exhibition. The activists of the *Gedenkstätten-Verein* furthermore complained that Reich refused to darken the former cells in order to present an authentic picture of the state of complete isolation from the outside world, which prisoners had to bear.[133] A collection of mostly former inmates reacted by founding a kind of protest group, the *Zeitzeugen-Initiative* (Eyewitness Initiative), which organized vigils in front of the site and became increasingly hostile to the Memorial leadership. According to journalist Peter Jochen Winters, this Eyewitness Initiative was led primarily by Bodo Platt (a former inmate) and Dirk Jungnickel (a film maker), who used personal attacks and polemics against Reich. In mid-2011, Jungnickel and Rüdiger collected signatures and campaigned for the removal of Reich. They argued that she lacked the appropriate sensitivity to deal with victims, and worse, that victims felt that "they are being used merely as historical sources."[134] Tensions further escalated when Reich accused a former UOKG executive committee member and Gulag inmate Lothar Scholz of physically attacking and threatening her in March 2012. She pressed official charges, while

---

[131] See Interviews, Gisela Rüdiger. This sentiment was echoed in other interviews, for instance with Hugo Diederich and Anna Kaminsky.

[132] 'Die zwei Wahrheiten ', 'Die zwei Wahrheiten.'

[133] Gedenk- und Begegnungsstätte Ehemaliges KGB-Gefängnis Potsdam e.V. 'Offener Brief an das Kuratorium' Potsdam, 7 November 2009 as well as September 16, 2012.

[134] 'Gisela Rüdiger für Abberufung,' 'Gisela Rüdiger für Abberufung.'

Scholz maintained that it was merely a scuffle during a dispute about the *Leistikowstrasse*.[135] On both sides, accusatory language was no longer within the reasonable parameters of public debate.

The apex of this conflict happened in the fall of 2011, when Reich submitted the texts for the planned permanent exhibit to the *Beirat* for approval. The majority of the *Beirat*, along with most of the civic memory activists, strongly rejected them. Anna Kaminsky of the *Stiftung Aufarbeitung* called them "problematic."[136] According to my conversations with several *Beirat* members, not only was there reluctant cooperation with the *Beirat* at best, but the texts were problematic for several reasons. The central critique was that the exhibition focused on the actions of Soviet counterintelligence in the context of the Cold War, thereby underemphasizing the specific criminality of this site and its embeddedness in the Communist system of rule. This, according to Kaminsky, amounted to a trivialization of Soviet human rights violations. Moreover, the suffering and fate of the victims at *Leistikowstrasse* did not take centerstage, with an emphasis placed instead on the biographies and artifacts of the perpetrators. Some GDR memory activists would have liked a more gripping and emotional representation of the suffering of victims (though memorial experts warned not to overwhelm visitors with drastic representations and language).[137] While the *Beirat* and the activists acknowledged that some former Nazis were also incarcerated at *Leistikowstrasse*, they argued that there was little distinction made between them and the great majority of innocent inmates. As the *Gedenkstätten-Verein* put it: "we do not want a KGB Museum!" but instead a place to remember and honor the victims.[138]

The *Beirat* commissioned an external expert opinion and then worked itself to implement the demanded revisions. Through this intervention, the exhibition texts were revised and are now regarded as acceptable by many observers, though the *Gedenkstätten-Verein* and the *Zeitzeugen Initiative* remain opposed. The behind-the-scenes procedure that led to the ultimate formulation of the exhibit is not openly acknowledged by the Memorial leadership. Despite the compromise, memory activists mobilized against the inauguration of the exhibit in April 2012 – by one account attracting about 150 protesters.[139] Critics, including Hubertus Knabe and former oppositionist Vera Lengsfeld, continued to voice

---

[135] Jander, 'Kultur der Aufrechnung' p. 129.
[136] See Interviews, Anna Kaminsky.
[137] Meyer and Brauckmann, 'Geschichtspolitik und Ausstellungsdidaktik' p. 221.
[138] See Interviews, Anna Kaminsky, Ulrike Poppe, and Gisela Rüdiger. See also www.kgb-gefaengnis.de/.
[139] Meyer and Brauckmann, 'Geschichtspolitik und Ausstellungsdidaktik' p. 221.

concerns about the exhibit, called for its revision, and admonished Reich for her inability to work with the activists.[140]

In response to their dissatisfaction with the official memory work at *Leistikowstrasse*, the *Zeitzeugen Initiative* has sought to become a memorializer itself and to put up a bronze plaque in the prison court-yard. The proposed inscription combined a quote by Solzhenitsyn with the text "Tormented – Tortured – Exiled – Shot. In memory of our comrades as well as all victims of the Soviet Secret Police NKVD/KGB." The plaque initially received support from Brandenburg's Minister President Matthias Platzeck and was approved by the *Beirat* and the *Kuratorium*. The activists collected about €1,000 and had the plaque produced in January 2013. Shortly thereafter, however, sharp criticism was voiced by the Central Council of Jews in Germany. Its General Secretary, Stephan Kramer, wrote in a local newspaper that particularly the phrase "all victims of the NKVD" amounted to "an unprecedented scandal" because it included perpetrators in the commemoration and thereby discredited the real victims of Stalinist repression. Moreover, Kramer criticized the dearth of memory about Jewish life and suffering in Potsdam.[141] The *Zeitzeugen Initiative* rejected the accusation that the plaque honored perpetrators, but agreed to change the text to "In memory of our comrades as well as all the *innocent* victims of the Soviet Secret Services" (my emphasis). The Central Council of Jews did not respond to further attempts at negotiation, and so, the plaque with the new text was produced and dedicated on the 23rd of August 2013 (the European day of commemoration for the victims of totalitarianism, which is controversial in Germany).[142]

The *Zeitzeugen Initiative* has continued to publicize what it sees as unacceptable behavior on the part of the Memorial leadership. This is expressed in a 2012 flyer that I quote here at length:

> Since the Brandenburg Memorial Foundation took over, we have had to watch powerlessly how the site of our suffering and trauma has been stripped of its horror. Dark dungeons, screening panels (Sichtblenden), and window bars have mostly vanished. Cells are now flooded with sun and light and indicate a regular prison. Solitary confinement and torture are no longer comprehensible. Knowledge, experience, and memories of witnesses are rejected as bothersome. Exhibition texts were manipulated through their selection and wording. Documentation and memories, interviews with witnesses and by Memorial Germany and the Verein Ehemaliges

---

[140] 'Leistikowstraße: Reich zum Rücktritt ', 'Leistikowstraße: Reich zum Rücktritt.
[141] 'Zentralrat der Juden kritisiert Gedenkkultur in Potsdam.' www.epd.de/landesdienst/land esdienst-ost/schwerpunktartikel/zentralrat-der-juden-kritisiert-gedenkkultur-potsda.
[142] Gisela Rüdiger, email communication October 20, 2014.

KGB-Gefängnis Potsdam were boycotted or confiscated. As a result, the members of the Zeitzeugen-Initiative have since 2010 suspended their activities at the site and demanded the recall of the current Director Dr. Reich. She acts on behalf of and with the support of Prof. Dr. Morsch, Director of the Brandenburg Memorial Foundation. Since the 1990s, he has been responsible for countless conflicts with former prisoners of the Sachsenhausen Special Soviet Camp ... Why is there a tendency to relativize the crimes of the Soviet secret police KGB/NKVD in this exhibition? Why are the fates of victims, their murder, their persecution as well as their suffering in the Gulag overshadowed by countless KGB files?[143]

The sense of the loss of control over the memory of the *Leistikowstrasse* and over the governance of the site itself, as well as a fundamental mistrust of the memorial officials, becomes clear here.

Overall, the *Leistikow* dispute has become somewhat less heated since 2013 – activists and memorial staff seem to have developed a working relationship with some former prisoners who support the Memorial's approach. The *Gedenkstätten-Verein* engages in a limited set of activities at the Memorial.[144] Nevertheless, there remains much mistrust.[145] To a large extent, the escalation of the conflict can be explained by preexistent tensions between activists and memorial officials derived from earlier contention in Brandenburg and elsewhere in which the protagonists were involved. In other words, there was little mutual trust at the outset. Another important factor was the lack of sensitivity on the part of Ines Reich when it came to dealing with victims of GDR repression – some of whom may be suffering from posttraumatic stress. As Anna Kaminsky points out, a special approach is needed here: I am not of the opinion that one needs to implement everything that is demanded by the victims ... But it is a matter of fairness: one cannot, from one day to the next, show those the door who have worked for fifteen years to create this memorial, who made sure the site was accessible. One cannot just say "okay, now we are a memorial and now we will undertake professional work here. And throw out everything that was accomplished before and declare that it is worth nothing."[146]

Beyond this local breakdown of the relationships necessary to build a functioning interchange between civil society and state actors, a more widely relevant point emerges from this case study: that the nature of the integration of memory activists, particularly of former victims, into the work of official memorials is key to their democratic quality.

---

[143] Flyer, April 2012, www.kgb-gefaengnis.de/files/flyer_zzi_2.pdf.
[144] See Interviews, Martin Gorholt.
[145] See Interviews, Claus Peter Ladner and Ulrike Poppe.
[146] See Interviews, Anna Kaminsky.

This is the crux of the matter: the activists do not feel that they have helped *make the rules* by which they are able to participate in memorialization, even though they believe that their personal suffering and their civic efforts entitle them to this. As a flyer of the *Gedenkstätten-Verein* states: "The rights of the witnesses to autonomous work in this memorial have since 2009 been curtailed in an *illegitimate* manner."[147] Probably due to the interpersonal problems surrounding the *Leistikowstrasse* and the suspicion felt on both sides, the "system" of memorialization became more visible and acquired an elevated importance. When civic, state, and hybrid actors develop good working relationships, the rules of their engagement are shaped mutually and the dividing lines between civil society and state are blurred. At *Leistikowstrasse*, the identity of activists as "civil society against the state" became highly pronounced – despite the fact that in reality many of them straddled that line – and they resisted the imposition of memory policy by officials. Again, I want to stress that what matters here is not the opposition between activists and government, but the process of shaping memory through their complex interaction.

Conclusion

Despite government institutions' occasional stalling or resistance to memorial initiatives, the situation for GDR memory campaigners was overall more favorable than before 1990 in West Germany. Compared to the History and Memorial Site Movements, and even more so compared to the conditions faced by the memory activists of the 1950s–1970s, GDR initiatives generally encountered institutions that acknowledged the important role of civil society in the memorialization process. Moreover, many of the relevant actors within the state had been actively engaged in civic initiatives in their own careers or at least highly supportive of them. Through the activism of the 1980s and 1990s in the West, institutions had emerged that were strongly shaped by civic activism or are even run by former activists. The origin of these institutions in the civic struggle to commemorate the Nazi past also, however, makes for a problematic relationships between the old and new memory advocates and their competing priorities. The existing "memory infrastructure" profoundly influences the strategies used by activists in their GDR memory work and protest. But they have also creatively shaped their own unique approach to reckoning with life and repression in East Germany. They stress the importance of recognizing resistance to dictatorship and the contribution made to democratic values in the present.

[147] Flyer of the Gedenkstätten-Verein www.kgb-gefaengnis.de/ (my emphasis).

The case study of the *Leistikowstrasse* Memorial poignantly illustrates that civil society matters for our understanding of the development of democratic memory – not because activists are positioned against the state per se, but because their engagement with contentious sites is essential for the meaning of democratic remembrance in practice. Activists here and elsewhere have demanded their right to emotional remembrance and to autonomy in memorialization – even and especially when their approaches question existing frameworks espoused by the "memory establishment." Whether or not such demands can be accommodated is a major challenge for the future of Germany's memory culture. And it is this tension between established and newer mnemonic norms that drives contemporary memorial conflicts. In the concluding chapter, I examine more closely the ways in which activists and "professionals" interact in memorial institutions, as well as the implications of this interaction for democratic memory.

7   Hybrid Memorial Institutions
and Democratic Memory

The core goal of this book has been to place contentious civic activism at the center of our understanding of German memory politics from the postwar era to the present. Throughout, I have highlighted shifts from memory work to memory protest as crucial moments when social movements and civil society are able to transform salient norms about what and how we should remember the past. I make the argument that since 1945, grassroots activists have not only been vigorously engaged in shaping the public landscape of remembrance, but that they have often been *the* driving force behind memorialization efforts without which German memory culture would look very different today. Over the decades, the identity of the activists involved in promoting various "pasts," and their effectiveness in transforming the state institutions that govern public memory, have changed dramatically. I have illustrated this complex story by providing a detailed political history of German memory politics from the neglected perspective of civic activism.

Shortly after the end of hostilities in 1945, groups of Holocaust survivors were among the first memory activists of post-Nazi Germany. Together with Allied forces, they erected monuments to recall their fallen comrades and their own suffering. From then on, victims' associations have been among the most important creators of public memory, demanding tirelessly that German society confront its recent past. However, these efforts were initially overshadowed by civic action of a different variety: veterans, expellees, and anti-Communist campaigners more effectively influenced the early memory landscape in West Germany. They initiated thousands of markers in public places commemorating fallen soldiers, lost homelands, and communist atrocities – all without reference to Nazi terror and Germans' participation in it. In East Germany, the memory of Communist resistance to fascism was elevated to state ideology while the majority of Nazism's victims were not represented – nor were the memories of expulsion or wartime suffering.

Thus, during the first decades of the two German states, mnemonic civil society groups were highly active and – and least in the West – influential in

determining government remembrance policy. However, the most successful of them perpetuated Germans' uncritical reading of their recent past
and buttressed the Cold War rhetoric of the era. The victims of Nazism did
manage to achieve the creation of a few key memorial sites – most notably
at the Dachau and Bergen Belsen concentration camps, and the Memorial
to German Resistance in Berlin – and these were used periodically by
politicians for official ceremonies. But for the most part, a self-critical
reflection on the Nazi past did not find its way into the mainstream of
German society in the first postwar decades. At this time, German public
memory was democratic in the sense of enjoying broad support within the
population and being highly representative of Germans' attitudes toward
the past. However, it was not yet normatively democratic. It did not reflect
those norms of tolerance and self-critique that would have supported
a consolidation and deepening of German democratic political culture.

In the wake of the student uprisings of the 1960s, and supported by the
efforts of liberal intellectuals and artists, confronting the Nazi past finally
became a central topic in the German public sphere. But this debate did
not yet translate into major changes in the material commemorative
culture or memorial landscape. However, building on the gradual shift
in public attitudes starting in the '60s, two social movements emerged in
the 1980s that I contend transformed the memorial politics of West
Germany. Through their local historical research and advocacy for public
remembrance, the Memorial Site and the History Movements not only
initiated and reinvented countless memorials, they also profoundly
shaped the state institutions that fund, support and regulate public memory in the Federal Republic to the present day.

Initially, most of these memorial projects had to be pushed through
against the resistance of local and federal authorities – and the resulting
memory protest saw a diverse and creative repertoire of movement strategies. The activists positioned themselves as the critical opposition to the
Kohl government's memorial projects. The official memory politics were
responding to the same public demand for engagement with German
history that drove the social movements, but offered an anodyne and
traditionalist form of memorial representation. However, the increased
popular demand for critical history and the political recognition that the
issue of German responsibility for the past would not disappear, meant
that critical memory groups and governmental actors often gradually
became partners rather than opponents. This did not mean that grassroots memory activists no longer faced resistance, or that their projects
received generous funding across the board. In fact, to this day, a large
proportion of memorials and locations for historical education could not
survive without strong civic backing and enthusiastic volunteers.

Figure 7.1. Topography of Terror memorial in the heart of today's Berlin.[1]

However, since the 1980s and 1990s, both the memorial landscape and the practice of German memory culture have been transformed. Government officials (often themselves former movement members) pride themselves on intensive cooperation with grassroots activists at the local, state, and federal levels. The resulting decentralized landscape of memory – strongly supported by civic institutions that helped create it – has become the hallmark of Germany's self-critical approach to history, which has done much to contribute to a "deepening" of its democracy. The transformation of the Topography of Terror site – from an idea put forward by a passionate group of memory activists in the early 1980s to a "Memorial of Nation-Wide Importance" by 2010 – neatly captures this process (Figure 7.1).

In 1989, the Iron Curtain was dismantled and a "new past" was propelled into public view. The relationship between civil society and the state in the public memory of West Germany was still in the midst of its renegotiation process. A new community of memory activists now

[1] Stefan Müller, 2010.

sought to commemorate life and repression in East Germany. They emerged in the midst of changing institutional arrangements in memory politics, and they both clashed with and influenced them in turn. The victories of the Memorial Site and the History Movements were as yet very new and anxiously guarded by their (former) members – many of whom now had leadership positions in state-funded memorials. Moreover, unification created a new situation in both East and West, as the federal state transformed the funding models for memorials "of nationwide importance" and so heightened the contest over resources and recognition.

The victims' associations of the GDR, the former dissidents and others who sought to commemorate repression under the Communist regime, employed many of the same strategies as previous activist groups. But they also sometimes espoused a different political culture and conflicting memorial goals. Most centrally, memorialization for some of these civic groups was a highly emotional affair, fed by fresh personal memories of suffering, and determined by the need to educate the public about the deeds of perpetrators, some of whom were still active in public life. These passionate movements encountered resistance from established memorial organizations focused on confronting the Nazi past and wary of any comparison or relativizing between the two German dictatorships. These conflicts were particularly acute in the context of memorial sites that were the location of *both* NS and Soviet or SED crimes.

This persistent clash of memory politics, the necessity for accommodation between new and old memory activists, and the impact of these dynamics on memorial institutions is where I pick up the narrative in this concluding chapter. Drawing on the empirical evidence presented throughout the book, I analyze how civil society and state have become intertwined through the collective action of the Memorial Site and History Movements since the 1980s. I have already demonstrated how this process of intermeshing occurred through case studies and by detailing the Movements' impact on memorial design ideas. Now, I draw attention specifically to the Movements' "infiltration" of memorial institutions through staff, the mainstreaming of key activist principles, and the exercise of growing control over the governing rules of the memorial landscape. This process of activist-to-institution integration began in the 1980s with West German movements focused on the Nazi past. From the 1990s onward, memorial advocates focused on the GDR past have become involved in institutions in comparable ways. I argue that, as a result, we have seen the creation of "hybrid institutions" that exhibit characteristics of what are routinely regarded as separate state and civil society sectors.

The regulatory framework that has been devised to deal with memorial policy in Germany has therefore not been unidirectionally imposed by the state on civil society, but rather shaped by both. Nevertheless, it is crucial to understand that there *is* a regulatory framework that has been influenced and challenged by a new generation of GDR memory activists in recent years. My main and conclusive point here is that civil society and state are closely intertwined in the field of memorialization, and that the history of memory activism in Germany must be taken into account when trying to grasp how the interaction between the various actors works today. Particularly important are moments when the (quieter) work of memorialization by civil society turns contentious. I contend that it is at such intersections of memory work and memory protest that both institutional and normative change is likely to happen.

Focusing on the relationship between activists and state, and their entanglement in the current institutional setting, also allows me to make an argument about the meaning of memory for the development of democracy. I have referred throughout this study to the changing balance between representative and normative components of public memory. In this concluding chapter, I raise some concerns related to this dynamic about the increasingly professionalized nature of public remembrance and consider the significance of recent controversial actions, particularly as carried out by victims of the GDR regime. The key question here is whether German memorial culture is able to grant public space and autonomy to civic groups that may not adhere to the framework that has been worked out between state and civic actors through preceding contentious politics. In other words, what does it mean for the norms of democratic memory when they are challenged by memory activists who do not "play by the rules?" As the GDR memory activists stake their claim to representation in a democratic memory politics, they challenge the normative democratic values in the existing memory culture that resist comparison of Nazism to any other form of totalitarianism and view potentially nationalist sentiments (such as the expellee groups allied with GDR activists) with suspicion. This is the tension that characterizes today's memory political debates. But it cannot be understood outside the context of the history of memory activism that it follows.

Of course, this is a political debate about values and ideas. But it is shaped by individuals and organizations that have developed a hybrid institutional structure of memory politics in Germany that blurs traditional boundaries between civil society and the state. This is true at the federal level – but also at the state and local level. This integration has been referenced episodically throughout the book, but I present it here in a more comprehensive form to tie together the threads of history to describe this phenomenon.

The Intermeshing of State and Civil Society in Memorial Politics

The 1980s witnessed a remarkable expansion of public interest in history and the creation of numerous new museums and memorial sites. This is what I have referred to as the "dual memory boom," since it was driven both by the representative politics of state institutions and by myriad local citizens' initiatives under the auspices of the Memorial Site and the History Movements. As a result, many of the individuals who were active in or socialized through these social movements found employment both in institutions that they had helped to create (such as the enlarged foundations running the concentration camp memorials), but also in museums that had been initiated "from above." In the course of the 1980s and 1990s, these staff members – whether consciously or unconsciously – carried out a "march into the institutions," usually without leaving them again. They brought with them their civic identity, memorialization principles developed in the Memorial Site and History Movements, and the objective to shape institutions in a way that included civil society through their organizational structure.

After 1989, memorial policy was greatly expanded as a field of state action, and with it the size and financial resources of memorial institutions. This was because the large official GDR memorials were in dire need of reinvention, and because the federal government recognized that unification necessitated a clear commitment to the memory of the Nazi past. The first *Gedenkstättenkonzeption* (memorial concept) of the Berlin Republic therefore included funding, not only for East German sites, but also for the Topography of Terror, the Memorial to German Resistance, and the Memorial House of the Wannsee Conference.[2] State funding was gradually increased over subsequent years and became more regularized partly as a result of the creation of a federal cultural ministry (BKM). Activists from the GDR *Aufarbeitungsszene* also joined some of the new institutions (and helped to create new ones), variously adopting some of the same ideas brought in by previous grassroots leaders or challenging them. The relationships among activists of different backgrounds and with memorial officials are key to understanding that transformation of the institutions of memory, as well as the clash of pasts, over the last thirty years or so.

Staff in Hybrid Institutions

Activists from the Memorial Site and History Movements found employment in local museums, *Gedenkstätten* and institutions of historical

---

[2] Garbe, 'Die Gedenkstättenkonzeption des Bundes.'

education – both in positions of leadership and in lower-level research or educational posts. Michael Brown explains why former volunteers often become paid staff in hybrid institutions: "People acquire skills and specialized information while volunteering that make them appropriate candidates to hire. Often by volunteering they more readily hear about job openings. The increasing willingness of the state to fund projects or contracts means more people *can* be paid to do work that either had not been done before or had been done by volunteers."[3]

Civil society activists developed historical expertise and practical skills in making the kinds of exhibitions that were in increasing demand since the mid-1980s. Furthermore, these activists continued to be highly motivated by what they saw as their personal responsibility to commemorate and educate about the past. Getting paid to do this did not change their principled commitment – in fact, it allowed them to spend more time on memory work. In my interviews, I asked a standard question about civic activism in relation to official capacities. More often than not, state employees responded that engaging with civil society and attending public meetings was part of their job as well as their personal interest: they did not distinguish between their roles as state actors and citizens. For Thomas Lutz, the idea of playing the state against citizen initiatives was "nonsense."[4] As Brown points out, the distinction between state and civil society, or between bureaucrat and activist, is not empirically borne out in the arena of hybrid institutions, which have become spaces where "relations of state and civil society weave together."[5]

Numerous of my interviewees argued that the Movement "lives on" through the individuals in these organizations.[6] As a result, such institutions have a lesser need to be pressured "from below." Staff in hybrid institutions also tend to be highly motivated. According to Norbert Kampe, Director of the House of the Wannsee Conference memorial, his team members have a commitment to their workplace that is above and beyond a "normal" job – they are willing to work long hours and collectively assure that the memorial is running smoothly.

Their commitment to civil society and their self-image as activists-at-heart notwithstanding, memorial leaders and staff have become settled in a comfortable status quo. Their progressive identity is likely reinforced by colleagues with a similar background and by the important role they have come to play in German memorial politics. However, critics point out that many of the former protagonists of the Memorial Site and History

---

[3] Brown, *RePlacing citizenship* p. 94.   [4] See Interviews, Thomas Lutz.
[5] Brown, *RePlacing citizenship* p. 86.
[6] See Interviews, Christine Fischer-Defoy, Martin Düspohl, and Bernt Roder.

Movements have lost their critical edge and the ability to recognize new trends and needs in political education. Gabriele Camphausen, who herself does not come from this Movement background, but has worked in several Berlin institutions, analyzes this contradictory attitude:

> I think that these representatives do not see themselves as representatives of the state, because the state – this is a holdover from the old days – the state as such is not something to which you profess allegiance unequivocally. Thus, state administration is automatically to be regarded with suspicion. They see themselves as representatives of a special culture, their own culture, and I believe that they at times become quite self-satisfied and self-righteous. And I think that there is not much left of the original civic consciousness in the face of acquiring power and influence. But I think that this is not critically reflected upon . . . I can imagine that the representatives that I am thinking of now are convinced that they are continuing to pursue their civic ideals, but in their everyday conduct with their staff, this is not the case . . . There are those who are convinced that they continue to practice the old "*WG-Küchenkultur*" [culture of community living, open discussion]. But what happens on a daily basis – it's the worst power politics.[7]

Despite the fact that former activists who work in memorials may not view themselves as state representatives and may genuinely attempt to implement Movement ideas, they are nevertheless subject to the "corrupting influence" of power. They adopt the interests of the organization, as well as the needs of their own power preservation, as a top priority. As Cornelia Siebeck argues, "particularly the state-funded NS-memorials have since the 1990s experienced an intensive process of institutionalization, musealization, scienticization, and professionalization. As is common during such processes, a relatively small circle of experts has developed a set of specific standards, determining how historical sites of perpetration and suffering were to be 'correctly' managed in political, historiographical, aesthetic, and pedagogical terms." This, Siebeck maintains, has both been productive in the development of reflexive cultural memory, but also had a strongly a standardizing effect.[8]

It is not surprising, then, that some of those activists who remain outside of institutional boundaries are frustrated with their former comrades – despite the undeniable successes of the memorial institutions in publicizing a critical approach to the past. The hybrid nature of these institutions has produced tensions in the work and identity of the individuals who have traversed the space from movement to institution. They are a symbol of civil society's profound success; but they are also practical examples of its normalization and integration into the status quo.

---

[7] See Interviews, Gabriele Camphausen.
[8] Siebeck, 'Gedächtnisarbeit zur NS-Vergangenheit ' p. 9.

This assessment is highly relevant for understanding what happened once representatives of GDR memory initiatives – especially members of victim groups and former dissidents – entered these memorial institutions, including the large concentration camp memorials and the memory foundations in the East German *Bundesländer*. Here, they encountered people who had been socialized by the Memorial Site and History Movements and remained adamant that the Nazi past must remain the top mnemonic priority. The political left in the West had on the whole not been overly concerned with human rights violations taking place in socialist states and had accepted the existence of two German states as permanent – or even as a justified outcome of Nazi aggression. By contrast, there was a long-standing and strong conservative lobby that fostered the commemoration of victims of communism in the Cold War context. The ritual pronouncements by West German leaders on June 17 (the day of the 1953 uprising) should be understood in this light. During this time, civic groups such as the Victims of Stalinism (VOS) enjoyed considerable clout within conservative circles. After 1989, these same voices immediately supported the explicit condemnation of repression in the GDR and demanded compensation payments and the safeguarding of memory sites. It follows that West German conservative memory activists and political leaders were quickest to build alliances with the new East German *Aufarbeitungszene*. This created a complex politics, as West Germans from the left-leaning history movements began to dominate many memorial institutions. And while the sentiments and tactics of the East German activists were often similar to those of the earlier West German Movements, the political content and alliances of the GDR memory activists challenged the norms and democratic values of the memory culture built through the 1980s in the West. Jan Kubik and Michael Bernhard have offered a distinction between mnemonic warriors and pluralists (next to two other categories) that usefully captures how actors relate to one another in the field of memory politics. They write that "The content of memory appears to warriors as largely nonnegotiable; the only problem is how to make others accept their 'true' vision of the past."[9] This characterization applies to many victims' groups (of both the Nazi and the GDR eras), whose rhetoric is shaped primarily by personal (and sometimes quite fresh) memories of suffering. In such instances, what is claimed by historical research matters little because first-hand knowledge is simply more powerful. By contrast, the majority of staff in German memorial institutions may be described as pluralists who

[9] Kubik and Bernhard, 'A Theory of the Politics of Memory' p. 13.

believe that the others *are entitled* to their own visions. If they disagree with those visions, they are ready to engage in dialogue whose principal aim is the orderly pursuit of 'the truth,' discovery of the areas of overlap among the competing visions, and articulation of common *mnemonic fundamentals* that allow discussion among competing versions ... A serious concern for the pluralists is how to construct a field of memory politics that accommodates competing visions and provides a platform for a dialogue among them.[10]

However, far from being neutral actors in the German memory policy field, pluralists often espouse rigid frameworks and standards, determining what may be recognized as acceptable commemoration, worthy of official funding. Pluralist staff members of memorial institutions tend to reject the emotional approach of the warriors on the grounds of being "unprofessional," rather than historically inaccurate.

Thus, long-standing and often partisan disagreements, together with this fundamental clash between warriors and pluralists, help to explain how the meanings of the two German dictatorships have been negotiated since the 1990s. This conflict is reflected in everyday practice and working relationships for those involved in memorial sites. As Joachim Scherrieble, of the border memorial at *Marienborn*, recalls: "During my first meeting with memorial site leaders, I was almost lynched when I used the term "dictatorship" [in reference to the GDR], especially by West German colleagues who almost all came from memorials of the Nazi past and feared the minimization [*Bagatellisierung*] of fascism."[11]

Scherrieble's experience must also be seen in the context of a series of conflicts that engulfed concrete memorial sites with "double pasts" – pre- and post-1945 – and the memorial foundations that were created in all the East German states after 1990. These disputes dominated the early work (and in turn affected the governance structures) of state memorial foundations, especially in Brandenburg and Saxony.[12] The key issue was the meaning of the Nazi and the Stalinist/GDR pasts in German history and collective self-understanding. To put it simply, the victims of fascism and their advocates were concerned that their hard-won battles to get Germans to take responsibility for Nazism and the Holocaust (with their far-reaching implications for political education and culture) would be sidelined by the memory of the dictatorship after 1945. They accused GDR memory activists of attempting to *relativize* the Holocaust and even of right-wing tendencies. They also worried about commemorating Nazi victims alongside those Nazi perpetrators who had been held in Soviet Special Camps. On the other side, advocates for victims of Stalinism and

[10] Ibid. p. 13 (emphasis in original).   [11] quoted in Finger, 'Was war die DDR?'
[12] Leo, 'Keine gemeinsame Erinnerung', Pearce, 'An Unequal Balance?'

GDR repression were adamant that their plight deserved recognition and argued that denial of adequate remembrance amounted to a *minimization* of their suffering. While most GDR memory activists drew a clear distinction between the enormity of Nazi crimes and what occurred in East Germany after the war, they argued that individual suffering must nevertheless be equally recognized. There were those, however, who contended that communism had an even higher body count than fascism and, employing theories of totalitarianism, that the two ideologies were two sides of the same coin.[13] Another argument here was that some of the former victims of Nazism became perpetrators in the GDR.

Thus, from the perspective of the memory-political opponents, neither victim group could any longer be regarded as unproblematically innocent. The existence of vocal hard-liners on either side resulted in oversimplified accusations being leveled at the entire groups of activists. These disputes – and the often very personal and hurtful attacks that accompanied them – rocked memorial institutions across East Germany for years. In some cases, such as Saxony and Brandenburg, pivotal organizations, such as the Central Council of Jews, withdrew from governing structures in protest and separate committees were set up to address sites of Nazi and GDR pasts.

In the early 1990s in the context of the conflicts over Buchenwald and Sachsenhausen, historian Bernd Faulenbach – member of both *Enquete Commissions* on confronting the East German dictatorship and later in the leadership of the *Stiftung Aufarbeitung* – put forward an ethical principle with which to address the conflict between the Nazi and GDR past: "Nazi crimes may not be relativized through the reckoning with Stalinist crimes. Stalinist crimes may not be minimized through the reference to Nazi crimes." According to Thomas Lindenberger, though this "Faulenbach formula" was developed to address local contention, it has become a general guideline for state memory politics and for the development of large memorial sites.[14] It has since been cited time and again, including in the final report of the second *Enquete Commission*.[15]

Despite the availability of this guiding "rational approach," disputes have continued to flare up. The reason for this lies less in the subject matter itself, than in the relationships damaged as a consequence of the

---

[13] Background to these arguments is the debate on totalitarianism, dating back at least to the 1980s (Herbert, 'Der Historikerstreit') and has international dimensions (Courtois and others, *Das Schwarzbuch des Kommunismus*).

[14] Lindenberger, 'Governing Conflicted Memories' p. 79.

[15] Deutscher Bundestag, 13. Wahlperiode, 'Schlußbericht der Enquete-Kommission "Überwindung der Folgen der SED-Diktatur im Prozeß der deutschen Einheit"' Drucksache 13/11000, August 10, 1998, p. 240.

foregoing conflicts, the identity of the interlocutors, and their influence on the relevant institutions and civic groups. As Carola Rudnick writes,

> There is not a single memorial founded after 1990, the development of which was not accompanied by quarrels and disputes about the interpretation of suffering and crimes ... Victim groups and factions of historians clashed especially over the sites of successive dictatorships, in Saxony for instance at the memorials Münchner Platz, Torgau, and Bautzen. A high level of politicization of the memory landscape has been the consequence to this day. A reconstruction of the individual historical debates shows that the lines of conflict between former prisoners amongst each other, between former prisoners and historians, as well as at the parliamentary level, were always very similar, even stereotypical. This was the case no matter which concrete location of double dictatorial past was at hand. The issue here was less one of a "competition of remembrance," and more one of diametrically opposed value systems and life experiences, which were colliding.[16]

Here again we see the importance of the integration of civil society leaders from West German memorial movements in the public institutions that set the governance structure for memory politics writ-large after reunification. The political collision described here is one between individuals emerging from two very different sociopolitical histories. First, there were those who were socialized to a large extent in West Germany through the struggle to commemorate the Nazi past against the resistance of state actors during the 1980s and 1990s. And second were those who grew up in the GDR (or with connections to the GDR) with only a very limited ability to openly address the past through civic engagement. GDR memory actors have acknowledged the important accomplishments of these Western memory campaigners.[17] Nevertheless, the encounters between protagonists of the History and Memorial Site Movements (who have partly achieved positions of great influence) and the new generation of activists and memorial officials after 1989 have been challenging.

While during the 1980s, activists and historians reinvented memorial institutions from the ground up and even created new ones; the new actors who sought to commemorate the GDR past were confronted with those existing power structures and power brokers. And although they also benefited from the general recognition granted to civil society in memory politics, the contest over norms and values sharply divided the two groups. Gabrielle Camphausen contends that:

> One should not forget that many, who were engaged with the working through of the Nazi past in the old Federal Republic in the past twenty-five or thirty years, come from the left-liberal spectrum, and that they concentrated

---

[16] Rudnick, 'Wenn Häftlinge und Historiker streiten' p. 197.
[17] See Interviews, Siegfried Reiprich.

primarily on the Nazi past and were more reserved when it came to critique of the Communist dictatorships. Many of my colleagues might disagree, but I do think that this topic was approached with a certain "blindness on the left eye." This is the first point. The second point is that these people really had to fight for a long time for the Nazi past to have a recognized position in society and in politics. And when you have fought for something for a very long time, then there is probably a fear that this might be taken away again. The third point has to do with power, with preservation of the status quo, with interpretive dominance – these are all not pretty concepts, which my colleagues might be reluctant to own up to. But this really *does* have to do with power and influence. And with the fear that one may no longer be the only one with something to say about history, about history politics, about working through dictatorship – that they have to stand in line next to others, who also have something to say. I think that this prospect is very frightening for some. But this is not addressed openly, but instead they argue that relativization is happening, that Nazi crimes are being minimized, that old conservatives are returning to take over etc. etc. On the other side, on the side of memory work on communism, there are similar clichés that are repeated over and over.[18]

For the local and federal politics of confronting the GDR past then, it matters greatly which individual actors are involved and to what extent they have found ways to communicate with actors who approach memory through different lenses of socialization and experience. For example, Günter Morsch (head of the Sachsenhausen Memorial and the Brandenburg Memorial Foundation), who was profoundly influenced by the movements of the 1980s,[19] has done much to shape the relationship between the two pasts in this state. His unapologetic prioritization of the Nazi past through words and resources at Sachsenhausen and his reliance on a network of similarly inclined staff members in Brandenburg have helped produce mistrust and hurt feelings on both sides.[20] By contrast, the large influence of GDR victim groups and the leadership of the state's memorial foundation by a former political prisoner in Saxony have led to a different situation. Here, post-1945 memory advocates feel they receive adequate conditions for participation, while the representatives of Nazi victims lament the difficulty of memory work here.[21]

Often – though by no means always – it is also a question of the degree to which individuals are removed from direct experiences of repression. While the History and Memorial Site Movements and West German historians are mostly the children or grandchildren of the *"Erlebnisgeneration"*

[18] See Interviews, Gabrielle Camphausen.
[19] See Interviews, Günter Morsch.
[20] Meyer and Brauckmann, 'Geschichtspolitik und Ausstellungsdidaktik' p. 229, See Interviews, Ulrike Poppe.
[21] Ibid. p. 229, Rudnick, 'Wenn Häftlinge und Historiker streiten' p. 209, 'Rückkehr unter Bedingungen.'

(experiential generation), many of those active in East Germany have direct experience of repression and personal trauma. Herein also lies an explanation for why these memory "factions" clash not only over historical interpretation, but also over whether memorials should emphasize "neutral facts" or "emotional remembering." This issue became especially poignant during the discussions over the Memorial *Leistikowstrasse*, discussed in the previous chapter. It is one that should be kept in mind when we consider the role of normative and representative memory in democratic societies.

Despite these clashes between old and new memory activists within memorial institutions, many GDR memory advocates have found their place in hybrid organizations and have adopted a compatible approach to memorialization. As a result, however, they have grown distant from activists who have remained outside – a dynamic that we have seen with previous activist generations as well. "Outsiders" lament that even those formerly critical dissidents deradicalize and become accommodationist once they are in positions of influence.[22]

Memory Work in Hybrid Institutions

As memory activists entered memorial institutions in Germany, they implemented there the ideas they had developed during their Movement days. Local museums, *Gedenkstätten*, and other organizations have thus taken on tasks that were previously performed or begun by civil society initiatives. Their purpose is continuously using the memory of the Nazi past as a source of "self-unsettlement" (Selbstbeunruhigung) and as a vantage point for critical reflection about past and present.[23] Hybrid institutions work with methods championed by the Memorial Site and History Movements: oral history, self-reflection, public participation, and so forth. Udo Gößwald described his work in the Neukölln Museum in contradistinction to conventional museums:

> This defines our work: the interaction with concrete people, recording their biography, collecting their objects, and thereby creating a kind of connection. So this is a very concrete cooperation, which of course draws its own audience at every exhibit opening ... This is therefore really a citizen-oriented museum and history work – it has its own character that does not take place in the large museums.[24]

Former activists not only try to implement a cooperative working environment, but they continue to understand their work as a contribution to emancipatory memory work. One of their major goals is not merely to

---

[22] See Interviews, Carl-Wolfgang Holzapfel.
[23] Siebeck, 'Gedächtnisarbeit zur NS-Vergangenheit ' p. 4.
[24] See Interviews, Udo Gößwald.

investigate and exhibit history, but to open the museum/memorial to the public and to tap into existing societal developments. For example, the Kreuzberg Museum in Berlin – in addition to its efforts to lay *Stolpersteine* and examine the history of protest movements – has cooperated closely with its immigrant community to develop exhibits and events on the issues of migration and diversity.[25] Salient topics are thus supposed to emerge from the community, rather than from museum professionals. Local museums carefully cultivate relationships with neighborhood schools, initiatives, and political players.

Local museums in particular have become known in their neighborhoods as a first point of contact – for local civic groups, parliaments, and officials – to put together an exhibit or help erect a memorial. A good example of this can be found in Berlin, where local museums have been instrumental in researching and commemorating Nazi forced labor. In response to federal debates about financial compensation for forced laborers, members of the Working Group of Local Museums (ABR) argued that such an approach to the issue was degrading and did not account for the many individual fates involved. In response, local museums not only organized a joint exhibit and locally specific ones but also embraced activities that were taking place in the realm of civil society. In Berlin-Spandau, the museum leadership counseled and aided an artist who had created a memorial to forced laborers as part of a civic initiative. In Berlin-Pankow, the museum not only collected and exhibited the biographies of forced laborers but also made explicit the connection of former sites of Nazi forced labor to the present neighborhood – very much in sync with the History Movement's idea of evoking links between past and present.[26] In such ways, these institutions have had a profound influence on the local landscape of memory, as well as supporting less permanent ongoing historical work.

With the wide variety and expanding range of tasks for hybrid memory institutions, they have almost inevitably grown or been consolidated into larger entities. The effects of growth and consolidation are in some ways contradictory. The expansion of an entity like the Topography of Terror or a concentration camp memorial brings increased funding and staff, as well as greater outreach capacity and more public visibility. Another advantage is usually the improvement of facilities – both in terms of material resources and office space. However, the administrative consolidation of museums can also mean reduced budgets for local history work and a smaller overall staff. Both developments bring with them a greater

---

[25] See Interviews, Martin Düspohl; http://www.kreuzbergmuseum.de/.
[26] See Interviews, Andrea Theissen and Bernt Roder.

degree of bureaucratization of memory work, a decline in the informal relationships, which had buoyed the Memorial Site and History Movements, and larger barriers to the participation of nonprofessionals. Such a shift contributes to making a memorial institution appear more like the state than like a community organization.[27]

Nevertheless, *Gedenkstätten* and local museums distinguish themselves from "conventional" state agencies through an organizational culture that links directly to their roots in social movements. I have already described this with respect to the Topography of Terror Foundation. Christian Staffa, the long-standing Managing Director of the civic organization Action Reconciliation/Service for Peace (ASF), told me:

> Well, you can't style [*durchstylen*] a *Gedenkstätte* like a ministry. They use their organizational form as a protective shield to some extent – which is not typical for a state organization. This is expressed in various constructions – in the House of the Wannsee Conference, in their governing council or curatorium there are representatives of societal groups. In the international memorial council [*internationaler Gedenkstätten-Beirat*] in Brandenburg, Thomas Lutz is our representative for the ASF, not the *Topo* for example. Such constructions show an acceptance that these could not become pure governmental organizations. And you can feel this in how these institutions function – some of the "NGO-flair" is still present there.[28]

Former political prisoners and dissidents in the GDR have also carried their agenda and political culture into existing and newly founded memorial institutions. The leadership of the federal and state authorities dealing with the Stasi files (the LStU and the BStU) is made up entirely of former GDR dissidents. They not only know each other from joint oppositional work, but they share a political culture fostered through their East German political biographies. They are generally able to connect directly to former political prisoners based on experiences of persecution by the regime. Many of the staff working at memorials that emerged from GDR memory activism explicitly regard themselves as advocates for the victims who suffered at these locales and actively seek input from former prisoners. Thus, employees of the Andreasstrasse Memorial in Erfurt, the Moritzplatz Memorial in Magdeburg, or the Human Rights Center at Cottbus not only practice historical education and remembrance, but counsel former inmates on ways to acquire financial compensation or how to live with their personal past. Such emotional commitments can mean that staff in memorial institutions who came out of the GDR memory scene must find a delicate balance between

---

[27] Brown, *RePlacing citizenship* p. 111.   [28] See Interviews, Christian Staffa.

upholding the institutions' guidelines concerning a nonemotional approach to history and carrying their own civic principles into them.

Hybrid Institutions as Mediators

The hybrid nature of institutions that are shaped by (former) civic activists allows them to act as a kind of mediator between the state – embodied by federal and local agencies, parliaments, and governments – and civil society groups. They are seen by grassroots initiatives as "closer to the ground" and more trustworthy than an entity that is closely identified with the state – such as the German Historical Museum (DHM). This role is crucial for the continued legitimacy of hybrid institutions and it is therefore important to foster relationships with civic associations.

Bernt Roder, Director of the Prenzlauer Berg Museum, describes his task as creating a "membrane" between civic engagement and state actors. The creation of a memorial at the site of a former Soviet prison on Prenzlauer Allee in Berlin is an example of the Museum's role. In response to pressure from former prisoners, the local parliament tasked the Museum with researching the history of the site and marking it. Meanwhile, a citizens' initiative was founded and triggered a lively debate not only on how this location should be commemorated, but also on the basic question of how the immediate postwar period and the actions of Soviet authorities should be evaluated. The memorialization process was complicated by the fact that the local government was represented by the post-Communist party (PDS/Die Linke), which had a very different historical interpretation than the victims of the prison and hence was mistrusted by them. Here, the Museum was pivotal in mediating, organizing exchanges, and coming up with a mnemonic solution. Since there was no consensus on the meaning of the site, it was decided that the memorial, for which an artistic competition was announced in 2002, should allow for both reflection about the prison and various interpretations.[29] The winning design is made up of a banner on the building on which questions are written that are meant to evoke reflection. In addition, there are two information panels, as well as regular events with witnesses – all very typical of the memorial aesthetics of the Memorial Site and History Movements.

Similarly, the Brandenburg Memorial Foundation works to build a network of initiatives as partnerships. This has involved an Internet platform for civic initiatives, help publicizing events, and annual conferences where the Foundation seeks to convey its expertise to initiatives, for

---

[29] See Interviews, Bernt Roder, Roder, 'Lokale Akteure und Initiativen.'

instance on interviewing techniques or archeology. The Foundation has also guided the development of new exhibit at the former Soviet Special Camp at Lieberose, organizing the negotiation process among civic and state stakeholders. "We see ourselves as a service agency," says Director Günter Morsch.[30] Though the Foundation may appear to be taking a neutral supportive role here, the intervention in GDR memorial sites by individuals such as Günter Morsch is highly contentious. As we have seen in the context of the *Leistikowstrasse* Memorial in Potsdam, Morsch in particular is eyed with much suspicion in the GDR *Aufarbeitungsszene* due to his prioritizing of the Nazi past over the Stalinist past at the Sachsenhausen Memorial. Again, the individuals who shape frameworks of memorialization are critical.

Another way for memorial institutions to act as mediators is by providing a physical home to civic groups. The Memorial to German Resistance (GDW) in Berlin offers expertise, joint projects, and office space to initiatives, including the Active Museum, the Union of the Persecuted of the Nazi Regime (VVN-BdA), "Against Forgetting, For Democracy," the International Auschwitz Committee, and a coordination office for *Stolpersteine* – among others. Johannes Tuchel, Director of GDW, understands his institution as a kind service and support entity. "This means we do not understand ourselves as purely a state agency, but rather we work very consciously with these associations according to *their* ideas and substantive guidelines and we support them a little with our know-how." Tuchel stresses that there is no attempt to influence or dominate these groups, but rather to encourage joint projects and foster an exchange about memory politics, though he does concede that some of the groups involved were "taken in" at the behest of the federal government.[31] There is clearly direct involvement of the state happening here.

Similar arrangements have also been made at newer institutions, including ones focused on the GDR past. In Stuttgart, the coalition pushing for the Hotel Silber (the former local Gestapo headquarters), is planning to create space in the refurbished building for several of the groups involved so that they can remain closely engaged in the running of the completed memorial, which is scheduled to open in 2018.[32] At the former Stasi facilities at Moritzplatz in Magdeburg, at Bautzener Strasse in Dresden, and at Normannenstrasse in Berlin, associations such as the *Vereinigung der Opfer des Stalinismus* (VOS), the *Bund Stalinistisch*

---

[30] Horst Seferens in Kongress der LStU and Stiftung Aufarbeitung, 'Über Grenzen und Zeiten' p. 157, see Interviews, Günter Morsch.
[31] See Interviews, Johannes Tuchel.
[32] See Interviews, Elke Banabak, email communication August 29, 2016.

Verfolgter (BSV), *Gegen Vergessen, Für Demokratie*, and the UOKG have offices and are thus routinely involved in memorial events and debates.[33]

In sum, the lasting success of the Memorial Site and the History Movements has been to carry its brand of critical memory into the main-stream and to persuade the state to take on the task of confronting the Nazi past in a continuous manner. Because a major linchpin of the Movements was suspicion of state authority, an acceptable way of organizing state funded memory work has been to create or transform institutions and locate them at the intersection of state and society. This "shadow state" sector runs memorials, provides for discussion, and innovates with new projects in the memory field. Such hybrid institutions – *Gedenkstätten*, local museums, foundations, and other entities emerging out of civic activism – have taken over tasks from mnemonic civil society, provided services to activists, and acted as mediators. Members of civic groups demanding the memorialization of the GDR past have often adopted these mechanisms and successfully become part of institutions. However, the meeting of former and new memorial activists in institutional settings has also caused much conflict that will no doubt take many years to resolve.

Making Memory Policy Through Hybrid Institutions

The memory institutions of the "shadow state" have been arguably more effective and visible in their memory work than autonomous civil society. Those former movement members who have taken salaried positions in these institutions usually identify simultaneously with the institution and their civil society background and see the same principles embodied in their professional work. However, not all activists regard the development of the shadow state as an unequivocal success, as it has come with significant concessions and disappointments. Those outside the institutions continue to view these institutions with a suspicious eye and maintain their role as "watchdogs" and innovators for new memory concerns. They lament the decline in activist enthusiasm and atmosphere in memory work today, as well as their lack of direct influence even on hybrid institutions. They feel excluded from decision-making processes and structures, see that their former fellow activists have become "professionals," and criticize efforts to control public memory on the part of the state.

There is in fact evidence of hybrid organizations migrating "out of the shadows" and become more "state-like": some are displaying tendencies to centralize control over memorials and becoming more concerned with

---

[33] Harald Wernowsky in: Kongress der LStU and Stiftung Aufarbeitung, 'Über Grenzen und Zeiten', see Interviews, Herbert Wagner, and Jörg Drieselmann.

the representative needs of the state. According to Harald Schmid, a staff member in the foundation that runs memorials in the state of Schleswig-Holstein, with rising levels of federal funding, "the pressure on actors to legitimize and professionalize has increased perceptively." The result is that memorials are no longer politicized spaces, critical of state and society, but rather driven by the goal of efficiency and to meeting the expectations of the state as the primary funder.[34]

These tendencies have an impact on the practical work of remembrance for visitors to these sites, as even some who help to run memorials to the Nazi past have recently lamented. Habbo Knoch, until 2014 the managing director of the Memorial Foundation of Lower Saxony, argues that memorials have become highly regulated and specialized spaces. They are equipped with powerful codes, rules, and rituals concerning what may legitimately be said and done and even felt in response to the gruesome history of the Holocaust. Knoch calls memorials "hermetic and hegemonic places that tend, in spite of best intentions and laudable practices, to become prisoners of their own pretensions, victims of the empathy they themselves seek to embody."[35] The result may be that memorials and the discourses about the past that they foster will find themselves far removed from the concerns of most citizens.

Despite this looming disconnect, state agencies are concerned with fostering and creating a framework for civil society activity. The nature of hybrid institutions is thus not set in stone, but subject to change. There are two – on the surface contradictory – tendencies in the relationship between government actors, civil society, and hybrid institutions. On the one hand, representatives of the state have taken on public memory as a policy field by founding hybrid memorial institutions and taking over tasks from civil society. On the other hand, the state has increasingly tried to fund and foster civil society organizations, and even helped to create some. While critics argue that this amounts to a shirking of responsibility to deal with memory, it can also be seen as a way to regulate the sphere of civil society.

Representatives of the state routinely stress how important civil society has been to the development of the German memory landscape, as well as the limited role that the state should play therein. Rainer Klemke, formerly of the Berlin Senate Administration for Culture, argued that "citizen initiatives are absolutely indispensable in the memorial arena. Because we also don't want state prescribed commemoration!"[36] The central involvement of civil society in memorial institutions is seen as a guarantee for their autonomy from state direction. The municipal administration of Dresden

[34] Schmid, 'Mehr Gegenwart in die Gedenkstätten!'
[35] Knoch, 'Wohin Gedenkstätten?'   [36] See Interviews, Rainer Klemke.

similarly stresses that the city hopes to consciously support and integrate civic associations in the memorialization process and provide a platform for it, without prescribing its content.[37] Federal agencies also emphasize the limited role of the state. Christian Freiesleben, a staff member of the Federal Cultural Ministry (BKM) and responsible particularly for GDR memory, highlights the remoteness of statist interests ("*Staatsferne*") in the cultural politics at the federal level. Due to budgetary responsibility, decisions must ultimately be taken by the BKM, but it does not prescribe an interpretation of history. The Ministry "does not make memory policy; that would negate democracy."[38]

In the past few decades, the state has transformed its image from that of a reluctant listener to an active supporter of civil society. This shift is apparent not only in the memory field but also more broadly. There has recently been a call to a "new spirit of volunteerism" (*neue Ehrenamtlichkeit*)[39] and the federal government has created a commission to draw up recommendations for how to encourage this. The commission's report calls for the "development of an encompassing culture of recognition, which contributes to a sustained valuing, encouragement, and public visibility of civic engagement."[40] The state, according to this document, must open itself to society, institutionalize modes of participation, and impart responsibility to citizens, while citizens for their part should voluntarily adopt some socially necessary tasks. The commission posits a very harmonic and mutually supportive relationship, which makes no mention of the role of civil society in keeping the state in check from an independent vantage point.

It fits into this picture that formerly oppositionist veterans of the History Movement such as Berlin History Workshop's Gisela Wenzel, as well as civic campaigners of the GDR memorial scene such as Harald Fiss, have been the recipients of the Order of Merit of the Federal Republic of Germany. Such encouragement of civic activity also exists on the local and regional level, where citizenship prizes are being awarded by governments and administrations engage in "participation management."[41] Erik Meyer argues that beginning with the *Enquete Commissions* of the 1990s,

---

[37] Lunau, 'Identität durch bürgerschaftliches Selbstbewusstsein' p. 126.
[38] Christian Freiesleben, email communication, September 28, 2007.
[39] Wollmann, 'Die Doppelstruktur der Stadt.'
[40] 'Bericht der Enquete-Kommission "Zukunft des Bürgerschaftlichen Engagements"' Drucksache 14/8900, June 3, 2002, p. 6.
[41] Wollmann, 'Die Doppelstruktur der Stadt ', www.amadeu-antonio-stiftung.de/die-stiftung-aktiv/buergerstiftungen/aktuelles/foerderpreis-2010/. Citizen participation programs are also being funded by corporations and foundations. See www.aktive-buergerschaft.de/aktive_buergerschaft; www.die-deutschen-buergerstiftungen.de/, www.buergerstiftungen.de/cps/r de/xchg/buergerstiftungen.

memorial institutions and the cultural departments of the federal government have established a routine system of participatory consultation of with civic actors through which initiatives provide input and expertise on memorial issues. This process has become systematic and professionalized – it no longer requires citizens to fight for it.[42]

While civil society groups, among them memorial initiatives, have benefited from these arrangements, they have also lost some autonomy and critical potential. State actors may be able to use their intimate relationship with civil society as a way of legitimating their own actions, often preventing citizens from being a highly disruptive (and corrective) force to state policy. The ability of the state to argue that it has merely listened to citizens and is implementing their wishes can take the wind out of opponents' sails. Sabine Weißler (herself an activist who has moved into the Berlin government) makes an insightful distinction between genuine citizens' initiatives and civic engagement.

> I think that civic engagement and citizens' initiatives are different. Citizens' initiatives have a clearly traceable structural and organizational history in the Federal Republic. The first citizens' initiatives were not history initiatives, but were concerned with environmental questions, the *Startbahn West* [a protest against a runway at Frankfurt airport], the antinuclear movement – that's where this form of political protest comes from. This form was then appropriated by many causes, but it was always used by people to represent their own interests. The term civic engagement is increasingly being used to delegate responsibilities that the state no longer wants to honor ... This is then presented in rosy colors. Citizens' initiatives define their own interests, and they are often in opposition to those of the state. To struggle against them, with one's own ideas, and to want to push them through, that is a completely different thing than adopting tasks set by the state."[43]

When applying this critique to the erection of memorials, the argument could be made that the state's reliance on civil society for the initiation and promotion of remembrance amounts to a shirking of responsibility. Thomas Lutz (again a memorial official himself) has also noted that civic engagement is touted particularly when the state does not want to take on the burden of commemoration.[44]

A prominent example of this dynamic was the creation in 1997–1998 of the Wall Memorial association at *Bernauer Strasse* in Berlin. The Berlin government had received the mandate from the federal level to create a documentation center on the history and memory of the Berlin Wall at this location of both historical significance and previous civic

---

[42] Meyer, 'Die Gedenkstättenkonzeption des Bundes' p. 107.
[43] See Interviews, Sabine Weißler.
[44] See Interviews, Thomas Lutz.

action.[45] The cultural administration in Berlin first created a working group in which it participated, but soon withdrew and encouraged the remaining members to register the group as a civic association. Gabriele Camphausen, who took part, notes that the participants were not particularly aware that the state was outsourcing its responsibility, but merely saw the task at hand. She describes the development as follows:

> We had the state side, that recognized that something had to be done, but did not want to get into that boat themselves. They delegated the whole thing to a private association [*Trägerverein*], to which they provided financial support, but otherwise left us mostly to fend for ourselves. And then this association generated such a powerful effect and so much public attention, that the state felt pressure to become more involved after all. Consequently, the small association was transformed into a public foundation, a foundation of the state of Berlin partially financed at the federal level, a foundation analogous to the Topography of Terror Foundation or the Memorial Berlin-Hohenschönhausen Foundation. Here, you can see the very peculiar interweavings between state action and civic initiative.[46]

State actors have thus intervened in civic memorialization efforts both directly and indirectly. Four of the five Eastern federal states (*Länder*) set up memorial foundations in the early 1990s. Mecklenburg-Western Pomerania chose a route similar to the one used for the Berlin Wall, founding an association called "Politische Memoriale e.V." that provides expert support, training and networking opportunities.[47] These hybrid organizations are all responsible for governing and financing sites from both before and after 1945, which has led to the bitter conflicts between the respective victim groups and their supporters, as I have already discussed. Key civic or interest groups send representatives to the councils of the foundations, formalizing civic participation in its governance but also crystallizing the clash between the different "pasts."[48]

The executive director of the Saxon Memorial Foundation Siegfried Reiprich, a former oppositionist who was recently embroiled in controversy, is critical of the nature of the state's relationship with memory activists.[49] Reiprich argues that the memorial foundations are "too etatistic. They do not censor, but of course one is dependent on them. It is impossible to develop a 'corporate culture' that departs from the mainstream. When you look at the private sector, such as the GDR Museum in

---

[45] See Interviews, Manfred Fischer and Maria Nooke. See Wüstenberg, 'Transforming Berlin's Memory.'
[46] See Interviews, Gabriele Camphausen.
[47] Wagner, 'The Evolution of Memorial Sites' p. 153.   [48] Pearce, 'An Unequal Balance?'
[49] 'Stiftung Sächsische Gedenkstätten', 'Stiftung Sächsische Gedenkstätten', 'Plattform sendet Protestbrief an den Herausgeber der Zeitung "Die Zeit"' March 11, 2016, https://www.stsg.de/cms/stsg/aktuelles/.

Berlin, there other things are possible that are very popular with the audience."[50] When I asked him what he meant by a "mainstream corporate culture" in the arena of memory, he explained that since the move of the German capital to Berlin, cultural politics had become more centralistic, driven crucially by the *Stiftung Aufarbeitung* in downtown Berlin. Reiprich contended that because of these structural conditions, conflicts were primarily carried out within bureaucracies, rather than in society writ-large. Though there were individuals and organizations working against this trend, the centralized structure meant that some controversial avenues for commemoration might not be explored. This assessment is closely tied to the sentiments of many local memorial activists I have spoken to. They point to the existence of an official "way of doing things" when it comes to standards for exhibitions, artistic representation of the past, the language used in memorials, and hiring practices for staff. These unspoken guidelines propel some civic campaigners – such as in Cottbus – to seek independence from state regulation, though almost all remain financially reliant to a great degree.

What some identify as a homogenous memory culture is rooted in a fundamental transformation of German cultural politics since unification. This transformation was not simply imposed from above. It is rather the result of a complex interplay between civic, state and hybrid stakeholders. As I have argued in the previous chapter, the state was directly involved in commemorative action from the beginnings of GDR memory activism in the early 1990s. The creation of the two *Enquete Commissions* and the foundation of the Stasi File authority (BStU) and the *Stiftung Aufarbeitung* meant that GDR memory was negotiated centrally in Berlin from the beginning. In a more general sense, cultural politics experienced centralization through the creation of what is essentially a ministry of culture – the Federal Government Commissioner for Culture and Media (BKM – *Bundesbeauftragte(r) für Kultur und Medien*) – which is directly attached to the Chancellor's office. This was an important shift since culture had traditionally been the domain of the states in the Federal Republic. Among the most significant responsibilities of the BKM was the enhanced funding and renewal of the large memorial sites, especially concentration camps, but also some GDR sites. The BKM also drove forward such pivotal projects as the unified German Historical Museum and the Foundation Memorial to the Murdered Jews of Europe.

In addition to the creation of formal administrative bodies to oversee and fund activity that was previously civically run, state actors have organized forums within which civil society groups can coordinate their

---

[50] See Interviews, Siegfried Reiprich.

projects and exchange ideas with each other and their government partners. Such an effort exists in Thuringia, for instance, where the *Geschichtsverbund Thüringen* was founded in 2009 in order to link and support civic groups and memorials working on the SED dictatorship.[51] Rainer Klemke, responsible for memorials for the Berlin city government, was proud to have inaugurated working groups AK1 and AK2 (Arbeitskreis 1 for the Nazi past and Arbeitskreis 2 for the GDR past) for civic associations:

> In principle, we try to organize the field of memorials as remote from the state (*staatsfern*). This means I provide impulses but then I try to let them run things. The state should not sit there and say "you have to do it this way and that way." Instead I analyze the situation, say, this is what you need, an instrument of communication and a forum, which can be a partner and to which one can delegate particular topics and say: you should look at this. So I took the initiative for the working groups and then it has to sustain itself. And in order for this to happen, we have to push a bit, but I remain in the background.[52]

Despite the stated commitment on the part of government representatives to the autonomy of civil society, the regulation of professional standards and the prevailing funding criteria in effect do amount to a regulatory framework. When state representatives are pressed on the details of the state's dealings with memorial actors, it becomes clear that the approach is not quite as hands-off as it appears on the surface. Knut Nevermann, who was the Ministerial Director in the BKM until late 2005, explained his conception of the state to mean:

> not a civil servant [*Beamter*] who run things, but in the sense of a cultural entity, meaning autonomous and free, with a professional director, and surrounded by people who come from supportive associations, victims organization etc. and who determine everything. The state should not tell them how to do things. God forbid. The state should tell them: *you are a professional, you are not a professional.* But not more.[53]

Thus, state actors are mindful to include various stakeholders in memory debates and create financial mechanisms to support nonstate initiatives. Andrew Beattie has made a useful distinction between "official" and "state-mandated" memory in this context: the former term denotes memory produced directly by state organs or representatives, while the latter means memory promoted by other actors, which is subsidized or endorsed by the state.[54] Memory policy is a mixed field, in which state

---

[51] www.geschichtsverbund-thueringen.de/.
[52] See Interviews, Rainer Klemke.
[53] See Interviews, Knut Nevermann (my emphasis).
[54] Beattie, 'The Politics of Remembering the GDR' p. 25.

agents operate both proactively and more indirectly. Beattie contends that new state funding instruments after 1990 did not result in state control: "Indeed, the ongoing conflict over GDR memory has not only or primarily been between state and society. Much conflict has occurred within and around state institutions, as diverse actors compete for influence over official memory."[55] I concur that direct intervention in memorialization was not the dominant approach of federal institutions; however, *state actors did do much to determine memory indirectly through the creation of frameworks of funding and memorial site organization*. Although civil society actors have worked hard to shape these frameworks as well, the existence of rules for memorialization becomes most evident when contention erupts between state and civic actors.

This account of how memorial policy-making is organized supports my argument (drawing on Thomas Lindenberger's) that the state does not seek to control memorialization directly, but rather works to create a framework for guiding such policy in cooperation with nonstate actors. The creation of forums for exchange among activists but under the roof of official institutions and with state encouragement is a useful tool for accomplishing this. It is important to stress that government actors such as Klemke do not seek to surreptitiously influence the process without owning up to it; but they nevertheless set certain parameters by acting as the initiator of activist networking and influence the standards that must be met to have access to influence and resources.

One key goal – and simultaneously one of the criteria for admission into such forums – is "professionalism" on the part of the institutions and actors involved, as Nevermann stated clearly. The use of "professionalism" as a distinction is meant to invoke a whole set of principles of conduct, including most importantly an objective handling of historical facts, an unemotional and reasoned approach to memorialization, and restraint in politicizing remembrance. These are principles that were developed in the context of the Memorial Site Movement and in the process of turning former sites of Nazi terror into venues for democratic political education. The resulting institutions have become the standard-bearers for "professional conduct" in German memorialization. However, these ideas privilege historians and other experts over victim advocates who approach commemoration through experience. According to Lindenberger, this grants scholarly experts a crucial role in legitimating professionalism and valuing it higher than the needs of "nonneutral witnesses" to the past.[56] When I asked Martin Sabrow – very much a representative of the mnemonic expert community – how the needs of victims' organizations could be

---

[55] Ibid. p. 24.   [56] Lindenberger, 'Governing Conflicted Memories' p. 83.

reconciled with professionalism, he said: "You cannot fully reconcile them, because the suffering of the victims cannot be compensated or healed even through – from their perspective – the best and most emotional remembrance; this fire cannot be put out. One has to achieve an honorable commemoration, but it is like the justice system – it should not be placed in the hands of victims, so that we do not get a justice of revenge."[57]

This means that those who do not speak the language of professionalism – but who have important memory political concerns to voice in a democratic process of working through remembrance – may be denied access to crucial memory policy forums. This can even result in an inability to realize their memorialization goals. More broadly – these practical and institutional dividing lines that are present even in the hybrid institutions of civic-state memory politics in Germany, speak to the tension between normative and representative democracy in memorialization.

Democratic Memory in Germany

Eighty years after Hitler's ascent to power in 1933, the President of Germany's Federal Parliament, Norbert Lammert, underscored the important role played by public remembrance for German society and in international relations: "This memory culture is an indispensable prerequisite for the restitution of German standing in the world, and it was the condition for the recovery of an upright gait for a people who had gone politically astray, were militarily defeated, economically destroyed, and morally discredited."[58]

The cover image of this book shows a scene in 1985, when memory activists of the Active Museum literally started digging up the past at the former Gestapo headquarters in Berlin. It was civil society's challenge to the state's memory politics that was instrumental in placing the Holocaust and Nazi terror in the center of political culture and international public relations. As Lammert's speech illustrates, representatives of the German state display an unapologetic pride in the accomplishments of civic memory work – a pride that is buttressed by the many favorable comparisons that have been drawn with other countries' attempts to interrogate traumatic episodes of national history. German memorial officials and activists have even traveled abroad to offer their advice on how remembrance "is done" democratically.

---

[57] See Interviews, Martin Sabrow.

[58] Norbert Lammert, speech in Hamburg, April 11, 2013, www.norbert-lammert.de/01-lammert/texte2.php?id=120.

Throughout this study, I have analyzed how the engagement of civil society in memory politics has altered the balance between the representative and normative components of democratic memory. I have argued that we must pay attention *both* to the extent to which public commemoration is reflective of widespread attitudes about past experiences (whether historically accurate or not) *and* to the normative values embodied in the mnemonic narratives that are displayed publicly. While the dominance of memory about expulsion, war experiences, and Communist repression in the first postwar decades accurately represented the majority's reading of the past, the marginalization of the Holocaust indicated a very "shallow" level of democratization. For this reason, the challenge launched by the Memorial Site and History Movements to propel a critical examination of the Nazi past – not only into intellectual circles, but also into the everyday life of German citizens – had a revolutionary effect. Without this civic activism, the memory landscape in Germany would look very different, and we would not have seen a deepening of democratic values in political culture in the same way. Of course, these Movements stood on the shoulders of others and worked alongside like-minded intellectuals and government officials. But the memory activists of the 1980s and 1990s were decisive in compelling more than a superficial, centralized acknowledgement of guilt. Their localized actions and the aesthetic principles they popularized meant that the reckoning with the Nazi past was distributed across many aspects of social life and found its way into the normative cultural understanding of the Federal Republic.

The civically driven and detail-oriented memory work of the activists was adopted by agencies of the state – official memorials, state-funded museums, and cultural administrations – through the mechanisms I have described in this chapter. This made the accomplishments of the social movements more lasting. And it means that they are now backed by powerful interests. The merging of the *norms* of Holocaust memory with their *representativeness* – in the sense of both widespread presence in the memory landscape and functionality for the state – is clearly a victory for advocates of democratic memory. It is clear from pronouncements such as Lammert's that a critical approach to the Nazi past is no longer an option – it is part of a code of conduct that has become institutionalized. However, this high level of institutionality does not mean that is has been automatically adopted by the public. In fact, there is evidence that the lessons for which the Memorial Site and History Movements labored and that are so neatly presented in memorials across Germany, are not widely recognized by citizens. Knoch cites a survey conducted on the seventieth anniversary of the liberation of Auschwitz that found that 81 percent of respondents would prefer to "leave behind" the history of the Holocaust.[59] Such findings beg the question of whether a memory that is as established as Holocaust memory has become in Germany today, loses its ability to be a support structure for democratic norms. Established memory spaces could be so ingrained that they no longer function as venues to "unsettle" those norms about the past that visitors bring with them. Arguably, an experience of "unsettlement" and of personal investment in a particular understanding of the past is needed in order to foster democratic participation.

Though representatives of the state continuously emphasize the important role played by civil society in memory politics past and present, they are not willing to relinquish control entirely over the regulatory framework that governs memory culture. As I have argued, this framework was built jointly by memory activists and individuals employed by the state – and many that straddle this dividing line. One might assume that when civil society input is structurally embedded in the organization of memory culture in this way, that this signifies a highly democratic state of affairs. This would be very much in line with Robert Putnam's argument about the democratic effect of social capital in the functioning of institutions more generally.[60] In the introductory chapter, I cited Andreas Nachama, the Director of the Topography of Terror, taking this position when he lauded the civic origins of the site: "if you put more civic engagement in on one side, more democracy will also come out the other end."

However, as my investigation of civic activism has made clear, this equation cannot be applied universally and in fact masks the tension that remains between civil society and state – even as they cooperate and intertwine in hybrid institutional arrangements. Neither state nor civil society should be regarded uncritically in this relationship. A demand for remembrance that emanates from the grassroots, even from victims of repression, is not automatically democratic. According to philosopher and theologian Richard Schröder,

> Civil society should not replace the state. A permanent plebiscite of those most concerned (der Betroffenen) would mean anarchy. Personal affliction (Betroffenheit) is not democratic legitimation for decision-making. Citizens' initiatives can receive the right to be consulted and informed. The right to make decisions and take final responsibility must always remain with those who have been elected and appointed. Otherwise responsibility fades. When everyone is responsible for everything and everyone is included in decision-making, nobody is responsible in reality. Civil society should collect, coordinate, and channel what will then become politically binding according to the rules and jurisdiction of the

---

[59] Knoch, 'Wohin Gedenkstätten?'   [60] Putnam, *Making Democracy Work.*

constitution and the legal order. Civil society should shape the state in the direction of more transparency of official action, in the direction of the state as a service provider, not as lord of the citizens.[61]

Closer examination of this statement helps spotlight the tension. On the one hand, it is true that memory activists have not been democratically elected and sometimes espouse views that are not only marginal but highly problematic from the standpoint of democratic values. An extreme example of this are the actions of the activist Gustav Rust who displays anti-Semitic and nationalist propaganda while claiming to uphold the memory of those who perished at the Berlin Wall – all in a very prominent location on Berlin's main tourist route. Here, the collective memory of repression in the GDR – and Rust's personal affliction as a former political prisoner – are clearly not serving democratic memory. Representatives of the democratic state are elected – or appointed by those who are elected – to maintain a memory culture that operates in accordance with the law.

However, just as problematic, I argue, is when the framework for governing memory has become so ingrained that it is no longer open to challenge. As I have shown, because the formerly oppositional activists of the 1980s and 1990s have been deeply involved in building the framework that exists in German memory culture today, and because they have become firmly embedded in it, it is very difficult for "outside" activists (or even just rebellious youth) to contest it. The critical norms of Holocaust remembrance have become the raison d'état, and they have thus become immensely powerful – with both a positive and a negative effect on democratic remembrance. The positive effect lies in the fact that ethics based on Holocaust memory (and therefore the protection of the weak, tolerance of difference, of self-critical reflection) can be linked to mainstream memory policy. This is of course no guarantee for a democratic political culture, but it makes for a strong support structure.

The negative effect of the strength of the Nazi past in current public memory (and of those activists who got it there) is that these important mnemonic norms are bound up with codes of conduct that are often defended for their own sake. Ideas such as nonemotionality in representation, nonpartisanship, and a particular language for articulating the meaning of the past are part of this code of conduct. Whoever violates it can quickly be labeled "unprofessional" and thus not worthy of state support and funding. In other words, the norms that were established through the struggle to commemorate the Nazi past are now defended by

---

[61] Richard Schröder 'Vom Wert der Freiheit' in: Konferenz der LStU, 'Vom Wert der Freiheit' pp. 42–43.

taboos about how acceptable memory activists are supposed to behave. These taboos are also ingrained in memorials themselves – in their exhibitions, their aesthetic conformity, their seminars and workshops – and send a powerful message to visitors about appropriate responses to a confrontation with violent pasts. As Habbo Knoch recognizes, the perpetuation of such hegemonic discourses of acceptable memory may not only produce discomfort in response to moral expectations conjured up there. Worse, they entail the danger of evoking active resistance to memorials and the norms they encapsulate as places that now represent the raison d'état.[62] In other words, memorial sites' loss of civic identity and openness to challenge from the outside may lead not only to a disconnect with society writ-large, but to a rejection of the normative messages about democracy that the Movements of the 1980s fought so hard to popularize. It is not far-fetched to suggest that recent xenophobic mobilization by the likes of *Pegida* and the *Alternative für Deutschland* are made possible by a partial failure to spread democratic norms beyond the confines of memorial sites.

Many of the former political prisoners and dissidents in East Germany have found ways to make their demands heard while adhering to this code of conduct. They have themselves become successful members of the "memory establishment," thereby working to reproduce the memorial framework and thus doing much important work to integrate the GDR past into German political culture. However, there are also those who have not been able or willing to adopt these rules of engagement and who have ruffled feathers by using words and memorial aesthetics that do not easily fit in. What I argue is that it is precisely *because* these activists challenge mainstream modes of memory, that they have a crucial contribution to make to the development of democratic memory.

There are several reasons for this. First, and at the most basic level, many of these activists have personally experienced the human rights violations that they seek to commemorate. It is a demand of justice not only to allow them to do so, but to grant them public space for this without prescribing how it must be used. It is a matter of respect for these people's personal memories and their struggle to come to terms with the past that they should not be compelled to remember as previous generations of activists saw fit. If emotionality, dramatization of the past, and even its politicization is important for them, then it is not appropriate for memorial officials to denigrate this approach. Of course, if undemocratic values are promoted in the course of such remembering, then they need to be called out on this.

---

[62] Knoch, 'Wohin Gedenkstätten?'

Second, controversial activists have a contribution to make to democratic political education. The past that they seek to represent speaks of repression, collaboration, and opposition in recent (communicative) memory. Victims, perpetrators, bystanders, those who accommodated themselves to the regime, and those who resisted, are all still around to bear witness and use their experiences to address the contemporary challenges to democracy. The fact that the way in which activists speak about these complex legacies cannot easily be controlled is all the more reason to address them directly, rather than to marginalize them through "rules and regulations." Future generations of democrats will not learn to defend democratic norms if there are taboos that prevent them from being discussed. When commemoration problematically conjures up discourses of German nationalism, of simplistic friend-enemy divisions reminiscent of the Cold War, or of a lack of consciousness of the causes of the Second World War and Holocaust, they need to be addressed head-on. The consolidation and deep adoption of democratic norms needs to happen continuously, and this requires debate about historical complexity, about inconsistencies in individual and collective remembering, and about emotions. German democracy will be much stronger if it does not require the erection of taboos about the past for its self-defense.

Finally, the challenge to mainstream memory brought by "outsiders" is important for a fundamental reason raised by scholars of social movements. Since previous civic memory campaigners have become intertwined with the state, it has become difficult for them to function as checks and balances on state power. Though I have argued that we need to disaggregate the state and analyze the critical forces that exist within, we also need to take seriously the pressure on them to secure their own position and to defend the ideas that brought them there. Thus, it is vital that memory culture and the institutions that support it are called into question persistently, so that they do not become static. The measure of democratic memory will not be whether particular norms are adhered to, but how the practice of commemoration and discussion about the past is organized and to what extent it can propel critical thought processes among citizens. The tension between normative and representative elements in public remembrance must be continuously negotiated and reinvigorated – and civil society will continue to be crucial to this process.

Interviews

Name	Affiliation	Date and Place
Elke Banabak	Co-Chair, Initiative Lern- und Gedenkort Hotel Silber e.V. (Initiative for memorial at former Gestapo headquarters), Stuttgart	February 7, 2014, Stuttgart
Renate Bauschke	Member, Arbeitskreis Bürger gestalten ein Mahnmal, Hannover-Ahlem	September 1–6, 2016, email communication
Wolfgang Benz	Historian & Director, Zentrum für Antisemitismusforschung (Center for Anti-Semitism Research) Technical University, Berlin	May 30, 2006, Berlin
Peter Boeger	Head of initiative for Checkpoint Bravo Memorial	November 23, 2012, Berlin
Andreas Bräutigam	Executive Committee Member of the Berliner Geschichtswerkstatt (Berlin History Workshop)	December 10, 2012, Berlin
Eva Brücker	Staff at Stiftung Denkmal für die ermordeten Juden Europas, member Berlin History Workshop	August 22, 2007, Berlin
Gabrielle Camphausen	Head of Political Education, Bundesauftragter für Stasiunterlagen (Federal Commissioner for the Records of the Stasi), Head of Berliner Mauerverein (Berlin Wall Association)	August 21, 2007, Berlin
Peter Conradi	Architect, 1972–98 SPD Member of Bundestag (Socialdemocratic Party)	June 12, 2006, email communication
Hans Coppi	Head of Vereinigung der Verfolgten des Naziregimes (Union of the Persecuted of the Nazi Regime) in Berlin	August 23, 2007, Berlin
Michael Cramer	Member of the European Parliament, the Green Party	May 22, 2006, Berlin
Michael Cullen	Author and publicist	November 14, 2005, Berlin

(cont.)

Name	Affiliation	Date and Place
Thomas Dahnert	Gedenkbibliothek für die Opfer des Stalinismus (Memorial Library for the Victims of Stalinism), Berlin	May 16, 2006, Berlin
Hugo Diederich	Head of Vereinigung der Opfer des Stalinismus (Union of Victims of Stalinism), Berlin	December 13, 2012, Berlin
Eberhard Diepgen	Partner, law firm Tümmel-Schütze & Partner, Former Mayor of Berlin	May 24, 2006, Berlin
Jörg Drieselmann	Director, Stasi Museum, Berlin Normannenstrasse, Managing Director of ASTAK e.V.	August 15, 2007, Berlin
Martin Düspohl	Director Kreuzberg Museum, Berlin, founding member Berlin History Workshop	May 30, 2006, Berlin
Günter Dworek	Staff for Green Party in the Bundestag, Initiative on Homosexual Victims of Nazism	November 25, 2005, Berlin
Andreas Eberhard	Executive Director, Gegen Vergessen, Für Demokratie (Against Forgetting, for Democracy)	November 16, 2005, Berlin
Stefanie Endlich	Author, professor at Universität der Künste, Berlin, member of Active Museum	August 27, 2007, Berlin
Manfred Fischer †	Protestant Minister, Initiator of Wall Memorial at Bernauer Strasse	November 22, 2005, Berlin
Peter Fischer	Gedenkstättenreferent (responsible for memorials), Zentralrat der Juden in Deutschland, Central Council of Jews in Germany	May 22, 2006, Berlin
Christine Fischer-Defoy	Head of Active Museum	November 17, 2005, Berlin
Harald Fiss	Initiator Memorial Refugee Camp Marienfelde	June 2, 2006, Berlin
Bodo Förster	History teacher, Sophie-Scholl-Oberschule, Berlin	May 26, 2006, Berlin
Edeltraut Frankenstein	Staff in Berlin coordinating office for Stolpersteine	November 17, 2005, Berlin
Christian Freiesleben	Staff, Beauftragter der Bundesregierung für Kultur und Medien (Federal Commissioner for Culture and Media)	September 28, 2007, email communication
Detlef Garbe	Head of Concentration Camp Memorial Neuengamme, Hamburg	August 21, 2013, Hamburg
Ruth Gleinig & Oliver Igel	Staff, Stiftung Aufarbeitung (Foundation for Working Through the SED Dictatorship)	May 16, 2006, Berlin
Kristian Golla	Member of Bonner Friedensplenum/ Netzwerk Friedenskooperative	May 19, 2009, email communication

(cont.)

Name	Affiliation	Date and Place
Martin Gorholt	State Secretary, Ministry of Science, Research and Culture, Brandenburg	July 28, 2016, Potsdam
Udo Gößwald	Director, Museum Berlin-Neukölln, founding member Berlin History Workshop	August 13, 2007, Berlin
Michael Heiny	Treasurer, Marburger Geschichtswerkstatt	September 9, 2016, email communication
Alexandra Hildebrandt	Director Museum at Checkpoint Charlie	November 25, 2005, Berlin
Helga Hirsch	Freelance journalist, formerly with *Die Zeit*	May 3, 2006, Berlin
Jörg Holl and Melanie Roeser	Members of Bürgerverein Luisenstadt e.V. (local Berlin civic association)	November 16, 2005, Berlin
Carl-Wolfgang Holzapfel	Head of association 17. Juni e.V.	November 21, 2012, Berlin
Walter Homolka	Rabbi, Abraham-Geiger-Kolleg (rabbinical seminary in Berlin)	May 31, 2006, Berlin
Ulrike Hoppe	Head of Stadtteilarchiv Bramfeld (local Hamburg archive)	August 21, 2013, Hamburg
Friedrich Hossbach	Member of Initiative Synagoge Haus Wolfenstein and Mirror Wall in Berlin-Steglitz	August 15, 2007, Berlin
Michael Jeismann	Editor/journalist, *Frankfurter Allgemeine Zeitung*	April 19, 2006, Frankfurt am Main
Anna Kaminsky	Managing Director Stiftung Aufarbeitung (Foundation for Working Through the SED Dictatorship)	February 10, 2014, Berlin
Norbert Kampe	Director, Haus der Wannsee Konferenz (Memorial House of the Wannsee Conference)	May 4, 2006, Berlin
Jürgen Karwelat	Head of Berliner Geschichtswerkstatt (Berlin History Workshop)	December 10, 2012, Berlin
Peter Kenzelmann	Entrepreneur, founder of the DDR Museum (GDR Museum)	August 25, 2007, Berlin
Diethart Kerbs †	Founding member Berlin History Workshop	Spring 2010, email communication
Birgit Kipfer	Executive Committee, DDR Museum (GDR Museum) Pforzheim	November 19, 2013, Pforzheim
Jupp Klegraf	Long-time member of Stuttgart Geschichtswerkstatt (History Workshop)	November 20, 2013, Stuttgart
Rainer Klemke	Gedenkstättenreferent (responsible for memorials), Berliner Senatsverwaltung (Berlin Senate Administration for Science, Research and Culture)	May 18, 2006, Berlin
Volkhard Knigge	Director, Gedenkstätte Buchenwald und Mittelbau-Dora (Memorial Buchenwald and Mittelbau-Dora)	October 17, 2013, Buchenwald near Weimar

(*cont.*)

Name	Affiliation	Date and Place
Gerd Koch	Executive Committee Galerie Morgenland/ Geschichtswerkstatt Eimsbüttel, History Workshop in Hamburg	February 6, 2013, Berlin
Stephan Konopatzky	Staff, Bundesauftragter für Stasiunterlagen (Federal Commissioner for the Records of the Stasi), co-founder Bürgerkommittee 15. Januar e.V.	November 25, 2005, Berlin
Angelika Krüger-Leissner	Member of Bundestag, SPD (Socialdemocrats)	June 3, 2006, Berlin
Jörg Kürschner	Journalist, Head of Förderverein Gedenkstätte Hohenschönhausen (Friends of Memorial Hohenschönhausen association)	May 5, 2006, Berlin
Claus Peter Ladner	Retired Judge, head of Fördergemeinschaft Lindenstrasse 54 (association for Memorial at Lindenstrasse 54), Potsdam	December 18, 2012, Potsdam
Thomas Lindenberger	Historian, Zentrum für Zeithistorische Forschung (Center for Contemporary History), Potsdam, founding member Berlin History Workshop	March 5, 2013, Potsdam
Jürgen Litfin	Initiator of memorial to his brother, Günter Litfin, in watch tower at Kieler Eck	May 3, 2006, Berlin
Susanne Lohmeyer	Former head and long-time member of Geschichtswerkstatt Eimsbüttel, Hamburg	August 20, 2013, Hamburg
Gesine Lötzsch	Member of Bundestag, Die Linke (The Left Party)	May 23, 2006, Berlin
Andreas Ludwig	Historian, former Director, Dokumentationszentrum Alltagskultur der DDR (Documentation Center Everyday Culture in the GDR) Eisenhüttenstadt, member Berlin History Workshop	August 14, 2007, Eisenhüttenstadt
Thomas Lutz	Gedenkstättenreferent (responsible for memorials), Stiftung Topography des Terrors (Foundation Topography of Terror)	May 18, 2006, Berlin
Beate Meyer	Historian, Institut für die Geschichte der deutschen Juden (Institute for the History of German Jews), member Geschichtswerkstatt Eimsbüttel	August 22, 2013, Hamburg
Sonja Miltenberger	Archivist, Museum Charlottenburg-Wilmersdorf, member and archivist of the Berlin History Workshop	January 15, 2013, Berlin
Günter Morsch	Historian/Director, Stiftung Brandenburgische Gedenkstätten (Memorial Foundation Brandenburg)	August 17, 2007, Berlin-Oranienburg

(cont.)

Name	Affiliation	Date and Place
Andreas Nachama	Director, Stiftung Topography des Terrors (Foundation Topography of Terror)	November 24, 2005, Berlin
Knut Nevermann	Until late 2005, Ministerial Director in the Chancellor's Office, Federal Commissioner for Culture and Media	November 15, 2005, Berlin
Uwe Neumärker	Managing Director, Stiftung Denkmal für die ermordeten Juden Europas (Foundation Memorial to the Murdered Jews of Europe)	November 18, 2005, Berlin
Günter Nooke	Human Rights representative of the federal government (2006–10), before that Member of the Bundestag, CDU (Christian Democrats) for Berlin, initiator of Unity and Freedom Memorial in Berlin	May 12, 2006, Berlin
Maria Nooke	Project coordinator, Gedenkstätte Berliner Mauer (Wall Memorial) Bernauer Strasse, Berlin	April 28, 2006, Berlin
Rainer Potratz	Staff, Gedenkstätte Deutsche Teilung (Memorial German Separation) at Marienborn, head of Berlin-Brandenburg History Workshop	August 16, 2007, Berlin
Ulrike Poppe	Landesbeauftragte zur Aufarbeitung der Folgen der kommunistischen Diktatur Brandenburg (State Commissioner for the Records of the Stasi)	January 10, 2013, Berlin
Peter Radunski	Publicis-PR/Consultants, formerly Cultural Senator in Berlin and election manager for Helmut Kohl	May 10, 2006, Berlin
Matthias Rau	City guide, Stattreisen e.V.	June 1, 2006, Berlin
Siegfried Reiprich	Executive Director, Stiftung Sächsische Gedenkstätten zur Erinnerung an die Opfer politischer Gewaltherrschaft (Saxon Memorial Foundation), Dresden	January 16, 2013, Dresden
Bernt Roder	Director, Prenzlauer Berg Museum, Berlin	June 2, 2006, Berlin
Volker Römer	Head of Gegen das Vergessen e.V./DDR Museum, association Against Forgetting/ GDR Museum, Pforzheim	November 19, 2013, Pforzheim
Gisela Rüdiger	Active for Leistikowstrasse and Lindenstrasse Memorials, Potsdam	March 5, 2013, Potsdam
Reinhard Rürup	Historian, former Research Director of Topography of Terror	May 19, 2006, Berlin
Gustav Rust	Memorial activist, stages private memorial between Reichstag and Brandenburger Tor	May 11, 2006, Berlin
Martin Sabrow	Historian, Director of Zentrum für Zeithistorische Forschung (Center for Contemporary History), Potsdam	August 30, 2007, Potsdam

(cont.)

Name	Affiliation	Date and Place
Günter Schlusche	Planning Director, Gedenkstätte Berliner Mauer (Berlin Wall Memorial) at Bernauer Strasse	January 15, 2014, Berlin
Gerhard Schoenberner †	Co-founder Aktives Museum Widerstand und Faschismus Berlin e.V. (Active Museum), founding Director Memorial House of the Wannsee Conference	August 23, 2007, Berlin
Rainer Schubert	Founder of Aufarbeitungsinitiative Deutschland e.V. (Initiative for Working Through the Past), Berlin	November 21, 2005, Berlin
Jakob Schulze-Rohr †	Co-founder of Förderkreis Denkmal für die ermordeten Juden Europas (Initiative Memorial for the Murdered Jews of Europe)	November 22, 2005, Berlin
Tom Sello	Staff, Robert-Havemann-Gesellschaft/ Archiv der DDR Opposition (Robert-Havemann-Society oppositional archive)	May 8, 2006, Berlin
Hermann Simon	Director Centrum Judaicum, since 1988	May 23, 2006, Berlin
Christian Staffa	Executive Director, Aktion Sühnezeichen/ Friedsdienste (Action Reconciliation/ Service for Peace)	May 17, 2006, Berlin
Annegret Stephan	Founding Director, Gedenkstätte Moritzplatz Magdeburg	August 2, 2016, Magdeburg
Renata Stih and Frieder Schnock	Artists, designed the memorial at Bayrischer Platz	May 9, 2006, Berlin
Andrea Theissen	Director of Kunstverwaltung (Art Administration) Spandau and of Zitadelle Spandau (local museum)	August 16, 2007, Berlin
Johannes Tuchel	Director, Gedenkstätte Deutscher Widerstand (Memorial to German Resistance)	May 15, 2006, Berlin
Peter von Becker	Journalist, *Der Tagesspiegel*	May 22, 2006, Berlin
Jesko von Samson	Staff of Erika Steinbach (CDU Member of Bundestag) and of Stiftung Zentrum gegen Vertreibungen (Foundation Center against Expulsions)	November 21, 2005, Berlin
Herbert Wagner	Head of Erkenntnis durch Erinnerung e.V. (association Insight Through Remembrance), former mayor of Dresden	January 16, 2013, Dresden
Rainer Wagner	Head of Union der Opferverbände Kommunistischer Gewaltherrschaft (Union of Victims Associations of Communist Dictatorship)	August 24, 2007, Berlin

(cont.)

Name	Affiliation	Date and Place
Sabine Weißler	Fachbereichsleiterin für Kultur und Bibliotheken (Director of culture and library administration) in Berlin-Steglitz-Zehlendorf, member Active Museum	June 1, 2006, Berlin
Gisela Wenzel	Historian & Political Scientist, founding member Berlin History Workshop	May 11, 2006, Berlin and subsequent meetings and correspondence
Dieter Winkler & Harald Hampel	Social Democratic Party, local branch Berlin-Pankow	May 17, 2006, Berlin
Eberhard Zastrau	Member of the governing council of the Stiftung Brandenburgische Gedenkstätten (Brandenburg Memorial Foundation), Initiative on Homosexual Victims of Nazism	November 28, 2005, Berlin

Bibliography

Ahonen, Pertti, *After the Expulsion: West Germany and Eastern Europe 1945–1990* (Oxford: Oxford University Press, 2003).

Alexander, Jeffrey C, *The Civil Sphere* (Oxford: Oxford University Press, 2006).

Alscher, Mareike, Dietmar Dathe, Eckhard Priller, and Rudolf Speth, "Nähe und Distanz. Die Zivilgesellschaft braucht den Staat, aber auch Unabhängigkeit," *WZB Mitteilungen*, 121 (2008), 18–21.

Anschütz, Janet, and Irmtraud Heike, *"Wir wollten Gefühle sichtbar werden lassen" Bürger gestalten ein Mahnmal für das KZ Ahlem* (Bremen: Edition Temmen, 2004).

Apelt, Andreas H, ed., *Der Weg zum Denkmal für Freiheit und Einheit* (Schwalbach/Ts.: Wochenschauverlag, 2009).

Applebaum, Anne, *Iron Curtain. The Crushing of Eastern Europe, 1944–1956* (New York: Doubleday Press, 2012).

Arbeitsgruppe Stattbuch 3 Berlin, ed., *Stattbuch 3 Berlin – Ein Wegweiser durch das andere Berlin* (Berlin: Stattbuch Verlag GmbH, 1984).

Arenhövel, Mark, *Demokratie und Erinnerung – Der Blick zurück auf Diktatur und Menschenrechtsverbrechen* (Frankfurt: Campus Verlag, 2000).

Art, David, *The Politics of the Nazi Past in Germany and Austria* (Cambridge: Cambridge University Press, 2006).

Assmann, Aleida, *Der lange Schatten der Vergangenheit: Erinnerungskultur und Geschichtspolitik* (Munich: C.H. Beck, 2011).

Assmann, Jan, *Das kulturelle Gedächtnis. Schrift, Erinnerung und politische Identität in frühen Hochkulturen* (Munich: C.H. Beck, 1999).

Religion and Cultural Memory – Ten Studies. trans. Rodney Livingstone (Stanford: Stanford University Press, 2006).

Assmann, Aleida, and Ute Frevert, *Geschichtsvergessenheit – Geschichtsversessenheit. Vom Umgang mit deutschen Vergangenheiten nach 1945* (Stuttgart: Deutsche Verlags-Anstalt, 1999).

Bacia, Jürgen, and Cornelia Wenzel, *Bewegung bewahren: Freie Archive und die Geschichte von unten* (Berlin: Archiv der Jugendkulturen Verlag KG, 2013).

Barber, Benjamin R, *A Place for Us – How to Make Society Civil and Democracy Strong* (New York: Hill and Wang Press, 1998).

"'Barfuß-Historiker' ohne Boden," *Frankfurter Rundschau*, 23 April 1992.

Baukloh, Anja Corinne, "'Nie wieder Faschismus!' Antinationalsozialistische Proteste in der Bundesrepublik der 50er Jahre im Spiegel ausgewählter

Tageszeitungen," in *Protest in der Bundesrepublik – Strukturen und Entwicklungen,* ed. by Dieter Rucht (Frankfurt: Campus Verlag, 2001).

Baum, Karl-Heinz "Für Meinungsfreiheit und Mitbestimmung – Die Friedenswerkstatt vor 25 Jahren," *Horch und Guck,* 57 (2007), 4–8.

Baumann, Leonie "Vorwort" in Stefanie Endlich 1990 (ed) *Denkort Gestapogelände* (Berlin: Schriftenreihe Aktives Museum).

Baumgärtner, Ulrich "Schuld oder Scham? Theodor Heuss' Gedenkrede in Bergen-Belsen 1952." *Praxis Geschichte,* December 06/2007.

Beattie, Andrew H, "The Politics of Remembering the GDR: Official and State-Mandated Memory since 1990," in *Remembering the German Democratic Republic: Divided Memory in a United Germany,* ed. by David Clarke and Ute Wölfel (Basingstoke: Palgrave Macmillan Press, 2011).

Behling, Heidburg, and Klaus Möller, "Gegen das Verdrängen – Für ein würdiges Gedenken," in *Herbert Schemmel (1914–2003) Überlebender und Chronist des KZ Neuengamme. Mahner gegen das Vergessen,* ed. by Freundeskreis KZ-Gedenkstätte Neuengamme e.V. (Hamburg: 2004).

Behrens, Heidi, Paul Ciupke, and Norbert Reichling, "... und im nachhinein ist man überrascht, wie viele Leute sich das auf die Fahnen schreiben und sagen, ich habe es gemacht." Akteursperspektiven auf die Etablierung und Arbeit von Gedenkstätten in Nordrhein-Westfalen," *GedenkstättenRundbrief,* 171 (2013), 3–18.

Benz, Wolfgang, "Probleme mit der Erinnerung und dem Gedenken. Einleitung.," in *Ein Kampf um Deutungshoheit. Politik, Opferinteressen und historische Forschung. Die Auseinandersetzung um die Gedenk- und Begegnungsstätte Leistikowstrasse Potsdam,* ed. by Wolfgang Benz (Berlin: Metropol Verlag, 2013).

ed., *Ein Kampf um Deutungshoheit. Politik, Opferinteressen und historische Forschung. Die Auseinandersetzung um die Gedenk- und Begegnungsstätte Leistikowstrasse Potsdam.* ed. by Wolfgang Benz (Berlin: Metropol Verlag, 2013).

Berg, Manfred, and Bernd Schaefer, "Introduction," in *Historical Injustice in International Perspective – How Societies Are Trying to Right the Wrongs of the Past,* ed. by Manfred Berg and Bernd Schaefer (Cambridge: Cambridge University Press and and Washington, D.C.: German Historical Institute, 2009).

Berg, Stefan, and John Goetz "Protest am Reichstag: Der Mann, der Berlin blamiert," *Der Spiegel* (31 March 2008).

Berger, Thomas U., "The power of memory and memories of power: the cultural parameters of German foreign policy-making since 1945,' in *Memory & Power in Post-War Europe – Studies in the Presence of the Past,* ed. by Jan-Werner Müller (Cambridge: Cambridge University Press, 2002).

Berger, Thomas U, *War, Guilt, and World Politics after World War II* (New York: Cambridge University Press, 2012).

Berliner Geschichtswerkstatt e.V., ed., *Alltagskultur, Subjektivität und Geschichte: zur Theorie und Praxis von Alltagsgeschichte* (Münster: Westfälisches Dampfboot, 1994).

ed., *Sackgassen – Keine Wendemöglichkeit für Berliner Straßennamen* (Berlin: Verlag Dirk Nishen, 1988).

Berliner Kulturrat e.V., ed., *1933 Zerstörung der Demokratie. Machtübergabe und Widerstand. Ausstellungen und Veranstaltungen Programm 1983* (Berlin: 1983).

Berman, Sheri, "Civil Society and the Collapse of the Weimar Republic," *World Politics*, 49 (1997), 401–29.

Bermeo, Nancy, *Ordinary People in Extraordinary Times: The Citizenry and the Breakdown of Democracy* (Princeton: Princeton University Press, 2003).

Beßmann, Alyn, and Insa Eschebach, eds., *Das Frauen-Konzentrationslager Ravensbrück. Geschichte und Erinnerung, Schriftenreihe der Stiftung Brandenburgische Gedenkstätten* (Berlin: Metropol Verlag, 2013).

Best, Michael, ed., *Der Frankfurter Börneplatz. Zur Archäologie eines politischen Konflikts* (Frankfurt: Fischer Taschenbuch Verlag, 1988).

Boeger, Peter, and Lydia Dollmann, *FREUNDwärts, FEINDwärts. Die deutsch-deutsche Grenzübergangsstelle Drewitz/Dreilinden* (Berlin: Verlag Willmuth Arenhövel, 2011).

Böge, Volker, "'... Treffpunkt, Meinungsumschlagplatz für kritische, unbändige Entwürfe' Zur Vor- und Frühgeschichte der Galerie Morgenland 1978–1984," in *25 Jahre Galerie Morgenland/Geschichtswerkstatt Eimsbüttel – Festschrift*, ed. by Volker Böge, Beate Meyer, and Sielke Salomon (Hamburg: Galerie Morgenland e.V., 2003).

"Zur Einleitung," in *Geschichtswerkstätten gestern – heute – morgen. Bewegung! Stillstand. Aufbruch?*, ed. by Volker Böge (München: Dölling und Galitz Verlag, 2004).

Bonner Friedensplenum Arbeitskreis "Von der Fahne," ed., *Für die unbekannten Deserteure – Dokumentation zum Projekt*. Ergänzte und durchgesehene Auflage Stand Anfang Juni 1989 edn (1989).

Borsdorf, Ulrich, and Heinrich Theodor Grütter, eds., *Orte der Erinnerung – Denkmal, Gedenkstätte, Museum* (Frankfurt: Campus Verlag, 1999).

Brown, Michael P, *RePlacing Citizenship: AIDS Activism and Radical Democracy* (New York: The Guilford Press, 1997).

Brubaker, Rogers, *Nationalism Reframed. Nationhood and the National Question in the New Europe* (Cambridge: Cambridge University Press, 1996).

Brumlik, Micha, Hajo Funke, and Lars Rensmann, *Umkämpftes Vergessen – Walser-Debatte, Holocaust-Mahnmal und neuere deutsche Geschichtspolitik*. Second edn (Berlin: Verlag Hans Schiler, 2004).

eds., *Umkämpftes Vergessen – Walser-Debatte, Holocaust-Mahnmal und neuere deutsche Geschichtspolitik*. Second edn (Berlin: Verlag Hans Schiler, 2004).

Büchten, Daniela, and Anja Frey, eds., *Im Irrgarten deutscher Geschichte. Die Neue Wache 1818–1993* (Berlin: Schriftenreihe Aktives Museum, 1994).

Buggeln, Marc, and Inge Marszolek, "Concrete Memory. The Struggle over Air-Raid and Submarine Shelters in Bremen after 1945,' in *Beyond Berlin. Twelve German Cities Confront the Nazi Past*, ed. by Gavriel D Rosenfeld and Paul B Jaskot (Ann Arbor: The University of Michigan Press, 2008).

Camphausen, Gabriele, "Constructing Remembrance – Dealing with the German Experience of Dictatorship,' in *Goethe-Institut – Dossier: Constructing Remembrance* (2007).

Camphausen, Gabriele, and Manfred Fischer, "Die bürgerschaftliche Durchsetzung der Gedenkstätte an der Bernauer Straße,' in *Die Mauer.*

Errichtung, Überwindung, Erinnerung, ed. by Klaus-Dietmar Henke (München: Deutscher Taschenbuch Verlag, 2011).

Confino, Alon, "Collective Memory and Cultural History: Problems of Method," *The American Historical Review,* 102 (1997), 1386–403.

Courtois, Stéphane, Nicolas Werth, Jean-Louis Panné, Andrzej Paczkowski, Karel Bartosek, and Jean-Louis Margolin, *Das Schwarzbuch des Kommunismus. Erweiterte Studienausgabe edn* (Munich: Piper Verlag, 2000).

Cruz, Consuelo, "Identity and Persuasion – How Nations Remember Their Pasts and Make Their Futures," *World Politics,* 52 (2000), 275–312.

Cullen, Michael S, ed., *Das Holocaust-Mahnmal – Dokumentation einer Debatte* (Zürich: Pendo Verlag, 1999).

"Das Interesse für das Projekt 'Bürger gestalten ein Mahnmal' in Ahlem ist groß," *Hannoversche Allgemeine Zeitung,* 5 March 1987.

Davis, Belinda, "New Leftists and West Germany – Fascism, Violence, and the Public Sphere, 1967–1974," in *Coping with the Nazi Past – West German Debates on Nazism and Generational Conflict, 1955–1975,* ed. by Philipp Gassert and Alan E Steinweis (New York: Berghahn Books, 2006).

Davis, Belinda, Thomas Lindenberger, and Michael Wildt, "Einleitung," in *Alltag, Erfahrung, Eigensinn – Historisch-anthropologische Erkundungen,* ed. by Belinda Davis, Thomas Lindenberger and Michael Wildt (Frankfurt: Campus Verlag, 2008).

Davis, Belinda, Wilfried Mausbach, Martin Klimke, and Carla MacDougall, eds., *Changing the World, Changing Oneself. Political Protest and Collective Identities in West Germany and the U.S. in the 1960s and 1970s* (New York: Berghahn Books, 2012).

della Porta, Donatella, *Can Democracy Be Saved?* (Cambridge: Polity, 2013).

Der LStU Freistaat Thüringen, ed., *Von der Überwindung kommunistischer Diktaturen zum vereinten Europa – Erinnerung als Chance für die Zukunft – Gemeinsamer Kongress der LStU und der Bundeszentrale für politische Bildung mit den Opferverbänden und Aufarbeitungsinitiativen (3. Verbandstreffen) vom 18. bis 20. Juni 1999 in Gera* (Erfurt: 1999).

Der LStU Mecklenburg-Vorpommern, ed., *Demokratie braucht Erinnerung. Gemeinsamer Kongress der LStU mit den Opferverbänden und Aufarbeitungsinitiativen (4. Verbandstreffen) vom 12. bis 14. Mai 2000 in Schwerin* (2001).

"Der Stein des Anstoßes," *Der Tagesspiegel,* 1 June 2006.

Der Spiegel, "'Ein kräftiger Schub für die Vergangenheit' Spiegel-Report über die neue Geschichtsbewegung in der Bundesrepublik," in *Historisches Lernen in der Erwachsenenbildung,* ed. by Ulrich Kröll (Münster: Verlag Regensburg, 1984).

Deutscher Bundestag, ed., *Formen und Ziele der Auseinandersetzung mit den beiden Diktaturen in Deutschland. Vol. IX, Materialien der Enquete-Kommission "Aufarbeitung von Geschichte und Folgen der SED-Diktatur in Deutschland" (12. Wahlperiode des Deutschen Bundestags)* (Badan-Baden: Nomos Verlagsgesellschaft, 1995).

"Die Geschichtswerkstatt e.V. stellt sich vor," *MOZ – Moderne Zeiten,* 4 (1984).

"Die zwei Wahrheiten von Sachsenhausen," *Süddeutsche Zeitung,* 13 July 2006.

Doßmann, Axel, "Geschichtswerkstatt-Initiativen im Osten – ein ernüchterndes Fazit," in *Alltagskultur, Subjektivität und Geschichte: zur Theorie und Praxis von Alltagsgeschichte*, ed. by Berliner Geschichtswerkstatt e.V. (Münster: Westfälisches Dampfboot, 1994).

Dowe, Christopher, "Symbol des Widerstandes. Die Einschätzungen des Attentäters Stauffenberg haben sich seit dem Krieg stark gewandelt," *Momente. Beiträge zur Landeskunde von Baden-Württemberg*, 4 (2006), 29–33.

Dowe, Dieter, "Geschichtspolitik als wesentliche Aufgabe in der demokratischen Gesellschaft – einige Schlussbemerkungen," in *Geschichtspolitik und demokratische Kultur. Bilanz und Perspektiven*, ed. by Beatrix Bouvier and Michael Schneider (Bonn: Dietz Verlag, 2008).

Dubiel, Helmut, *Niemand ist frei von der Geschichte – Die nationalsozialistische Herrschaft in den Debatten des Deutschen Bundestages* (München: Carl Hanser Verlag, 1999).

Düspohl, Martin, "20 Jahre Berliner Geschichtswerkstatt – Ein persönlicher Rückblick," in *Immer noch Lust auf Geschichte. 20 Jahre Berliner Geschichtswerkstatt e.V.*, ed. by Berliner Geschichtswerkstatt e.V. (2001).

Eley, Geoff, *Forging Democracy – The History of the Left in Europe, 1850–2000* (Oxford: Oxford University Press, 2002).

Endlich, Stefanie, "Gestapo-Gelände: Entwicklungen, Diskussionen, Meinungen, Forderungen, Perspektiven," in *Zum Umgang mit dem Gestapo-Gelände. Gutachten im Auftrag der Akademie der Künste*, ed. by Akademie der Künste (Berlin: 1988).

"Projekte für ein Freiheits- und Einheitsdenkmal in Berlin und Leipzig," *Deutschland Archiv* (2015).

Wege zur Erinnerung. Gedenkstätten und -orte für die Opfer des Nationalsozialismus in Berlin und Brandenburg (Berlin: Metropol Friedrich Veitl-Verlag, 2006).

Eppelmann, Rainer, Thomas Krüger, and Markus Meckel, "Zum Geleit," in *Orte des Erinnerns – Gedenkzeichen, Gedenkstätten und Museen zur Diktatur in SBZ und DDR*, ed. by Annette Kaminsky (Leipzig: Forum Verlag, 2004).

Eyerman, Ron, "Social movements and memory," in *Routledge International Handbook of Memory Studies*, ed. by Anna Lisa Tota and Trever Hagen (Oxon: Routledge, 2016).

Faulenbach, Bernd, "Diktaturerfahrungen und demokratische Erinnerungskultur in Deutschland," in *Orte des Erinnerns – Gedenkzeichen, Gedenkstätten und Museen zur Diktatur in SBZ und DDR*, ed. by Annette Kaminsky (Leipzig: Forum Verlag, 2004).

Faust, Hans, "Vorläufer des Bundes der Verfolgten des Naziregimes Berlin e. V.," *Die Mahnung* (1983).

Fein, Elke, Nina Leonhard, Jens Niederhut, Anke Höhne, and Andreas Decker, *Von Potsdam nach Workuta. Das ehemalige NKGB/MGB/KGB-Gefängnis Potsdam-Neuer Garten im Spiegel der Erinnerung deutscher und russischer Häftlinge* (Potsdam: Brandenburgische Landeszentrale für politische Bildung, 2002).

Finger, Evelyn, "Was war die DDR? Und was soll von ihr bleiben? Eine Reise zu den Gedenkstätten des untergegangenen deutschen Staates, von Marienborn über Leipzig nach Bautzen.," *Die Zeit* (2006).

Fischer, Jan Otakar, "Memento Machinae. Engineering the Past in Wolfsburg," in *Beyond Berlin. Twelve German Cities Confront the Nazi Past*, ed. by Gavriel D Rosenfeld and Paul B Jaskot (Ann Arbor: The University of Michigan Press, 2008).

Fletcher, Roger, "Review: History from Below Comes to Germany: The New History Movement in the Federal Republic of Germany," *The Journal of Modern History*, 60 (1988), 557–68.

Forster, Reinhold, "Antworten lesender Augsburger – Die Geschichte der Geschichtswerkstatt Augsburg," *Geschichte quer – Zeitschrift der Geschichtswerkstätten in Bayern*, 13 (2006), 43–45.

Fox, Thomas C. *Stated Memory – East Germany and the Holocaust* (Rochester, NY: Camden House, 1999).

Francois, Etienne, ed., *Deutsche Erinnerungsorte*. Vol. 1–3 (Frankfurt: C.H. Beck Verlag, 2003).

Frank, Sybille, "Der Mauer um die Wette gedenken," in *Dossier: Geschichte und Erinnerung* (Bundeszentrale für politische Bildung, 2011).

Frei, Alfred Georg, "2. Geschichtsfest – Tango und Theoriearbeit," *Journal für Geschichte*, 5 (1985), 4–6.

"3. Geschichtsfest der Geschichtswerkstätten – Alltagstrott bei den Alltagshistorikern?," *Journal für Geschichte*, 1 (1987), 6–9.

"Die Geschichtswerkstätten in der Krise," in *Alltagskultur, Subjektivität und Geschichte: zur Theorie und Praxis von Alltagsgeschichte*, ed. by Berliner Geschichtswerkstatt e.V. (Münster: Westfälisches Dampfboot, 1994).

"Die Zukunft liegt in der Vergangenheit – Geschichtswerkstaetten, Tendenzwende und demokratische Alternativen," *MOZ – Moderne Zeiten*, 4 (1984), 3–6.

"Geschichtswerkstätten," in *Geschichte entdecken – Erfahrungen und Projekte der neuen Geschichtsbewegung*, ed. by Hannes Heer and Volker Ullrich (Reinbek bei Hamburg: Rowohlt Verlag, 1985).

"Geschichtswerkstätten als Zukunftswerkstätten – Ein Plädoyer für eine aufklärerische Geschichtsarbeit," in *Die andere geschichte: Geschichte von unten, Spurensicherung, ökologische Geschichte, Geschichtswerkstätten*, ed. by Gerhard Paul and Bernhard Schoßig (Köln: Bund-Verlag, 1986).

Frei, Norbert, *1945 und Wir – Das Dritte Reich im Bewusstsein der Deutschen* (Munich: C.H. Beck, 2005).

Vergangenheitspolitik – Die Anfänge der Bundesrepublik und die NS-Vergangenheit (Munich: C.H. Beck, 1997).

ed., *Hitlers Eliten nach 1945* (München: dtv, 2003).

Freisberg, Andrea, and Thomas Werther, "Was wir wollten, was wir taten: die alte Geschichtswerkstatt," in *Grabe, wo Du stehst! 15 Jahre Geschichtswerkstatt Marburg e.V.*, ed. by Geschichtswerkstatt Marburg (Marburg: 2003).

Friedrich, Klaus-Peter, Albrecht Kirschner, Katharina Nickel, and Autorenkollektiv Zeitgeschichtliche Dokumentationsstelle Marburg, "Zur Geschichte und Nachgeschichte der 'Marburger Jäger,'" ed. by Marburger Geschichtswerkstatt (Marburg: 2013).

Fritz, Anja, "1950–1958. Schlussstrich und Integration" in *Was bleibt: Nachwirkungen des Konzentrationslagers Flossenbürg. Katalog zur Dauerausstellung*, ed. by Jörg Skriebeleit (Wallstein Verlag, 2011).

Garbe, Detlef, *Die Arbeit der KZ-Gedenkstätte Neuengamme 1981 bis 2001. Rückblicke – Ausblicke. Eine Dokumentation der Aktivitäten 20 Jahre nach der Eröffnung des Dokumentenhauses in Hamburg-Neuengamme.* Second edn (Hamburg: KZ-Gedenkstätte Neuengamme, 2002).

"Die Gedenkstättenkonzeption des Bundes: Förderinstrument im Geschichtspolitischen Spannungsfeld," *Gedenkstättenrundbrief,* 182 (2016), 3–17.

"Von den 'vergessenen KZs' zu den 'staatstragenden Gedenkstätten'?," *Gedenkstättenrundbrief,* 100 (2001), 75–82.

Gedenkstätte Buchenwald, ed., *Die Geschichte der Gedenkstätte Buchenwald. Begleitheft zur Dauerausstellung* (Weimar: 2007).

George, Alexander L, and Andrew Bennett, *Case Studies and Theory Development in the Social Sciences* (Cambridge, MA: MIT Press, 2005).

Gerstenberger, Heide, and Dorothea Schmidt, eds., *Normalität oder Normalisierung? Geschichtswerkstätten und Faschismusanalyse* (Münster: Westfälisches Dampfboot, 1987).

Gerstenberger, Heide, and Dorothea Schmidt, "Von den Festen zu den Alltagen und zu neuen Aufgaben," *Geschichtswerkstatt* 24 (1991).

Geschichtswerkstatt Marburg, *Grabe, wo Du stehst! 15 Jahre Geschichtswerkstatt Marburg e.V.* (2003).

Gilcher-Holtey, Ingrid, "'1968' – Eine versäumte Kontroverse?," in *Zeitgeschichte als Streitgeschichte – Große Kontroversen nach 1945,* ed. by Martin Sabrow, Ralph Jessen and Klaus Große Kracht (München: Verlag C.H. Beck, 2003).

"Gisela Rüdiger für Abberufung von Ines Reich," *Potsdamer Neueste Nachrichten* (26 May 2011).

Goldberg, Werner, "Gerechtigkeit und Sühne als Zielsetzung vor 50 Jahren. Rede zur Festveranstaltung zum 50. Jahrestag der Gründung des Bundes der Verfolgten des Nazi-Regimes Berlin e.V. am 27. Juni 1996," *Die Mahnung,* 43 (1996).

Goldhagen, Daniel Jonah, *Hitler's Willing Executioners – Ordinary Germans and the Holocaust* (London: Little, Brown and Company, 1996), p. 622.

"Modell Bundesrepublik – Nationalgeschichte, Demokratie und Internationalisierung in Deutschland," *Blätter für deutsche und internationale Politik* (1997), 424–43.

Goldman, Natasha, "Marking Absence. Remembrance and Hamburg's Holocaust Memorials," in *Beyond Berlin. Twelve German Cities Confront the Nazi Past,* ed. by Gavriel D Rosenfeld and Paul B Jaskot (Ann Arbor: The University of Michigan Press, 2008).

Görtemaker, Manfred, *Geschichte der Bundesrepublik Deutschland – Von der Gründung bis zur Gegenwart* (Munich: C.H. Beck, 1999).

"'Grabe wo du stehst.' Geschichte von unten' *die tageszeitung* (23 June 1981).

Großbölting, Thomas, "Die DDR im vereinten Deutschland," in *Dossier: Geschichte und Erinnerung* (Bundeszentrale für politische Bildung, 2010).

Haase, Norbert, "Berlin-Charlottenburg, Witzlebenstraße 4–10. Anmerkungen zur Auseinandersetzung um eine Erinnerungstafel für die Opfer des Reichskriegsgerichts," *Dachauer Hefte,* 6 (1994), 206–16.

Habermas, Jürgen, "Über den Öffentlichen Gebrauch der Historie – Warum ein "Demokratiepreis" für Daniel Goldhagen?," *Blätter für deutsche und internationale Politik* (1997), 408–16.

Hamel, Irene, "Denk-Steine setzen. Bericht über die Denk-Stein-Aktion der Geschichtswerkstatt Bayreuth," *Geschichte quer – Zeitschrift der Geschichtswerkstätten in Bayern*, 13 (2006).

Hartmann, Christian, Johannes Hürter, and Ulrike Jureit, eds., *Verbrechen der Wehrmacht. Bilanz einer Debatte* (Munich: C.H. Beck, 2005).

Haß, Matthias, *Gestaltetes Gedenken – Yad Vashem, das U.S. Holocaust Memorial Museum und die Stiftung Topographie des Terrors* (Frankfurt: Campus Verlag, 2002).

Haß, Ulrike, "Mahnmaltexte 1945 bis 1988 – Annäherung an eine schwierige Textsorte," *Dachauer Hefte*, 6 (1994), 135–61.

Hattig, Susanne, Silke Klewin, Cornelia Liebold, and Jörg Morré, *Geschichte des Speziallagers Bautzen. 1945–1956. Katalog zur Austellung der Gedenkstätte Bautzen.* ed. by Stiftung Sächsische Gedenkstätten (Dresden: Michel Sandstein Verlag, 2004).

Stasigefängnis Bautzen II. 1956–1989. Katalog zur Austellung der Gedenkstätte Bautzen. ed. by Stiftung Sächsische Gedenkstätten (Dresden: Michel Sandstein Verlag, 2004).

Haunss, Sebastian, and Darcy K Leach, "Social movement scenes – Infrastructures of opposition in civil society," in *Civil Societies and Social Movements – Potentials and problems*, ed. by Derrick Purdue (Oxon: Routledge Press/ECPR studies in European political science, 2007).

Hausmann, Brigitte, *Duell mit der Verdrängung? Denkmäler für die Opfer des Nationalsozialismus in der Bundesrepublik Deutschland 1980 bis 1990* (Münster: Lit Verlag, 1997).

Heer, Hannes, Walter Manoschek, Alexander Pollak, and Ruth Wodak, *Wie Geschichte gemacht wird: Zur Konstruktion von Erinnerungen an Wehrmacht und Zweiten Weltkrieg* (Wien: Czernin Verlag, 2003).

Heer, Hannes, and Volker Ullrich, "Einleitung: Die 'neue Geschichtsbewegung' in der Bundesrepublik. Antriebskraefte, Selbstverstaendnis, Perspektiven," in *Geschichte entdecken – Erfahrungen und Projekte der neuen Geschichtsbewegung*, ed. by Hannes Heer and Volker Ullrich (Reinbek bei Hamburg: Rowohlt Verlag, 1985).

Heimann, Siegfried "Wie der Popanz 'Zeitzeuge' in der Geschichtswerkstatt verhindert, sich einer 'Geschichte von unten' zu nähern," *Berliner Geschichtswerkstatt Rundbrief*, 2 (1983).

Heimrod, Ute, Günter Schlusche, and Horst Seferens, eds., *Der Denkmalstreit – das Denkmal? Die Debatte um das „Denkmal für die ermordeten Juden Europas". Eine Dokumentation* (Berlin: Philo Verlag, 1999).

Heinrich, Christoph, *Strategien des Erinnerns: der veränderte Denkmalbegriff in der Kunst der achtziger Jahre* (München: Verlag Silke Schreiber, 1993).

Heisler, Martin O, "The Politics of Managing the Past: Democratic Norms, Democratization and the Collective Self-Concept in the Face of Unpalatable Revelations," in *the Annual Meeting of the American Political Science Association* (Washington, D.C.: 2005).

Heller, Agnes, "A Tentative Answer to the Question: Has Civil Society Cultural Memory?," *Social Research*, 68 (2001), 1031–40.

Herbert, Ulrich, "Der Historikerstreit. Politische, wissenschaftliche, biographische Aspekte," in *Zeitgeschichte als Streitgeschichte – Große Kontroversen nach 1945*, ed. by Martin Sabrow, Ralph Jessen and Klaus Große Kracht (München: Verlag C.H. Beck, 2003).

Herf, Jeffrey, *Divided Memory – The Nazi Past in the Two Germanys* (Cambridge: Harvard University Press, 1997).

Hertle, Hans-Hermann, and Maria Nooke, "Die Todesopfer an der Berliner Mauer 1961–1989," (Potsdam/Berlin: Zentrum für Zeithistorische Forschung Potsdam, Stiftung Berliner Mauer, 2011).

Hettling, Manfred, and Jörg Echternkamp, eds., *Bedingt erinnerungsbereit. Soldatengedenken in der Bundesrepublik* (Göttingen: Vandenhoeck & Rupenrecht, 2008).

Hildebrandt, Alexandra, "Die Freiheit verpflichtet – Das Freiheitsmahnmal am Platz Checkpoint Charlie," *Technische Universität Berlin Sozialwissenschaften*, 34 (2005).

Hinske-Gengnagel, Ursula, "Die eigene Vergangenheit finden ... 10 Jahre Frauengeschichtswerkstatt Memmingen e.V.," *Geschichte quer – Zeitschrift der Geschichtswerkstätten in Bayern*, 13 (2006).

Hirschman, Albert O, "Exit, Voice, and the Fate of the German Democratic Republic: An Essay in Conceptual History," *World Politics*, 45 (1993), 173–202.

Holtmann, Everhard, "Politische Interessenvertretung von Vertriebenen: Handlungsmuster, Organisationsvarianten und Folgen für das politische System der Bundesrepublik," in *Vertriebene in Deutschland – Interdisziplinäre Ergebnisse und Forschungsperspektiven*, ed. by Dierk Hoffmann, Marita Krauss and Michael Schwartz (München: Oldenbourg Verlag, 2000).

Horn, Gerd-Rainer, *The Spirit of '68 – Rebellion in Western Europe and North America, 1956–1976* (Oxford: Oxford University Press, 2007).

Horst, Uwe, "Stolpersteine – auch in Bielefeld," in *Geschichte und Geschichtsvermittlung – Festschrift für Karl Heinrich Pohl*, ed. by Olaf Hartung and Katja Köhr (Bielefeld: Verlag für Regionalgeschichte, 2008), pp. 259–74.

Hoss, Christiane, and Martin Schönfeld, *Gedenktafeln in Berlin – Orte der Erinnerung an Verfolgte des Nationalsozialismus 1991–2001*. Vol. 9 (Berlin: Schriftenreihe Aktives Museum, 2002).

Howard, Marc Morjé, *The Weakness of Civil Society in Post-Communist Europe* (Cambridge: Cambridge University Press, 2003).

Huntington, Samuel P, *Political Order in Changing Societies* (New Haven: Yale University Press, 1968).

Hüttner, Bernd, *Archive von unten – Bibliotheken und Archive der neuen sozialen Bewegungen und ihre Bestände* (Neu-Ulm: AG SPAK Bücher, 2003).

Initiative Deserteur Denkmal für Stuttgart, ed., *Stuttgart braucht ein Denkmal für Deserteure* (Stuttgart: 2002).

Initiative Haus Wolfenstein, ed., *Von Juden in Steglitz. Beiträge zur Ortsgeschichte* (Berlin: 1990).

Jander, Martin, "Kultur der Aufrechnung: Erneuerte deutsche Opfermythologie und radikaler Antikommunismus. Die Union der Opferverbände Kommunistischer Gewaltherrschaft (UOKG)," in *Ein Kampf um Deutungshoheit. Politik, Opferinteressen und historische Forschung. Die Auseinandersetzung um die Gedenk- und Begegnungsstätte Leistikowstrasse Potsdam*, ed. by Wolfgang Benz (Berlin: Metropol Verlag, 2013).

Jarausch, Konrad H, "Critical Memory and Civil Society: The Impact of the 1960s on German Debates about the Past," in *Coping with the Nazi Past – West German Debates on Nazism and Generational Conflict, 1955–1975*, ed. by Philipp Gassert and Alan E Steinweis (New York: Berghahn Books, 2006).

Die Umkehr: Deutsche Wandlungen, 1945–1995 (Munich: Deutsche Verlagsanstalt, 2004).

Jaskot, Paul B, "The Reich Party Rally Grounds Revisited. The Nazi Past in Postwar Nuremberg," in *Beyond Berlin. Twelve German Cities Confront the Nazi Past*, ed. by Gavriel D Rosenfeld and Paul B Jaskot (Ann Arbor: The University of Michigan Press, 2008).

Jaspert, Bernd, "Vorwort," *Hofgeismarer Protokolle: Geschichte von unten – Modelle alternativer Geschichtsschreibung. Dokumentation einer Tagung der Evangelischen Akademie Hofgeismar, 6.-8.2.1990.*, 274 (1990).

Jeggle, Utz, "Heimatkunde des Nationalsozialismus – Vier lokale Versuche, verwischte Spuren zu sichern," *Dachauer Hefte*, 6 (1994), 162–81.

Jeismann, Michael, *Auf Wiedersehen Gestern. Die deutsche Vergangenheit und die Politik von morgen* (Stuttgart: 2001).

ed., *Mahnmal Mitte – Eine Kontroverse* (Köln: DuMont Buchverlag, 1999).

Jones, Sara, *The Media of Testimony. Remembering the East German Stasi in the Berlin Republic*, Palgrave Macmillan Memory Studies (Basingstoke: Palgrave Macmillan, 2014).

Jordan, Jennifer A, *Structures of Memory: Understanding Urban Change in Berlin and Beyond* (Stanford: Stanford University Press, 2006).

Judt, Tony, "The past is another country: myth and memory in post-war Europe," in *Memory & Power in Post-War Europe – Studies in the Presence of the Past*, ed. by Jan-Werner Müller (Cambridge: Cambridge University Press, 2002).

Postwar – A History of Europe since 1945 (New York: Penguin Books, 2005).

Kaminsky, Annette, and Ruth Gleinig, "Vorwort," in *Orte des Erinnerns – Gedenkzeichen, Gedenkstätten und Museen zur Diktatur in SBZ und DDR*, ed. by Annette Kaminsky (Leipzig: Forum Verlag, 2004).

eds., *Orte des Erinnerns. Gedenkzeichen, Gedenkstätten und Museen zur Diktatur in SBZ und DDR*. Third edn (Berlin: Ch. Links Verlag, 2016).

Kansteiner, Wulf, "Losing the War, Winning the Memory Battle: The Legacy of Nazism, World War II and the Holocaust in the Federal Republic of Germany," in *The Politics of Memory in Postwar Europe*, ed. by Richard Ned Lebow, Wulf Kansteiner and Claudio Fogu (Durham: Duke University Press, 2006).

Kattago, Siobhan, *Ambiguous Memory – The Nazi Past and German National Identity* (Westport, CT: Praeger Press, 2001).

Kierdorf, Alexander, and Uta Hassler, *Denkmale des Industriezeitalters – Von der Geschichte des Umgangs mit Industriekultur* (Tübingen: Ernst Wasmuth Verlag und Lehrstuhl für Denkmalpflege und Bauforschung der Universität Dortmund, 2001).

Kinter, Jürgen, Manfred Kock, and Dieter Thiele, *Spuren suchen – Leitfaden zur Erkundung der eigenen Geschichte* (Hamburg: VSA-Verlag, 1985).

Kirsch, Jan-Holger, "'Hier geht es um den Kern unseres Selbstverständnisses als Nation.' Helmut Kohl und die Genese des Holocaust-Denkens als bundesdeutsche Staatsräson," *Potsdamer Bulletin für Zeithistorische Studien*, 43/44 (2008).

Klemke, Rainer, "Das Gesamtkonzept Berliner Mauer," in *Die Mauer. Errichtung, Überwindung, Erinnerung*, ed. by Klaus-Dietmar Henke (München: Deutscher Taschenbuch Verlag, 2011).

Knabe, Hubertus, "Das Aufarbeitungskombinat: Merkwürdige Vorschläge zur Neuorganisation des DDR-Gedenkens," *Die Welt*, 8 May 2006.

Die Täter sind unter uns: Über das Schönreden der SED-Diktatur (Berlin: List Verlag, 2008).

Knobloch, Heinz, *Mißtraut den Grünanlagen! Extrablätter* (Berlin: Transit Verlag, 1996).

Knoch, Habbo, "Wohin Gedenkstätten? Ein Plädoyer für mehr Selbstkritik und Mitgestaltung," *Gedenkstättenrundbrief*, 178 (2015), 3–8.

Koch, Angela, "Historikerinnentreffen – Entstanden aus Betroffenheit," *Journal für Geschichte*, 4 (1985), 6–7.

Kohlstruck, Michael, "Erinnerungspolitik: Kollektive Identität, Neue Ordnung, Diskurshegemonie," in *Politikwissenschaft als Kulturwissenschaft – Theorien, Methoden, Problemstellungen*, ed. by Birgit Schwelling (Wiesbaden: Verlag für Sozialwissenschaften, 2004).

Konferenz der LStU, ed., *Vom Wert der Freiheit. 8. Kongress der LStU und der Stiftung zur Aufarbeitung der SED-Diktatur mit den Verfolgtenverbänden und Aufarbeitungsinitiativen, Mai 2004 in Jena* (Erfurt: 2004).

Kongress der LStU, and Stiftung zur Aufarbeitung der SED- Diktatur, eds., *Über Grenzen und Zeiten. Für Freiheit, Recht und Demokratie. 7. Kongress der LStU und der Stiftung zur Aufarbeitung der SED-Diktatur mit den Verfolgtenverbänden und Aufarbeitungsinitiativen. 23. bis 25. Mai 2003 in Brandenburg an der Havel* (Berlin: 2003).

König, Helmut, *Politik und Gedächtnis* (Weilerswist: Velbrück Wissenschaft, 2008).

Koselleck, Reinhart, "Die Transformation der politischen Totenmale im 20. Jahrhundert," in *Zeitgeschichte als Streitgeschichte – Große Kontroversen nach 1945*, ed. by Martin Sabrow, Ralph Jessen and Klaus Große Kracht (München: Verlag C.H. Beck, 2003).

Koshar, Rudy, *From Monuments to Traces: Artifacts of German Memory, 1870–1990* (Berkeley: University of California Press, 2000).

Kramer, Dieter, "Zum kulturpolitischen Standort der Heimat- und Regionalmuseen," in *Experiment Heimatmuseum. Zur Theorie und Praxis regionaler Museumsarbeit*, ed. by Oliver Bätz and Udo Gößwald (Marburg: Jonas Verlag für Kunst und Literatur, 1988).

Kubik, Jan, "Hybridization as a Condition of Civil Society's Portability," in *Building Civil Society and Democracy in New Europe*, ed. by Sven Eliaeson (Newcastle: Cambridge Scholars Publishing, 2008).

Kubik, Jan, and Michael Bernhard, "A Theory of the Politics of Memory," in *Twenty Years After Communism. The Politics of Memory and Commemoration*, ed. by Michael Bernhard and Jan Kubik (Oxford: Oxford University Press, 2014).

Kühling, Gerd, "Die Auseinandersetzung um das Haus der Wannsee-Konferenz (1966/67)," *Zeithistorische Forschungen – Studies in Contemporary History*, 5 (2008), 211–35.

KZ-Gedenkstätte Neuengamme, ed., *Die KZ-Gedenkstätte Neuengamme – Ein Überblick über die Geschichte des Ortes und die Arbeit der Gedenkstätte* (Hamburg: 2010).

Lachauer, Ulla, "Geschichte wird gemacht – Beispiele und Hinweise, wie man am eigenen Ort 'Geschichte machen' kann," in *"Die Menschen machen ihre Geschichte nicht aus freien Stücken, aber sie machen sie selbst" Einladung zu einer Geschichte des Volkes in Nordrhein-Westfalen*, ed. by Lutz Niethammer, Bodo Hombach, Tilman Fichter and Ulrich Borsdorf (Essen: Klartext Verlag, 2006 [1984]).

Lammert, Norbert, "Bikini-Verkäufer am FKK-Strand? Der Staat und die Erinnerungskultur," in *Jahrbuch für Kulturpolitik 2009. Thema: Erinnerungskulturen und Geschichtspolitik*, ed. by Institut für Kulturpolitik der Kulturpolitischen Gesellschaft and Bernd Wagner (Essen: Klartext Verlag, 2009).

Landeshauptstadt Potsdam der Oberbürgermeister, ed., *Das Denkmal des unbekannten Deserteurs* (Potsdam: 1999).

Lange, Dirk, "Politische Alltagsgeschichte. Ein Konzept zur historischen Erforschung neuer sozialer Bewegungen," in *Vorwärts und viel vergessen. Beiträge zur Geschichte und Geschichtsschreibung neuer sozialer Bewegungen*, ed. by Bernd Hüttner, Gottfried Oy and Norbert Schepers (Neu-Ulm: AG SPAK Bücher, 2005).

Langenbacher, Eric, "Changing Memory Regimes in Contemporary Germany?," *German Politics and Society*, 21 (2003), 46–68.

Ledig, Georg, "Geschichte von unten – das Archiv der Münchner Arbeiterbewegung e.V.," *Geschichte quer – Zeitschrift der Geschichtswerkstätten in Bayern*, 13 (2006).

Leggewie, Claus, and Erik Meyer, *"Ein Ort, an den man gerne geht" Das Holocaust-Mahnmal und die deutsche Geschichtspolitik nach 1989* (München: Carl Hanser Verlag, 2005).

"Shared Memory – Buchenwald and Beyond," *Tr@nsit online*, 22 (2002).

Le Goff, Jacques, *History and Memory* (New York: Columbia University Press, 1992).

Leiserowitz, Ruth, "Eine eigene Öffentlichkeit herstellen – Die Friedenswerkstatt vor 25 Jahren," *Horch und Guck*, 57 (2007), 9–10.

'Leistikowstraße: Reich zum Rücktritt aufgefordert Kritiker drängen auf Zeitplan zur Überarbeitung der Dauerausstellung im ehemaligen KGB-Gefängnis," *Potsdamer Neueste Nachrichten*, 20 August 2012.

Leo, Annette, "Keine gemeinsame Erinnerung – Geschichtsbewusstsein in Ost und West," *Aus Politik und Zeitgeschichte*, 40–41 (2003), 27–32.

"Unscharfe Konturen – scharfe Konkurrenzen," *Gedenkstättenrundbrief* 131 (2005).

Levy, Daniel, and Julian B Dierkes, "Institutionalising the past: shifting memories of nationhood in German education and immigration legislation," in *Memory & Power in Post-War Europe – Studies in the Presence of the Past*, ed. by Jan-Werner Müller (Cambridge: Cambridge University Press, 2002).

Levy, Daniel, and Natan Sznaider, *Erinnerung im globalen Zeitalter: Der Holocaust*. ed. by Ulrich Beck, *Edition Zweite Moderne* (Frankfurt: Suhrkamp Verlag, 2001).

Lewins, Ann, and Christina Silver, *Using Software in Qualitative Research. A Step-by-Step Guide* (London: Sage Publications, 2007).

Lindenberger, Thomas, "Governing Conflicted Memories: Some Remarks about the Regulation of History Politics in Unified Germany," in *Clashes in European Memory. The Case of Communist Repression and the Holocaust*, ed. by Muriel Blaive, Christian Gerbel and Thomas Lindenberger (Innsbruck: StudienVerlag, 2011).

"Werkstattgeflüster. Überlegungen zu Selbstverständnis und Praxis radikalde-mokratischer Geschichtsforschung aus der Berliner Geschichtswerkstatt," in *Demokratie- & Arbeitergeschichte*, ed. by Franz-Mehring-Gesellschaft Stuttgart (Weingarten: Drumlin-Verlag, 1983).

Lindenberger, Thomas, and Michael Wildt, "Radikale Pluralität – Geschichtswerkstätten als praktische Wissenschaftskritik," *Archiv für Sozialgeschichte*, 29 (1989), 393–411.

Lindqvist, Sven, *Grabe wo du stehst. Handbuch zur Erforschung der eigenen Geschichte*. trans. Manfred Dammeyer (Bonn: Verlag J.H.W. Dietz, 1989).

Lohmeyer, Susanne, ed., *Stolpersteine in Hamburg-Eimsbüttel und Hamburg-Hoheluft-West. Biographische Spurensuche* (Hamburg: Landeszentrale für politische Bildung und Institut für die Geschichte der deutschen Juden, 2012).

Lotz, Christian, *Die Deutung des Verlusts. Erinnerungspolitische Kontroversen im geteilten Deutschland um Flucht, Vertreibung und die Ostgebiete (1948–1972)*. *Vol. 15, Neue Forschungen zur Schlesischen Geschichte* (Cologne: Böhlau, 2007).

Lübbe, Hermann, "Der Nationalsozialismus im politischen Bewußtsein der Gegenwart," in *Deutschlands Weg in die Diktatur: Internationale Konferenz zur nationalsozialistischen Machtübernahme im Reichstagsgebäude zu Berlin*, ed. by Martin Broszat (Berlin: Siedler Verlag, 1983).

Lüdtke, Alf, ed., *Alltagsgeschichte. Zur Rekonstruktion historischer Erfahrungen und Lebensweisen* (Frankfurt: Campus Verlag, 1989).

Ludwig, Andreas, "Das "33-Projekt," in *Immer noch Lust auf Geschichte. 20 Jahre Berliner Geschichtswerkstatt e.V.*, ed. by Berliner Geschichtswerkstatt e.V. (2001).

Lunau, Ralph, "Identität durch bürgerschaftliches Selbstbewusstsein und kritische Auseinandersetzung," in *Jahrbuch für Kulturpolitik 2009. Thema: Erinnerungskulturen und Geschichtspolitik*, ed. by Institut für Kulturpolitik der Kulturpolitischen Gesellschaft and Bernd Wagner (Essen: Klartext Verlag, 2009).

Lupu, Noam, "Memory Vanished, Absent, and Confined. The Countermemorial Project in 1980s and 1990s Germany," *History & Memory*, 15 (2003), 130–64.

Lutz, Thomas, "Gedenkstätten für die Opfer des NS-Regimes – Landmarken gegen die Wende-Geschichtsschreibung," in *Normalität oder Normalisierung? Geschichtswerkstätten und Faschismusanalyse*, ed. by Heide Gerstenberger and Dorothea Schmidt (Münster: Westfälisches Dampfboot, 1987).

"Von der Bürgerinitiative zur Stiftung. Der Bildungsgehalt der öffentlichen Debatte um den Umgang mit dem Prinz-Albrecht-Gelände in Berlin," in *Bilden und Gedenken: Erwachsenenbildung in Gedenkstätten und an Gedächtnisorten*, ed. by Heidi Behrens-Cobet (Essen: Klartext-Verlag, 1998).

Maier, Charles S, *The Unmasterable Past – History, Holocaust, and German National Identity* (Cambridge, MA: Harvard University Press, 1988).

Marcuse, Harold, "Das ehemalige Konzentrationslager Dachau. Der mühevolle Weg zur Gedenkstätte 1945–1968," *Dachauer Hefte*, 6 (1994), 182–205.

Legacies of Dachau. The Uses and Abuses of a Concentration Camp, 1933–2001 (Cambridge: Cambridge University Press, 2001).

Marcuse, Harold, Frank Schimmelfennig, and Jochen Spielmann, *Steine des Anstoßes. Nationalsozialismus und Zweiter Weltkrieg in Denkmalen 1945–1985* (Hamburg: Museum für Hamburgische Geschichte, 1985).

Margry, Peter Jan, and Cristina Sanchez-Carretero, eds., *Grassroots Memorials. The Politics of Memorializing Traumatic Death* (New York: Berghahn Books, 2011).

Markovits, Andrei S, and Simon Reich, *The German Predicament – Memory and Power in the New Europe* (Ithaca: Cornell University Press, 1997).

Martin, Angela, "Bewegung! Stillstand. Aufbruch? Eine Tagung zu Geschichte und Zukunft der Geschichtswerkstätten," *Berliner Geschichtswerkstatt Rundbrief*, 2 (2003).

Maser, Peter, "Der lange Weg in die Andreasstraße. Anmerkungen zur Aufarbeitung der SED-Diktatur in Thüringen," in *Zwischenbilanzen. Thüringen und seine Nachbarn nach 20 Jahren*, ed. by Hans-Joachim Veen (Wien: Böhlau Verlag, 2012).

Maser, Peter, Hans-Joachim Veen, and Jochen Voit, eds., *Haft Diktatur Revolution. Thüringen 1949–1989. Das Buch zur Gedenk- und Bildungstätte Andreasstraße Erfurt* (Weimar/Erfurt: Stiftung Ettersberg, 2015).

McAdams, A. James, *Judging the Past in Unified Germany* (Cambridge: Cambridge University Press, 2001).

Meckel, Markus, and Martin Gutzeit, eds., *Opposition in der DDR – Zehn Jahre kirchliche Friedensarbeit – kommentierte Quellentexte* (Köln: Bund-Verlag, 1994).

Meyer, Beate, "Zwischen Anspruch und Wirklichkeit – stadtteilbezogene Geschichtsforschung 1984–1989. Ein Erfahrungsbericht," in *25 Jahre Galerie Morgenland/Geschichtswerkstatt Eimsbüttel – Festschrift*, ed. by Volker Böge, Beate Meyer and Sielke Salomon (Hamburg: Galerie Morgenland e.V., 2003).

Meyer, Erik, "Die Gedenkstättenkonzeption des Bundes als Instrument geschichtspolitischer Steuerung," in *Jahrbuch für Kulturpolitik 2009. Thema: Erinnerungskulturen und Geschichtspolitik*, ed. by Institut für Kulturpolitik der Kulturpolitischen Gesellschaft and Bernd Wagner (Essen: Klartext Verlag, 2009).

"Memory and Politics," in *Cultural Memory Studies – An International and Interdisciplinary Handbook*, ed. by Astrid Erll and Ansgar Nünning (Berlin: Walter de Gruyter, 2008).

Meyer, Winfried, and Roland Brauckmann, "Geschichtspolitik und Ausstellungsdidaktik. Ein Streitgespräch über die Dauerausstellung in der Gedenk- und Begegnungsstätte Leistikowstraße Potsdam," in *Ein Kampf um Deutungshoheit. Politik, Opferinteressen und historische Forschung. Die Auseinandersetzung um die Gedenk- und Begegnungsstätte Leistikowstrasse Potsdam*, ed. by Wolfgang Benz (Berlin: Metropol Verlag, 2013).

Michels, Robert, *Soziologie des Parteiwesens – Untersuchungen über die Oligarchischen Tendenzen des Gruppenlebens*. 4th edn (Stuttgart: Alfred Kröner Verlag, 1989).

Misztal, Barbara A, "Memory and Democracy," *The American Behavioral Scientist*, 48 (2005), 1320–38.

Mitchell, Timothy, "Society, Economy, and the State Effect," in *State/Culture – State-Formation after the Cultural Turn*, ed. by George Steinmetz (Ithaca: Cornell University Press, 1999).

Moeller, Robert G, "Remembering the War in a Nation of Victims – West German Pasts in the 1950s," in *The Miracle Years – A Cultural History of West Germany, 1949–1968*, ed. by Hanna Schissler (Princeton: Princeton University Press, 2001).

War Stories – The Search for a Usable Past in the Federal Republic of Germany (Berkeley: University of California Press, 2001).

Morina, Christina, *Legacies of Stalingrad. Remembering the Eastern Front in Germany since 1945* (New York: Cambridge University Press, 2011).

Morsch, Günter, "Sachsenhausen – auf dem Weg zur Neugestaltung und Neukonzeption der Gedenkstätte," in *Gedenkstätten im vereinten Deutschland – 50 Jahre nach der Befreiung der Konzentrationslager*, ed. by Jürgen Dittberner and Antje von Meer (Oranienburg: Stiftung der Brandenburgischen Gedenkstätten und Edition Hentrich, 1994).

Moses, A Dirk, *German Intellectuals and the Nazi Past* (Cambridge: Cambridge University Press, 2007).

Mosse, George L, *Fallen Soldiers – Reshaping the Memory of the World Wars* (Oxford: Oxford University Press, 1990).

Mühl-Benninghaus, Wolfgang, "Vergeßt es nie! Schuld sind sie! Zu Kriegsdeutungen in den audiovisuellen Medien beider deutscher Staaten in den vierziger und fünfziger Jahren," in *Schuld und Sühne? Kriegserlebnis und Kriegsdeutung in deutschen Medien der Nachkriegszeit (1945–1961)*, ed. by Ursula Heulenkamp (Amsterdam: Editions Rodopi B.V., 2001).

Müller, Bernhard, "Die Sozialdemokraten entdecken die Geschichte von unten (Stimmungsbericht eines Frustrierten von einem Kongreß in Bonn)," *Berliner Geschichtswerkstatt Rundbrief*, 1 (1985).

"Zur Beteiligung der BGW an der 750 Jahrfeier," *Geschichtswerkstatt*, 14 (1988).

Müller, Jan-Werner, "Introduction: The Power of Memory, the Memory of Power and the Power over Memory," in *Memory & Power in Post-War Europe – Studies in the Presence of the Past*, ed. by Jan-Werner Müller (Cambridge: Cambridge University Press, 2002).

Myers Feinstein, *Margarete, Holocaust Survivors in Postwar Germany, 1945–1957* (New York: Cambridge University Press, 2010).

Neue Gesellschaft für Bildende Kunst e.V., ed., *Stolpersteine für die von den Nazis ermordeten ehemaligen Nachbarn aus Friedrichshain und Kreuzberg. Dokumente, Texte, Materialien* (Berlin: 2002).

'Neue Initiative für Freiheits- und Einheitsdenkmal," *Berliner Morgenpost*, 16 June 2016.

Niethammer, Lutz, ed., *Lebenserfahrung und kollektives Gedächtnis: die Praxis der "Oral history"* (Frankfurt am Main: Syndikat, 1980).

Niven, Bill, ed., *Germans as Victims. Remembering the Past in Contemporary Germany* (Basingstoke: Palgrave Macmillan Press, 2006).

Noetzel, Thomas, "Erinnerungsmanagement. Von der Vorgeschichte zur Geschichte," in *Erinnerungsmanagement. Systemtransformation und Vergangenheitspolitik im internationalen Vergleich*, ed. by Joachim Landkammer, Thomas Noetzel and Walter Ch Zimmerli (München: Wilhelm Fink Verlag, 2006).

Nora, Pierre, "General Introduction: Between Memory and History," in *Realms of Memory*, ed. by Pierre Nora and Lawrence D Kritzman (New York: Columbia University Press, 1996).

Olick, Jeffrey K, "Collective Memory: The Two Cultures," *Sociological Theory*, 17 (1999), 333–48.

The Politics of Regret – On Collective Memory and Historical Responsibility (London: Routledge Press, 2007).

"What Does It Mean to Normalize the Past?: Official Memory in German Politics since 1989," in *States of Memory – Continuities, Conflicts, and Transformations in National Retrospection*, ed. by Jeffrey K Olick (Durham: Duke University Press, 2003).

Olk, Thomas, Daphne Reim, and Jenny Schmithals, "Qualitative Studie," in *Entwicklung der Zivilgesellschaft in Ostdeutschland*, ed. by Thoas Gensicke, Thomas Olk, Daphne Reim, Jenny Schithals and Hans-Liudger Dienel (Wiesbaden: VS Verlag für Sozialwissenschaften, 2009).

Ostertag, Roland, and Martin Schairer, eds., *70 Jahre Deportation. Dokumentation der Gedenkfeier am 1. Dezember 2011 für die aus Stuttgart, Würtemberg und Hohenzollern deportierten Menschen jüdischen Glaubens, Sinti und Roma* (Stuttgart: 2012).

Palmowski, Jan, *Inventing a Socialist Nation. Heimat and the Politics of Everyday LIfe in the GDR, 1945–1990* (Cambridge: Cambridge University Press, 2009).

Panne, Kathrin, "Erinnerungspolitik – Erinnerungsspuren. Zur Funktion symbolischer Erinnerung an Flucht und Vertreibung im öffentlichen Raum. Eine Skizze.," in *Zwischen Heimat und Zuhause – Deutsche Flüchtlinge und Vertriebene in (West) Deutschland 1945–2000*, ed. by Rainer Schulze (Osnabrück: secolo Verlag, 2001).

Paul, Gerhard, and Bernhard Schoßig, "Geschichte und Heimat," in *Die andere geschichte: Geschichte von unten, Spurensicherung, ökologische Geschichte, Geschichtswerkstätten*, ed. by Gerhard Paul and Bernhard Schoßig (Köln: Bund-Verlag, 1986).

eds., *Die andere geschichte: Geschichte von unten, Spurensicherung, ökologische Geschichte, Geschichtswerkstätten* (Köln: Bund-Verlag, 1986).

Pearce, Caroline, "An Unequal Balance? Memorializing Germany's "Double Past" since 1990," in *The GDR Remembered. Representations of the East German State since 1989*, ed. by Nick Hodgin and Caroline Pearce (Rochester, NY: Camden House, 2011).

Poppe, Ulrike, "Gesellschaftliche Aufarbeitung," in *Es ist noch lange nicht vorbei. Erinnerungen und die Herausforderungen bei der Aufarbeitung der DDR-Vergangenheit*, ed. by Bundesstiftung zur Aufarbeitung der SED-Diktatur and Stiftung Gedenkstätten Sachsen-Anhalt (Berlin: Metropol Verlag, 2012).

Prowe, Diethelm, "The 'Miracle' of the Political-Cultural Shift – Democratization between Americanization and Conservative Reintegration," in *The Miracle Years – A Cultural History of West Germany, 1949–1968*, ed. by Hanna Schissler (Princeton: Princeton University Press, 2001).

Putnam, Robert, *Making Democracy Work* (Princeton: Princeton University Press, 1993).

Putnam, Robert D, *Bowling Alone – The Collapse and Revival of American Community* (New York: Simon & Schuster Press, 2000).

Putsch, Jochen, "Die Solinger Geschichtswerkstatt im Auf und Ab ihrer eigenen Geschichte," in *Macht Geschichte von unten: Handbuch für gewerkschaftliche Geschichte vor Ort*, ed. by Manfred Scharrer (Köln: Bund-Verlag, 1988).

Reading, Anna, and Tamar Katriel, eds., *Cultural Memories of Nonviolent Struggles. Powerful Times* (Basingstoke: Palgrave Macmillan, 2015).

Redies, Rainer, ed., *Zehn Jahre Stolpersteine für Stuttgart. Ein bürgerschaftliches Projekt zieht Kreise* (Stuttgart: Markstein Verlag, 2013).

Reich, Ines, and Maria Schultz, eds., *Sowjetisches Untersuchungsgefängnis Leistikowstraße Potsdam*. Vol. 33, *Schriftenreihe der Stiftung Brandenburgische Gedenkstätten* (Berlin: Metropol Verlag, 2012).

Reichel, Peter, *Politik mit der Erinnerung – Gedächtnisorte im Streit um die nationalsozialistische Vergangenheit*. Revised edn (München: Carl Hanser Verlag, 1999).

Vergangenheitsbewältigung in Deutschland – Die Auseinandersetzung mit der NS-Diktatur von 1945 bis heute (Munich: C.H. Beck, 2001).

Reuter, Elke, "Die VVN in der SBZ/DDR," in *60 Jahre Vereinigung der Verfolgten des Naziregimes. Lesebuch zu Geschichte und Gegenwart der VVN*, ed. by Hans Coppi and Nicole Warmbold (Berlin: 2007).

Richter, Alexander, "Aus der Geschichte der VOS," in *Vergeßt uns nicht – wenn auch die Tage wandern und die Jahre. Eine Festschrift zum 50-jährigen Bestehen der Vereinigung der Opfer des Stalinismus*, ed. by Vereinigung der Opfer des Stalinismus e.V. (Berlin: 2000).

Roder, Bernt, "Lokale Akteure und Initiativen der Erinnerungsarbeit," in *Urbane Erinnerungskulturen im Dialog: Berlin und Buenos Aires*, ed. by Peter Birle, Elke Gryglewski and Estela Schindel (Metropol Verlag, 2008).

Roediger, Henry L, III, and James V Wertsch, "Creating a New Discipline of Memory Studies," *Memory Studies*, 1 (2008), 9–22.

Roloff-Momin, Ulrich, *Zuletzt: Kultur* (Berlin: Aufbau Verlag, 1997).

Rosenfeld, Gavriel, "A Mastered Past? Prussia in Postwar German Memory," *German History*, 22 (2004), 505–35.

Roth, Jürgen, "Notizen zu einem Jubiläum aus der Provinz," in *Grabe, wo Du stehst! 15 Jahre Geschichtswerkstatt Marburg e.V.*, ed. by Geschichtswerkstatt Marburg (Marburg: 2003).

Rothberg, Michael, "Multidirectional Memory in Migratory Settings: The Case of Post-Holoaust Germany," in *Transnational Memory: Circulation, Articulation, Scales*, ed. by Chiara de Cesari and Ann Rigney (Berlin: de Gruyter Press, 2014).

Rucht, Dieter, and Jochen Roose, "Von der Platzbesetzung zum Verhandlungstisch? Zum Wandel von Aktionen und Struktur der Ökologiebewegung," in *Protest in der Bundesrepublik – Strukturen und Entwicklungen*, ed. by Dieter Rucht (Frankfurt: Campus Verlag, 2001).

'Rückkehr unter Bedingungen. Der Zentralrat der Juden will wieder in der Stiftung Sächsische Gedenkstätten mitarbeiten," *Jüdische Allgemeine*, 14 January 2010.

Rudnick, Carola S, *Die andere Hälfte der Erinnerung. Die DDR in der deutschen Geschichtspolitik nach 1989* (Bielefeld: transcript Verlag, 2011).

"Wenn Häftlinge und Historiker streiten. Konflikte um sächsische Gedenkstätten," in *Ein Kampf um Deutungshoheit. Politik, Opferinteressen und historische Forschung. Die Auseinandersetzung um die Gedenk- und Begegnungsstätte Leistikowstrasse Potsdam*, ed. by Wolfgang Benz (Berlin: Metropol Verlag, 2013).

Rürup, Reinhard, ed., *Netzwerk der Erinnerung. 10 Jahre Gedenkstättenreferat der Stiftung Topographie des Terrors* (Berlin: 2003).

ed., *Topographie des Terrors. Gestapo, SS und Reichssicherheitshauptamt auf dem "Prinz-Albrecht-Gelände" – Eine Dokumentation* (Berlin: Verlag Willmuth Arenhövel, 2004).

Sa'adah, Anne, *Germany's second chance: trust, justice, and democratization* (Cambridge: Harvard University Press, 1998).

Sabrow, Martin, "Der Weg der Erinnerung. Entgegnung auf die Kritik an den Empfehlungen der Expertenkommission für eine künftige "Aufarbeitung der SED-Diktatur," *Vierteljahrshefte für Zeitgeschichte*, 54 (2006).

"Die DDR im aktuellen Gedächtnis in Deutschland," in *Gedächtnis der Deutschen. Gedächtnis des Politischen vom 19. bis 21. Jahrhundert* (GHI Warsaw: 2006).

"Es geht nicht um Moral. Historische Selbstkritik hat Deutschland stark gemacht. Eine Antwort auf Heinrich August Winklers Essay über die Asyldebatte und das angebliche 'deutsche Moralmonopol'" *Die Zeit* 21 (2016).

Sabrow, Martin, Rainer Eckert, Monika Flacke, Klaus-Dietmar Henke, Roland Jahn, Freya Klier, Tina Krone, Peter Maser, Ulrike Poppe, and Hermann Rudolph, eds., *Wohin treibt die DDR-Erinnerung? Dokumentation einer Debatte* (Bonn: Bundeszentrale für politische Bildung, 2007).

Samuel, Ralph, "Das britische Modell – Die englische History-Workshop-Bewegung und ihre Ziele," *MOZ – Moderne Zeiten*, 4 (1984), 7–9.

Sander, Andreas, "Die 'Rote Insel,'" in *Immer noch Lust auf Geschichte. 20 Jahre Berliner Geschichtswerkstatt e.V.*, ed. by Berliner Geschichtswerkstatt e.V. (2001).

Sander, Andreas, and Erika Bucholtz, "Das 'Hausgefängnis' der Gestapo-Zentrale in Berlin. Terror und Widerstand 1933–1945," *GedenkstättenRundbrief*, 127 (2005).

Scharrer, Manfred, *Macht Geschichte von unten: Handbuch für gewerkschaftliche Geschichte vor Ort* (Köln: Bund-Verlag, 1988).

Scheer, Regina, *Der Umgang mit den Denkmälern. Eine Recherche in Brandenburg*. ed. by Brandenburgische Landeszentrale für politische Bildung and Forschung und Kultur des Landes Brandenburg Ministerium für Wissenschaft (2003).

Schießl, Sascha, *"Das Tor zur Freiheit "Kriegsfolgen, Erinnerungspolitik und humanitärer Anspruch im Lager Friedland (1945–1970)* (Göttingen: Wallstein Verlag, 2016).

Schikorra, Christa, "Sommer 1945–1950. Übergang und Neuordnung," in *Was bleibt: Nachwirkungen des Konzentrationslagers Flossenbürg. Katalog zur Dauerausstellung*, ed. by Jörg Skriebeleit (Wallstein Verlag, 2011).

Schildt, Axel, "The Long Shadows of the Second World War: The Impact of Experiences and Memories of War on West German Society," *Bulletin of the German Historical Institute London*, XXIX (2007).

"Zur Einleitung," in *Geschichtswerkstätten gestern – heute – morgen. Bewegung! Stillstand. Aufbruch?*, ed. by Volker Böge (München: Dölling und Galitz Verlag, 2004).

Schissler, Hanna, ed., *The Miracle Years – A Cultural History of West Germany, 1949–1968* (Princeton: Princeton University Press, 2001).

Schmid, Harald, "Mehr Gegenwart in die Gedenkstätten! Erinnerungsorte in Zeiten des Memory-Drains und der Entpolitisierung," *Gedenkstättenrundbrief*, 177 (2015), 11–16.

Schmidt, Alexander, and Bernd Windsheimer, "Geschichtskultur, Geschichtsmarkt und Neuer Stadttourismus," *Geschichte quer – Zeitschrift der Geschichtswerkstätten in Bayern*, 2 (1992/1993).

Schmidtke, Michael, "The German New Left and National Socialism," in *Coping with the Nazi Past – West German Debates on Nazism and Generational Conflict, 1955–1975*, ed. by Philipp Gassert and Alan E Steinweis (New York: Berghahn Books, 2006).

Schneider, Ulrich, "Die VVN in der BRD," in *60 Jahre Vereinigung der Verfolgten des Naziregimes. Lesebuch zu Geschichte und Gegenwart der VVN*, ed. by Hans Coppi and Nicole Warmbold (Berlin: 2007).

Scholz, Stephan, *Vertriebenendenkmäler. Topographie einer deutschen Erinnerungslandschaft* (Paderborn: Ferdinand Schöningh Verlag, 2015).

Schönborn, Susanne, "The New Börneplatz Memorial and the Nazi Past in Frankfurt am Main," in *Beyond Berlin. Twelve German Cities Confront the Nazi Past*, ed. by Gavriel D Rosenfeld and Paul B Jaskot (Ann Arbor: The University of Michigan Press, 2008), pp. 273–93.

Schönfeld, Martin, *Gedenktafeln in Ost-Berlin*. Vol. 4 (Berlin: Schriftenreihe Aktives Museum, 1991).

Gedenktafeln in West-Berlin. Vol. 6 (Berlin: Schriftenreihe Aktives Museum, 1993).

Schornstheimer, Michael, *Bombenstimmung und Katzenjammer – Vergangenheitsbewältigung: Quick und Stern in den 50er Jahren* (Köln: Pahl-Rugenstein Verlag, 1989).

Schöttler, Peter, "Die Geschichtswerkstatt e.v. Zu einem Versuch, basisdemok-ratische Geschichtsinitiativen und -forschungen zu 'vernetzen'," *Geschichte und Gesellschaft*, 10 (1984), 421–24.

Schrafstetter, Susanna, "The Long Shadow of the Past. History, Memory and the Debate over West Germany's Nuclear Status 1954–69," *History & Memory*, 16 (2004), 118–45.

Schröter, Ursula, "Gründungsphase der Berliner Geschichtswerkstatt," in *Immer noch Lust auf Geschichte. 20 Jahre Berliner Geschichtswerkstatt e.V.*, ed. by Berliner Geschichtswerkstatt e.V. (2001).

Schulze, Rainer, "Auf dem Weg zu einer gemeinsamen Erinnerung – Einführung," in *Zwischen Heimat und Zuhause – Deutsche Flüchtlinge und Vertriebene in (West) Deutschland 1945-2000*, ed. by Rainer Schulze (Osnabrück: secolo Verlag, 2001).

Schwan, Gesine, *Politics and Guilt – The Destructive Power of Silence*. trans. Thomas Dunlap (Lincoln: University of Nebraska Press, 2001).

Schwelling, Birgit, "Die 'Friedland-Gedächtnisstätte'," *Zeithistorische Forschungen – Studies in Contemporary History*, 5 (2008), 189–210.

""Verlorene Jahre"? Die sowjetische Kriegsgefangenschaft in den Erinnerungen ddes Verbandes der Heimkehrer," in *Russlandheimkehrer. Die sowjetische Kriegsgefangenschaft im Gedächtnis der Deutschen*, ed. by Elke Scherstjanoi (Munich: Oldenbourg Verlag, 2012).

ed., *Reconciliation, Civil Society, and the Politics of Memory. Transnational Initiatives in the 20th and 21st Century* (Bielefeld: transcript Verlag, 2012).

Seferens, Horst, *Ein deutscher Denkmalstreit. Die Kontroverse um die Spiegelwand in Berlin-Steglitz* (Berlin: Edition Hentrich, 1995).

"Zwei Jahrzehnte Diskussion um staatliche Erinnerungssymbole in Bonn und Berlin," *GedenkstättenRundbrief*, 100 (2001), 83–90.

Siebeck, Cornelia, "Gedächtnisarbeit zur NS-Vergangenheit als gesellschaftspo-litisches Projekt. Eine geschichtskulturelle Spurensuche," *Aktives Museum Mitgliederrundbrief*, 75 (2016).

Siegfried, Detlef, "Die Rückkehr des Subjekts – Gesellschaftlicher Wandel und neue Geschichtsbewegung um 1980," in *Geschichte und Geschichtsvermittlung – Festschrift für Karl Heinrich Pohl*, ed. by Olaf Hartung and Katja Köhr (Bielefeld: Verlag für Regionalgeschichte, 2008), pp. 125–46.

"Subversiver Alltag – Geschichtswerkstätten zwischen Politik und Wissenschaft," in *25 Jahre Galerie Morgenland/Geschichtswerkstatt Eimsbüttel – Festschrift*, ed. by Volker Böge, Beate Meyer, and Sielke Salomon (Hamburg: Galerie Morgenland e.V., 2003).

"Urbane Revolten, befreite Zonen. Über die Wiederbelebung der Stadt und die Neuaneignung der Provinz durch die 'Gegenkultur' der 1970er Jahre," in *Stadt und Kommunikation in bundesrepublikanischen Umbruchszeiten*, ed. by Adelheid von Saldern (Stuttgart: Franz Steiner Verlag, 2006).

Siegmund, Jörg, *Opfer ohne Lobby? Ziele, Strukturen und Arbeitsweise der Verbände der Opfer des DDR-Unrechts* (Berlin: Berliner Wissenschafts-Verlag, 2002).

Sierp, Aline, "Memory, Identity and a Painful Past: Contesting the Former Dachau Concentration Camp," in *Excavating Memory: Material Culture*

Approaches to Sites of Remembering and Forgetting, ed. by M.T. Starzmann and
J.R. Roby (Gainesville: University Press of Florida, 2016).

Sierp, Aline, and Jenny Wüstenberg, "Linking the Local and the Transnational:
Rethinking Memory Politics in Europe," *Journal of Contemporary European
Studies*, 23 (2015), 321–29.

Skriebeleit, Jörg, ed., *Was bleibt: Nachwirkungen des Konzentrationslagers
Flossenbürg. Katalog zur Dauerausstellung* (Wallstein Verlag, 2011).

Soss, Joe, "Talking Our Way to Meaningful Explanations. A Practice-Centered
View of Interviewing for Interpretive Research," in *Interpretation and Method:
Empirical Research Methods and the Interpretive Turn*, ed. by Dvora Yanow and
Peregrine Schwartz-Shea (Armonk, N.Y.: M.E. Sharpe Press, 2006).

Sperner, Eva, *Die neue Geschichtsbewegung, Geschichtswerkstätten und
Geschichtsprojekte in der Bundesrepublik* (Bielefeld: Kooperationsprojekt
Historisch-politische Arbeiterjugendbildung in der Region, 1985).

Spielmann, Jochen, *Denk – Mal – Prozesse. Eine Bilanz der in den achtziger Jahren
mit Denkmalen geführten Auseinandersetzungen über den Nationalsozialismus*
(Berlin: Senatsverwaltung für Bau- und Wohnungswesen, 1991).

"Gedenken und Denkmal," in *Gedenken und Denkmal – Entwürfe zur Erinnerung
an die Deportation und Vernichtung der jüdischen Bevölkerung Berlins (Katalog
der Ausstellung vom 4. November 1988 bis zum 8. Januar 1989 im Martin-
Gropius-Bau Berlin)*, ed. by Berlinische Galerie and Der Senator für Bau-
und Wohnungswesen (Berlin: Berlinische Galerie, 1988).

Stephan, Annegret, "'Ich hatte gedacht, es besser überwunden zu haben … '
Rückblick auf die Anfangsjahre in der Gedenkstätte," in *Es ist noch lange
nicht vorbei. Erinnerungen und die Herausforderungen bei der Aufarbeitung der
DDR-Vergangenheit*, ed. by Bundesstiftung zur Aufarbeitung der SED-
Diktatur and Stiftung Gedenkstätten Sachsen-Anhalt (Berlin: Metropol
Verlag, 2012).

Stephan, Annegret, Matthias Puhle, and Daniel Bohse, "Vorwort," in *Es ist
noch lange nicht vorbei. Erinnerungen und die Herausforderungen bei der
Aufarbeitung der DDR-Vergangenheit*, ed. by Bundesstiftung zur
Aufarbeitung der SED-Diktatur and Stiftung Gedenkstätten Sachsen-
Anhalt (Berlin: Metropol Verlag, 2012).

Stickler, Matthias, "Die deutschen Vertriebenenverbände – Interessengruppen
mit gesamtnationalem Anspruch," in *Flucht, Vertreibung, Integration –
Begleitbuch zur Austellung*, ed. by Stiftung Haus der Geschichte der
Bundesrepublik Deutschland (Bielefeld: Kerber Verlag, 2006).

Stiehl, Wolfgang, "Die VOS 50 Jahre 'gesamtdeutsch'; seit 10 Jahren auch
territorial," in *Vergeßt uns nicht – wenn auch die Tage wandern und die Jahre.
Eine Festschrift zum 50-jährigen Bestehen der Vereinigung der Opfer des
Stalinismus*, ed. by Vereinigung der Opfer des Stalinismus e.V. (Berlin:
2000).

Stiftung niedersächsische Gedenkstätten, ed., *Bergen-Belsen. Geschichte der
Gedenkstätte – History of the Memorial* (Celle: 2012).

Stiftung Sächsische Gedenkstätten, ed., *Spuren Suchen und Erinnern.
Gedenkstätten für die Opfer politischer Gewaltherrschaft in Sachsen* (Dresden:
Gustav Kiepenheuer Verlag, 1996).

'Stiftung Sächsische Gedenkstätten: Wut und Willkür," *Die Zeit* (2016).

Stifung Topographie des Terrors, and Bundesamt für Bauwesen und Raumordnung, eds., *Realisierungswettbewerb Topographie des Terrors. Berlin. 309 Entwürfe – Katalog zur Ausstellung der Wettbewerbsarbeiten* (Berlin: 2006).

Stoltzfus, Nathan, *Resistance of the Heart: Intermarriage and the Rosenstrasse Protest in Nazi Germany* (New York: W.W. Norton, 1996).

'Streit um Denkmal in Berlin-Mitte Thierse und Nooke stellen Aus für Einheitsdenkmal infrage,' *Der Tagesspiegel*, 16 June 2016.

Strnad, Maximilian, "'Grabe, wo Du stehst': Die Bedeutung des Holocaust für die Neue Geschichtsbewegung," in *Der Holocaust in der deutschsprachigen Geschichtswissenschaft*, ed. by Michael Brenner and Maximilian Strnad (Göttingen: Wallstein Verlag, 2012).

Szejnmann, Claus-Christian W, "Die Bedeutung der Regionalgeschichte für die Erforschung des Nationalsozialismus und des Holocausts," in *Geschichte und Geschichtsvermittlung – Festschrift für Karl Heinrich Pohl*, ed. by Olaf Hartung and Katja Köhr (Bielefeld: Verlag für Regionalgeschichte, 2008).

Szodrzynski, Joachim, "Altern in Würde oder Aufbruch zu neuen Ufern?," in *25 Jahre Galerie Morgenland/Geschichtswerkstatt Eimsbüttel – Festschrift*, ed. by Volker Böge, Beate Meyer and Sielke Salomon (Hamburg: Galerie Morgenland e.V., 2003).

"Einleitung," in *25 Jahre Galerie Morgenland/Geschichtswerkstatt Eimsbüttel – Festschrift*, ed. by Volker Böge, Beate Meyer and Sielke Salomon (Hamburg: Galerie Morgenland e.V., 2003).

Tarrow, Sidney, *Power in Movement – Social Movements and Contentious Politics*. Second edn (Cambridge: Cambridge University Press, 1998).

Ther, Phillipp, "The Integration of Expellees in Germany and Poland after World War II: A Historical Reassessment," *Slavic Review*, 55 (1996), 779–805.

Thomas, Marcel, "Coming to Terms with the Stasi: History and Memory in the Bautzen Memorial," *European Review of History: Revue européene d'histoire*, 20 (2013), 697–716.

Till, Karen E, *The New Berlin – Memory, Politics, Place* (Minneapolis: University of Minnesota Press, 2005).

Tismaneanu, Vladimir, *Fantasies of Salvation – Democracy, Nationalism, and Myth in Post-Communist Europe* (Princeton: Princeton University Press, 1998).

'Tobias Hollitzer wechselt den Job: Gedenkstätte Museum in der 'unden Ecke" hat jetzt einen eigenen Leiter' *Leipziger Internetzeitung* (1 April 2007).

Tocqueville, Alexis de, *Democracy in America* (Chicago: The University of Chicago Press, 2000).

Tomberger, Corinna, *Das Gegendenkmal. Avantgardekunst, Geschichtspolitik und Geschlecht in der bundesdeutschen Erinnerungskultur* (Bielefeld: transcript Verlag, 2007).

Torpey, John, "Introduction: Politics and the Past," in *Politics and the past: on repairing historical injustices*, ed. by John Torpey (Oxford: Rowman & Littlefield Publishers, 2003).

Uehling, Greta, "Social Memory as Collective Action: The Crimean Tatar National Movement," in *Globalizations and Social Movements – Culture, Power, and the Transnational Public Sphere*, ed. by John A Guidry, Michael

D Kennedy and Mayer N Zald (Ann Arbor: University of Michigan Press, 2000).

Ullrich, Volker, "Vorwort," in *25 Jahre Galerie Morgenland/Geschichtswerkstatt Eimsbüttel – Festschrift*, ed. by Volker Böge, Beate Meyer and Sielke Salomon (Hamburg: Galerie Morgenland e.V., 2003).

"Weltuntergang kann nicht schlimmer sein," in *Ein Volk von Opfern? Die neue Debatte um den Bombenkrieg 1940–45*, ed. by Lothar Kettenacker (Berlin: Rowohlt Verlag, 2003).

"Wie alles anfing. Die 'neue Geschichtsbewegung' der achtziger Jahre," in *Geschichtswerkstätten gestern – heute – morgen. Bewegung! Stillstand. Aufbruch?*, ed. by Volker Böge (München: Dölling und Galitz Verlag, 2004).

van Laak, Dirk, "Alltagsgeschichte," in *Neue Themen und Methoden der Geschichtswissenschaft*, ed. by Michael Maurer (Stuttgart: Philipp Reclam jun., 2003).

Vandamme, Ralf, *Basisdemokratie als zivile Intervention – Der Partizipationsanspruch der Neuen sozialen Bewegungen* (Opladen: Leske + Budrich Verlag, 2000).

Vees-Gulani, Susanne, "The Politics of New Beginnings: The Continued Exclusion of the Nazi Past in Dresden's Cityscape," in *Beyond Berlin. Twelve German Cities Confront the Nazi Past*, ed. by Gavriel D Rosenfeld and Paul B Jaskot (Ann Arbor: The University of Michigan Press, 2008).

von Hegel, Andrea, "Der Sinnlosigkeit einen Sinn geben. Zur Kriegsgefangenenausstellung des Verbandes der Heimkehrer, 1951–1962," in *Russlandheimkehrer. Die sowjetische Kriegsgefangenschaft im Gedächtnis der Deutschen*, ed. by Elke Scherstjanoi (Munich: Oldenbourg Verlag, 2012).

von Plato, Alexander, "Ambivalenter Etablierungsprozess. Michael Zimmermann und die lebensgeschichtlichen Tücken einer 'Geschichte von unten'," *Werkstatt Geschichte*, 50 (2008), 69–72.

von Saldern, Adelheid, "Markt für Marx. Literaturbetrieb und Lesebewegungen in der Bundesrepublik in den Sechziger- und Siebzigerjahren," *Archiv für Sozialgeschichte*, 44 (2004), 149–80.

"'Schwere Geburten'. Neue Forschungsrichtungen der bundesrepublikanischen Geschichtswissenschaft (1960–2000)," *Werkstatt Geschichte*, 40 (2006).

"Stadtgedächtnis und Geschichtswerkstätten," *Werkstatt Geschichte*, 50 (2008), 54–68.

Wagner, Andreas, "The Evolution of Memorial Sites in Mecklenburg-West Pomerania since 1990," in *The GDR Remembered. Representations of the East German State since 1989*, ed. by Nick Hodgin and Caroline Pearce (Rochester, NY: Camden House, 2011).

Wagner, Michael, "Mahnmal für Todesmarsch aufgestellt," *Geschichte quer – Zeitschrift der Geschichtswerkstätten in Bayern*, 2 (1992/1993), 30.

Wegner, Gregory, "In the Shadow of the Third Reich: The 'Jugendstunde' and the Legitimation of Anti-Fascist Heroes for East German Youth," *German Studies Review*, 19 (1996), 127–46.

Weigelt, Andreas, ed., *Chronik der Initiativgruppe Lager Mühlberg e.V. Mit einer einleitenden Betrachtung zur Wahrnehmung der Speziallager in der Zeit zwischen dem Ende des 2. Weltkrieges 1945 und der Gründung der Initiativgruppe 1991* (Mühlberg/Elbe: Initiativgruppe Lager Mühlberg e.V., 2010).

Wenzel, Gisela, ""Die zwölf Jahre werden Euch begleiten ... " Erinnerungen an Theo Pinkus," in *Immer noch Lust auf Geschichte. 20 Jahre Berliner Geschichtswerkstatt e.V.*, ed. by Berliner Geschichtswerkstatt e.V. (2001).

"'Grabe, wo du stehst." Zwei Jahrzehnte Berliner Geschichtswerkstatt," in *Geschichtswerkstätten gestern – heute – morgen. Bewegung! Stillstand. Aufbruch?*, ed. by Volker Böge (München: Dölling und Galitz Verlag, 2004).

Wenzel, Gisela, and Angela Martin, "NS-Zwangsarbeiterlager Berlin-Schöneweide. Eröffnung des Dokumentationszentrums im Herbst 2006 Erfolg und Elend des Bürgerengagements?," *Berliner Geschichtswerkstatt Rundbrief*, 1 (2006).

'Wider die geplanten historischen Wiederaufbereitungsanlagen der Bundesregierung – Entschließung des Vorstands der GW e.V.," *Geschichtswerkstatt*, 9 (1986).

Wildt, Michael, "Die große Geschichtswerkstattschlacht im Jahr 1992 oder: wie WerkstattGeschichte entstand," *Werkstatt Geschichte*, 50 (2008), 73–81.

"WerkstattGeschichte – Ein Zeitschriftenprojekt," in *Geschichtswerkstätten gestern – heute – morgen. Bewegung! Stillstand. Aufbruch?*, ed. by Volker Böge (Hamburg: Dölling und Galitz Verlag, 2004).

Wille, Manfred, "Compelling the Assimilation of Expellees in the Soviet Zone of Occupation and the GDR," in *Redrawing Nations – Ethnic Cleansing in East-Central Europe, 1944–1948*, ed. by Phillip Ther and Ana Siljak (Lanham, MD: Rowman & Littlefield Publishers, 2001).

Winkler, Heinrich August "Es gibt kein deutsches Moralmonopol. Lehren und Irrlehren aus der Geschichte: Bemerkungen zur Asyldebatte' *Die Zeit* 18 (2016).

Winter, Jay, "The Generation of Memory: Reflections on the "Memory Boom" in Contemporary Historical Studies," *Bulletin of the German Historical Institute*, Fall (2000), 69–92.

Winter, Jay, and Emmanuel Sivan, "Setting the framework," in *War and Remembrance in the Twentieth Century*, ed. by Jay Winter and Emmanuel Sivan (Cambridge: Cambridge University Press, 1999).

Winters, Peter Jochen, "Der Streit um die Leistikowstraße in Potsdam," in *Ein Kampf um Deutungshoheit. Politik, Opferinteressen und historische Forschung. Die Auseinandersetzung um die Gedenk- und Begegnungsstätte Leistikowstrasse Potsdam*, ed. by Wolfgang Benz (Berlin: Metropol Verlag, 2013).

Wirsching, Andreas, *Geschichte der Bundesrepublik Deutschland. Abschied vom Provisorium 1982–1990* (München: Deutsche Verlagsanstalt, 2006).

Wolfgram, Mark A, *Getting History Right: East and West German Collective Memories of the Holocaust and War* (Lewisburg: Bucknell University Press, 2010).

Wolfrum, Edgar, "Die beiden Deutschland," in *Verbrechen erinnern – Die Auseinandersetzung mit Holocaust und Völkermord*, ed. by Volkhard Knigge and Norbert Frei (Bonn: Bundeszentrale für politische Bildung, 2005).

"Die Massenmedialisierung des 17. Juni 1953," *Aus Politik und Zeitgeschichte*, B40–41 (2003).

Geschichtspolitik in der Bundesrepublik Deutschland: der Weg zur bundesrepublikanischen Erinnerung 1948–1990 (Darmstadt: Wissenschaftliche Buchgesellschaft, 1999).

Wollmann, Hellmut, "Die Doppelstruktur der Stadt als politische Kommune und zivilgesellschaftliche Bürgergemeinde," *vorgänge*, 1 (2004), 20–28.

Wüstenberg, Jenny, "The struggle for European Memory – New contributions to an emerging field," *Comparative European Politics*, 14 (2016), 376–89.

"Transforming Berlin's Memory: Non-State Actors and GDR Memorial Politics Today," in *Remembering the German Democratic Republic: Divided Memory in a United Germany*, ed. by David Clarke and Ute Wölfel (Basingstoke: Palgrave Macmillan Press, 2011).

"Vom alternativen Laden zum Dienstleistungsbetrieb: the Berliner Geschichtswerkstatt – A Case Study in Activist Memory Politics," *German Studies Review*, XXXII (2009), 590–618.

Wüstenberg, Jenny, and David Art, "Using the Past in the Nazi Successor States from 1945 to the Present," *The Annals of the American Academy of Political and Social Science*, 617 (2008), 72–87.

Young, James E, *The Texture of Memory: Holocaust Memorials and Meaning* (New Haven: Yale University Press, 1993).

Zeichen der Erinnerung e.V., *Zeichen der Erinnerung. Gedenkstätte im Stuttgarter Nordbahnhof für die aus Stuttgart, Württemberg und Hohenzollern deportierten Menschen jüdischen Glaubens* (Stuttgart: Karl Krämer Verlag, 2006).

Zeitgeschichte/Amsterdam, ID-Archiv im Internationalen Institut für, ed., *Reader der "anderen" Archive* (Amsterdam: Verlag Diederich, Hoffmann, Schindowski, 1990).

Zimmermann, Michael, "Haben Geschichtswerkstätten Zukunft?," in *Geschichtswerkstätten gestern – heute – morgen. Bewegung! Stillstand. Aufbruch?*, ed. by Volker Böge (München: Dölling und Galitz Verlag, 2004).

Index

Action Reconciliation/Service for Peace (ASF), 277. *See also* Aktion Sühnezeichen/Friedensdienste
Active Museum – Fascism and Resistance in Berlin, 1–2, 30, 105–14, 106*f*, 113*f*, 115–17, 121, 197
activist-to-institution integration, 265
Adenauer, Konrad, 25, 37, 38, 85, 219
Ahlem concentration camp memorial, 97, 178–80
Aktion Sühnezeichen/Friedensdienste (ASF), 43, 55, 98
Alexander, Jeffrey, 20
Allied bombing raids, 35
alternative archives, 139–40
alternative city guides *(Stattbücher)*, 141
Amicale Internationale de Neuengamme, 76, 86
Amnesty International, 252, 253
anti-cosmopolitan campaign, 39
anti-German heroism, 24
anti-monumentality memorial aesthetics, 192–98, 198*f*
anti-Semitism, 39, 58, 85, 107
Antistalinistische Aktion (ASTAK), 223, 235
Arbeitsgemeinschaft Verfolgter Sozialdemokraten (Working Group of Persecuted Social Democrats), 51
Arbeitsgruppe Neuengamme (AGN), 86
Arbeitskreis Berliner Regionalmuseen (ABR), 119
Arbeitskreis Bürger gestalten ein Mahnmal (Working Group Citizens Design a Memorial), 178. *See also* Ahlem concentration camp memorial
Arbeitskreis Regionalgeschichte Neustadt (Working Group Regional History Neustadt), 163
Archiv der Münchner Arbeiterbewegung e. V. (Archive of the Munich Workers' Movement), 142

Art, David, 17
Aschrott Fountain, 195–96
Association Human Rights Center Cottbus, 240
Aufarbeitungsszene (memorial scene), 216, 219, 226, 229, 246, 270
Auschwitz trial, 58
Außerparlamentarische Opposition (APO), 62
authenticity in memorial aesthetics, 187–92, 190*f*
autonomous activism, 133, 166

Banabak, Elke, 96
Barbe, Angelika, 237
Baum, Herbert, 197
Baumann, Leonie, 110–11
Bayrischer Platz memorial, 184–85, 185*f*
Beattie, Andrew, 245, 250, 286–87
Benz, Wolfgang, 206
Bergen-Belsen camp, 82–84, 83*f*, 85, 263
Bergen-Belsen Jewish Committee, 82
Bergen-Belsen Working Group, 94
Berger, Thomas, 17
Berlin Cultural Council, 105
Berlin Jewish Museum, 179, 191
Berlin Senate Administration for City Development, 118
Berlin Wall
  fall of, 3, 34, 68
  Gestapo terrain and, 103
  post-wall memory politics, 68–73, 102, 283–84
  reaction to building of, 231
Berman, Sheri, 22–23
Bermeo, Nancy, 20–21
Bernauer Strasse memorial, 233
Bernhard, Michael, 16, 270
Biermann, Wolf, 203*f*
Blindenwerkstatt Otto Weidt, 190
Boeger, Peter, 227–28
Böge, Volker, 162

Böll, Heinrich, 76
bottom-up motives for memorialization, 75
Brandenburg Memorial Foundation, 207,
    254, 255, 258, 278
Brandt, Willy, 58, 76
Brauckmann, Roland, 210
"Brexit" vote in the United Kingdom, 71
Brown, Michael, 27, 268
Brubaker, Rogers, 29
Brücker, Eva, 150
Bubis, Ignatz, 70
Buchenwald Komitee, 237
Bund der Verfolgten des Naziregimes (BVN),
    50, 86
Bund der Vertriebenen (BdV), 44, 119
Bund Stalinistisch Verfolgter (BSV), 220
Bundesbeauftragte(r) für die Unterlagen des
    Staatssicherheitsdienstes der ehemaligen
    Deutschen Demokratischen Republik
    (BStU), 214, 216, 223, 225–27, 234,
    277. See also Stasi File authority
Bundesministerium für Gesamtdeutsche Fragen
    (BGF), 44
Bundeszentrale für politische Bildung (Federal
    Agency for Political Education), 99
Bürgerbüro Berlin group, 247
Bürgerkomittee (Citizens' Committee)
    Erfurt, 223

Camphausen, Gabriele, 186–87, 214–15,
    269, 273–74, 284
Center for Anti-Semitism Research, 207
Central Council of Jews, 70, 192, 258, 272
Checkpoint Charlie in Berlin, 4, 5f, 243, 245.
    See also Museum Checkpoint Charlie
Christian Democratic Party (CDU), 62
Christian-Jewish cooperation, 3, 56
civic associations (Vereine), 21
civic autonomy, 26
Cold War, 45, 51, 66, 111, 174
collective action repertoire, 133
collective memory, 16, 291
Comité International de Dachau (CID), 85
commemoration, 183
communal property, 16
Communist Party of West Germany
    (KPD), 51
community of conviction, 24
concentration camp memorials, 68, 81–88,
    83f. See also specific memorials
Confino, Alon, 14
Cottbus Menschenrechtszentrum, 210, 240,
    241f
counter-democracy, 21
counter-monuments, 12, 194, 196

critical memory, 142–61, 146f, 151f, 155f,
    158f, 159f, 160f, 263
cultural memory, 137

Dachau concentration camp, 85, 184, 263
Dammeyer, Manfred, 153
Dampfergruppe (steam ship group), 127
DDR Bürgerbewegung (GDR citizens'
    movement), 43, 68, 222, 240
DDR Museum (GDR Museum), 229, 230f
decentralization in memorial aesthetics,
    182–87, 187f
definitional power over memory, 161–70,
    169f
Demnig, Gunter, 185–86
democracy
    counter-democracy, 21
    development of, 266
    German political culture, 59
    memory activism and, 6–10, 24–26,
        166–67
    safeguarding human rights, 53
democratic memory, 20, 266, 288–93
denazification, 69
Denk-Steine (thinking-stones), 193
Diederich, Hugo, 219, 220, 243
Diepgen, Eberhard, 87, 164, 191–92
direct-democratic (basisdemokratische)
    public history, 188
dissidents in East German memory politics,
    222–26
diversity in memorial aesthetics, 199–202,
    201f, 203f
Dombrowski, Dieter, 219
Drieselmann, Jörg, 234–35, 247

East German Communism, 28
East German memory politics. See also
    German Democratic Republic
    dissidents, 222–26
    for-profit memory initiatives, 229–34,
        230f
    framing of memory activism, 234–38
    GDR memorial scene, 214–16
    institutionalizing GDR memory, 245–51
    Leistikowstrasse Memorial, 210, 251–60,
        253f, 261
    pragmatics, 226–29
    strategies for memory activism, 238–44,
        241f
    summary of, 206–11, 260–61
    unification and, 211–14
    victims' associations/organizations, 216,
        217–22
Eberhardt, Andreas, 196–97

Endlich, Stefanie, 119
Eppelmann, Rainer, 235–36
Erhard, Ludwig, 57
Erinnerungspolitik (memory politics/policy),
    12–13
Erlebnisgeneration (experiential generation),
    274–75
euthanasia program, 118, 199
expert commissions *(Enquete-Kommissionen)*,
    69
extra-parliamentary opposition (APO), 135
Eyerman, Ron, 16

Faulenbach, Bernd, 272
Federal Agency for Civic Education, 98. *See
    also* Bundeszentrale für politische
    Bildung
Federal Government Commissioner
    for Culture and Media (BKM),
    282, 285
Federal Ministry for Pan-German
    Questions (BGF), 50. *See also*
    Bundesministerium für
    gesamtdeutsche Fragen
Federal Republic of Germany (FRG), 7,
    35–38, 56, 131
Federation of Expellees (BdV), 217
Federation of Lesbians and Gays in
    Germany (LSVD), 124
Feinstein, Margaret Myers, 83
Finn, Gerhard, 217
Fischer, Peter, 192
Fischer-Defoy, Christine, 106, 115,
    116, 183
Fiss, Harald, 227, 228
Flossenbürg camp, 84, 85
for-profit memory initiatives, 229–34, 230*f*
forgotten victims, 92, 199, 200
Forster, Reinhold, 172
frame alignment, 166, 237
Frank, Sibylle, 229
Frei, Norbert, 12
Freiesleben, Christian, 282
Freiheitsglocke (Freedom Bell), 220
French Revolution, 15
Frevert, Ute, 59
Friedland-Gedächtnisstätte (Friedland
    Memorial), 47
Friends of Refusers of Military Service
    (Wehrdiensttotalverweigerer), 202

Garbe, Detlef, 122
Gauck, Joachim, 212, 246
Gedenkstätte Deutscher Widerstand
    (Memorial to German Resistance),
    55, 191

Gedenkstättenbewegung (Memorial Site
    Movement)
    activists and, 125, 237
    disparate groups in, 215
    impact of, 65, 289
    lasting success of, 280
    memory boom, 80
    memory landscape, 182–83
    Nazi terror commemoration, 89–102,
        100*f*, 103, 114
    structure of, 80–81
    success of, 121
    summary of, 30, 124–26
Gedenkstättenkonzeption (federal memorial
    concept), 68, 90, 91, 267
Geistig-moralische Wende, 62
German Center for Tourism, 112
German Democratic Republic (GDR).
    See also East German memory
    politics
    citizens' movement, 222. *See also* DDR
        Bürgerbewegung
    memorial scene, 38–42, 214–16
    memory activism in, 66–68, 69
    Nazi prisons, 81–82
    summary of, 9
German Historical Museum (DHM), 89,
    163, 172, 278
German History Movement. *See
    Geschichtsbewegung*
German Social Democracy, 23
German war graves, 89
Germany, 35–38, 42–57
Gerz, Jochen, 194, 195
Geschichte für alle e.V. (History for All), 152
Geschichtsbewegung (History Movement)
    access to, 134–42
    activists and, 237
    critical memory and, 142–61, 146*f*, 151*f*,
        155*f*, 158*f*, 159*f*, 160*f*
    definitional power over memory, 161–70,
        169*f*
    differences in, 154
    disparate groups in, 215
    impact of, 65, 289
    lasting success of, 280
    mainstreaming memory, 170–77
    memory landscape, 182–83
    overview, 127–30, 128*f*, 129*f*
    structure of, 80–81
    summary of, 30, 130–34
Geschichtsfeste (history festivals),
    147–48, 165
Geschichtspolitik (history politics/policy),
    12–13
Geschichtsverbund Thüringen, 286

Geschichtswerkstatt, 131, 171–72, 193. *See also* History Workshop
Alexander-Seitz-Geschichtswerkstatt, 158
Geschichtswerkstatt Augsburg, 172
Geschichtswerkstatt Barmbek (History Workshop Barmbek), 142, 164, 165–72
Geschichtswerkstatt e.V., 132, 146–47, 172–73
Geschichtswerkstatt Hamburg-Eimsbüttel, 154
Werkstatt für Ortsgeschichte Köln-Brück e. V. (Workshop for Local History Köln-Brück), 142
Gestapo terrain, 102–4, 107–8, 288. *See also* Topography of Terror
Glotz, Peter, 72–73
Goldhagen, Daniel, 70
Gößwald, Udo, 275
Grass, Günter, 72–73
grassroots agency, 14, 21, 168, 262
Green Party, 62, 71, 74, 91, 96, 109, 115, 135, 149, 164, 184, 190, 202, 245
Grenzturmverein (Border Tower Association), 240
Großbölting, Thomas, 211
GULag system, 251
Gutzeit, Martin, 67

Haase, Norbert, 136
Hansen, Nicoline, 53
Haß, Matthias, 17, 109–10, 114–15
Haß, Ulrike, 60
Hassemer, Volker, 109
Haunss, Sebastian, 140
Hausmann, Brigitte, 188
Heer, Hannes, 163
Heimann, Siegfried, 168
Heimatgeschichtliche Wegweiser (Homeland History Guides), 152
Heimkehrermahnmal (Monument to Homecomers), 47
Heinemann, Gustav, 150
Heinrich, Christoph, 180
Heller, Agnes, 15
Herf, Jeffrey, xiv, 7, 36, 39, 58
Heuss, Theodor, 36, 83
Hildebrandt, Alexandra, 232–34
Hildebrandt, Rainer, 231
Hilfswerk 20. Juli 1944 group, 53
history politics, 64–65
History Workshop. *See also* Geschichtswerkstatt
Bavarian, 184
Berlin, 105, 119, 120, 127, 129*f*, 138, 159*f*

Frauengeschichtswerkstatt (Women's History Workshop), 175
Galerie Morgenland/Geschichtswerkstatt Eimsbüttel, 162
Marburg, 143, 159, 161, 200, 201*f*
Neuhausen, 175
Oberhausen, 175
Rostock, 175
Solingen, 155
Hitler's Willing Executioners (Goldhagen), 70
Hoheisel, Horst, 193, 195–96
Hollitzer, Tobias, 224
Holocaust
legacy of, 66, 281, 289–90
Memorial to the Homosexual Victims of the Holocaust, 81
memory regime, 9, 63, 72
representativeness of, 33, 289
survivors, 3, 137
US Holocaust Memorial Museum, 112, 179
Holzapfel, Carl-Wolfgang, 49, 242
Hossbach, Friedrich, 189
Hrdlicka, Alfred, 97
human rights, 53, 68
hybrid memorial institutions
democratic memory and, 288–93
mediation through, 278–80
memory policy through, 280–88
memory work in, 275–78
staff in, 267–75
state and civil society, 267
summary of, 21, 262–66, 264*f*

individual memories, 11
induction ritual Free German Youth in the GDR (*Jugendweihe*), 40
Initiative Dokumentationsstätte Neuengamme, 76, 98
Initiative Haus Wolfenstein, 96, 189–90
Initiative Hotel Silber, 97–98
Initiative Mahnmal (Memorial Initiative), 218
"inner" democratization, 8
institutionalizing GDR memory, 245–51
instrumentalization of memory, 20, 33, 214
insurgent narratives, 17
integrationist debate culture, 148
International Auschwitz Committee, 55
International Camp Committee at Buchenwald, 82. *See also* Buchenwald Komitee
International Exhibition of Construction and Design (IBA), 103
intersubjectively held memories, 11

Jarausch, Konrad, 8
Jaspers, Karl, 36, 87
Jewish memory. *See also* Holocaust
    anti-Semitism, 39, 58, 85, 107
    Bergen-Belsen Jewish Committee, 82
    Berlin Jewish Museum, 179, 191
    Central Council of Jews, 70, 192,
        258, 272
    Christian-Jewish cooperation, 3, 56
    identity of Nazi victims, 39, 41, 181
    memorial practices, 66–67
    Memorial to the Murdered Jews of
        Europe, 81, 102, 122, 123, 191,
        192, 196
Jewish Museum, 102
Jordan, Jennifer, 17–18, 188, 191
judicial process of transition, 70
Jungnickel, Dirk, 256

Kaminsky, Anna, 206, 232, 255,
    257, 259
Kampe, Norbert, 268
Kansteiner, Wulf, 17, 169
Katriel, Tamar, 18
Kattago, Siobhan, 122
Kirsch, Jan-Holger, 65, 70, 122
Kissinger, Henry, 178
Klemke, Rainer, 192, 244, 281
Kley, Joe, 200
Klier, Freya, 246–47
Knabe, Hubertus, 254, 255, 257
Knabe, Klaus, 239
Kneist, Gisela, 256
Knigge, Volkhard, 12
Knobloch, Heinz, 66
Knoch, Habbo, 281, 289–90, 292
Kocka, Jürgen, 149
Kogon, Eugen, 36
Kohl, Helmut, 62, 64–65, 73–74,
    94–95, 138
Kolb, Eberhard, 86
*Komitee der Antifaschistischen
    Widerstandskämpfer* (Committee of
    Antifascist Resistance Fighters), 43
Koshar, Rudy, 17, 92, 183
Kramer, Stephan, 258
*Kreuzberg antifaschistisches
    Gedenktafelprogramm* (Anti-Fascist
    Commemorative Plaque
    Program), 184
Kreuzberg Museum in Berlin, 276
Kubik, Jan, 16, 270
Kulturrat (Cultural Council), 143

Kunert, Günter, 66
Kuratorium Unteilbares Deutschland
    (KUD), 49

Ladner, Claus Peter, 226–27, 242, 243
Lammert, Norbert, 245, 288
Landesbeauftragte der Stasiunterlagenbehörde
    (LStU), 225–26, 236
Langenbacher, Eric, 72
Leach, Darcy, 140
*Lebenserfahrung und kollektives Gedächtnis
    (Life Experience and Collective Memory)*
    (Niethammer), 149
leftist survivor organizations, 33
Leggewie, Claus, 17
Leiserowitz, Ruth, 67
Leistikowstrasse Memorial, 210, 251–60,
    253*f*, 261
lieux de mémoire (realms of memory), 11
Lindenberger, Thomas, 19, 28–29, 59,
    130, 133, 166, 175–76, 204, 250,
    272
Lindqvist, Sven, 153
Litfin, Jürgen, 221–22
Lübbe, Hermann, 36
Lübke, Heinrich, 52*f*, 52
Ludwig, Andreas, 133, 171, 173, 239
Lupu, Noam, 194
Lutz, Thomas, 98, 268, 277, 283

mainstreaming memory, 170–77
majoritarian approach to memory, 8
Marburger Jäger Memorial, 160*f*, 160
Marcuse, Harold, 88, 92–93, 182
Marienfelde Refugee Center Memorial
    (*Erinnerungsstätte Notaufnahme-Lager
    Marienfelde e. V.*), 227
Martin, Angela, 120
Marxism, 132–33, 146
Marxist "K-groups," 61
McAdams, James, 211
Meckel, Markus, 67
mediation through hybrid memorial
    institutions, 278–80
memorial aesthetics
    anti-monumentality and reflexivity,
        192–98*f*, 198*f*
    authenticity in, 187–92, 190*f*
    decentralization, 182–87*f*, 187*f*
    principles of, 182
    specificity and diversity, 199–202,
        201*f*, 203*f*
    summary of, 178–82, 179*f*, 203–5

Memorial Germany, 252, 253
Memorial to German Resistance, 102, 124,
    263. *See also* Gedenkstätte Deutscher
    Widerstand
Memorial to the Homosexuals Persecuted
    under the National Socialist Regime,
    81, 124
Memorial to the Murdered Jews of
    Europe, 81, 102, 122, 123, 191,
    192, 196
Memorial to the Victims of
    Communism, 249
memorialization initiatives, 218
memorials to Nazi terror
    Active Museum, 1–2, 30, 105–14, 106*f*,
        113*f*, 115–17, 121
    communist resistance to fascism, 262
    early activism, 81–88, 83*f*
    Gedenkstättenbewegung and, 89–102, 100*f*
    Gestapo terrain, 102–4, 107–8
    instrumentalization of memory, 214
    nation-wide importance of, 121–24
    summary of, 76–81, 77*f*, 79*f*, 124–26
memory activism
    agency in, 14–19
    civic activism, 7, 124
    cultural memory, 137
    democracy and, 6–10, 24–26
    East/West Germany, 42–57, 232
    framing of, 234–38
    German Democratic Republic, 66–68
    Holocaust, 9, 63, 72
    key concepts, 10–13
    movements and, 19–24
    outlook, 29–31
    postwar, 33
    public memory, 10
    state actors and, 26–29
    strategies, 238–44, 241*f*
    summary of, 1–6, 2*f*, 5*f*
    work of memory, 8
memory actors, 11
memory boom, 61, 63, 78–80, 89, 138,
    203–5, 267
memory entrepreneurs, 229
memory establishment, 292
memory-making process, 167
memory movements, 182
memory policy through hybrid memorial
    institutions, 280–88
memory politics
    after 1945, 35
    boom in, 62–64
    civil society action in, 5, 214, 263, 267,
        268, 283

    contrasting developments, 62
    democratic memory, 20, 24, 266
    Federal Republic of Germany, 35–38
    German Democratic Republic, 38–42
    history politics, 64–65
    National Socialism, 65, 88, 124
    post-wall memory politics, 68–73
    since 1945, 32–35
    summary of, 12, 20, 73–75
    turning point for, 57–61
    understanding, 262–66
    unification and, 211–14
memory protest, 157–58
    examples, 158–59, 243
    initiatives, 157
    memory work as, 6, 8, 9, 18, 29, 125,
        238–39, 262, 266
    tactics of, 18
memory work, 18–19, 275–78
memory work as memory protest, 6, 8, 9,
    18, 29, 125, 238–39, 262, 266
"mercy of late birth" *(Gnade der späten
    Geburt)*, 64
Merkel, Angela, 71, 72, 248
Meyer, Beate, 131, 148, 154
Meyer, Erik, 12–13, 15–16, 17, 282–83
Meyer, Winifried, 210
Miltenberger, Sonja, 140
"Mirror Wall" memorial, 190*f*, 190
Misztal, Barbara, 16
Mitchell, Timothy, 27
mnemonic fundamentals, 271
Moeller, Robert G., 36
Monument against Fascism, War and
    Violence, 194–95
Morina, Christina, 45
Morsch, Günter, 90, 255–56, 274, 279
Moses, Dirk, 58
Mosse, George, 48–49
mourning work, 164
movements and memory activism, 19–24
Müller, Bernard, 139
Müller, Jan-Werner, 14
Müller, Roland, 200
Museum Haus am Checkpoint Charlie,
    231–34
Memorial House of the Wannsee
    Conference, 68, 87, 96, 192, 199,
    267, 277
Museum "Runde Ecke" (Museum Round
    Corner), 223–24

Nachama, Andreas, 6–7, 112, 290
National Day of Mourning *(Volkstrauertag)*,
    47, 158

National Socialism
  analysis of guilt, 60, 67–68, 123–24
  Communist resistance to, 73
  forgotten victims of, 92
  indigenous structure of, 125
  local topography of, 94
  memorialization of victims, 37, 43, 53,
    54f, 220
  memory of, 65, 88, 124
  responsibility for, 35
  terror of, 3
  victims of, 37, 54f, 73, 97, 220, 256
Nazi victims
  Jewish identity of, 39, 41, 181
  memory of, 35, 36, 38, 47, 71
Nazism
  church-based resistance to, 55
  communist resistance to, 40
  criminal prosecution, 58
  denazification, 69
  euthanasia program, 118
  public opinions on, 57
neo-Nazism, 58
Neue Wache Memorial, 121–22, 123
Neuengamme concentration camp, 76,
  84–85, 86, 90, 93, 95, 98, 178
Neumann, Bernd, 248
Neumärker, Uwe, 187
Nevermann, Kurt, 286
new social movements (NSMs), 130,
  135, 141
New Society for Fine Arts (Neue
  Gesellschaft für Bildende Kunst), 105
Niethammer, Lutz, 149
non-contentious memory work, 19
Nooke, Maria, 67, 255
Nora, Pierre, 11
Notaufnahmelager (refugee camp), 227. See
  also Marienfelde

Ohnesorg, Benno, 59
Oldenburg, Claes, 181
Olick, Jeffrey, 64
"Ostalgie" (Nostalgia for the East), 69

Panne, Katrin, 45
Paris Commune (1871), 157
peace movement, 56, 76, 91, 98, 132, 161,
  185, 200–1
Peaceful Revolution, 28
Platt, Bodo, 256
political prisoners, 102
political process of transition, 70
Politics and Guilt (Schwan), 25–26
politics of memory. See memory politics
Poppe, Ulrike, 216, 238, 255

post-wall memory politics, 68–73
pragmatics in East German memory
  politics, 226–29, 234
Preußen-Versuch einer Bilanz, 63
prisoners of war (POWs), 35, 45–47
professionalism goal, 287–88
Prowe, Diethelm, 57
public memory, 10
Putnam, Robert, 22, 290

Radmacher, Norbert, 196
Rau, Matthias, 68
Reading, Anna, 18
Reagan, Ronald, 94–95, 138
reflexivity in memorial aesthetics, 192–98,
  198f
Reich, Ines, 256, 259
Reiprich, Siegfried, 284–85
Richter, Gunnar, 99
Robert-Havemann-Society and Archive in
  Berlin, 235, 239, 247
Roder, Bernt, 91, 278
Römer, Volker, 228
Rosa-Luxemburg-Bridge activism, 127–28,
  129f, 159
Rothberg, Michael, 16
Rüdiger, Gisela, 253
Rudnick, Carola, 273
Rürup, Reinhard, 110
Rust, Gustav, 222, 291

Sa'adah, Anne, 24
Sabrow, Martin, 245, 246, 247, 248, 255,
  287–88
Sachsenhausen Concentration Camp
  Memorial, 90
Saldern, Adelheid von, 131, 135, 136
Saxon Memorial Foundation, 284
Schäfer, Hermann, 248
Scherrieble, Joachim, 271–72
Schlusche, Günter, 250
Schmid, Harald, 281
Schmidtke, Michael, 59
Schoenberner, Gerhard, 87, 115
Scholz, Lothar, 256–57
Scholz, Stephan, 44
Schönfeld, Martin, 41, 43, 51
Schöttler, Peter, 163
Schröder, Gerhard, 71, 72
Schröder, Richard, 246, 290–91
Schubert, Rainer, 222
Schüler, Horst, 206, 219
Schumacher, Kurt, 36
Schütz, Klaus, 87
Schwan, Gesine, 25–26
Schwelling, Brigit, 18, 43–44

Sebald, W.G., 72–73
Sello, Tom, 235
Shalev-Gerz, Esther, 194
Shoah victims, 38
Siebeck, Cornelia, 269
Siegfried, Detlef, 141, 170–71, 176
Sinti and Roma Memorial, 81, 124
Social Democrats, 104, 107, 139
Soviet Counterintelligence SMERSH,
    251
Soviet Secret Police (NKVD), 41,
    237, 258
Soviet Special Camps, 219, 237, 255, 256,
    271, 279
Sozialistische Einheitspartei (SED), 41,
    211, 214
specificity in memorial aesthetics, 199–202,
    201f, 203f
Sperner, Eva, 162
Spielmann, Jochen, 60
Stacheldraht (Barbed Wire), 220
Stadtteilarchiv Ottensen (Neighborhood
    Archive Ottensen), 142
staff in hybrid memorial institutions,
    267–75
Staffa, Christian, 56, 277
Stalinism, 54f, 251, 271
Stasi file authority (BStU), 69, 212, 285
state actors and activism, 26–29
Stephan, Annegret, 241
Stiftung Aufarbeitung (Foundation for
    Working Through the Past), 206,
    212–13, 214, 216, 217–18, 220, 228,
    249, 285
Stiftung Berliner Mauer (Berlin Wall
    Foundation), 228
Stolpersteine (stumbling blocks) memorial,
    185–86, 276, 279
Stölzl, Christoph, 164
Strnad, Maxililian, 131
Studienkreis Deutscher Widerstand
    (Association for Studying German
    Resistance), 152
Szodrzynski, Joachim, 176

Tarrow, Sidney, 23, 135
Thüringer Archiv für Zeitgeschichte
    "Matthias Domaschk" (ThürAZ),
    240
Till, Karen, 17
Tischker, Robert, 49
Topography of Terror
    expansion of, 276
    founding of, 111–12
    impact of, 81, 117–18, 189
    memorial design, 90, 264f

overview, 101f, 102, 121, 126
summary of, 1–2, 2f, 6, 30
Topography of Terror Foundation,
    117–18
topography of traces, 188
tourist industry, 215
transitional justice, 25
Tuchel, Johannes, 88, 279
Twenty Years After Communism (Bernhard,
    Kubik), 16, 270

Ullmann, Micha, 66, 198
Ullrich, Volker, 163
unification and memory politics,
    211–14
Union der Opferverbände Kommunistischer
    Gewaltherrschaft (UOKG),
    217–20
Union of Victims of Nazi Military
    Justice, 199
US Holocaust Memorial Museum,
    112, 179

Verband der Heimkehrer, Kriegsgefangenen
    und Vermisstenangehörigen (VdH)
    group, 45–47, 48f
Verband der Opfer der Nürnberger Gesetze
    (OdN), 50
Verein Freiheit e.V. (Assocation Freedom),
    242, 243
Vereinigte Ostdeutsche
    Landsmannschaften, 44
Vereinigung der Opfer des Stalinismus (VOS),
    49, 219–20, 270
Vereinigung der Verfolgten des Naziregimes
    (VVN), 40, 41, 42–43, 50–51, 86
Vergangenheitspolitik, 12
veterans' groups, 45
victims' associations/organizations, 216,
    217–22
victims of National Socialism, 37, 54f, 73,
    97, 220, 256
Vogel, Thomas, 99
Volksbund Deutsche Kriegsgräberfürsorge
    (VDK), 47–49
Volksbund für Frieden und Freiheit (Popular
    Alliance for Peace and Freedom), 49
Volkshochschulen (adult education
    centers), 175

Wagner, Herbert, 243–44
Wagner, Rainer, 218–19
Walser, Martin, 70
war commemoration, 74
war memorial inscriptions, 45, 46f
Wehler, Hans-Ulrich, 149

Weidt, Otto, 191
Weißler, Sabine, 96, 165
Weizsäcker, Richard von, 55, 63, 65, 89, 104
Wenzel, Gisela, xiii, 120, 165, 282
Wildt, Michael, 204
Wille, Manfred, 41–42
Willy-Bredel-Society, 142
Winter, Jay, 17
Winters, Peter Jochen, 256
Wittelsbach dynasty in Munich, 89
Wolfgram, Mark, 39
Wolfrum, Edgar, 38, 57

Wolle, Stefan, 229
work of memory, 8
Working Group of Local Museums (ABR), 276. *See also* Arbeitskreis Berliner Regionalmuseen
Wulf, Josef, 87

Yad Vashem in Jerusalem, 112, 179
Young, James, 103

Zeitzeugen-Initiative (Eyewitness-Initiative), 256, 258–59
Zimmermann, Michael, 167